T0342224

IMAGINED FUTURES

IMAGINED FUTURES

Fictional Expectations and Capitalist Dynamics

JENS BECKERT

HARVARD UNIVERSITY PRESS
Cambridge, Massachusetts
London, England
2016

To Annelies and Jasper

and the happiness they have brought

Second printing

Library of Congress Cataloging-in-Publication Data

Names: Beckert, Jens, 1967– author.
Title: Imagined futures : fictional expectations and capitalist dynamics / Jens Beckert.
Description: Cambridge, Massachusetts : Harvard University Press, 2016. | Includes bibliographical references and index.
Identifiers: LCCN 2015040447 | ISBN 9780674088825 (alk. paper)
Subjects: LCSH: Capitalism. | Economics. | Time and economic reactions. | Economic forecasting. | Decision making—Economic aspects.
Classification: LCC HB501 .B37384 2016 | DDC 330.12/2—dc23
    LC record available at http://lccn.loc.gov/2015040447

CONTENTS

ACKNOWLEDGMENTS

MORE THAN thirty years ago Benedict Anderson introduced the term "imagined communities" to argue that national identities are based on social imaginaries. In this book, I claim that the dynamism of the capitalist economy is in no lesser way based on imaginaries. But this book differs from Anderson's because it explores imaginaries of the future rather than imaginaries of the present and the past. Furthermore, I focus on the development of the modern capitalist economy rather than on processes of nation building. Given the complexity of economic relations and the uncertainty of future developments, actors making decisions on investments, innovations, credits, or consumption develop imaginaries on how the future will look and how the decisions they make will influence outcomes. I call these imaginaries "fictional expectations," and argue that they are a fundamental force fueling the dynamism of modern capitalist economies.

I should like to begin by expressing my gratitude to the Institut d'études avancées (IEA) in Paris, where I was a fellow during the 2012–13 academic year. Without the opportunity to focus for almost a whole year on writing this book, I would never even have begun. Many thanks to Gretty Mirdal and Patrice Duran and to the formidable staff at the IEA, in particular to Marie-Thérèse Cerf, its administrative head. I would also like to thank the other fellows of the IEA, with whom I spent the year in Paris, for sharing their thoughts about my project in both informal conversations and during a seminar.

Paris was crucial to this project in many other ways as well. It was in Paris in 2010, in Olivier Favereau's Economix seminar in Nanterre that I first presented the ideas from which this book grew. During the writing process, I presented parts of the book in seminars at Sciences Po, the Ecole Normale Superieur, the Ecole des Hautes Etudes en Sciences Sociales, and at the Université Sorbonne Nouvelle Paris 3. I also presented the project on many other occasions beyond Paris: at meetings of the American Sociological Association in Las Vegas and Denver, the SASE meetings in Madrid and Milan, and at seminars at the Instituto Juan March in Madrid, the University of Leicester, University College Dublin, and Oxford University, to name just a few. I gained vital insights from all of these seminars.

The support I received at my home institution, the Max Planck Institute for the Study of Societies in Cologne, was equally crucial to the project. Wolfgang Streeck, with whom I co-directed the Max Planck Institute for close to ten years, was a critical source of inspiration. Without his insistence on developing an economic sociology that moves closer to the concerns addressed in political economy, this book would have looked very different. I also discussed parts of this project in seminars at the institute, in meetings of my research group, and with guest researchers in Cologne. My thanks to all the colleagues and students who, with their comments and questions, helped my thinking during the writing process.

Jenny Andersson, Robert Boyer, Benjamin Braun, Richard Bronk, John Campbell, Bruce Carruthers, Christoph Deutschmann, Frank Dobbin, Nigel Dodd, Heiner Ganssmann, Ariane Leendertz, Renate Mayntz, Alfred Reckendrees, Werner Reichmann, Lyn Spillman, Wolfgang Streeck, Jakob Tanner, Christine Trampusch, and two anonymous reviewers have read the whole manuscript or chapters from it and provided me with invaluable suggestions for revisions. I also benefited greatly from conversations with Nina Bandelj, Henri Bergeron, Francesco Boldizioni, Gérald Bronner, Timur Ergen, Ted Fischer, Neil Fligstein, Marion Fourcade, Brooke Harrington, Kieran Healy, Martin Hellwig, Peter Katzenstein, Wolfgang Knöbl, Karin Knorr Cetina, Sebastian Kohl, Patrick LeGalès, Mark Lutter, Fabian Muniesa, Christine Musselin, Claus Offe, Birger Priddat, Werner Rammert, Akos Rona-Tas, Fritz Scharpf, Charles Smith, David Stark, Philipp Steiner, Richard Swedberg, Laurent Thévenot, Cornelia Woll, and Martha Zuber. Many thanks to all of them. Despite many rounds of revision encouraged by the immensely helpful comments, what Paul Valéry once said about poems rings very true to me: an academic book is never finished, only abandoned.

Writing a book is not just an intellectual task; it is also an organizational undertaking. I am indebted to the many people at the Max Planck Institute who helped to make this book possible through their practical and organizational support. First of all I would like to thank Christine Claus, who has supported me in all organizational matters since I arrived at the institute. She added the endnote references to the chapters of this book, meticulous work that demands attention to detail and mastery of the software, and patience with its many pitfalls. Heide Haas researched and edited most of the figures in the book. I also want to thank the librarians at the Max Planck Institute: Susanne Hilbring and her staff have done a formidable job obtaining the literature I needed. My gratitude also extends to the publications department of the Max Planck Institute, in particular to Ian Edwards, Astrid Dünkelmann, Cynthia Lehmann, and Thomas Pott, who accompanied the manuscript on its journey from my desk to the staff of Harvard University Press and eventually to the printer.

Parts of the findings presented in this book grew out of earlier discussions and studies that appeared in an edited volume (Beckert 2011) and in the journals *Politics and Society* (Beckert 2013a) and *Theory and Society* (Beckert 2013b).

If this book reads well, it is to the merit of Miranda Richmond Mouillot, who did a fantastic job editing the chapters. Ian Malcolm, my editor at Harvard University Press, has supported the project from the time he heard me mention it in a conversation in Paris in 2012. I would like to thank him for many years of trustful collaboration. *Imagined Futures* is now the third book project we have worked on together.

Paris has not only been important to me as a source of intellectual stimulus in recent years; it was also the city where I met Annelies. For me, our relationship and our son, Jasper, embody more than anything else what this book is about: Imagined Futures. This book is dedicated to them.

It is certain that a very large part of what we experience in life depends not on the actual circumstances of the moment so much as on the anticipation of future events.

—WILLIAM STANLEY JEVONS, *The Theory of Political Economy*

ONE

INTRODUCTION

THROUGHOUT MOST of history, the level of economic wealth has changed very little. Only with the onset of the industrial revolution did it begin to accelerate, leading to unprecedented levels of economic production and affluence (Figure 1.1). This shift began in a few European countries and in North America, but ultimately, over the course of the twentieth century, it spread to almost all regions of the world; today economic and social development across the globe is shaped by the dynamics of capitalism, in the form of growth as well as recurrent economic crises. What explains the extraordinary momentum of the capitalist economy?

Scholars of capitalism trace the dramatic creation of wealth that began in the late eighteenth century to a plethora of factors: among them are technological advances, institutional changes, the division of labor, the expansion of trade, commodification processes, competition, exploitation, the increase in production factors, and cultural developments.[1] The deep crises capitalism has witnessed again and again are attributed to overaccumulation, regulatory failure, lack of investment and consumption, psychological factors, and miscalculations of risk.[2]

As comprehensive as these explanations are, they pay only limited attention to another, no less essential aspect of capitalist dynamics: its temporal order. Changes in temporal orientations of actors and the enlargement of time horizons into an unknown economic future are crucial components of the genesis of the capitalist order, and of its dynamics. This holds for economic growth as well as for economic crises. Capitalism is a system in which actors—be they firms, entrepreneurs, investors, employees, or consumers—orient

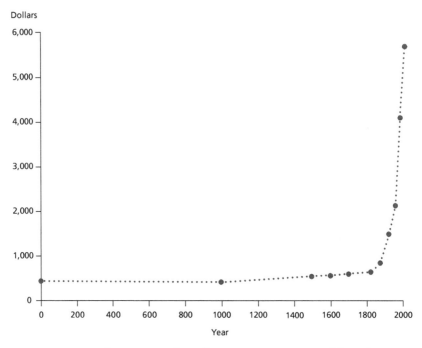

FIGURE 1.1. Growth per capita of world GDP. *Data source*: Maddison (2001: 264, Table B-21).

their activities toward a future they perceive as open and uncertain, containing unforeseeable opportunities as well as incalculable risks. The spread of competitive markets and the expansion of monetary exchange have anchored this temporal orientation toward an open future in the institutional fabric of the economy and society. But it is also anchored in the unique human ability to imagine future states of the world that are different from the present. As they seek to make profit, augment their income, or increase their social status, actors create imaginaries of economic futures, the achievement or avoidance of which motivates their decisions. The temporal disposition of economic actors toward the future, and the capability to fill this future with counterfactual economic imaginaries, is crucial to understanding both how capitalism diverges from the economic orders that preceded it and its overall dynamics. This book investigates the impact of such imagined futures on the dynamics of capitalism.

The Future Matters

Making imagined futures a cornerstone of understanding the dynamics of capitalism is a distinct departure from most current scholarship on the economy in sociology and political science. Over the past thirty years the slogan "history matters" has become a rallying cry for both historical institutionalism and sociology. To explain current outcomes, historical institutionalists investigate the long-term structural trajectories that form developmental paths and shape choices in the present (Mahoney 2000). Institutional paths differ from country to country and cannot be easily abandoned; in general, only external shocks are seen to cause a shift in these trajectories. Sociological institutionalists, though they place a stronger emphasis on cognition, are similarly oriented toward the past, and see social change as a process of isomorphic adaptation to existing institutional models (DiMaggio and Powell 1991).[3] Political scientists and sociologists concur in their assumption that present outcomes are formed by past occurrences.

But not all disciplines in the social sciences agree that the present is largely determined by the past. In a chapter on the concept of temporality in sociology, Andrew Abbott (2005) pointed out that sociologists and economists apply opposing strategies when explaining events in the present. "While sociologists see present events as a final outcome emerging from the past, economists reason backwards from the future: Decisions are explained by the present value of expected future rewards" (406). In a similar vein, Arjun Appadurai (2013: 286) observes that "economics has consolidated its place as the primary field in which the study of how humans construct their future is modeled and predicted." While much of economics includes the future in explanatory models (see Chapter 3), the capacity to imagine futures should play a much larger role in explanations of economic action in sociology and political science. This is particularly true when it comes to the capitalist economy.

The capacity to imagine counterfactual futures is of course a human characteristic that exists independent of capitalism. Imagined futures are crucial to understanding the development of modernity in general; and they exist, though in different forms, in traditional societies as well. Religious eschatology, for instance, projects futures unrelated to the economy. By the same token, the capitalist economy's orientation toward an open economic future does not exist solely at the level of action orientations: the capitalist economy *institutionalizes* specific systemic pressures that enforce a temporal orientation toward future economic opportunities and risks. Only by closely examining these institutionalized pressures may we comprehensibly shed light on the role of actors' temporal orientations with regard to economic processes.

In particular, two institutional mechanisms enforce the future orientation of actors in capitalism: competition and credit. The ceaselessly changing environment that has accompanied the spread of market competition has forced actors to remain alert to threats from other actors who deviate from established practices as they seek new opportunities and ways to overcome threats they themselves perceive. Constant forward momentum is necessary if one is not to fall behind. Competition forces firms to seek more efficient forms of production and introduce new products to the market. As one firm increases productivity or offers new products, all its competitors are pressured to innovate and develop even more efficient forms of production and better products. The pressure to succeed in competition has also been transferred to employees, whose prospects and social status depend on their success in the labor market. Competition forces them to acquire and maintain marketable skills by anticipating and adjusting to new labor market demands (Chapter 6). The pressure extends also to consumers, in that they express their social status through the purchase of ever-new consumer items (Chapter 8).

The "expansive dynamism of capitalism" (Sewell 2008) is also institutionalized through the credit-based financing of investments. Credit provides access to resources to which no "normal claim" (Schumpeter 1934: 107) exists. The claim is only justified through future success. Credit is a central pillar of capitalist growth because it allows firms to engage in economic activities that could not otherwise be undertaken, using resources they have yet to earn. At the same time, the interest charged for credit forces firms to produce products of higher market value than the investments being made in them. The "claim" to capital must be earned through the expansion of economic value. In this way, the credit system both provides opportunities for growth and enforces that growth. Firms that fail to produce sufficient surplus lose access to capital and are eventually wiped out from their markets.

Economic and social competition and the financial system create both opportunities *and* a systematic demand for dynamic change, which forces actors to pursue the economic opportunities to be found in imagined futures. This "restlessness" (Sewell 2008) keeps capitalist economies in "dynamic disequilibrium" (Beckert 2009), which is constantly upended through the decentralized decisions of market actors operating within the institutional constraints of competitive markets and a monetary economy. Capitalist economies destabilize and stabilize themselves by continuously undermining their own historical forms: firms relentlessly seek new profit opportunities, employees strive to build careers, consumers hunt for new consumption experiences. Surviving and thriving in an environment in which current forms will not last demands that firms, employees, and consumers be constantly oriented toward a future they cannot yet see.

Although temporal orientation toward the future is a cornerstone of capitalism, it is not a cornerstone of the study of capitalism; it is taken up far more often in popular culture than in the social sciences. The "American dream" is perhaps the most significant cultural representation of imagined futures assumed to shape economic attitudes and motivation. The dream of upward social mobility based on equal opportunity is a crucial motivating and integrating force in American society. But despite the obvious importance of imagined futures, few sociologists have seen them as particularly useful, let alone central, to understanding capitalist dynamics. Two notable exceptions are Max Weber ([1930] 1992), in his studies on Protestant ethics, and Pierre Bourdieu (1979, 2000), particularly in his accounts of the social and economic transformations in Algeria in the mid-twentieth century (see Chapter 2). Scholars from other disciplines have highlighted the role of imagined futures in general and, more specifically, the role of imaginaries. In economics, George Shackle (1979) has assigned the greatest significance to the role of imaginaries in the economy, thus foreshadowing many of the arguments developed in this book. More recently, Richard Bronk (2009) advanced the idea that the way we imagine the indeterminate future structures much of economic behavior. Bronk discusses in detail the work of many economists and philosophers since the Enlightenment and the role of imaginaries in their thinking. The anthropologist Arjun Appadurai (1996, 2013) has called attention to the role of imaginaries of the future in the creation of the modern subject and of political participation. Benedict Anderson's (1983) now classic *Imagined Communities* highlights the role of imaginaries in the process of nation building, but Anderson focuses more on the past and the present than on the future. There have also been efforts to integrate the role of imagined futures into the field of general sociology (see Chapter 3).[4] Most prominent, perhaps, are the works of Alfred Schütz (1962), Niklas Luhmann (1976), and Cornelius Castoriadis (1998). More recently, Ann Mische (2009, 2014) embarked on the project of a sociology of the future, critiquing sociological approaches that explain present action only in light of past occurrences.[5] Finally, in specialized sociological fields such as innovation and technology studies, there is a vibrant discourse on the role of projections of the future in the development of new technologies (see Chapter 7). These move forward through imaginaries, which are a "cultural resource that enables new forms of life by projecting positive goals and seeking to attain them" (Jasanoff and Kim 2009: 122).

This book builds on these formative contributions, arguing that imaginaries of the future are a crucial element of capitalist development, and that capitalist dynamics are vitally propelled by the shaping of expectations. Institutional trajectories from the past are not irrelevant to explaining outcomes, of course, but, based on the contributions mentioned above, sociologists would do well to shift more of their attention to the future, particularly to the images of the future that actors nourish. Furthermore, temporal orientations and perceptions of the future are relevant far beyond the economic realm investigated here, and may indeed underpin a fresh paradigm in sociology. This, then, is the core hypothesis of this book: "history matters," but the future matters just as much.

Microfoundations

Investigating economic phenomena is an important area of research in sociology *and* political science. However, economic sociology and political economy often differ in the level of analysis they choose. Economic sociologists have, for the most part, investigated the "embeddedness" of economic action in order to show that economic outcomes can only be explained with reference to social life—its structure, institutions, and culture—and the way it shapes opportunity structures and actors' beliefs. Often embeddedness is seen as a means of allowing the reduction of uncertainty. Economic sociology has focused on the micro- and mesolevels of analysis, and scholarship in this field frequently consists of case studies showing the different ways in which economic action in contemporary economies is embedded.

The institutional approach of political economy, by contrast, focuses on explaining macrolevel outcomes, investigating the development of the capitalist economy in relation to the state and to dominant interest groups. Much research in this tradition has attempted to explain the institutional differences among developed capitalist regimes, as well as the macroeconomic consequences of these differences (Hall and Soskice 2001b). More recently, the investigation of capitalism as such has (again) become a topic of increasing interest (Streeck 2011).

Some institutional approaches in political economy are founded on the assumption that changes at the macrolevel—in the law, in consumer demand, in inflation, in wealth distribution, or in technologies—need not be described with any specific reference to actors (Thelen and Steinmo 1992). In other words, they see no need to attend to the processes of social interaction that underlie the macrodevelopments they observe. The recourse to the distribution of power resources, for instance, explains individual decisions and collective outcomes (Hall and Taylor 1996; Korpi 1985). Other approaches in political economy do focus on the microfoundations of economic dynamics, but assume that actors are rational agents or that they follow cognitively determined scripts (Hall and Taylor 1996; Korpi 1985; McDermott 2004; Shepsle 2006).

Capitalist development stands at the center of political economy, and it is the topic addressed in this book.[6] However, the book does not provide a new structural explanation of capitalist dynamics, nor establish a more refined rational actor theory, behavioral approach, or power resource model. Rather, it explores how macrodynamics are anchored in social interaction and interpretations of social reality. In this sense, it draws insight from those strands of economic sociology that focus on the interactional level; however, unlike most of this scholarship, here it is only a starting place in an attempt to understand and explain the broader question of capitalist dynamics.

Thus, this book proceeds from a microperspective and uses action theory as its starting point. Any approach to capitalist dynamics that includes the openness of the future must proceed from the social interactions that take place in the economy. An analysis of imagined futures as a force in capitalist dynamics focuses on the social interactions that underlie both the buoyant expansion and sudden crises of capitalist economies. The future enters social interactions through perceptions of the social world, which are anchored in actors, even if these perceptions are socially shaped and should thus not be understood in purely individualistic terms.

Laying the microfoundations for an understanding of capitalist dynamics is an interpretative approach that makes it possible to bring economic sociology and political economy into closer dialogue with one another, using instruments primarily developed in the field of sociology to explore a question that has in current scholarship been addressed mostly by political economists.

This implies that the book sympathizes with endeavors in economics and political science that attempt to discern the microfoundations of macroeconomic processes. However, economic macrodevelopment and capitalist dynamics cannot be explained by approaches rooted in rational actor theory (see Chapter 3). The assumption that decisions in economic contexts may be understood as rational calculations based on full knowledge of all (available) information has been broadly criticized. One chief objection to this assumption is the issue of uncertainty: future states of the world are not predictable because of the complexity of situations in which decisions are made; unforeseeable effects of interactions; genuine novelty brought about by unpredictable innovations; and the contingency of other actors' choices. Particularly in situations of rapid economic change or crises (Bronk 2009, 2015), which are characteristic of modern capitalism, uncertainty prevails.

This objection to rational actor theory differs from those in the sociological tradition, whose critiques are based in the fact that some decisions in the economy are "nonrational"; that is, based on habit and routines, inconsistent, or normatively oriented toward goals other than the maximization of utility or profit (Beckert 2002). While routines, mistakes, and value-rational action also play an undeniable role in contemporary economies (Beckert 2002; Camic 1986; Etzioni 1988), they are of limited significance if our goal is to understand an economic system that legitimizes utility maximization and socializes its actors accordingly.

Instead, if actors *intend* to maximize what they understand as utility, and that they consider their goals, means, and conditions for action accordingly, their decisions must be based on expectations of presumed outcomes. Expectations are understood here as the value economic agents assume a given variable will have in the future (see also R. Evans 1997: 401). Rational actor theory does not fail because actors do not wish to maximize their utility, but because it is unable to address the consequences of genuine uncertainty. As theories of bounded rationality have argued persistently, actors often simply do not have the information or the computational capacity to make optimizing choices. Under conditions of uncertainty, the parameters and probabilities that would make it possible to choose the optimal course of action are unknowable.

Ever since Frank Knight ([1921] 2006) introduced the distinction between risk and uncertainty, uncertainty has been an important concept in mainstream economics, as well a crucial point of reference for dissenting voices in economics and in economic sociology.[7] Starting from the assumption that it is possible to calculate optimal choices, mainstream economics has directed all its efforts into creating a theory that does away with uncertainty—in Knight's sense of the term—by reducing it to calculable risk (Beckert 2002, Hodgson 2011). By contrast, heterodox approaches and economic sociologists have asserted that introducing uncertainty has much greater implications than standard economics has acknowledged, arguing that uncertainty can be a vantage point for a renewed understanding of economic phenomena.

Fictional Expectations

This book uses these observations on the limits of rational actor theory in situations characterized by uncertainty as the starting point for a theory of capitalist dynamics. If actors are oriented toward the future and outcomes are uncertain, then how can expectations be defined? What are expectations under conditions of uncertainty? That is the central question to which this book seeks an answer. If we take uncertainty seriously instead of conflating it with risk, it becomes evident that expectations cannot be probabilistic assessments of future states of the world. Under genuine uncertainty, expectations become interpretative frames that structure situations through imaginaries of future states of the world and of causal relations. Expectations become determinate only through the imaginaries actors develop.

The term "fictional expectations" refers to the images actors form as they consider future states of the world, the way they visualize causal relations, and the ways they perceive their actions influencing outcomes. The term also refers to the symbolic qualities that actors ascribe to goods and that transcend the goods' material features. This is often a feature of actors' relationships to consumer goods, but it also holds for the ascription of value to tokens that circulate as money. Actors use imaginaries of future situations and of causal relations as well as the symbolically ascribed qualities of goods as interpretative frames to orient decision-making *despite* the incalculability of outcomes.

As Chapter 4 explains in detail, the term "fictional" should not be taken to mean that these expectations are false or mere fantasies, only that expectations of the unforeseeable future inhabit the mind not as foreknowledge, but as contingent imaginaries. Actors, motivated by an imagined future state, organize their activities based on this mental representation and the emotions associated with it. Expectations under conditions of uncertainty and ascribed symbolic meanings may be seen as a kind of *pretending*, which creates confidence and provokes actors to act *as if* the imaginary were the "future present," or a good's material quality.[8] Actors act *as if* the future were going to develop in the way they assume it will, and *as if* an object had the qualities symbolically ascribed to it. Decisions in the economy thus share traits with "make-believe games," another term that is elaborated in Chapter 4.

As is the case with fiction in literature, the defining feature of fictional expectations in the economy is that they create a world of their own into which actors can project themselves (see Chapter 4). In the creation of fictional expectations, a "doubling of reality" (Luhmann 1996) takes place. Expectations and the symbolic meanings ascribed to objects are significant as images of a future that actors believe in and use as a reference point for their decision-making. In economic practice, fictional expectations take a narrative form, and become articulated as stories that tell how the future will look and how the economy will unfold into the future from the current state of affairs. Alternately, the stories ascribe meaning to objects, associating them with intangible ideals. For this, narratives make use of theories, models, plans, marketing instruments, and forecasts as "instruments of imagination" (Chapters 9 and 10).

The notion of fictional expectations is used here in contrast to the concept of "rational expectations," which proposes that actors' expectations, at least in the aggregate, equal the statistically expected value for a variable. According to rational expectations theory, actors make use of all available information, which suggests that outcomes do not differ systematically from the forecasts made by the dominant economic model. Conversely, the concept of fictionality points to the openness of the future, which makes expectations *contingent*. Contingency negates the idea that expectations are correct in the aggregate: the notion of fictional expectations contrasts with rational expectations in that it posits that very different expectations can exist under conditions of uncertainty, and that no one is able to predict which of them will be accurate. In other words, the future is "an ambiguous canvas capable of multiple interpretations" (DiMaggio 2002: 90).

Implications for Understanding Capitalism

Fictional expectations have four sets of implications for the dynamics of capitalist economies.

First, fictional expectations can help economic actors work in concert in the face of uncertainty: if they share a conviction that the future will develop in a specific way and that other actors will thus behave in foreseeable ways, they may use these expectations to *coordinate* their decisions. Imaginaries of the future are thus a crucial component of social and economic order. By coordinating action, they also contribute to the dynamics of capitalism, since the correspondence of expectations, or "frame alignment" (Snow and Benford 1992), anchors decisions for investment and innovation.

A second, related implication is that there are real-world consequences of expectations. Because expectations can help actors coordinate their efforts, they are able to *affect* the future. Sociology has used the idea of the self-fulfilling prophecy—generally known today as performativity—to describe this phenomenon (Merton 1957) with reference to economic theories and models. It has been the subject of important discussions in social studies of finance (Callon 1998b; MacKenzie 2006). Whereas the performativity approach likens economic theory to the social world in its claim that economic theory shapes the economy, this book understands the performative effects of expectations more broadly and in several ways. Economic theories are not the only framing of a situation with the potential to influence outcomes, and expectations do not *necessarily* lead to the anticipated future; rather, in a world characterized by uncertainty and an open future, the influence of theories is manifold and unpredictable.

The contingency of expectations is also a source of *innovation* in the economy, giving rise to new ideas *despite*—or, even better, *because of*—uncertainty. Because they are not confined to empirical reality (although the actors who hold them may claim the opposite), expectations can represent radical departures from the present, and become a creative and stimulating force within the economy (Bronk 2009; Buchanan and Vanberg 1991; Esposito 2011). Deviations from established economic practices and existing technologies rely on imagined futures.

Finally, the contingency of expectations gives rise to the *politics of expectations*. Even if the future they represent is imaginary, expectations motivate real decisions that have distributional consequences and may thus become the object of interest struggles among actors in economic fields. Actors seek to influence expectations in different ways, including by shaping the social and political structures that underlie them. The degree to which they succeed in this depends on their economic, social, and cultural resources. Indeed, this is one of the main tasks of firms and political actors and a major goal of speech acts uttered in the field of the economy. Material interests in the economy are swayed by the expectations of competitors, consumers, researchers, employees, and employers, and so the politics of expectations are an important element in the microfoundation of capitalist dynamics. Power is expressed in the creation and influencing of expectations—in other words, fictional expectations are central to the market struggle. This stands in stark contrast to the theory of rational expectations, which denies the possibility that attempts to influence expectations may shape economic outcomes. Rational expectation theorists argue that rational actors will always perceive a commodity's intrinsic value and therefore cannot be blinded in their expectations.

These implications are crucial elements in this analysis of the role of expectations in the dynamics of capitalism. Chapters 5 through 8, which form the second and main part of the book, describe how fictional expectations coordinate action, have performative effects, help to create newness, and are contested among actors in four key fields of the capitalist economy: money and credit, investment decisions, innovation processes, and consumption choices.

Fictionality, far from being a lamentable but inconsequential moment of the future's fundamental uncertainty, is a constitutive element of capitalist dynamics, including economic crises. An economy without uncertainty would be an economy without fictional expectations in which actors could act fully rationally, but it would also be a static economy without novelty and without time, in which everything happens at once. The mathematical models of general equilibrium theory brought this idea to its logical conclusion in the 1950s (Arrow and Debreu 1954).

By contrast, Keynes ([1936] 1964) asserted that it was important for actors to evoke desirable future states of the world to keep the economy running despite the incalculability of outcomes. Keynes used the notion of animal spirits to express the idea that calculation is not the only factor driving economic growth and crises. Animal spirits counter feelings of insecurity that arise when actors perceive the future's uncertainty, which might lead to inaction and stagnation. As contemporary behavioral economists have so often shown, people tend to grossly overestimate their chances for success in economic ventures (Taleb 2010: 180). This overconfidence underpins the very functioning of capitalism—and is a far cry from the rationality assumptions of neoclassical economics. Keynes also coined the term "liquidity preference" to express the consequences of actors' lack of confidence in the potential profitability of new investments, which shrinks their time horizons, reduces investment and consumption, and leads to the underemployment of economic factors—in other words, to economic crises. Capitalism needs the evocative overload of fictional expectations in order to operate.

The Social Bases of Fictional Expectations

If they cannot be formed from information alone, then where exactly do expectations come from? Contrary to behavioral approaches in economics, images of future outcomes and the confidence to act in the face of uncertainty—or, conversely, the sudden collapse of this confidence—cannot be comprehensively understood by focusing on cognitive regularities expressing themselves through overconfidence, loss aversion, or decision heuristics. Instead, expectations are social phenomena, in the sociological tradition of Emile Durkheim and American pragmatism.

The idea that expectations are social and not individual phenomena has important roots in the sociology of Emile Durkheim, who, in his sociology of religion, set out to investigate how religious belief systems are formed and reinforced (Durkheim [1912] 1965). Durkheim argues that religious beliefs are collective representations shaped and renewed through ritualistic practices in which the members of a clan come together and experience situations of collective effervescence. Though it may at first seem farfetched to compare the behavior of deliberately rational actors in contemporary capitalist economies with the behavior of tribal community members, Durkheim's analysis offers unique insight into the emergence and dynamics of expectations held in the capitalist economy. These expectations are also shaped by collective beliefs formed through communicative practices, albeit in a very different context. Discourses among expert communities and beliefs held by laypeople are crucially important to the formation of the imagined futures formed within the capitalist economy. Such discourses, and the imaginaries prevailing at any given point in time, are framed by powerful actors such as firms, politicians, experts, and the media.

The discourses likewise take place in the context of cultural and institutional frames, which actors use to interpret the economic world, and which inform their expectations. These frames include economic theories and institutions as well as beliefs in concepts such as calculability, the goal of economic growth, or the solution of problems through technological progress.

In *Imagined Communities,* Benedict Anderson (1983) explains how maps or shipping schedules in newspapers helped people imagine their nations. This also applies to how actors imagine their economic futures. While the expectations formed from within these cognitive frames are oriented toward the future, the frames themselves are strongly influenced by the past, in the form of the distribution of resources, historically shaped cultural norms, social networks, and the use of historical information. Macroeconomic forecasts, to give one example, are based on the statistical examination of past events. More generally, assessments of the future are influenced by past experiences and their interpretation, as well as established structures, implying that the way the future is imagined differs between historical periods, countries, and social groups. The discursive constitution of expectations is also structurally shaped through economic and social stratification. Position in the stratified social order as well as economically or politically powerful actors and experts influence the construction of imagined futures and the alleged causal relations that underpin them. Just as a priest guides believers in religious practice, the power exercised by firms through advertising and lobbying, as well as the mass media, plays a hugely important role in the enunciation of economic imaginaries. The archaic world described by Durkheim lives on in capitalist modernity.

If expectations are understood to be both contingent and dependent on collective processes influenced by culture, history, and power relations, then they are an inherently sociological phenomenon. Moreover, the idea of fictional expectations is associated with a *sociological* understanding of action, because of its focus on the intersubjective processes by which expectations are formed and contested. Action in this context is not understood in the teleological sense, as driven by an end originating from an individual actor and independent of the process by which it is produced. Instead, action is seen in pragmatist terms, as a process in which ends and strategies are formed and revised based on contingent and changing interpretations of an emerging situation. Expectations and goals are the outcome of a process unfolding in time, based on past experiences and through interactions with others, by which actors develop and enact projects, plans, and strategies. In this sense, fictional expectations are similar to Dewey's ends-in-view, "foreseen consequences which influence present deliberation" (Dewey [1922] 1957: 223). Pragmatist thinking sees the future as a process; it unfolds in a nonlinear way as actors investigate it and make decisions based on their imaginaries of what the future will look like.

OVERVIEW OF THE BOOK

The first part of this book critically engages existing approaches to expectations in sociology and economics in order to develop the idea of fictional expectations, beginning with a discussion of the temporal order of capitalism and its consequences for the time orientation of actors. It first reviews the relevant work of sociologists, historians, and economists on this subject, then shows that the dominant temporal orientation of actors in capitalist modernity is toward an open future.

Chapter 3 opens with a critical assessment of general equilibrium theory and rational expectations theory as the most powerful ways to conceptualize expectations in modern economics. This chapter also covers dissenting approaches in economics by economists such as John Maynard Keynes, George Shackle, and Paul Davidson, which foreshadow arguments regarding expectations in economic action. It continues with a discussion of the more limited literature on expectations in sociology.

Chapter 4 develops the concept of fictional expectations, discussing the notion of fictionality in literary theory, in particular that of John Searle (1975), and the philosophy of arts (Walton 1990). It relates the notion of fictional expectations to concepts such as hope, fear, beliefs, ideology, imaginaries, ideas, and promises. It then examines the political dimension of expectations salient in the *politics of expectations*. Chapter 4 closes with a discussion of the social sources of imaginaries of the future, with special attention to the pragmatist theory of action.

Part 2, which forms the main, empirical segment of the book, discusses, chapter by chapter, the concept of fictional expectations with reference to what are considered to be four building blocks of capitalist economies. Chapter 5 discusses the operation of money and credit, arguing that their chief precondition is belief in the stability of the monetary system and in the future credibility of debtors. The belief in the stability of the monetary system, which is indispensable for the expansion of capitalism, depends on actors' expectations that they will be able to exchange tokens, which are worthless in and of themselves, for valuable commodities at a future point in time. It discusses the question of how this "fiction of a monetary invariant" (Mirowski 1991: 580) is maintained and what happens if belief in the future value of money vanishes. Linked to money is the notion of credit, another building block for capitalist growth in which uncertainty is inherent, since a debtor's willingness and ability to repay his debt cannot be fully known.

Assessments of the risks associated with credit and the future stability of money are both forms of fictional expectations that are at least partly institutionally anchored and enforced through the power of creditors and the state to impose compliance.

Chapter 6 turns to investments as another crucial building block of capitalist dynamics, and discusses investments in plants and equipment, financial investments, and human capital investments. These investments are motivated by the desire for profit or, in the case of investments in human capital, by expectations of income, social status, or employment security. As its high failure rate shows, investment is a fundamentally uncertain practice: actors often cannot know in advance which investment will maximize utility and therefore must rely on imaginaries of future states of the world (as well as on conventions) when deciding on specific investments. Financial markets in particular are rife with examples of investment motivated by fictional expectations, conveyed as stories of how asset prices will develop in the future.

Chapter 7 investigates innovation processes as a third crucial element of capitalist dynamics. Economic growth theories have attributed the unprecedented growth over the past 250 years in large part to technological innovation (Roemer 1990; Solow 1957). Schumpeter (1934) examined the microlevel and observed that innovative processes are inspired by actors' imaginaries. Following in his footsteps, contemporary innovation studies investigate the roots of technological progress in "projections" of future worlds, and this chapter uses these studies to show the role of fictional expectations in the innovation process.

The final chapter in Part 2 examines consumption. Capitalist growth in affluent consumer societies requires that demand outstrips necessity, and consumers' perceptions of the value of goods or services depends on expectations regarding the symbolic "performance" of these goods once they are purchased. In affluent societies, the value of goods is increasingly based on symbolic meanings, which must be created and maintained through communications between producers and consumers for purchases to take place. The imaginaries of value that consumers attribute to purchasable products is another instance of fictional expectations.

In all four chapters of Part 2, the topic of valuation plays a central role: actors pursue money, investments, innovations, and consumption only if they believe the objects they obtain through market exchange will have value in the future. Their expectations of value take many forms: they accept money because they believe in its future purchasing power; they accept the risk of capital investments and innovation because they expect profit; they purchase consumer goods based on dreams of future satisfaction and expected social status. Valuation and imagined futures are closely intertwined. Current value is based on fictional expectations regarding future outcomes and, vice versa, fictional expectations express assumptions about future value. Looking at how value is based on the expectations created in markets can contribute to the sociology of valuation (see also Beckert and Aspers 2011; Beckert and Musselin 2013).

The final part of this book focuses on two *instruments* used to generate fictional expectations. Chapter 9 discusses forecasting (macroeconomic forecasts and technological projections) as a technology that helps to establish fictional expectations. It examines the question of why substantial resources continue to be spent on economic forecasts even though they have been widely shown to be unreliable and erroneous. They are analyzed as instruments for the creation of fictional expectations that help actors to make decisions under conditions of uncertainty. In the same vein, Chapter 10 investigates how economic theories and models may be interpreted as instruments that help generate fictional expectations by providing accounts of causal relations with which actors form a cognitive map for predicting the future consequences of present decisions. In addition to their function in the coordination of economic decisions, economic and technological forecasts and economic theories are analyzed according to how they help contribute to newness, as well as their role as tools in the politics of expectations.

The conclusion reviews the book's findings with a discussion of their implications for a theory of capitalist modernity. It critically questions Max Weber's view of the development of the capitalist economy as a process of rationalization and disenchantment. Weber ([1930] 1992) identified the religious motifs present in the origins of modern capitalism, but believed these nonrational influences disappeared as capitalism evolved, arguing that the "iron cage" of self-propelled economic mechanisms would ultimately force actors into instrumentally rational behavior. His view of modernity's development has been highly influential, but the central role of fictional expectations shows that capitalist dynamics are still partly animated by nonrational beliefs, or "secular enchantment." This is not a trivial phenomenon or a romanticization of modern capitalism; rather, it reconceptualizes the notion of the "iron cage" as colonizing creative and non-economically motivated expressions of agency, feeding into capitalism's restlessness.

Using the processes of social interaction in the economy—an approach typical of economic sociology—to explore the broad question of the dynamics of capitalism strengthens the connection between economic sociology and political economy, and shows the contribution micro-oriented sociology can make to the understanding of macroeconomic processes.

This book is an "essay" in the formal sense of the term: it is a broad-ranging attempt to develop an innovative perspective on capitalist dynamics and to offer a response to the very old question of how these dynamics are linked to the political and cultural order. More speculative in nature and more open to approaches from a variety of academic disciplines than many academic works on the topic of capitalism, it offers fresh ideas in a longstanding discussion, and opens a path for future empirical and theoretical work.

I

DECISION-MAKING IN AN UNCERTAIN WORLD

TWO

THE TEMPORAL ORDER
OF CAPITALISM

> The emphasis of modernism is on the present or on the future, but never on the past.
>
> —DANIEL BELL, *The Cultural Contradictions of Capitalism*

THE EMERGENCE of the capitalist economy is most visible in the expansion of markets and monetary exchange.[1] Beginning in the early modern period, markets expanded: processes of commodification accelerated, economies of scale could be realized, and depersonalized exchange oriented toward profit became increasingly prevalent. The labor process, too, came to be dominated by the competitive logic of the market mechanism as broad-scale labor markets emerged in the nineteenth century. The widespread use of monetary instruments made the expansion of credit-based investments and cost calculations possible. Though this process started in early modernity, it was only in the nineteenth and twentieth centuries that it became dominant in shaping economic processes, first in Western Europe and North America, and today globally.

Scholars of capitalism have described the preconditions for the development of capitalist markets in great detail: secure property rights, strong state power, double-entry bookkeeping, the development of labor markets, the construction of infrastructure, and the introduction of standardized measurement scales are all necessary conditions for capitalism to expand, and they are systematically foregrounded in historical accounts. A less-recognized precondition, however, is a change in the temporal disposition of actors; that is, a shift in the principal cognitive orientation of economic actors with regard to relevant time horizons (Bourdieu 1979). These orientations are an integral part of actors' belief systems and inform their practices; the perception of time is historically specific and is itself an aspect of the social construction of reality (Luhmann 1976: 34).

In this chapter, it is argued that the evolution of capitalism was accompanied by fundamental changes in the temporal orientations of actors; specifically, by an altered understanding of the future. This change in temporal orientations was both a cause and effect of capitalist transformations. Traditional societies generally viewed the future as part of a circular repetition of events whose occurrence was often cognitively represented through myths. Though these societies had trade relations and markets, they did not have a self-expanding market sphere (Polanyi [1944] 1957). By contrast, the temporal dispositions of capitalism portray the future as open, containing opportunities to be seized and risks to be calculated. Capitalism is characterized by "a belief in a future rather than a resignation to, or an investment in the present. The future, rather than the past, is this regime's distinctive temporal orientation" (Moreira and Palladino 2005: 69). Indeed, capitalism is an economic system in which the present is assessed principally through the lens of the future, which is itself considered using imaginaries of future states in order to anticipate as yet unrealized profit and loss. If modern capitalism "embeds itself into the future" (Giddens 1999: 2), it is necessary to analyze this temporal orientation and the corresponding dispositions of actors in order to lay the microfoundations required to understand capitalist dynamics.[2]

DETRADITIONALIZATION AND THE EMERGENCE OF THE FUTURE

One of the most insightful analyses of the historical development of capitalism from the perspective of changes in temporal dispositions is Pierre Bourdieu's (1979) description of the changes in the economic and social order of the Kabyle in Algeria. Bourdieu conducted his fieldwork in Algeria in the 1950s at a moment when the capitalist economy was starting to penetrate traditional Kabyle society; its established ways of life and forms of economic organization were undergoing profound changes. The monetized circuits of the capitalist economy were placing increasing pressure on the traditional economy, giving rise to intense conflicts and disorientations. Bourdieu describes changes to economic life and their effects on family structures and community relations using detailed ethnographic observations and statistical analyses. The study is most remarkable, however, in its description of the destruction of the Kabyle people's temporal order and its replacement with a new one, which came about primarily through the expansion of monetized market exchange.

Bourdieu's understanding of the relationship between the development of capitalism and changes in the temporal order of society was groundbreaking. He shows, from an analysis of daily economic practices, that actors must integrate new temporal orientations in order to achieve economic success in a capitalist economy. These new temporal orientations uproot traditional ways of life in which the future is seen mostly as a circular repetition of events from the past. This perception is based in practical experiences on the circular movements of nature: what has been will come again; what will come in the future has existed before. The future is closed, in other words. In the capitalist economy, by contrast, actors no longer understand the future as a continuation of a present informed by the past; rather, the future is an unending disruption of the present, a "restless" (Sewell 2008; Wagner-Pacifici 2010) social formation in which actors may refer to several possible futures to select their course of action. This shift in actors' dispositions, driven by the expansion of competitive markets and the spread of money-based exchanges, is a necessary corollary of the development of the capitalist economy.

The difference in temporal orientation does not mean traditional societies are indifferent to the future. As Bourdieu shows, peasants in Algeria plan for their future with great care. But they do so by planning for what Bourdieu (1979) calls "direct goods"; that is, goods that provide intrinsic satisfaction in the future and conform to an inherited "logic of honor" prevalent in the community. Food stock, land investments, and innovations to improve agricultural and domestic equipment are all planned in this way. The individual peasant "lives in the very rhythm of the world with which he is bound up" (27). The economic future is thus connected to the present as a single organic entity, and consists largely of products "forthcoming" from the next harvest, and positions of honor and prestige to be secured within the social order. To use the terminology of Karl Marx ([1885] 1993), the traditional Kabyle economy may be characterized as "simple reproduction"; that is, production for a stationary state. It serves "the reproduction of the group with its ties, values, and beliefs which ensure the cohesion of the group" (Bourdieu 1979: 17).

This assessment of the future contrasts greatly with the emerging capitalist economy Bourdieu observed, a new economic formation that "presupposes the constitution of a mediated, abstract future" (Bourdieu 1979: 10). The capitalist future is based on calculations of distant future states of the world that form "an absent, imaginary vanishing point" (7), a remote goal established by imaginaries of possible worlds and approached through calculation and rational action. These two opposing understandings of the future clashed with one another as Kabyle society modernized.

Kabyle peasants for the most part lacked the dispositions necessary to fulfill the expectations of the increasingly dominant capitalist economy, leading to profound social conflicts. These conflicts may be observed, for instance, in peasants' strong opposition to engaging with the abstract future of the market, which is seen as an unreal world (Bourdieu 1979: 15). Those who calculate the future and its possibilities are seen as excessive worriers seeking to make themselves "the associate of God." By the same token, actors are critical of money because it is an "indirect good," not a source of satisfaction in and of itself. Money's promise of utility in the future "is distant, imaginary, and indeterminate" (11). A similar critique is leveled against credit, the economic institution most alien to the logic of the precapitalist economy, in that it not only relies on an abstract future but also opposes solidarity by presupposing "the complete impersonality of the relationship between contracting parties" (14).

The rejection of an abstract and calculated future is also visible in peasants' lack of interest in proposed improvements to agricultural methods. Bourdieu observes that changes to production methods proposed by outsiders "often arouse only incomprehension and skepticism, the reason is that, being based on abstract calculation and entailing a suspension of adherence to the familiar 'given,' they are tainted with the unreality of the imaginary" (Bourdieu 1979: 10). Nothing, Bourdieu wrote, "is more foreign to the pre-capitalist economy than representation of the future [le futur] as a field of possibles to be explored and mastered by calculation" (8).

Bourdieu is not the only scholar of capitalism to describe changes in the temporal order and their attendant conflicts as crucial to capitalism's development. Many social and economic historians have investigated such changes, particularly in the context of European industrialization. E. P. Thompson's (1967) investigation of the emergence of new time regimes and work discipline in the process of industrialization in Great Britain has been particularly influential. Thompson shows that the temporal orientations demanded by industrial production processes clashed violently with workers' temporal dispositions. Workers in the early 1800s often arrived late to work, left early, and did not show up at all on Mondays and religious holidays. Once these conflicts were resolved, subsequent struggles by trade unions to shorten the workday indicated the continuing tension between the temporal order of capitalist production and the moral economy of workers—a conflict that still stands at the center of many labor disputes today. Thompson's study is just one example of many historical investigations of how industrialization disciplined workers with clocks, piece-rate pay schedules, timetables, and production line regimentation (Biernacki 1995; Le Goff 1960).[3]

Max Weber describes another aspect of traditional resistance to capitalist time orders in his early studies on Silesian peasants in the late nineteenth century (Weber [1927] 2003). Large-scale Silesian farmers sought to generate profits in the global capitalist market. Their workers, however, were traditional peasants, and wage incentives to work longer with greater discipline were a failure: instead of working longer hours to raise their living standards, the Silesian peasants decided to work less when wages were increased. Contrary to landowners' (and economists') expectations, "it was futile to double the wages of an agricultural laborer in Silesia who mowed a certain tract of land on a contract, in the hope of inducing him to increase his exertions. He would simply have reduced by half the work expended" (355). Similarly, the weavers working from their homes in the nineteenth century would work longer hours during economic downturns, when the prices they fetched were low, and reduce their work effort during times of prosperity, when they could draw higher prices and support their families with less effort (Kocka 2013: 68). Neither the Silesian peasants nor the weavers based their decisions on imaginaries of a future with higher living standards; instead, they embraced a traditional way of life. This does not mean that traditional societies have no ambition for the future: to them, however, the future is not an open realm waiting to be filled by a changed social reality. Instead, "established practices are used as a way to organizing the future. Thus the future is shaped without the need to carve it out as a separate territory" (Giddens 1994: 62).

As Max Weber observes, traditional time dispositions have a limiting effect on the development of modern capitalism. According to him, economic rationalism, while "partly dependent on rational technique and law . . . is at the same time determined by the ability and disposition of men to adopt certain types of practical rational conduct. When these types have been obstructed by spiritual obstacles, the development of rational economic conduct has also met serious inner resistance" (Weber [1930] 1992). The market subject of the capitalist economic order must free himself from traditionalism and systematically seek to maximize profits or income by seizing the opportunities he perceives in the future. Strangely enough, this idea can also be found in nineteenth-century debates on the abolition of slavery in the United States, in which both defenders and opponents of slavery expressed concern over the economic behavior of freed slaves. Both sides argued that freed slaves could only become productive members of American society if they did not limit their economic activities to the fulfillment of immediate needs, but also aspired to the satisfaction of "artificial wants," based on imaginaries of life beyond necessity. In other words, freed slaves would only be economically productive if they could project themselves into a superior future, motivated to work by imaginaries of a better life ahead of them (Oudin-Bastide and Steiner 2015: 161).

These historical observations show that the orientation toward a different and "better" future that holds the promise of increased consumption, higher profits, and new lifestyles should not be taken for granted. It is the product of a longstanding historical process of institutional and cultural transformation that has taken place over decades as the capitalist system unfolds. It is, in other words, part of the process of detraditionalization, which is never complete. Even in modern capitalist societies, many pockets of traditionalism persist and new ones emerge. Nevertheless, today a large percentage of the world population has been caught up in economic behavior that requires them to pursue unlimited profit through rational investment, or to continually increase their consumption with income they augment through hard and disciplined work. This behavior demonstrates the time dispositions of capitalism identified by Bourdieu and Weber.

THE OPENING OF THE FUTURE

But where did the temporal disposition specific to modern capitalism originate? Bourdieu and Thompson point to the disciplining of the workforce through coercion and incentives, as well as to the action logics introduced through the expansion of competitive markets and monetary exchange. The process can thus be understood as the outcome of changed forms of social domination and the effect of the systemic forces of capitalism. In capitalism, actors are structurally compelled to abandon traditional ways of life.

In a different vein, Max Weber investigated the abandonment of traditional ways of life at a moment when the capitalist forces were not yet an "iron cage." He famously concludes ([1930] 1992) that the dispositions rational capitalism requires of its actors are formed from religious doctrines to which actors are drawn (or which they fear), particularly from the Protestant doctrine of predestination. This doctrine is striking in its understanding of the future: its subscribers believe they cannot know whether their souls will be saved. Living in a constant state of existential fear and uncertainty, they seek signs from God that might indicate their future salvation. One such sign is economic success, which can only be the outcome of endless and systematic striving. The search for such signs motivates behaviors analogous to the behaviors demanded by capitalism, and encourages the temporal orientation toward the future. Weber's *Protestant Ethics* famously quotes Benjamin Franklin's biological analogy for the systematic investment of monetary resources: "Remember, that money is of the prolific, generating nature. Money can beget money, and its offspring can beget more, and so on. Five shillings turned is six, turned again it is seven and threepence, and so on, till it becomes a hundred pounds. The more there is of it, the more it produces every turning, so that the profits rise quicker and quicker. He that kills a breeding sow, destroys all her offspring to the thousandth generation" (Franklin, quoted in Weber [1930] 1992: 15).

Note that it is an imaginary future that justifies the demand for specific behavior on the part of actors. Current action will create future riches. Furthermore, rational economic pursuit is interpreted as a religious duty that is pleasing to God. These religious convictions and their integration into secular conduct operated as a force against economic traditionalism and encouraged the way of life Weber describes as contributing to the rise of modern rational capitalism. Weber shows that the pursuit of profit is not a natural propensity but a cultural construct: Protestant believers engage in activities that please their God and lessen their fears of a future experienced as wholly contingent. The new temporal dispositions conducive to the expansion of capitalism are the unintended side effect of a pervasive religious doctrine.

This is not to say that the rise of capitalism can be understood as based on cultural transformations alone. Nobody would reject such an assumption more than Weber himself. All I claim is that cultural transformations, particularly as they pertain to the temporal order, play a role in the construction of the "capitalist subject." Moreover, I argue with Bourdieu and Weber that capitalism can develop only if the temporal dispositions of traditional societies are altered. For Bourdieu, the Kabyle economy's transition into the global capitalist economy under colonial rule was a process driven by systemic forces. For Weber, investigating the *origins* of modern rational capitalism, actors were attracted to this economic behavior also for religious reasons. Only later would capitalism's religious roots become a *"caput mortuum* in the world" (Weber [1927] 2003: 368). Weber's metaphor of the iron cage expressed the idea that religious motivation would become irrelevant to the further development of capitalism once its mechanisms were in place and methodic profit-seeking and utility maximization became the rational responses to market system's pressures.

THE EXTENSION OF TIME HORIZONS IN MODERN SOCIETY

The idea that modernity developed in the context of a new understanding of the future is not limited to assessments of economic change. Historians have investigated longer term changes to the temporal orders of societies as far back as the Middle Ages, and have shown that understanding the future as the locus of events that are open and yet to occur emerged gradually, beginning in the seventeenth century (Hölscher 1999: 34; Koselleck 2004).

In the history of Christianity up to the sixteenth century, perceptions of the future were characterized by expectations of the world's apocalyptic end. Although the precise timing of this apocalyptic ending was theologically contested—prophecies were generally ambiguous and modified frequently—human history was seen as moving toward a predetermined and possibly imminent end. In the Last Judgment that followed this end, God would save the souls of some; all others would be sentenced to eternal damnation. The idea that the future was a realm that could be shaped through deliberate action was impossible in this worldview. The Church used eschatology to dominate and integrate society, and exercised close control over prophecy; any vision of the future required its authorization. The future was the "property of God," not the object of human will and discretion (Hölscher 1999: 36; Koselleck 2004: 11).

The Reformation destroyed this view of a predetermined future. The absolutist states, consolidating their power at that time, required a monopoly over interpretations of the future and suppressed competing or dissenting religious and political prophecies, including apocalyptic and astrological visions of the future. Eschatology was replaced by a new experience of time: human history was no longer seen as moving toward a predetermined endpoint; now it was a domain of "finite possibilities, arranged according to their greater or lesser probability" (Koselleck 2004: 18). The future began to be assessed using instruments of prognosis that relied on foresight and political calculation. Political actors attempted to anticipate developments in a future perceived as surprising and requiring preparedness. Still, the future remained within the confines of a traditional order: the time structure of prognoses was static, repetitive, or circular. "A politician could become more clever or even cunning: he could refine his technique; he could become wiser or more farsighted: but history never conveyed him into unknown regions of the future" (Koselleck 2004: 21). In this sense, prognoses of the future had not yet left the static horizon of Christian expectations.

The Enlightenment and the development of philosophies of progress changed all this. The notion of progress opened up a future that transcended the traditional order; there was, not incidentally, an important wave of utopian descriptions of future social orders produced in the eighteenth and early nineteenth centuries. In 1771, Louis-Sébastien Mercier published *L'An 2440, rêve s'il en fut jamais,* a novel that described society in the future. Tocqueville, Saint-Simon, Fourier, and Robert Owen all described in the early nineteenth-century utopian visions for the organization of society in the future. This interest in envisioning an uncertain and possibly completely different future has never vanished from modern society. At the close of the nineteenth century, books like Edward Bellamy's *Looking Backward* (1887), H. G. Wells's *The Time Machine* (1895), and multiple works by Jules Verne bear witness to this interest in the open future and to the hopes and anxieties brought by a time of heightened technological, social, and economic change. Science fiction has its roots in that era, and continues to fulfill that function today. Utopias, starting from a "strange spatial extraterritoriality—from this nonplace, in the literal sense of the word—[ensure] that we are able to take a fresh look at our reality; hereafter, nothing about it can continue to be taken for granted" (Ricoeur 1991: 184).

Underlying this new orientation toward a future imagined to be fundamentally different from the present social order were contemporary experiences of accelerating social change. The philosophies of history emerging from the Enlightenment described stages of human development and thus anticipated processes of future social change. Both the imagining of a counterfactual future and the description of the process leading to it became the object of scientific reflection. Hegel, for example, analyzed the movement of the mind, while Marx described history as a logical progression of class struggles, which would ultimately lead to a classless communist society. Comte, on the other hand, argued that the development of human knowledge took place in three stages, ending with the positive stage of rationality, at which it would not only be possible to discern the present, but also to predict future developments according to scientific laws.

Hegel and Comte imagined an end stage to this process of change, at which history itself would conclude. This might be interpreted as romantic nostalgia, expressing the hope that capitalism's restless dynamic would eventually settle. Liberal economic theory went beyond this view, describing the future as an *endless* process of accumulating wealth. Economic development was seen as an infinite source of progress through which all actors and nations could ultimately increase their well-being. At the same time, the concept of self-regulating markets rationalized short-term hardship for the sake of an as-yet-unrealized economic future. Competition, unemployment, or dislocation were to be borne for the sake of future gains in economic welfare. This process had no final goal: wealth could increase infinitely because the future was imagined to be an endless source of unfulfilled needs. In this sense, liberal economic theory was both an emphatically modern social theory and a theory of capitalism. The socialist utopias that emerged from the labor movement were a corresponding shift toward anticipations of a utopian future. However, the form of this future, the classless communist society, was seen as a fixed vanishing point. Imagining the possibility of an open future different from the present is the cultural basis of the notion of progress. The consciousness of actors becomes enmeshed in a "not yet," possessing the structure of a perennial imperative (Hölscher 1999: 39; Koselleck 2004: 23).

CALCULATION AND UTOPIAS

Niklas Luhmann (1976) has argued that the temporal order of modernity should be understood as one in which utopias of progress mix with prognoses and calculation. To Luhmann, traditional societies think of themselves as living in an enduring or even eternal present, as Bourdieu observed was the case for the Kabyle. In accord with Koselleck, Luhmann finds that perceptions of the future changed in the eighteenth century, with the advent of bourgeois society, which turned the future into "a storehouse of possibilities" (Luhmann 1976: 131). The future was thought of in the present as containing several mutually exclusive possibilities for how it would actually unfold. The future was thus experienced "as a generalized horizon of surplus possibilities that have to be reduced as we approach them" (141). Werner Sombart described this change long before Luhmann in relation to the emergence of modern capitalism. Sombart observed that in early modernity, a social type was already appearing that he called the "projector." These were "inventive and resourceful leaders whose lives were dedicated to forging reforms and restructuring plans, and to gaining support for these from the country's rich, great, and titled." (Sombart [1902] 1969: 872, own translation). With the advent of modern capitalism, these projectors turned into entrepreneurs, setting up businesses and trying to convince others of their visions. The founders of companies "dreamed the colossal" and attempted to persuade others of plans that became imaginable in a context in which the future was perceived as open.

This hints also at the loss of control modern societies experienced as result of their changing perception of the future: the future became a space of promises and hopes, but also a cosmos of possible threats. Though traditional societies also perceived danger, particularly from uncontrollable natural events, the deliberate extension of courses of action into uncharted territories gave rise to a new form of insecurity and a new experience of dangers. In part, this development of a social world perceived as increasingly risky can be attributed to the characteristics of modernity: increasing functional differentiation and role segmentation which undermine the familiarity that traditional communities take for granted and that cause the social world to appear more contingent (Seligman 1997).

The concept of risk shares similar historical roots with that of the open future, for risk emerges when courses of action are decided upon using projections of a counterfactual future, which may turn out differently than predicted, and when any resulting damage is attributed to these decisions (Esposito 2011: 32). Indeed, a new attitude toward the imponderability of the future first surfaced in the twelfth and thirteenth centuries in the Italian city-states, when merchants and explorers ceased to perceive risks as dangers to be passively endured or avoided and began seeing them as bearing opportunities to improve their welfare (Zachmann 2014: 6). The notion of risk became prominent in the sixteenth and seventeenth centuries, in the context of Western explorations of the world, and was originally a literal reference to sailing into uncharted waters (Giddens 1999: 1). The social location of the idea of risk in explorers, merchants, and financiers was confirmed in subsequent historical developments: in the late seventeenth and the early eighteenth centuries the insurance market expanded, with London as its center. Insurance made it necessary to calculate insurance premiums, thus motivating further developments in probability theory. Risk and the notion of an open future belong together: "Risk refers to hazards that are actively assessed in relation to future possibilities. It only comes into wide usage in a society that is future-oriented—which sees the future precisely as a territory to be conquered or colonized" (1).

Medieval Europe and traditional Kabyle society had no concept of risk in the modern sense. They also had no need for the concept. Whether time would eventually end, as medieval thinkers would have had it, or whether it repeated itself endlessly, as the Kabyles believed, the disappointment of prophecy or the disturbance of cycles could be interpreted in many ways and attributed to factors beyond individual control. Catastrophes such as droughts, floods, or earthquakes were attributed to fate, not to decisions based on erroneous expectations—certainly, they did not call into question the normative validity of traditional rules (Seligman 1997: 172). Imaginaries of the future were restricted by an overarching and unquestioned order.

For actors, a world with an open future that depends on risky decisions devalues responses based on habit or tradition and forces them into calculative and reflexive modes of action. Arjun Appadurai (2013: 298–99) points out that the "world of habitus has been steadily eroded by the pressures of improvisation," meaning that imagination, anticipation, and aspiration with regard to the future are crucial elements of the development of modern societies. Imagination has "become part of the quotidian mental work of ordinary people" (Appadurai 1996: 5); indeed, the imagination of future possibilities has become a vital resource in social processes and projects. Mass media, migration, and life in diaspora communities also push actors to consider a wider set of possible lives. Like Bourdieu, Appadurai (1996: 53) sees detraditionalization as an antidote to the finitude of social experience in traditional societies. For him, however, future orientation is not primarily associated solely with the experience of a loss; rather, it is a resource that opens up possibilities for new courses of action. Aspirations and imaginaries, he argues, can be building blocks of democratic politics and empowerment of the poor.

Appadurai's interpretation of the modern understanding of the future dovetails with my own argument, although my focus is on the role of imagined futures in the dynamics of the capitalist economy. Just as Appadurai argues they are for polities, I posit that imaginaries of the future are a cognitive and emotional force that helps orient and animate the capitalist economy, although, by the same token, they can also produce disorientation and fear. If actors perceive opportunities, the open future is an energizing and dynamic factor in capitalist development. The capitalist economy depends on such perceptions, since investments, whose outcomes are uncertain and will often be known only in the distant future, are necessary for capitalism to operate. Likewise, the capitalist economy depends on consumers purchasing new consumer items whose utility they anticipate. Capitalism can only expand if actors embrace the unpredictability of the future. If imaginaries of a distant, better future fade away or are obscured by fear, time horizons shrink and actors forego opportunities for further, future growth. As a result the capitalist dynamic slows. One may indeed say that capitalism "would not survive a considerable shrinkage of time horizons" (Luhmann 1976: 150–51)

CONCLUSION

Economic orders are characterized by distinct temporal orders. In conjunction with the unfolding of capitalism, a new temporal order of the economy emerged, one with an altered understanding of the future. This remains true even when accounts of this historical process by Bourdieu, Giddens, Koselleck, and Luhmann can be criticized for over-emphasizing the contrast between the temporal orientations of traditional and modern societies. Expectations that the past will continue are still relevant in modern societies, and not every actor in traditional societies confines himself to traditional mental constructs. Explorers, for example, who ventured into hitherto unknown parts of the world in search of new profit opportunities came of age in societies largely dominated by tradition. Vice versa, the thriving postwar capitalist economy of Japan prospered by *continuing* an existing economic model and imitating products first developed elsewhere (Miyazaki 2003). The stark contrast described by the scholars cited above is most useful as an ideal type rather than as a comprehensive description of historical forms. Concurrent movements of traditionalization and detraditionalization exist within capitalism. Linear time and cyclical time coexist. And yet, even with this qualification in mind, it is still the case that a major transformation in the temporal orientation of actors took place concurrently with the development of the capitalist economy. The pervasive perception of the future in modern societies is of an open space waiting to be filled by contingent events prompted by actors making decisions with only limited control over their outcomes.

Sociologists, historians, and anthropologists have described the ways in which the rise of this new time disposition has caused profound social conflict. It is also true, however, that the new time dispositions were crucial to the advance of the capitalist economy: capitalism's development cannot be understood in terms of technological advances, institutional changes, the division of labor, or other macrofactors alone. Changes in cognitive orientations through new temporal dispositions are crucial components in the genesis of the capitalist order, and must be taken into account in any explanation of capitalist dynamics. While this is perhaps evident when it comes to describing growth dynamics, it is also true of economic crises: economic crises should be understood as the collapse of hitherto assumed futures. Such breakdowns open up space for new imaginaries, through which capitalism adjusts and regains its momentum.

The temporal orientation of the capitalist order has social, political, and institutional preconditions: specifically, it requires a social structure open to social mobility and institutions that allow for innovation and the expansion of market competition. Once the future is recognized as open, the question of how actors contend with the uncertainty of future events becomes highly salient. How do actors become convinced that the risks associated with their decisions are worth taking? The answer to this question lies in the expectations actors have when deciding to take them. The probabilistic calculation of risks and opportunities and utopian imaginaries of future states are two cognitive devices modern societies use to come to terms with the open future. They both allow for the *feigning* of future presents, a process that takes place within the confines of social and institutional structures, as well as in the context of power relations that influence expectations.

My focus on capitalist economies in no way implies that *other* modern social orders do not also enlarge time horizons through imaginaries of the future. Socialist thinkers and politicians, for example, have made fierce use of utopian images of how the *socialist* future would unfold. Indeed, these imaginaries play a central role in socialist countries as well as in the labor movements in the West (Hölscher 1989, 2002, Müller and Tanner 1988). This book, however, is limited to examining the role of imagined futures in the dynamics of capitalism.

THREE

EXPECTATIONS AND UNCERTAINTY

The present of future things is expectations.

—AUGUSTINE OF HIPPO, *Confessions*

IN THE PAST thirty years the catchphrase "history matters" has been a rallying cry across the social sciences. Studies in political science and sociology have insisted on explaining current states of the world with reference to past events, and concepts such as path dependence, increasing returns, trajectories, and institutions have been employed to describe the causal influence of the past on the present. William Sewell (1996) summarizes this approach succinctly: "what happened at an earlier point in time will affect the possible outcomes of a sequence of events occurring at a later point in time" (262). That "history matters" is largely taken for granted in sociology and political science.[1]

There is no doubt that understanding historical trajectories is indispensable to understanding the social phenomena of the present. However, events in the social world cannot be explained by the past alone. Actors' decisions are determined by more than existing structures and past experiences—they are shaped in equal measure by perceptions of the future. When making decisions, actors associate certain future results with the course of action they are contemplating, connecting numerous outcomes with different possible decisions. These perceptions are known as expectations.

If expectations are relevant to understanding social action, then social scientists must take more than just the past into account if they are to explain outcomes in any satisfactory way: they must also look to the future. Or, to be more precise, they must consider the expectations of the future that actors hold in the present with regard to the outcomes of the decisions they make. These "present futures" are actors' images of how the world will look at a future point in time; they are the "temporal horizon of the present" (Luhmann 1976: 139) through which decisions are shaped. Like a geographic horizon, a temporal horizon can never be reached, but the images making up this horizon help actors to define situations, and hence to decide on courses of action which will shape future outcomes. Certainly, "history matters," but the future matters, too.[2]

The catchphrase "the future matters" summarizes the approach outlined in this chapter, which includes the role of expectations in economics and in sociology, disciplines that differ profoundly in the role they assign to the future. Expectations of the future stand front and center in contemporary economics, whereas only a few authors or schools in sociology pay attention to expectations, aspirations, and projections.

Despite the apparent differences between the two disciplines in the importance they assign to the future, the dominant branches of economics and sociology have both failed to account for important aspects of the role of the future in social interactions. In the prevailing approaches in economics, expectations are seen deterministically because actors' expectations are believed to be rational. This view of expectations occludes the ways in which actors' decisions are creative responses to situations that are based on contingent interpretations of what the future holds, and minimizes the myriad ways actors may make sense of that future. Sociologists, on the other hand, have dealt "only peripherally, when at all, with the impact of the imagined future on social events" (Mische 2009: 695).[3] Several sociologists who have addressed expectations in their work—including Talcott Parsons and Alfred Schütz—see conceptions of the future largely as shaped by socially anchored templates. Such approaches do no more justice than economics does to the contingent ways in which actors perceive the future and act upon their perceptions.

There are, however, some approaches in both economics and sociology that show how expectations can be conceptualized in a way that truly takes into account the openness of the future and the contingency of interpretations of future developments. These approaches identify the future not only as a "cultural capacity" (Appadurai 2013: 182), but also as an economic capacity. The concept of uncertainty plays a crucial role in all of these approaches, and the contingency of imaginaries necessarily assumes a central role if uncertainty is taken seriously.

EXPECTATIONS IN ECONOMICS

Within the social sciences, economics is undoubtedly the discipline in which expectations play the most important role. This has not always been the case, but starting in the early twentieth century, economics mostly ceased to be a historical discipline and began using the future to explain decisions in the present.[4] Economists analyze social situations by assuming that actors are forward-thinking and will try to figure out which decisions will optimize their resources and maximize their future welfare. Decisions are based on expected future payoffs, discounted to present value. Game theory, for instance, speaks of the "shadow of the future"; that is, an actor's belief that there will be further interactions in the future helps him or her to overcome opportunistic behavior in the present (Dal Bó 2005). The role of the past is limited to explaining what specific institutional restrictions are in place and to providing the statistical data for projections of the future. In all other respects, the past is a "done deal." Sunk costs, the term economists use to describe investments from the past that may influence current decisions, should, they argue, be ignored in decision-making. Economics, in other words, is all about the future: "Economists look ahead to potential rewards, not back to sunk costs. They use discounting to pull uncertain future results back into the present, where decisions are made" (Abbott 2005: 406). This theory's orientation toward the future corresponds particularly well to the temporal order of capitalism. In this way, it would seem to be an ideal discipline to study in order to better understand how the future enters into the action process.

General Equilibrium Theory

General equilibrium theory and rational expectations theory are the two main approaches modern economics uses to understand how the future is perceived. General equilibrium theory, whose development in the second half of the twentieth century is mostly associated with the work of Kenneth Arrow and Gerald Debreu (1954), seeks to provide mathematical evidence for the existence of a general competitive equilibrium in the economy, and to show that this equilibrium fulfills the condition of Pareto optimality.[5] The future plays a crucial role in the Arrow-Debreu model, which introduces the idea of "dated contingent commodities" that are "made possible" by the assumption of complete future markets. Goods, they posit, are defined by four attributes: physical qualities, place, time of delivery, and external conditions at the time of availability. A special market exists for every good thus defined in their equilibrium model, which would produce a specific price for umbrellas supplied during a rain shower in Paris on May 18, 2064, for example. Since all future markets exist, firms and households can "determine their entire production and consumption plans, for they know the prices of all goods in all future periods, and they can insure themselves against all eventualities" (Backhouse 1985: 290). If there are complete future markets, then the future may be fully integrated into the equilibrium model and a Pareto optimal equilibrium may be expected (Arrow [1969] 1983: 142; Starr 1997: 180).

Curiously, although the Arrow-Debreu model concerns itself with future exchanges, it actually extinguishes time. All exchange processes can take place simultaneously in the present because all possible conditions of the world in future periods are known already, and can thus be included in contingent contracts at time t_0. In this way, the model reduces the economy to a static equilibrium in which time and an open future do not call the rationality of decisions into question. When future prices are discounted to their present value, the future can be concatenated with the present.

The assumption of complete future markets shields general equilibrium theory against the consequences of an open future: it denies that anything may be unknown or unknowable. The existence of complete markets for contingent contracts, however, can be assumed only theoretically, not as a description of an actual, existing economy. It is entirely unrealistic to assume that all possible contingencies are known, that they are mutually exclusive, that the actors have no influence over the actual incidence of a given situation, and that all future markets actually exist. Moreover, according to this model, actors must always be able to see the actual state of the world and must be able to calculate at least subjective probabilities for the occurrence of every possible state. Actors must have perfect foresight and possess an exhaustive list of all possible events (Gravelle and Rees 1992; Starr 1997). Evidently, every one of these assumptions can be challenged (Postlewaite 1987: 133; Radner 1968; Vickers 1994). The *model* of an economy with a stable, market-clearing equilibrium should not be confused with the description of an existing economy.

Rational Expectations Theory

The premises of the Arrow-Debreu model are purely theoretical, and some of the assumptions it makes are avoided by rational expectations theory, the second prevailing approach to the future in economics today. Rational expectations theory was developed in the 1960s and 1970s, most notably in work by John Muth (1961) and Robert Lucas (1972), both of whom sought to formulate a microfoundation for macroeconomics. Rational expectation theory—with its corollary, the efficient market hypothesis—is the most influential approach to expectations in today's economics. It has played a prominent role in politics as well. This book concurs with rational expectations theory that expectations matter greatly; however, it takes issue with the assertion that actors' decisions are formed based on expectations that make efficient use of available information and that actors' expectations concur on the dominant macroeconomic model.

A "rational expectation" may be defined as an expectation based on the observation of the statistical distribution of events in the past using all presently available information. This statistical examination is represented in the dominant economic model, which predicts future outcomes correctly. This "true" model of the economy is assumed to be historically constant, meaning that the validity of the fundamental relations and laws governing economic activity do not themselves vary with time (Bausor 1983: 4). Under these conditions, the future can be predicted from the past; indeed, it is merely the "statistical shadow of the past" (Davidson 2010: 17).[6] Since expectations are "informed predictions of future events" they do not differ from those of the "true" economic model (Muth 1961: 316). The theory of rational expectations asserts that though individuals make decisions based on their subjective probability distributions, "if expectations are to be rational these subjective distributions must be equal to the objective probability distributions that will govern outcomes at any particular future date" (Davidson 2010: 16–17). This assumption is necessary for an equilibrium to be possible. Both rational expectations theorists and general equilibrium analysis assume that correct foresight is possible and thus advocate a deterministic model of expectations. The theories differ in that rational expectations theory assumes a stochastic conception of the real structures of the economy, while general equilibrium theory assumes perfect information.

This does not exclude the possibility that individual actors might be mistaken in their assessments of economically relevant variables concerning the future. In the aggregate, however, the predictions actors form are correct, because all individual errors are random. Put another way, their predictions are not correlated, and thus not systematically biased. Consequently, the rational individual can predict outcomes that do not differ systematically from the resulting market equilibrium. This reveals the rational-expectations hypothesis as the stochastic analogue of the perfect-information postulate (Bausor 1983: 8). Discrepancies from the expected outcome are caused only by random shocks, which cannot be predicted and are short-term disturbances. As such, they will eventually be overcome, and the system brought back to its predicted path.

Rational expectations theory has significant implications for economic policy. Rational actors, the theory proclaims, cannot be "fooled," and any public policy that attempts to "manipulate the economy by systematically making the public have false expectations" (Sargent 2008: 3) is doomed to failure. For example, the theory predicts that attempts to influence business cycles using short-term tax cuts or inflationary monetary policies cannot be successful because actors will anticipate long-term consequences and adjust current prices accordingly. This critique has most notably been leveled against Keynesian policy interventions, which assume the effectiveness of increased monetary supply and fiscal demand stimuli. Since the 1970s, rational expectations theory has been used extensively to justify the state's retreat from macroeconomic interventions. The theory has also been used to legitimize the deregulation of financial markets, based on the claim that uninhibited financial markets are the optimal device for the creation of efficient market prices, which are defined as prices that correspond to an asset's fundamental value. Used to quash market intervention, the theory reduces both policy-makers and market actors to passive executors of rules based on a fully predetermined economic model (Frydman and Goldberg 2007: 5). Following these rules leads to an efficient equilibrium and thus to an optimal use of economic resources.

As mentioned above, the corollary of rational expectations theory is the efficient market hypothesis (Fama 1965a), which states that market prices are efficient in the sense that they represent the best possible prediction of an asset's future value. An equilibrium price is efficient when it reflects the discounted future income generated by an asset—that is, the fundamental or intrinsic value. Financial markets will be efficient if prices are left to set themselves without outside interference, because actors will detect and seize unexploited profit opportunities stemming from inefficient prices. If securities are undervalued, their purchase will lead to price changes by pushing them toward the security's fundamental value. If one asserts that, given full information and unbridled competition, fundamental value and market prices will converge, then it is logical to conclude that any change in prices is caused by factors that could not be known beforehand. Price changes are thus a random walk.

Rational expectations theory and the efficient market hypothesis have been criticized on many grounds. One of the most frequent critiques is of the theory's track record for correct predictions: neither stock market bubbles nor empirically observable movements in currency markets confirm rational expectations theory (Frydman and Goldberg 2007: 113ff.). More specifically, Robert Shiller (2003) argues that there are significant differences between the volatility of stock prices and their underlying fundamental value, as indicated by company earnings. Volatility in markets seems to be too excessive to be explained by the efficient market hypothesis. This critique gained significant ground after the financial crisis of 2008: "Market expectations and pricing are now shown to have been misguided and even delusional for a long time, whilst the models produced by economists and internalized over a long period by most risk managers and other economic actors are revealed to have been systematically wrong, causing highly correlated 'errors' that were anything but random" (Bronk, forthcoming).

The bubble in real estate prices that preceded the 2008 crisis, overestimation of the value of Internet stocks, and the underestimation of the risks associated with bonds from the southern European periphery are all examples of the pervasiveness of valuations in financial markets that turn out to be wrong. In each of these instances, changes in asset prices were not attributable to new information about assets' fundamental values, but rather to revised interpretations of existing information, or revised expectations as to the behavior of market actors.[7] Actors make systematic errors in their prognoses; these mistakes have become a subject of investigation for behavioral economists.

The empirical record of rational expectations theory is not so much the issue as the assumptions it makes. The efficient market hypothesis assumes that assets have an objective value, expressed in their expected future earnings, which can be determined based on information from the past. It thus has "a world view that treats the future as implied in the present" (Buchanan and Vanberg 1991: 170). Rational expectations theory uses a linear concept of time and assumes stationary values in order to discount the unpredictability of future events, presupposing that all possible contingencies may be taken into account and remain valid in the future. This neglects the historically unique context within which each decision is made. It implies "a highly restricted view of uncertainty as mere random deviations from a fully predetermined model of behavior" (Frydman and Goldberg 2007: 4). Through its assumptions, rational expectations theory can show the coordinative properties of markets. But it does so only under restricted circumstances. Because expectations can only be correct if all the relations that may affect a situation are identified, rational expectations theory is at the same time, in the words of one of its founders, "restricted to the situation in which the relevant distributions have settled down to stationary values and can thus be 'known' to traders" (Lucas 1975: 1121). Unpredictable elements must be excluded from the model, and genuine surprise banished (Bausor 1983: 7).[8] The efficient market hypothesis assumes that external shocks are normally distributed (Muth 1961: 317). The use of normal distributions to predict future events is highly questionable in complex and open situations that are characterized by newness and singularity. If one assumes that the future is open and uncertain because economic events are nonlinear and vary with time, the intrinsic value of assets cannot be assessed with any true precision.

The second problematic assumption in rational expectations theory is that of the randomness of errors. Any systematic errors in forecasting will cancel themselves out because they will be eliminated in competitive markets. In the real world, however, "there is a division of knowledge among market participants, who forecast not only on the basis of different factors (their information sets), but also on the basis of different strategies (their knowledge) that map these factors into forecasts" (Frydman and Goldberg 2007: 52). Two people may analyze a situation in radically different ways, and no one can know ahead of time which of them, if not both, will turn out to be wrong. At the same time, it is possible to pool wrong assessments: as financial bubbles and panics show, there are no empirical grounds for assuming that, on average, market actors are correct. Herd behavior can cause market prices to deviate, for extended periods and in all directions, from the earnings of an asset.

The counter-thesis to rational expectations theory would be that under conditions of uncertainty expectations are contingent, because the openness of the future renders impossible the existence of a "true" economic model. Actors' expectations, rather than being rational forecasts, are "*wagers* concerning a future that . . . is not yet known" (Orléan 2014: 190). Seen in this light, expectations about the future and asset prices are better understood as based on communicatively established imaginaries that change as interpretations and judgments of a situation evolve. This view of expectations negates the claim that the future is already entailed in the past, as well as the idea of efficient markets in which prices reflect fundamental value. It does, however, raise interesting questions about how expectations, prices, and the dynamics of capitalism are constituted.

Uncertainty

The concept of uncertainty is crucial to understanding the contingency of expectations, and although it has received a lot of attention from economists, that attention has been tightly bounded. Standard economics seeks to interpret uncertainty in ways that make it possible to continue understanding actors' decisions as the outcome of rational calculations, and to see economies as equilibrium systems (Elster 2009; Hirshleifer and Riley 1992; Hodgson 2011). Such an understanding of uncertainty is limited, however, as Frank Knight has shown with great clarity in his seminal work on the subject from the early twentieth century.

As is well known, Knight ([1921] 2006) distinguished among three different types of probability situations. In the first, outcomes can be calculated based on a priori probability distributions, using absolutely homogeneous classifications of completely identical instances, as in a game of chance. In the second, that of "statistical probability," actors categorize instances as belonging to classes of incidence for which probabilities are known. While the actual risk of a case cannot be known, a probability calculus can be made. Knight calls the third type "estimates," in which cases are so entirely unique that there "is no possibility of forming in any way groups of instances of sufficient homogeneity to make possible a quantitative determination of true probability" (231). The uniqueness of these situations precludes calculability. Knight suggests collapsing the three types into two categories, which he calls "risk" and "uncertainty."[9]

Knight focuses on situations characterized by uncertainty, a type of situation he sees as crucial in "any typical business decision" (Knight [1921] 2006: 226). While Knight's distinction between risk and uncertainty is analytically sharp, it is difficult to determine whether any given situation is risky or uncertain. It is fairly safe to assume, though, that uncertainty is a prevailing condition in economic decision situations. The complexity and interdependencies of parameters, the unforeseeability of the reactions of relevant third parties, and the nonlinearity of economic processes make the (probabilistic) calculation of outcomes of decisions impossible. Even decisions that appear to be probabilistically calculable often involve elements of uncertainty that "contaminate" the risk calculation (Ortmann 2004: 133). Particularly in situations associated with change, novelty, and crisis, uncertainty is paramount. However, it is precisely these situations which are most closely related to the dynamics of capitalism. They demand decisions despite the unknowability of important information for the calculation of outcomes. In such situations, writes French economist André Orléan, "statistical rationality no longer applies, and an element of personal judgment unavoidably enters into the formation of expectations" (Orléan 2014: 193). For Orléan, who is primarily interested in the operation of financial markets, the consequence of recognizing Knightian uncertainty is that "it is impossible to determine the true value of a security" (Orléan 2014: 195). The central tenet of the efficient market hypothesis therefore does not hold. If future fundamental values cannot be known, then they cannot be the basis of the decisions being made.[10]

If uncertainty is taken into consideration, actors' decisions can no longer be understood as based solely on mathematical calculation; rather, Knight asserts that they are a matter of "opinion as to the outcome" ([1921] 2006: 237). Confidence in predictions is thus "in large measure independent of the 'true value' of the judgments and powers themselves" (242). In what is perhaps an unintentional reference to what sociologists know as the Thomas theorem, Knight writes that confidence "based on the strength of intuition may appear to be compounded to the point of nonsense, but in so far as there exist such feelings reached unconsciously or without deliberation and in so far as they may become the objects of deliberate contemplation, the situation is none the less real" (229).

For Knight, the importance of recognizing uncertainty and the limits of the rational calculation of outcomes lies not in the doubt it casts on economists' assumptions of rationality, nor in the more realistic understanding of business decisions it provides. The role Knight assigns uncertainty is more far-reaching than that: he argues that it is one of the cornerstones of capitalism itself.[11] This is because for him profit—the desired outcome that motivates investments in capitalism—is only possible under conditions of uncertainty. In situations with a certain outcome or known risk, the logic used in neoclassical equilibrium analysis holds, and profits are eliminated in the competitive process. In other words, actors faced with a situation whose outcomes are fully calculable would not be motivated to engage in entrepreneurial activities. This indicates that the dynamics of capitalism could not function without the openness of the future and the incalculability of outcomes of decision-making processes that follow from it.

Frank Knight's insight that business decisions are based on expectations that cannot be rationally calculated flies in the face of mainstream economic theory. Neoclassical economic theory is based on what Paul Samuelson

(1969) has called an "ergodic" view of the world; that is, the assumption that reality is predetermined and can be fully described by unchanging objective conditional probability functions (Davidson 1996: 479). Samuelson sees this as a necessary condition for scientific methodology in economics (see also Davidson 1996; North 1999; Samuelson 1969: 184), and it is therefore not surprising that much of economic thinking in the twentieth century has sought to do away with uncertainty in the Knightian sense of the term. Economics addresses "the question of the individuals' relation to the future by postulating that all likely outcomes can be objectively enumerated. In effect, then, uncertainty is reduced to a probabilizable list of events that can be defined in advance" (Orléan 2014: 70). This outlook has persisted, although some economists are keenly aware of the limits fundamental uncertainty imposes on their models. For Robert Lucas (1981), one of the key originators of rational expectations theory, it is obvious that the theory cannot "be applicable in situations in which one cannot guess which, if any, observable frequencies are relevant: situations which Knight called 'uncertainty'" (224).

Arguably, decisions in contemporary market economies are characterized by fundamental uncertainty; either actors do not fully understand all the parameters relevant to a situation's outcome because of complexity, or all of the relevant factors do not yet exist. In both cases, errors resulting from the lack of foresight need not be randomly distributed; indeed, in such situations it is particularly likely that actors will orient their decisions using a certain set of economic models, the decisions of others, or market trends, for example. If actors make decisions without being able to fully know their consequences—and it must be concluded that they do—then on what basis do they make them?

Expectations under Conditions of Uncertainty

The most influential discussion of expectations in economics based on the recognition of uncertainty in Frank Knight's sense of the term is to be found in the work of John Maynard Keynes. Expectations play a key role in Keynes's theory because he believes that investment and consumption decisions that influence the business cycle evolve largely due to changes in expectations. Keynes differs sharply from rational expectations theory in that he sees the future as only minimally predictable. "The considerations upon which expectations of prospective yields are based are partly existing facts which we can assume to be known more or less for certain, and partly future events which can only be forecasted with more or less confidence" (Keynes [1936] 1964: 147). For Keynes, expectations are indefinite because the future is uncertain: they "cannot be uniquely correct, since our existing knowledge does not provide a sufficient basis for a calculated mathematical expectation. In point of fact all sorts of considerations enter into the market valuation which are in no way relevant to the prospective yield" (152).[12]

Once the idea that the fundamental values of securities may be rationally forecasted is abandoned and the contingency of market valuations is accepted, what indicators can actors use for their assessments? Keynes sketches out three possible answers to this question: first, actors may assume that the "existing state of affairs will continue indefinitely, except insofar as we have specific reasons to expect a change" (152). If this is so, actors will make decisions based on conventions. The second answer Keynes offers is that under conditions of uncertainty actors base their decisions on emotions, which he captures in the notion of "animal spirits" and which prevent actors from retreating into a state of inactivity. "Individual initiative will only be adequate when reasonable calculation is supplemented and supported by animal spirits, so that the thought of ultimate loss which often overtakes pioneers, as experience undoubtedly tells us and them, is put aside as a healthy man puts aside the expectation of death" (162). Finally, Keynes proposes that individual investors in the stock market base their decisions on their expectations regarding the expectations of other investors, rather than on information regarding the fundamental value of assets. Investment decisions in markets are thus guided by the projection of short-term market opinion. Keynes explains this using the famous metaphor of a beauty contest in which the prize is awarded to the person whose choice corresponds most closely to the average opinion of all the other participants.

Keynes's treatment of expectations in *General Theory* is not worked out in detail, but has nevertheless been very influential. In the 1950s, George Shackle developed an approach within the Keynesian tradition that uses expectations under conditions of uncertainty as its starting point. For Shackle, expectations can only be understood with regard to the unknowability of the future. Because the "content of time-to-come is not merely unknown but nonexistent, and the notion of foreknowledge of human affairs is vacuous" (Shackle 1983: 33), any theory that assumes the future is knowable is misguided. For Shackle, however, as for Knight, the contingency of expectations is not primarily a threat. Rather, it offers the possibility of creative change in the economy, through choices based on imaginaries of future states of the world. Choice, according to Shackle, takes place "amongst imagined experiences" (12). In a universe of ultimately creative thought, imaginations of counterfactual futures are a driving force of capitalist dynamics.[13]

Uncertainty is a cornerstone for theories of decision-making also beyond the Keynesian tradition. The concept of "sunspots" refers to random influences on expectations that have no basis in economic fundamentals but become relevant because actors believe in their relevance (Cass and Shell 1983). They are a random variable based in beliefs. Sunspots are influences on economic equilibria that cannot be predicted using economic fundamentals, and which lead to inefficient outcomes such as the self-fulfilling prophecy of a bank run. In other words, and contrary to the claims of rational expectations theory, if sunspots influence outcomes, then a government is justified in intervening to stabilize fluctuations that arise from the fundamentally unfounded expectations of market participants.

Theories of bounded rationality (Simon 1957) share with Keynes the assumption that actors lack either the information necessary to calculate an optimal choice or the cognitive capabilities. Actors have different aspirations, assume different random events, and cannot precisely predict the behavior of their interaction partners (Güth and Kliemt 2010), making it impossible to predict equilibrium outcomes. Given the complexity of decision situations, choices inevitably involve judgments and mental shortcuts. Rather than acting rationally, individuals are more accurately characterized as coping sensibly with the complexity of decision situations. Simon coined the term "satisficing" to describe this process. Bounded rationality finds fault with rational expectations theory in the assumptions it makes about actors' true cognitive capacities: "How can one impute to the social agents the capacity to make the calculations that occupy many pages of mathematical appendixes in the leading journals and that can be acquired only through years of professional training?" (Elster 2009: 7).

Behavioral economics questions neoclassical models' assumptions of rationality in a similar vein, but goes beyond the concept of satisficing, seeking to understand the different types of cognitive biases present in decision-making in a systematic fashion. Behavioral economists identify numerous mechanisms at work in the decision-making process, including stereotypes, overconfidence, herd behavior, limited attention, the sunk-cost fallacy, or projection biases, all of which have the potential to divert actors from the optimal choice. Behavioral economists argue that according to the standards set by neoclassical models, agents act nonrationally. Expectations play a crucial role in their research: "herd behavior," for example, describes the way actors form expectations about the future behavior of other actors. The reasons for nonrational decisions are sought, however, in the cognitive limitations of individuals, not in the openness and unpredictability of the future. The goal of behavioral economists is therefore to develop a superior predictive theory by explaining precisely how certain cognitive mechanisms influence the decision-making process. Once cognitive "mistakes" are systematically understood, they can be accounted and corrected for. Correct as behavioral economics may be in its critique of the unrealistic assumptions of neoclassical models, it falls short by continuing to "embrace the conventional belief that economic models should generate sharp predictions" (Frydman and Goldberg 2007: 54) and by ignoring that expectations may be disappointed because the future is open and unforeseeable.

Austrian economics is another strand of economic research that has highlighted the importance of uncertainty, concurring with Keynes in its critical assessment of agents' capacity to foresee the future. Friedrich Hayek ([1968] 1969) shared the belief in an ergodic reality, but he and others recognized that it was not possible for individuals to have complete knowledge of it. Seen in this light, competition becomes a process by which hitherto unknown possibilities are discovered. While the majority of the Austrian School posited that such discoveries take place within a predefined realm of possibility, a few working in its tradition broke with this limited understanding of the future's openness and emphasized the role of genuine novelty.

One of the most interesting contributions in this vein was written by James Buchanan and Victor Vanberg (1991), who argued that the equilibrium view of the economy is wrong in assuming that there exists a predefined set of goods needing only to be allocated. They assert instead that "future parts of a market simply do not exist; they are by definition not present. There are, at any point in time, many *potential* futures imaginable, based on more or less informed reflections. Yet, which future will come into existence will depend on choices yet to be made" (176). The market is therefore more than the discovery process or information problem described by Hayek; it is a creative process in which the imaginative potential of actors creates genuine novelty. This focus on the unknowability of the future connects the concept of uncertainty to that of novelty, which is a central feature of the dynamics of capitalist economies. Expectations are shaped by the ability of humans "to see and do things in a novel way" (Dequech 1999: 422). At the same time the unknowability of the future leads to the "indeterminacy of rational beliefs" (Elster 2009: 4). The Austrian School argued that there was a political consequence to this line of thinking: free markets should be institutionalized so that individuals could pursue their ends and new ideas could find their way. In other words, allowing for the uncertainties of progress at the institutional level was the best way to ensure that progress would take place (Robin 2013: 13). This runs contrary to Keynes's conclusions about uncertainty: he argued that it may cause the underemployment of production factors, and should therefore be countered by state regulation and intervention.

EXPECTATIONS IN SOCIOLOGY

The investigation of sociological contributions to the role of the future in economic action is much less accessible. There is no "economic sociology of expectations" and, as mentioned above, even sociological scholarship writ large has, on the whole, taken limited interest in understanding the role of the future in action processes (Emirbayer and Mische 1998; Mische 2009; Tavory and Eliasoph 2013). Sociology tends to focus on "final-point outcomes, the results of an examined process at its end" (Abbott 2005: 405). In the words of Alfred Schütz (1962: 22), sociology is interested primarily in "because motives"; that is, the past experiences that determine an action. Only few strands of scholarship have addressed the roles that forethought and anticipation play. For them "in-order-to-motives" (Schütz 1962: 22) are vital elements in causal explanations of action. Actors anticipate certain consequences when making decisions, including the responses of other actors. While sociologists who include the intentions of actors in their explanations of social phenomena may not explicitly use the notion of expectation, they employ many related notions, such as beliefs, goals, sense-making, meaning, or ideas. These are all ways of expressing that outcomes can only be explained by including anticipated effects as a causal factor.

As is the case for economics, the way sociology has dealt with expectations is only partially convincing. Though approaches vary considerably, sociology, like economics, has attempted to "undo" the consequences of uncertainty and mask the openness of the future in its understandings of action. The future, in the eyes of most sociologists, is a prolongation of the past. Sociology differs from economics mostly in the path it sees leading to the future. Economists assume either perfect foresight or the existence of rational expectations based on the efficient use of available information, while sociologists tend to look to norms and social structures to explain assessments of the future. But some sociological approaches do recognize the future's openness and unpredictability.

Expectations as Norms

Talcott Parsons assigned expectations a prominent role in his explanation of the action process.[14] In *The Structure of Social Action* ([1937] 1949), Parsons sees "ends" as one of the constitutive elements of action, defining them as "a future state of affairs toward which the process of action is oriented" (44). Action is thus understood as a process in time that "always implies a future reference" (45). All action implies "the possibility of 'error'" (46) in the form of choosing the wrong means. The end in this case is an ideal for the actor, not a forecast of an actual future state of affairs. But if this is true, how can the integration of the social order be explained? Or, to use Parsons's terms to ask the same question: How can the problem of double contingency be resolved?

Parsons answers this question in his later theory (1951), but does so by greatly limiting the voluntarism characteristic of his early theory of action, introducing the idea of role expectations to analyze the connection between the social system and the personality system of actors. The contingency of an actor's possible goals and responses in a given situation is channeled through institutionalized norms of how an actor is supposed to act in that situation. These norms become anchored in the personality system of the actor through processes of internalization. Expectations are "the probable reactions of alter to ego's possible action, a reaction which comes to be anticipated in advance, and thus to affect ego's own choices" (5). The anchoring of role expectations in the personality system ensures (to varying degrees) compliance with social norms and (also to varying degrees) the sanctioning of those whose behavior violates role expectations. The function of expectations, therefore, is to explain how social interactions are coordinated in anticipation of the reactions of other actors. Expectations help to resolve the problem of double contingency—but they no longer imply that actors will act innovatively with regard to an open future. Instead, they help to banish this tendency to unpredictable novelty. While Parsons's discussion of expectations is part of his general social theory, the notion that expectations are structured through norms and institutions also informs his treatment of the economy (Parsons and Smelser [1956] 1984).

The same idea is present in many other sociological approaches, some of which are directly informed by the work of Parsons. The ethnomethodology of Harold Garfinkel (1967), a student of Parsons, posits that actors have expectations as to what a "normal" reaction to a specific social situation would be. Violating these expectations—as Garfinkel shows in his famous breaching experiments—leads to great distress, and, ultimately, to the collapse of social order.[15] Garfinkel differs from Parsons in seeing expectations as "how-to" rules that actors take for granted, rather than being primarily anchored in the social value system.

Other approaches in sociology also see expectations as informed by social context. In the tradition of Durkheim, for instance, Mary Douglas (1986: 48) asserts that "institutions encode expectations." The more fully they accomplish this, "the more they put uncertainty under control, with the further effect that behavior tends to conform to the institutional matrix." In a similar vein, Niklas Luhmann (1988) sees expectations as a means to reduce the scope of possibilities. Social systems use expectations to determine and limit their perceptions of the environment. Expectations can be anchored in formal rules or well-established habits and particularly in the codes and programs of social systems. Here again, they are seen as a means to process complex information, reducing complexity by "[preparing] possibilities of future events" (Luhmann 1988: 121). Luhmann is aware, however, that expectations do not foreshadow the future; they may turn out to be inaccurate. Cognitive expectations will be revised in this case: a learning process takes place. By contrast, normative expectations will be maintained in light of behavior that contradicts the norm.

Phenomenology is the most important sociological tradition to include expectations of the future. Indeed, Harold Garfinkel and Niklas Luhmann were both strongly influenced by the phenomenological tradition. Undoubtedly, though, its most important representative in sociology is Alfred Schütz. At first, Schütz would seem to lay the strongest theoretical foundations for a sociological understanding of the role of the future in economic action. The claim that action is directed into the future is crucial to his analysis. He asserts that courses of action are chosen by "projecting," which "consists in anticipation of future conduct by way of phantasying" (Schütz 1962: 20). Before engaging in the actual activity of attempting to realize a goal, an actor creates a fantasy of himself "at a future time, when this action *will* already *have been* accomplished" (20). In this sense, projects are "anticipated in the Future Perfect Tense" (20).

One might think that recognizing the role of fantasizing would lead Schütz to emphasize the creative potential of expectations in a way similar to Shackle or Buchanan and Vanberg, particularly since Schütz observes that modified life circumstances constantly change the experiences on which action is based. Nearly the opposite is true: Schütz posits that actors focus on a situation's similarities with what is known to them, not on its differences, and interpret situations using "schemes of reference" based on assumed knowledge collected from former experiences. Though all lived experiences "are as such unique and irretrievable events" (Schütz 1962: 20), actors are interested in what is typical about them, not in their uniqueness. Features that make projects "unique and irretrievable in the strict sense are . . . eliminated as being irrelevant" (21).

Schütz's strong focus on typicality makes his work therefore only partially helpful in understanding expectations as sources of capitalist dynamics. Although he sees expectations as crucial to the action process, he does not perceive them as a source of novelty, and therefore not as a dynamic force in society. For him action is mimetic; it relies on presumed scripts. This line of theorizing has greatly influenced sociological thinking since the 1960s. In addition to the works of Harold Garfinkel and Niklas Luhmann mentioned above, phenomenology informs the sociological constructivism of Peter Berger and Thomas Luckmann (1967) and is a building block in the new sociological institutionalism, which focuses on processes of isomorphism in the explanation of the diffusion of institutional and organizational models (DiMaggio and Powell 1991). Thus, the focus on routine practices has largely outplayed future orientations in cultural and institutionalist theories (Mische 2009: 702).

This is true also of Pierre Bourdieu. As shown in Chapter 2, Bourdieu assigns great importance to time and the role of expectations in his early anthropological work on the Kabyle and beyond. Bourdieu (2000: 213) has a clear vision of the indeterminacy of the social world and the uncertainty associated with investments.[16] At the same time, he emphasizes— with reference to Alfred Schütz—that objective probabilities prove that not everything is possible in the social world. The social world, he writes, "is not a game of chance" (214). Rather, future events are structured by actors' habitus, and by objective mechanisms and constraints such as the codification of practices, customs, conventions, and law. Subjective hopes are shaped by objective probabilities, which emerge from an actor's position in the economic field. People's wills "adjust to their possibilities, their desires to the capacity to satisfy them" (216). As in the sociological approaches discussed above, Bourdieu also downplays the theoretical consequences of the observation that the future is open. The imaginary freedom that might result from the openness of the future is subordinate to the structural forces that exert power over actors.

The relationship between aspirations and social stratification was the focus of a research field that was particularly vibrant in the 1950s and 1960s. Social stratification scholars—in opposition to Bourdieu, who claimed aspirations were determined by class position—took up the notion of role expectations and aspirations to search for an empirical understanding of the causal effects of adolescents' expectations on the reproduction of social inequality. Particularly germane was research on the effects of expectations on social outcomes such as fertility, life satisfaction, occupational attainment, retirement planning, and mental health (Mische 2009: 697). The work of stratification researchers on occupational aspirations and understanding educational and occupational outcomes shed light on the expectations adolescents held about their own future (Kahl 1953; see also Chapter 6). Their work aimed to show that stratification could be explained by the expectations held by actors in an adolescent's social context. "In particular, significant others—parents, teachers, and peers—define expectations that students then internalize as educational and occupational aspirations" (S. Morgan 2007: 1529).[17] Aspirations are investigated as a dependent variable only later on: because students from lower-class backgrounds are more likely to be exposed to social influences with low aspirations for them, they aim lower when defining professional career goals, and thus reproduce social inequality through their own decisions (see Chapter 6).

Just as the most influential economic theories make far too limited use of the concept of expectations, so too does structural functionalism, phenomenology, and research on stratification. These sociological approaches seek to explain actors' compliance with social demands and the sociostructural anchoring of perspectives on the future. But they do not account for the creativity engendered by expectations, for an actor's ability to imagine futures that deviate from existing norms and habits and create counterfactual worlds. Recognizing the importance of the creative force of expectations requires departing from static models that aim to explain the stability of the social order or the reproduction of social stratification. Capitalism legitimates the violation of existing norms; indeed, this is a crucial element of competition (Simmel [1908] 2009) and innovation (Merton 1957). Innovations occur, profits are made, and capitalist dynamics are propelled through divergent behavior.

Expectations and Creativity

Some sociological and philosophical approaches have offered a more open assessment of the impact of uncertainty on expectations. They understand expectations as contingent, variable, productive, and open to manipulation. These approaches, together with the heterodox approaches in economics discussed above, provide the building blocks for the understanding of expectations and their role in the dynamics of capitalist economies. The most important of these is American pragmatism.

Like Schütz, pragmatism recognizes the importance of projections into the future. It diverges from Schütz's thought in its notion of typicality, and it focuses on the role imaginations of future states play in the emergence of novelty. In particular, George Herbert Mead's *The Philosophy of the Present* ([1932] 2002) and John Dewey's *Human Nature and Conduct* ([1922] 1957) describe the creative role of images of the future. Both Mead and Dewey take the position that imagining future states of the world is a part of the decision process in the present. A temporal extension of the environment takes place through actors' imaginations, meaning that the future is contained in the present, and not external to the actors' situation.

Again, the role of expectations and future orientation in the work of the pragmatists is most visible in their conceptualization of the action process. Dewey ([1922] 1957 describes action as starting in habit. Action, he proposes, is normally an unreflective flow of activities in which "habits do all the perceiving, recalling, judging, conceiving and reasoning that is done" (177). The flow of activities, however, may be interrupted in the case of conflict between different habits, or by the release of impulses; in such cases, the actor is confronted with a new and surprising situation. The interruption of the action process creates "confusion and uncertainty in present activities" (207), making actors unsure about action goals and the means they should apply to reach their goals. When confronted with the unexpected, current action goals and means become obstacles to the action process, creating an impulse for what Dewey calls investigation: "a looking into things, a trying to see them, to find out what is going on" (181). Through investigation, actors seek to restore unity of conduct to their situation, so that action may again become an unreflective flow.

The imagination of future possibilities is crucial to the process of investigation. Whereas Alfred Schütz describes individuals projecting themselves into the future, Dewey sees them as engaging in a "dialogue" with the relevant social and natural objects, through a process he calls deliberation. Deliberation allows actors to experiment with a situation through "a dramatic rehearsal (in imagination) of various competing possible lines of action" (Dewey [1922] 1957: 190). The meaning, character, and consequences of objects and possible courses of action are tried out in the imagination without being enacted in reality.[18] Actors imagine the consequences of choices, which allow them to know the road "as we travel on it" (23). Imaginaries of the future thus help orient decisions. "Thought about future happenings is the only way we can judge the present; it is the only way we appraise its significance. Without such projection, there can be no projects, no plans for administering present energies, overcoming present obstacles" (267).

In the process of deliberation, actors form expectations about the outcomes of possible courses of action and the goals they will strive for. A new course of action is decided upon "when the various factors in action fit harmoniously together, when imagination finds no annoying hindrance, when there is a picture of open seas [and] filled sails" (Dewey [1922] 1957: 192). Dewey calls decisions reached through the process of deliberation "reasonable." They allow action to continue, but they are not based on a forecast of the future because the events arising from a given decision may differ from what has been anticipated, since not all relevant factors can be taken into consideration. The goal of deliberation is not a "final terminus" but rather a "way to act" (23). Any choice is a temporary solution, which will operate until habit stumbles upon new obstacles emerging from unexpected events and new impulses. Dewey does not claim it is possible to predict the future—that is not the purpose of foresight to him. Foresight serves "to ascertain the meaning of present activities and to secure, as far as possible, a present activity with a unified meaning" (25).

Ends play a central role in the process of deliberation, but not as in neoclassical economic theory, which sees ends as both fixed and external to the action process. For Dewey, ends emerge and change during the process of deliberation, and are part of the present, not a calculation of indeterminate future results. For this reason, to Dewey they are necessarily tentative. The new purposes and plans that emerge in the process of deliberation are not the result of external shocks, but of a different interpretation of the situation at hand. This gives action its dynamic and open character. Deliberation, for Dewey, "is work of discovery" ([1922] 1957: 216), which leads him to the idea of ends-in-view, that is, "foreseen consequences which arise in the course of activity and which are employed to give activity added meaning and to direct its further course" (225). Ends are "a means in present action: present action is not a means to a remote end" (26). To become relevant for social outcomes, however, ends-in-view must be worked out by investigating the concrete conditions available for their realization in order to determine which means are necessary to achieve them. Ends may therefore be revised as means are applied. Dewey gives the example of Thomas Edison: imagining a world with electricity led him to investigations and decisions about how to make this imaginary a reality.

The role of imaginary anticipations of the future in present action is an argument against utilitarian theories. Utilitarianism sees action goals (particularly the moral goals to which actors aspire) as fixed, and external to the action process. Utilitarian thinkers do not see goals as derived from or changing with experience, but as expressing universally valid principles derived from logical deductions or anthropological assumptions. Utilitarian theories axiomatically assume that action is taken to obtain positive future sensations. Dewey argues that we cannot know what our future preferences will be, which implies that it is impossible to calculate how to satisfy them in advance. The indeterminacy of future preferences is thus another element in the uncertainty that actors face, which makes decisions leading to the optimal satisfaction of future desires impossible. For Dewey, the view taken by the utilitarian approach that ends are fixed and external to action processes is a reaction to the fear that uncertainty inspires. "The more complicated the situation, and the less we really know about it, the more insistent is the orthodox type of moral theory upon the prior existence of some fixed and universal principal or law which is to be directly applied and followed" (238).

This can also be read as contradicting both Schütz's notion of typification and Parsons's role expectations. For Dewey, goals emerge and change with experience. Denying this empties present activity (and even the present itself) of all meaning, reducing it to a mere instrument for attaining a distant future—a future in which we can never live. We can live only in the present, which may be extended in its temporality by deliberation; that is, by imaginatively constructing representations of the future. But "deliberation is not calculation of indeterminate future results. The present, not the future, is ours" (Dewey [1922] 1957: 207).

Dewey's assessment of the action process provides the means to understand that the role of expectations in action's orientation toward the future is indeterminate. It is a process, not a fixed idea. Few sociologists have taken up this understanding of the creative role of expectations and imaginaries of future states of the world. Philosophers have shown much greater interest in the subject, in particular, Paul Ricoeur (1991) and Cornelius Castoriadis (1998). In his theory of action, Ricoeur (1991: 177ff.) relates closely to Alfred Schütz and the phenomenological tradition in emphasizing the role of projecting the future. Actors can "play" with different possible courses of action without realizing any of them by deploying anticipatory imagination that makes use of narrative structure. These anticipations are crucial sources of motivation in that they allow different courses of action to be evaluated against both an actor's desires and his ethical obligations. According to Ricoeur, actors take possession of their power through imaginative variations. Ricoeur, unlike Schütz, defines imaginaries as productive in the sense that they are not mere reproductions of something that exists already, but are visions that allow actors to try out new ways of seeing and understanding. In this way, they create new meaning. At the same time, because imagination is anchored in the rule-governed intentionality of language, it does not draw actors into a world of fantasy and escapism; instead, it allows for new references to reality that can be connected to sedimented paradigms and actual work.

Cornelius Castoriadis bases his theory of action in the concept of praxis.[19] For Castoriadis, when actors take practical action, they open themselves to the future, which he sees as uncertain and as the temporal terrain in which actors create novelty. To him, "to do something" always means "projecting oneself into a future situation which is opened up on all sides to the unknown, which, therefore, one cannot possess beforehand in thought" (Castoriadis 1998: 87). Imagination directs human praxis (127); it is the "elementary and irreducible capacity of evoking images." Central to his idea of social praxis is the interrelatedness of the imaginary and the structural elements of social reality, which are represented through language. The imaginary remains connected to the reality of the social world because it is bound to the symbolic forms of language. For Castoriadis, arguing against Marxism and the French structuralism of his time, this does not mean that the symbolic is deterministic. Rather, he believes it is itself subject to a continuous process of change as it intermingles with the creativity of the imaginary. The ontology of the indeterminate that follows from his line of reasoning addresses the consequences of uncertainty discussed in the previous section. "Because the symbolic rests upon the natural human capacity for imagination, because meanings are inseparably interwoven with the irreducible aspect of the imagination, meanings cannot be traced back to causal factors. The historical-social realm consists of chains of meaning which cannot be fully derived from chains of causality" (Joas and Knöbl 2009: 412).

The indeterminacy of the future means that there can be no foreknowledge of it; historical processes are non-linear. But that same indeterminacy is what gives action its creative force. Because the world is not a realm of closed causal relations, social praxis helps create processes of change: it is always possible to create a different social reality. For Castoriadis, this is a necessary precondition for freedom, which is brought about through collective action intended to institutionalize the new.[20]

CONCLUSION

Actors' expectations about future outcomes must be taken into account if we are to understand action in the economy. In this sense, the future matters just as much as history matters: actors use expectations and projections of counterfactual futures to consider alternative options.

Expectations are more prominent in economics than they are in sociology. And yet mainstream economic thinking ignores or occludes the fundamental uncertainty engendered by the openness of the future, and therefore does not do justice to the contingent nature of expectations. Indeed, rational expectations theory, the most prominent approach to expectations in economics, assumes that expectations are determined. This approach has been criticized from within the discipline. Economists have made use of alternative understandings of expectations in which uncertainty and the openness of the future play a role, the most influential of these being Knight and Keynes. Scholars like George Shackle, André Orléan, David Dequech, and Paul Davidson have further developed Keynes's assessment of expectations under conditions of uncertainty. Austrian economists have also taken issue with rational expectations theory, critiquing it for disregarding the future's unknowability (Buchanan and Vanberg 1991). These approaches provide useful starting points for further understanding the character of expectations and their role in the dynamics of capitalism.

There is no treatment of expectations in sociology specifically tailored to the investigation of economic phenomena, although expectations are significant in several theories that proceed from social interaction. Most of the sociological tradition, however, has failed to note the role of expectations in processes of change. Structural functionalism, for example, sees expectations as meaningful only in their role of stabilizing the social order, which they do by helping to coordinate social interaction. Weber, too, defines expectations narrowly; for him, they are either based on assessments of a given outcome's probability, or emerge from agreements between actors. The phenomenological approach, on the other hand, sees expectations more broadly. Alfred Schütz, who made the most significant contribution on expectations in this tradition, is, however, primarily interested in intersubjectively shared frames of reference and the typicality of situations. Though he emphasizes the role of projections into the future and the fluidity of objectives arising from changing social and temporal contexts, he is convinced that actors anchor decisions in what they experience as typical.

The phenomenological approach has been highly influential to sociology in the past forty years, first in ethnomethodology and later for sociological institutionalism. This has led to advances in sociological approaches to the economy, but they have focused mostly on processes of isomorphism, which has led them to place excessive emphasis on conformity and typicality. Their understanding of non-isomorphic change is weak at best (Beckert 1999, 2010), though advances based on the notions of institutional entrepreneurship and institutional work confront this shortcoming. The pragmatist tradition, by contrast, recognizes much more fully the contingency and creativity entailed in the imagining of future situations. Dewey ascertains that projections into the future are open and subject to change as new experiences and reinterpretations take place. Emerging ends-in-view make it possible to reassess a given action situation, to creatively reconstruct it, and to envision innovative courses of action. Actors constantly reassess their situation. Emirbayer and Mische (1998: 966), for example, argue, in the pragmatist spirit, that "choices are imagined, evaluated, and contingently reconstructed by actors in ongoing dialogue with unfolding situations." Expectations therefore create uncertainty in addition to reducing it, because imaginations of the future are able to contribute to "creative destructions" of existing worlds to make way for new ones. Rational expectations theory does no justice to this "dissonance" (Stark 2009), which characterizes many decision situations in the economy. If there are different interpretations of a situation, at least some of them must use available information "inefficiently."

We must nevertheless bear in mind that expectations in the economy are not free-floating fantasies: outlooks on the future and the courses of action that are based on them are socially constrained through the distribution of wealth and power, through cognitive frames, through networks, through formal and informal institutions, and through normative obligation. Among other things, families, companies, laws, inheritances, discrimination, social power, state subsidies, and marketing all influence imagined futures. The capitalist system is dynamic, not completely unstable. This is a crucial point to make for any contribution that highlights the contingency of present futures.

FOUR

FICTIONAL EXPECTATIONS

> Imagination bodies forth the forms of things unknown . . . and gives
> to aery nothing a local habitation and a name.
>
> —WILLIAM SHAKESPEARE, *A Midsummer Night's Dream*

USING FICTION in an analysis of economic action and capitalist dy-namics may at first appear farfetched, even misguided. After all, the economy is the realm of calculation and of instrumental rationality—the epitome of the "real." Fiction, by contrast, is "made up" by an author. What good is it, then, to fit the two together?

Yet the notion provides useful conceptual tools for understanding the dy-namics of the capitalist economy and its relation to expectations under conditions of uncertainty, as long as we are clear how we use the term "fic-tion." After the dotcom and real estate bubbles of the early 2000s burst, many commentators spoke of "fictional values" or a "fictional economy." They meant that the prices paid for stocks, houses, or financial derivatives at the peak of these bubbles were far removed from their "true" value, "fictional" in the sense that they deceived investors or cheated those who bought as-sets at inflated prices (Kormann 2011: 101). Economic commentators have also often used the term "fictional" in negative remarks about the abstrac-tion of financial products, suggesting that economic goods traded on finan-cial markets have lost all connection to an underlying economic reality, and are fictional in the sense of being devoid of any function in the "real" economy (Otte 2011: 37). Neither of these meanings applies here.

Rather, under conditions of uncertainty, assessments of how the future will look share important characteristics with literary fiction; most impor-tantly, they create a reality of their own by making assertions that go beyond the reporting of empirical facts. Fiction pretends a reality where the author and the readers act *as if* the described reality were true. By nature, of course, works of literary fiction do more than describe observable truths—but expectations regarding economic futures do, too. This is true in two ways. First, because the future is unknown at the moment expectations about it are created. Ontologically, in other words, the openness of the future rules out the possibility of restricting expectations to empirical reality. Second, because in the economy transcending qualities become ascribed to objects, and actors behave *as if* these qualities were part of the essence of the object, although they have no objective material correlate in the objects themselves. Literary fictions and expectations under conditions of uncertainty both have a "broken relationship to reality" (Burgdorf 2011).

Since literary theory is the academic discipline most specialized in the analysis of fiction, it is only natural to pursue the parallels observed between expectations under conditions of uncertainty and fiction by exploring this field. This idea is not actually new. Hayden White (1973) argues that historiography, though focused on the reconstruction of past events, can only be understood as a form of storytelling that uses the instruments of fiction. In his analysis of the works of nineteenth-century historians and philosophers of history, White lays out the literary tropes and genres that can be distinguished within historiography. Historical accounts, to White, are a form of fiction (1978: 121), although historians and authors of fiction have different goals: the former seek to describe facts, while the latter describe imagined possibilities. White claims, however, that facts can only be represented using the rhetorical means conventionally associated with the writing of fiction. Historians, in other words, are obliged to employ narrative tools to report facts. White makes an even stronger claim than the one pursued here, since historical facts have already happened and therefore inarguably exist as facts, which is not the case with events that take place in the future. If it makes sense to consult literary theory to understand historiographic accounts, then the utility of doing so for accounts of the future is even greater.

FICTION

As discussed in Chapter 1, "fictional expectations" refers to the imaginaries of future states of the world and of causal relations that inform actors' decisions. Under conditions of fundamental uncertainty, as explained in Chapter 3, expectations can never be actual forecasts of the future, merely projections, whose truth can be verified only once the future has become the present. If the future cannot be foreknown, then images of the future are a kind of fiction. In this sense expectations under conditions of uncertainty are fictional. The term "fictional expectations" can also be used to analyze the role of the attribution of symbolic qualities to objects. This is crucial not only for understanding the attraction of consumer goods but also relevant for understanding the operation of money and the credibility of predictions derived from economic theories.

The second and third parts of this book uses the term "fictional expectations" in the two meanings introduced above: as predictions of ontologically uncertain outcomes and as a way of describing the ascription of transcending qualities to goods or, in the case of economic theories, as an epistemological means to represent the economy. The common thread in the two uses of the term lies in the *as-if* nature of their relationship to economic reality. In both cases, expectations show a broken relationship to reality, though in different ways. In the first instance, the brokenness comes from the ontological uncertainty existing in any reference to expectations regarding the open future. In the second instance, the uncertainty is epistemological, leading to contingent interpretations of the qualities of goods and of economic processes. These interpretations and classifications become consequential for economic outcomes if they are intersubjectively shared.

An example may help clarify: in November 2011, commodities investor Jim Rogers predicted that gold would eventually rise to $2,000 per ounce (see BullionVault 2011). Predicting the future value of an asset in this way, to provide justification to invest (or to sell), is a fictional expectation. To the extent it is shared by investors, it may influence the price of the commodity.

The relevance of the terminology of fictional expectations is evident in the semantics of the word "fiction," which comes from the Latin *fictio*, which itself comes from the verb *fingere*, to shape, to construct, to form, to make up (Bunia 2010: 47; Vaihinger 1924: 81). Fiction is the product of these activities, and includes fictional assumptions, creations, and imaginaries. Although fictional texts are not bound to empirical reality, literary theorists do not see fiction's unreality as its defining characteristic—indeed, they see the opposition between fiction and reality as mistaken. The defining characteristic of fiction, they argue, is that it contrives a world of its own, "creates a space, in which one can in thought and imagination experience a different reality which can differ from real reality to any extent" (Bunia 2010: 47, own translation). The creative dimension of fiction is central to this. Fiction can "change reality" in the sense that fiction invents its own reality: fictions "do not refer in a 'reproductive' way to reality as already given, they may refer in a 'productive' way to reality" (Ricoeur 1979: 126). Quite aptly, Paul Ricoeur speaks of fiction as increasing reality. Fictions have the capacity to open and unfold new dimensions of reality, thus adding new layers to it.

Fiction is made possible by human beings' unique ability to evoke images of a counterfactual reality that may be situated in the future or the past, that may take place in any location, and that may presume all imaginable behaviors of actors, objects, and natural forces. This capability is what allows humans to plan ahead, because they can imagine and rank alternative futures (Bloom 2010: 163). The imaginative power of the human mind seems unlimited, and humans' "fiction-ability" *(Fiktionsfähigkeit)* (Iser 1993) is a fundamental anthropological quality.

As discussed above, literary theorists are not the only scholars to have identified the creation of worlds in the imagination as a defining feature of the human condition. Social scientists have also studied the role that the creation of imaginary worlds plays in social action. Since fictional texts in literature and expectations regarding economic futures have radically different goals, it is necessary to identify their sources of credibility and the similarities and differences between fictional expectations in the social world and in literary fiction.

The Credibility of Fiction

A world created in the imagination—a "doubling of reality," in other words— makes it possible for an actor to experience a reality that only exists in her or his imagination. This begs the question of why and in what sense imaginary worlds are taken seriously, and what lends credibility to fictional depictions. Plato very famously condemned poetry as a lie, and the enlightenment tradition rejects assertions about reality whose truth-claims cannot be proven. The arts, with their imaginary realities, exist nonetheless, as do imaginaries of future social action in general and economic decision-making in particular, raising the question of what makes fictional depictions interesting and credible, a topic broadly discussed in literary theory.

This is the famous paradox of fiction: if we know the facts presented in a literary text cannot in fact be observed, why do we not disregard them as uninteresting, unworthy, or even as contemptible lies? Why should things exist without the characteristics of reality (Iser 1983: 122) and how is it that we are moved by them? (Walton 1990: 5) Why do readers of fictional texts assume what Coleridge described in the early nineteenth century as "the willing suspension of disbelief" (Coleridge 1817)?

Analytical philosophy has made particularly influential investigations into the paradox of fiction (Searle 1975; Walton 1990; Zipfel 2001). These start from the idea that the credibility of a fictional text is not an attribute of the text itself, but rather is anchored in a specific attitude of the author (Searle 1975) or the recipient (Walton 1990). For John Searle, the "identifying criterion for whether or not a text is a work of fiction must of necessity lie in the illocutionary intentions of the author" (Searle 1975: 319). In a nonfictional text, the author commits to a truth-claim regarding the propositions he expresses and must be able and willing to provide evidence for their truth. The author of a fictional text, by contrast, makes no such commitment. In this sense, Searle (1975: 320) characterizes fiction as "nonserious," by which he means that an author of fiction isn't seriously committed to believing that the statements he makes are true propositions about the world.

What makes fiction credible, then, "is a set of extralinguistic, nonsemantic conventions . . . [that] enable the speaker to use words with their literal meanings without undertaking the commitments that are normally required by those meanings" (Searle 1975: 326). The author of fiction is "pretending" to make an assertion "or acting as if she were making an assertion" (324). By "pretending" Searle does not mean that the author intends to deceive the reader, but rather that the author is pretending in the sense of acting "as if." Readers share these conventions, and are willing to go along with the pretended assertions made by the author: they agree to suspend disbelief, in other words. Searle's definition of a story neatly summarizes his analysis of the characteristics of fiction: "A fictional story is a pretended representation of a state of affairs" (328).

The rule of nonseriousness relieves the author of making a commitment to the truth of the assertions he or she makes; the worlds created are therefore not confined to an empirically observable reality, but may instead be based on the author's imaginings. The reader of a fictional text knows its assertions are not serious, but pretends for the time of reading that they are real. In this sense, fiction involves an implicit contract between the author and the reader that the latter will not ask for proof of the assertions made by the former (Zipfel 2001; Künzel 2014: 145). This does not, of course, imply that there is no correspondence between fictional texts and reality; to the contrary, the assertions of fictional texts are often credible precisely because they are or could very well be true, because they are coherent, and because they are closely interwoven with nonfictional information.

While Searle focuses on the claims fiction authors make regarding the truth of propositions, Kendall Walton (1990) focuses on the attitude of the recipients of fictional oeuvres to understand why they generate interest, and, more specifically, why they generate emotional responses. Walton compares fiction to the make-believe games that children play, in which children pretend that an object stands for something else and act *as if* it were the object that it represents. He uses the example of a game in which children make believe the stumps in a forest are actually bears, and react to the stumps *as if* they had encountered a bear. The game they play thus creates a fictional world in which stumps are "props" that prompt images of bears and reactions that mimic the reactions they would have if they had encountered a real bear. The notion of make-believe corresponds to the notions of pretending and acting *as-if* used by Searle. For Walton (1990: 35), a proposition is fictional if it is "true in some fictional world."

"Props" are objects that trigger the imagination when they are encountered; within the context of a specific game, they generate fictional truths. Props may be the stumps in a children's game, but more importantly for a theory of art, they may be fictional productions such as a novel or a painting. Props create new worlds in the imagination.[1] At the same time, in make-believe games, props suggest certain images and reactions based on agreed-upon rules. The rules underlying fictional worlds are not necessarily explicitly agreed upon as they are in a game, but they may be based on socially shared conventions. When we read a novel, we know that the world described therein is a fictional one.

Props stimulate the imagination of fictional worlds, but they also cause emotions akin to those provoked by experiencing "real" events. Walton calls these emotions "quasi-emotions" to emphasize the difference between watching a movie scene in which somebody is shown dying, for example, and experiencing a similar event in reality.

An important part of the philosophical debate on the paradox of fiction centers on the question of what difference there is between emotions triggered by fiction and those provoked by nonfictional events (Schneider 2009). The less demanding position advocated by Walton is of particular interest. Walton claims that the emotions caused by a fictional event are akin, but not identical, to the emotions caused by a similar real event. These quasi-emotions do nevertheless make readers react to fiction in ways that are at least analogous to how they would react to the real events.

While Searle and Walton stress conventions as the basis for the credibility of fiction, Wolfgang Iser (1983, 1991) argues that our interest in fiction comes from the way it interconnects reality and the imaginary. Iser describes fictional texts as bringing together factually existing and imagined things (Iser 1983: 122). Fictional texts contain a great deal of reality, which does not become nonreal because it is part of a fictional text. Modern fiction makes a particular effort to hew to reality, which leads to the intermingling of the real and the nonreal.

Iser describes another device by which the credibility of a fictional text is strengthened: that of transposing the imaginary into a concrete gestalt. Texts in narrative or story form give the imaginary gestalt. As concrete gestalt, fictional representations differ from phantasms, projections, daydreams, and aimless ideations, through which the imaginary enters our experience directly. In a way, the imaginary's transformation into narrative moves it closer to the real. By giving concrete form to the imaginary, fiction may have tangible impact upon the real world. Iser therefore locates fiction somewhere between the imaginary and the real (Iser 1983: 150). He emphasizes the intermingling of the real and the nonreal as a condition for the effectiveness of literary texts more than Searle and Walton do, but he joins with them in stressing the "as-if" character of literary texts. Through its self-exposure as fictional, "the world organized in the literary text becomes an as-if" (Iser 1983: 139, own translation).

Parallels between Literary and Economic Fictions

To what extent can these assessments of what makes fictional texts credible inform an analysis of expectations under conditions of uncertainty in the economy and the transcending qualities ascribed to goods? The strongest similarity between literary texts and fictional expectations in the economy is that in both, actors proceed *as if* a described reality were true. The openness of the future and the nonobservability of transcending qualities ascribed to goods means that expectations must also be "make-believe" or "pretend" in the sense that they refer at least partly to nonobservable and nonforeseeable features. Expectations are in this sense fictional, based on imaginaries of the future or based on the ascription of transcending qualities, not on the foreknowledge of the future and the object as an empirical reality. From this perspective, expectations under conditions of uncertainty are inventions similar to fictional works: they are expressions of creativity, descriptions that surpass what we can empirically observe, and open up counterfactual horizons (Martinez and Scheffel 2003: 13). In the case of literary fiction, the suspension of disbelief is based on a convention; in the case of fictional expectations in the economy, the suspension of disbelief is based on the conviction that the imaginary of the future will become a future present, or is at least somewhat likely to do so. In the case of literary fiction, disbelief would lead the reader to dismiss the text; in the case of fictional expectations in the economy, it would lead the actor to dismiss the expectation as irrelevant to the decision-making process, and the ascribed qualities as nonexistent.

Another parallel may be identified in Walton's (1990: 21ff.) notion of "props." In the case of literary fiction or child's play, be they the sentences in a Jane Austen novel or stumps in a wood, props trigger the evocation of imaginaries. Such props may also be observed in the economic world. A business plan is a prop in this sense: if convincing, it triggers imaginaries of a successful future business. A lottery ticket is another such prop, one that evokes images of sudden wealth in which the ticketholder indulges before the lottery numbers are actually drawn, at which point the ticket becomes in all likelihood worthless (Beckert and Lutter 2009; Lutter 2012b). Advertisements may also be understood as props, since they are intended to prompt emotional reactions by evoking imaginaries of a desired world and to communicate the transcending qualities of a good (Burgdorf 2011: 112) (see Chapter 8). Actors may be aware that the future developments envisioned in their expectations will not be identical to the future when it becomes the present, but in anticipation of an expected event may nevertheless experience emotions akin to those they would experience in reality, and thus be provoked to act "as-if" the content of those expectations were real.[2]

As Milton Friedman (1953) so famously argued, economic theory is based on as-if assumptions (see Chapter 10). Theories, statistical methods, and models used by economic agents for prognoses of future situations and as bases for decisions must also be understood as props that evoke imaginaries of certain outcomes. Understanding theories as props offers an interesting alternative to the conventional ideas that economic models either predict future states of the world probabilistically or that predictive theories are performative.

A further parallel may be drawn between fictional texts and expectations in the economy. Fictional texts often gain credibility by intermingling invented elements with true facts; likewise, fictional expectations in the economy are not just fantasies devoid of reality—they make extensive use of known facts. This intermingling of fact and the imaginary adds credibility to depictions of future states of the world.

Wolfgang Iser's observation that fictional text is itself a part of reality is also true for fictional expectations. For Iser, a fictional text is a specific form of immersion in the world *(Weltzuwendung)* (Iser 1983: 125), one that must be pushed into being to become visible and effective, since it does not spontaneously exist on its own. Authors achieve this in a fictional text by selecting events and creating relationships among characters, and by deleting, adding, and weighting events and characters to create a world. A fictional text is not meant to describe an empirically existing world, but rather to make imaginable a world it has created by literary means. Authors show that the world can be perceived in the way they describe it, and this fictional description in turn becomes part of the real world. No rules bind authors in their descriptive choices, and while it would be clearly wrong to claim that no rules govern expectations regarding economic outcomes, uncertainty makes it impossible to account for all the elements that will influence future developments, let alone to calculate and weight them.[3] This is particularly evident in the economic forecasting practices described in Chapter 9. Fictional expectations are a real part of the world, and as such make the world comprehensible and may have an impact on actors' decisions.

Still another parallel between literary fictions and fictional expectations in the economy is in the narrative form expectations take. A typical fictional expectation in the economy is a point prediction of a future state; for example, a commodities investor or a bank predicting a gold price of $2,000 per ounce or an economic forecasting institute claiming that the inflation rate in the United States will be 2.1 percent next year (see Chapter 9). Such predictions, stripped down and straightforward as they may seem, are always sustained by narrative. Underlying any imaginary of a specific future state is a story of how the present will be transformed into the depicted future through causally linked steps. Forecasters provide such stories in their reports to make their final predictions appear well grounded in legitimate economic reasoning. Stories provide causal links to show how the gap between the present state of the world and the predicted future state will be closed, thus providing plausible reasons why one should expect the outcome the teller has chosen to depict.

Given the parallels between expectations under conditions of uncertainty and literary fiction, it is no coincidence that the concept of fiction has found attention in the social sciences. Marx, for example, talked of "fictitious capital" when referring to the net present value of future cash flows from financial assets. In economic history Karl Polanyi ([1944] 1957: 72) described labor, land, and money as "fictitious commodities." He argued that they could not be real commodities because they had not been produced for market exchange, but that the capitalist market system treated them *as if* they were commodities. Recently, sociologist Elena Esposito (2007, 2011) has made extensive use of the concept of fiction in the analysis of financial markets and Karin Knorr Cetina (1994) introduced the notion into the social study of science. In law, the notion of legal fictions describes the use of a legal rule in a field other than the one for which it was made.[4] A legal issue is treated *as if* it had the properties of the one for which the rule was originally created.[5]

Beyond the term "fiction" itself, related concepts such as story, narrative, fantasy, or imagination extend the analogy between social phenomena and literature even further.[6] For Karl Marx, human labor was distinct from coordinated activities in the animal world because humans anticipate the outcome of their labor in their imaginations before actually beginning the labor process. Emile Durkheim ([1912] 1965) observed how totemistic societies assign powers to natural objects and create classifications of kinship relations in which they portray themselves as related to animals or plants, a phenomenon that could reasonably be described as fictional. Alfred Schütz (1962: 20) developed a theory of action that sees acts as anchored in a fantasy, drawing an analogy between symbols in science and symbols in poetry (345). John Dewey ([1922] 1957) recognized the role of fantasies in social action, in the form of the ends-in-view, which are, at the beginning of the deliberation process, "only a phantasy, a dream, a castle in the air" (234). Hayden White (1973, 1978) made the widely influential claim that historiography is a form of storytelling. Finally, the sociologist Harrison White (1992) described networks as consisting of stories. With its focus on narrative structure, the concept of fictional expectations may be connected to a wide range of work in the social sciences on the role of stories, fantasy, imagination, and narrative.[7]

Economists have also pointed to the role of imagination and narrative in economic theory and decision-making. McCloskey (1990), for instance, sees the mathematical models used by economists as a form of storytelling. George Shackle (1970: 111) asserts that "the nonexistent knowledge of particulars which have not yet themselves come into existence is a void which can be filled only by imagination, by the creation of figments," while Kenneth Boulding ([1956] 1961: 90) argues that the "great over-all processes of economic life—inflation, deflation, depression, recovery, and economic development are governed largely by the process of reorganization of economic images." In a similar vein, and directly in line with the argument pursued here, Randall Bausor (1983: 2) posits that by facing "an unobservable future, individuals build expectations from creative acts of imagination and fantasy."[8]

Differences between Literary and Economic Fictions

There are also, of course, important differences between fictional texts and expectations under conditions of uncertainty. Readers of novels are not interested in putting fictional descriptions into practice, while actors in the economy base their real-world decisions on the expectations they hold. Alfred Schütz (2003: 148) distinguishes between "mere fantasies" not intended to be put into practice, and "design fantasies" *(Entwurfsphantasien)*, intended to be brought to fruition. Fictional expectations in the economy are "design fantasies," likely to be scrutinized by actors not just with regard to their inherent persuasiveness as narratives, but also to their practical credibility. Assessments of situations and possible future developments are made with regard to reality; they stand in a dialogical relationship with empirical information becoming available.

The differences between literary fiction and expectations under conditions of uncertainty may thus be perceived in the way they portray a broken relationship to reality. Both are representations whose truth-claims cannot be verified by evidence (Figure 4.1). Fictional literary writing has a broken relationship to reality because the stories it tells do not claim to be accurate representations of events. Expectations under conditions of uncertainty have a broken relationship to reality in the sense that actors cannot know that they are accurate forecasts of how the future will unfold.

Literary texts and fictional expectations thus differ in the way their relationship to reality is broken, which means that actors commit themselves to the two under different conditions: in literary texts, conventions make readers suspend disbelief, and a reader asking the author for proof of her assertions would clearly be violating these conventions. Kendall Walton ([1978] 2007: 111) remarks on the ease with which we can be made to play make-believe games when reading a book or viewing a painting.

By contrast, the credibility of fictional expectations is based on conviction, which may be the result of deliberation and calculation, but also of habit, assumption, ignorance, prejudice, and so forth. Making imaginaries

	Representations of real events only	Representations include nonreal events
Convention of "seriousness"	Nonfictional texts	Fictional expectations
Convention of "nonseriousness"		Fictional texts

FIGURE 4.1. Seriousness and nonseriousness in fictional and nonfictional texts.

credible is often difficult to achieve. Disbelief is only suspended if it seems plausible that the imaginary of the future in question could come true (Esposito 2007: 13). Actors suspend disbelief only if they are convinced of the likelihood that the future predicted will indeed transpire. They may arrive at their conviction from habit or naiveté, but more likely it is the outcome of a process of information gathering involving reflection about the situation at hand, calculation, and observation of other actors. Fictional expectations hence tend to remain fragile: doubt may be cast at any time on images of the future by imaginaries that predict other states of the world. The transcending qualities attributed to a good may lose their appeal and simply vanish. Fiction in economic contexts is vulnerable to contradictory assessments of the situation and experiences in the real world; this also makes expectations open to adaptation (Barbalet 2009: 6; Bronk 2009: 221, 2015: 9; Joas 1996; Putnam 2006: 282; Whitford 2002: 339). Actors do consider fictional expectations *as if* they were true, but only conditionally: "The rationality badge of the As If is by definition only for the present, subject to further reevaluation" (Riles 2010: 9) and is thus scrutinized in an ongoing stress test. As John Dewey ([1922] 1957: 234) asserts, the goal actors imagine can become an end "only when it is worked out in terms of concrete conditions available for its realization, that is in terms of 'means.'"

The way expectations are scrutinized and their vulnerability explains a further difference between literary fictions and fictional expectations in the economy. At least in the modern period, literary texts are openly fictional, while nonliterary fictions are not. A novel's cover informs readers in advance that the text they are holding is "a novel," leaving no doubt as to its fictional character. In this "self-disclosure of its fictionality, an important feature of the fictional text comes to the fore: it turns the whole of the world organized in the text into an 'as-if' construction" (Iser 1993: 12–13).

By contrast, actors go to great lengths to conceal the fictional character of expectations in the economy. The purported purpose of this masking is "to leave natural attitudes intact in order that the fiction may be constructed as reality capable of explaining realities" (Iser 1993: 13). Only when the fictional character of expectations and of transcending qualities is hidden do actors feel comfortable enough to make decisions whose outcomes are by nature unpredictable or based on the attribution of qualities that exist only as contingent meanings.[9] To borrow a notion from Pierre Bourdieu (1993), the nonfictional character of assertions is an *"illusio"* to be maintained in the economic field; the belief *(croyance)* that assessments of future states of the world are accurate anticipations of the future present must be protected to maintain actors' confidence.[10] But this confidence is never fully impervious to scrutiny from actors looking for evidence for or against an economic fiction. Generating confidence in future developments is an ongoing process, part and parcel of the market struggle in capitalist economies.

One means for the creation of confidence are probability assessments. Economic actors in modern societies aim to "transfer" uncertain futures into probable futures. Such risk calculations can only lead to probabilistic statements about the future if the future can be considered a statistical shadow of the past; that is, if the world is ergodic (Davidson 1996; Samuelson 1969). This is true of the risk calculation of life insurance or fire insurance, for example, in that the relevant regularities exist *ex ante* and can rationally be expected to hold *ex post*. In intensively dynamic and innovative systems such as modern capitalism, many highly important situations do not fall into this category (Bronk, forthcoming). Thus, assigning probabilities to outcomes may say less about the actual likelihood of future events than it does about actors' need to feel comfortable about unpredictable outcomes. Probabilistic frequency distributions, by representing values from the past, cannot support a prognosis for dynamic environments, nor are they suitable for the orientation of unique ("nondivisable" and "nonseriable") events such as many economic decisions (Wiesenthal 1990: 23). Probability assessments in situations characterized by Frank Knight as uncertain or by Paul Davidson as nonergodic thus serve to mask "the nonreality of the fictive reality" (Esposito

2007: 10). Formulating uncertainty in terms of probabilities (risks) is a way of increasing the chance that actors will believe in certain outcomes and engage in activities whose results are actually unpredictable. Probability statements in situations where parameters are unknown, nonlinear, and unstable are thus a realistic fiction creating a present future that becomes a basis for decision-making (Esposito 2007: 57).

One example of this is the calculation of default risks for the asset-backed securities that played a decisive role in the financial crisis of 2008. In 2006, the three-year default probability assumption of AAA-rated Collateralized Debt Obligations (CDOs) was calculated to be .008 percent. As of July 2009, the actual default rate was 0.1 percent. Much more dramatically, A-rated CDOs were calculated to have a three-year default probability of .088 percent in 2006; the actual rate was 29.21 percent. Even when buying CDOs rated BBB-, one of the lowest ratings, investors who took seriously the risk calculations of the rating agencies believed that their default risk was less than one percent. Three years later, in reality, nearly all these CDOs defaulted. The wide discrepancy can be explained by an underestimation of the correlation effects among defaults of the credits bundled in the securities when risk was calculated (MacKenzie 2012). The actual default risk was unknowable, because the crisis was a unique event that could not have been anticipated using historical data. Following this line of argument, it is too simplistic to state that investors were deceived when buying CDOs, even though conflicts of interest did play an important role in their rating. (The rating agencies were paid by the issuers of the financial products they rated, meaning that optimistic ratings would help to expand their market.) More importantly, though, the likelihood of default was unpredictable. Probability calculations merely helped actors feel as if they had made secure investments. After the financial crisis, credit-rating agencies followed a similar line of reasoning when they declared that their ratings were nothing but "opinions." Their supposedly exact assessments of the future were a kind of pretending.

It may thus be concluded that fictional expectations are best understood as "placeholders" (Riles 2010) in the decision-making process, used to help actors momentarily overlook the unknowability of future states of the world and courses of events. Future states are "feigned." To take seriously the notion of fundamental uncertainty is to accept that precise calculations of future states are impossible. It follows, therefore, that the expectations that these calculations represent are contingent, based on assumptions about future developments that can only pretend to describe a future reality.

Put another way, decisions can only be made using as-if assumptions about the future. Following a line of reasoning similar to that of Kendall Walton (1990: 35), the assertion that expectations under conditions of uncertainty are fictions implies that these expectations are perceived as true representations of a future reality by a person or a social group. The same is true of the attribution of intangible qualities to goods. This kind of truth, however, cannot be verified (or falsified) before the present future has actually become the present. Using John Searle's definition of fictional texts, expectations under conditions of uncertainty may be described as "pretended representations of a future state of affairs," which make it possible to overlook the uncomfortable fact that we cannot know what the future holds. Overlooking uncertainty prevents paralysis or avoids perceived randomness of decisions. It helps actors to behave purposefully with regard to the future, despite it being unknown, unpredictable, and therefore only pretend. John Maynard Keynes expressed this idea when he said that there are matters about which there is "no scientific basis on which to form any calculable probability whatever. We simply do not know. Nevertheless, the necessity for action and for decision compels us as practical men to do our best to overlook this awkward fact" (Keynes 1937: 214). The fictional character of expectations under conditions of uncertainty, however, also allows for the "politics of expectations," discussed below.

FICTIONAL EXPECTATIONS AS A MOTIVATING FORCE FOR ACTION

Just as the "fiction-ability" of humans (Iser 1993) is of social significance only if it moves them to act, expectations can only be economically relevant if they influence action. We must therefore examine what motivating forces fictional expectations possess.

In this regard, rational actor theory and sociological theories that focus on how action is guided through calculation, norms, institutions, or structures of social networks are of little help. Rational actor theory presupposes agents' ability to calculate outcomes at least probabilistically, and posits that actors will choose the alternative that maximizes their welfare. This, as explained above, runs counter to the idea of fictional expectations, which are based on as-if assessments of the future and only pretend foreknowledge. The sociological approaches discussed earlier stress the importance of compliance with cultural frames in decision-making, meaning that action is seen as motivated by the internalized desire to follow social norms (Parsons 1951), by fear of sanctions, or by the urge to maintain a state defined as "normal" (Garfinkel 1967). Other approaches focus on social structures or institutions as explanatory factors. Ultimately, these approaches see prevailing structures and isomorphism as causing economic outcomes.

John Maynard Keynes ([1936] 1964: 152) took up the sociological rationale when emphasizing the role of conventions in economic action, and argued that actors assume "that the existing state of affairs will continue indefinitely." Keynes was, however, keenly aware that conventions could only partly explain action under conditions of uncertainty, and argued that there were also functionalist and psychological aspects. Functionally, he argued, humans seek to prevent despair: we simply must act, even if we do not know the outcome. He also claimed there was a psychological basis for action, that of "animal spirits," the term he used to describe "a spontaneous urge to action rather than inaction" (161). Individual initiative "will only be adequate when reasonable calculation is supplemented and supported by animal spirits, so that the thought of ultimate loss which often overtakes pioneers, as experience undoubtedly tells us and them, is put aside as a healthy man puts aside the expectation of death" (162).

Keynes' notion of animal spirits remains unsatisfactory, little more than a black box into which he folds the difficulties of understanding how intentionally rational actors make decisions when outcomes are unforeseeable. But expectations are practically relevant because actors are attracted to (or fear) the anticipated state these expectations portray.

Actors' attraction to imagined futures has two sources, both of which may be present simultaneously in decision-making situations. On the one hand, decisions may be motivated by the hope of realizing an imaginary by undertaking certain activities in the present.[11] This idea has often been expressed: Schumpeter (1934), for example, posited that entrepreneurs were motivated to work by the desire to establish a dynasty—a motivation he readily accepted was "irrational," but which he argued is nonetheless real and helps entrepreneurs overcome their fears of the risks associated with their endeavors.

Tying this in with the differences between the commitment to literary fictions and fictional expectations, it is evident that the "realness" of decisions helps explain what motivates actors: fictional expectations may be critically scrutinized. However, fictional expectations also promise something that no literary fiction can offer: consequences in the real world. This makes their power of attraction potentially far greater than that of literary imaginaries. Reading a novel about an entrepreneur getting rich through industriousness may cause pleasurable sensations; being an entrepreneur, on the other hand, can make a person actually rich (or lead to actual economic failure).

Geny Piotti (2009) provides a useful example of the motivational power of imaginaries in her study of the decision-making processes of German firms outsourcing parts of their production to China. Piotti shows from interviews conducted with managers involved in these decisions that what motivated them to invest in China was not only economic calculation but also a general atmosphere of euphoria generated by the media and industry organizations such as chambers of commerce. Depictions of the opportunities in narratives by firms already operating in China inspired overly optimistic assessments and motivated decisions that sometimes led to spectacular profits, but sometimes to high losses. One manager explicitly compared the decision to outsource to China "to the Gold Rush in America" (Piotti 2009: 23). Narratives of the great opportunities opening up in China, strong normative pressures in the field, and sentiments of euphoria were major ingredients in decisions to relocate. Ralf Dahrendorf (1976: 14) applied the idea of the motivating force of anticipations of future states of the world to consumption, seeing actors' hopes of upward social mobility as a force that motivates economic industriousness. "Such hope motivates people to change their conditions, or their lives, in a variety of ways. It may be the stimulus for the individual to move, either geographically, or in the scales of social status" (14).

The second explanation for the attractiveness of fictional expectations has none of the teleological qualities of the first. Instead, it emphasizes present gains from practical engagement in activities with uncertain outcomes, emotions felt in the present when an actor commits to a project with a desired anticipated outcome. The anticipation of an outcome can become a source of satisfaction in the present, before the goal is reached (Bloom 2010: 170). This idea has a long history, which can be traced to Blaise Pascal in the seventeenth century; it was also articulated by romanticist writers. Richard Bronk (2009: 200) cites the romantic writer William Hazlitt: "We must imagine the interest that our imagined future selves would feel for this imagined future; and it is this imagined future interest in the imagined future consequences of action today that excites in us a current 'emotion of interest' sufficient to motivate us now."

The idea was taken up by twentieth-century economists and political scientists. For instance, in his *General Theory* Keynes stated that if "human nature felt no temptation to take a chance, no satisfaction (profit apart) in constructing a factory, a railway, a mine or a farm, there might not be much investment merely as a result of cold calculation" (Keynes [1936] 1964: 150). Just as a fictional text provokes emotional reactions in its readers, the imagined outcomes of decisions evoke emotions in the form of "enjoyment by anticipation" (Shackle 1979: 45), instant rewards for a personal commitment to a given action.[12] Through "imagination [an actor] can perceive an attainable state of thought and realize it as an attained satisfaction" (Shackle 1979: 47).

In a similar vein, Albert Hirschman (1986) investigated the enjoyment produced by the anticipation of a future state of the world in the realm of political commitments. Drawing on the thinking of Blaise Pascal, Hirschman draws parallels with religious beliefs.[13] "He who strives after truth (or beauty) frequently experiences the conviction, fleeting though it may be, that he has found (or achieved) it. He who participates in a movement for liberty or justice frequently has the experience of already bringing these ideals within reach." (Hirschman 1986: 150).

Hirschman shows how emotions arising from an actor's commitment are relevant to their general motivation: "This savoring, this fusion of striving and attaining, is a fact of experience that goes far to account for the existence and importance of noninstrumental activities. As though in compensation for the uncertainty about the outcome, and for the strenuousness and dangerousness of the activity, the striving effort is colored by the goal and in this fashion makes for an experience that is very different from merely agreeable, pleasurable, or even stimulating: in spite of its frequently painful character it has a well-known, *intoxicating quality*" (150).[14] To experience these "quasi-emotions" of an anticipated desired state, however, the actor must be committed to struggling toward the goal.

Imagined futures help to explain actors' willingness to commit themselves to endeavors despite the incalculability of outcomes and environmental pressures to conform to established behaviors. "The attachment to a fantasy converts the ambiguities of history into confirmations of belief and a willingness to persist in a course of action" (March 1995: 437). An entrepreneur contemplating whether to relocate her firm to China is already enjoying "profits," although they have yet to be made. Similarly, a lottery player who imagines himself winning the jackpot before the numbers have been drawn experiences some of the sensations he would experience if he actually were to win (Beckert and Lutter 2009). In psychological terms, "high-risk behavior, like play and exploration in organizations that insist on rationality, may heighten the intensity of feelings, and may motivate a commitment to, for example, projects that are at the same time imagined with a substantial amount of disbelief" (Augier and Kreiner 2000: 678). The emotional force drawn from commitment to a goal is a phenomenon observable in investment and consumption decisions, and is discussed prominently in the second part of the book.

The commitment to fictional expectations can also be understood as a commitment to specific belief systems. This makes it possible to explain actors' motivations in relation to group processes. Hirschman's reference to political struggles indicates that "intoxication" by envisioned goals is not a purely individual process, but one that takes place in the context of social interaction. In a similar vein, Emile Durkheim ([1912] 1965) describes how belief systems in totemistic societies become established and reinforced through collective ritualistic practices in which clan members experience states of collective effervescence. The emotions experienced in the group reinforce the belief system of the clan, and thus motivate action in accordance with that belief system. The belief system of the clan is fictional in the sense that it uses animistic thinking to identify causal forces, but is nonetheless a motivating force because the world as envisioned in the beliefs is real to the believer. By the same token, fictional expectations in the economy are not purely individual; rather, they have a social reality that is shared by the members of the collective. This can be seen in economic decision-making: the fictional expectations of the German entrepreneurs relocating to China mentioned emerged within a discursive context; in this case, a public discourse, meetings organized by chambers of commerce, and work with consulting firms (Piotti 2009). All of this led to shared convictions in the field. Collective beliefs that lead to commitments can also entail beliefs in specific cognitive devices such as the efficient market hypothesis or assumptions of rationality (Miyazaki 2003).

THE POLITICS OF EXPECTATIONS

Mainstream economics is built on the assumption that actors will make maximizing decisions. Rational expectations theory follows its lead and assumes that—at least on average—actors' expectations are based on the efficient use of all available information. This denies the possibility of pursuing political goals by deliberately influencing expectations. Since rational agents cannot be fooled, public policies intended to engender "wrong expectations" will necessarily be ineffective (Sargent 2008).

The notion of fictional expectations leads to fundamentally different conclusions. In all economic situations characterized by uncertainty, it assumes there is no "correct" economic model for actors to follow. Since the future is seen as open, actors' expectations are indeterminate and contingent, which means that actors' expectations are not directly determined by a situation (or the dominant economic model), but shaped by imperfect information and varying interpretations of that information. The correctness of decisions can only be ascertained after the fact; actors may make right decisions based on wrong assumptions, and vice versa.[15]

The contingency of expectations opens the way to a multitude of responses to any given situation. More than that, it is an entry point for the exercise of power in the economy. If expectations are contingent, if decisions depend on expectations, and if the decisions of others influence outcomes, then actors have an interest in influencing the expectations of other actors. How successfully actors are able to pursue this interest is an expression of the power they command.

The "market struggle" (Weber [1922] 1978) at the core of the capitalist economy is in large part a struggle to influence the expectations of third parties. This is a central goal in economic policy, as well as for businesses in their relations with competitors and consumers. In this sense, a focus on fictional expectations opens up a specific perspective of conflict in our understanding of the economy. In the economy, the power lies with actors who are able to influence others' expectations most effectively. This is done by defining situations and the imaginaries of probable or desired future presents. The more powerful the actor, the more effective he will be in shaping expectations. Command of economic resources and cognitive devices such as economic theories and techniques of forecasting is essential to the process of influencing convictions. In this sense, knowledge and power are closely interwoven (Foucault 1975). Drawing on legitimate normative models of economic goals and accepted means is also an important part of this process. Contrary to rational expectations theory, expectations in the economy are political: power is exercised in markets through the influencing of expectations. To have power means: My expectations count!

Although the political character of expectations is an important aspect of capitalist dynamics, it has often been overlooked, even by authors who acknowledge the centrality of uncertainty and expectations. Keynes, for example, in his discussion of market dynamics, argues that financial investors, instead of trying to assess the fundamental value of securities, must anticipate the expectations of other investors in the market (Keynes [1936] 1964); clearly, then, he sees outcomes as depending on the expectations of others. To him, though, this uncertainty is a coordination problem, which is resolved by resorting to conventions (Keynes 1937: 214, Orléan 2008), which actors use to coordinate their expectations and make behavior reciprocally predictable.[16] He does not view uncertainty from a power perspective.

Keynes shows a much clearer awareness of the political nature of expectations at the macroeconomic level: to him, "economic prosperity is excessively dependent on a political and social atmosphere which is congenial to the average business man" (Keynes [1936] 1964: 162). The political and social atmosphere is a determining factor for economic investment. A few years after Keynes, the Polish economist Michal Kalecki (1943) added a political twist to this argument, asserting that if employment depends on economic confidence, then "capitalists [are given] a powerful indirect control over Government policy: everything which may shake the state of confidence must be carefully avoided because it would cause economic crisis" (Kalecki 1943: 325). According to Kalecki, the business community exerts power over government policies because it will withhold investments if its expectations shift regarding the profitability of these investments. The government, since it depends on private investments for employment and tax receipts, subordinates its decisions to the will of business interests by orienting its policies toward the effects they will have on business expectations in order to avoid what has been called an "investment strike." Claus Offe (1975) has analyzed this dependency principle in detail to explain why state elites in capitalist economies adopt policies that enhance business confidence and a favorable business climate. State elites have an interest "in their own stability and development [which can] only be pursued if it is in accordance with the imperative of maintaining accumulation" (Offe 1975: 126). Violating this logic of accumulation would weaken or undermine state capacities to govern. At the same time, businesses gain the power to automatically trigger punishment in cases where they consider economic reforms to be detrimental to their interests. The change in expectations leads to declining investment, a sluggish economy and unemployment. The market can, in this sense, be said to imprison society (Lindblom 1982).

Today's economic reality is far from Kalecki's assumption that the power of businesses can be bridled through state investments that would make the economy less dependent on their expectations—large-scale government programs, Kalecki argues, would positively influence unemployment and wages, thus reducing the power of business. Particularly today, deregulation, privatization, and globalization have imposed significant limits on the power of the state while increasing that of businesses, which can now credibly threaten governments with taking their investments elsewhere (Streeck 2014). Contemporary states are dependent on the expectations of markets.

Maintaining favorable business expectations may be seen as a key goal of state policies and of the communicative efforts of the state and its agencies. The communication strategies of central banks are a good example of this (Abolafia 2010, Holmes 2009, Smart 1999). Their goal is to create confidence in the business community by "talking to the markets" through public statements: "Prices become anchored in the expectations of market participants who take these allegories seriously and adjust their practices and expectations. . . . Together with open market operations, the economic narratives of central banks thus become the second main determinant for price developments. Put differently, uncertainty is being reduced by discursive practices that rely on strategic rhetorical action with essentially pedagogical aims" (Nelson and Katzenstein 2010: 31–32).

Such communicative interventions have highly visible effects: at the peak of the European sovereign debt crisis in July 2012, for example, Mario Draghi, the president of the European Central Bank, announced at a global investment conference in London that the ECB would firmly defend the euro. Within its mandate, Draghi stated, "the ECB is ready to do whatever it takes to preserve the euro—believe me, it will be enough." Immediately after the speech, interest rates for the sovereign debt of the countries most affected by the crisis went down significantly (Figure 4.2). The speech did not change the objective economic situation of Greece or Portugal in the slightest, but it shifted investors' expectations, which in turn had an impact on the economic situation.

This influencing of expectations in markets is not limited to the state and its agencies. Stories are told by all market participants in order to influence investors' confidence that markets will develop in a certain direction. When a stock market analyst predicts the development of the price of a specific stock and gives justifications for why this would occur, his aim is to create confidence in a fictional expectation that would encourage investors to buy (or sell) the financial asset. This connection between discursive interventions and confidence levels has also been depicted by behavioral economists:

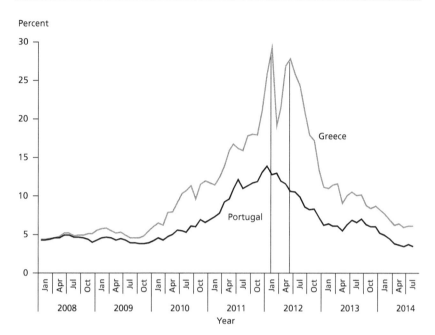

FIGURE 4.2. Long-term interest rate for Greece and Portugal, ten-year maturity. *Note*: The lines show the market reaction to the second rescue package in February 2012 and to the speech by ECB President Mario Draghi in July 2012. *Data source*: ECB Statistical Data Warehouse.

for example, Akerlof and Shiller (2009: 55) argue that market bubbles emerge because "high confidence tends to be associated with inspirational stories, stories about new business initiatives, tales of how others are getting rich." "Growth stories" feature prominently in investment justifications, and entail elements of prophecy. The circulation of such stories moves markets by influencing expectations, which in turn affects demand and prices: "Stories impart meaning, which is to say worth" (McCloskey 1990: 68).

Discursive interventions can destroy wealth in addition to creating it. In 1997, for example, a "Thai crisis" turned into an "Asian crisis" when investors took the economic downturn in Thailand as evidence of potential difficulties in other Asian countries, an expectation formed despite the fact that economic fundamentals varied greatly across Asia (Hellwig 1998: 715). When investors drew funds from other countries, such as Korea, they created the very difficulties that had been predicted by the "story." A more recent example is the exchange rate of the Hungarian forint. In early 2013, Hungary's economic minister blamed the research firm of the influential economist Nouriel Roubini for causing a slide in the Hungarian currency when Roubini recommended buying short positions in the forint in a note to investors, based on his expectation of a slide in the currency's value (Wall Street Journal 15 January 2013: 24).

Fictional expectations provide justification for investment decisions whose success is uncertain. It is difficult to argue against the claim that statements about expected future developments are made at least in part with the intention to influence the events they foresee. By influencing decisions, imaginaries of future states of the world can influence outcomes, causing the event anticipated in the fictional depiction to transpire (Esposito 2007: 112). This is what I mean when I connect economic power to the politics of expectations: predictions from influential investors or analysts about future prices in commodity or currency markets are not more or less certain than from other analysts, but their authority and the investments they command in the respective markets mean that the stories they tell are more likely to shape investor expectations, and in this way to shape investment decisions. The expectations these economists communicate create demand for that asset, eventually leading to the higher prices they asserted in their forecasts. In this sense, stories create "the economy itself as a communicative field and as an empirical fact" (Holmes 2009: 384). In hindsight, actors may interpret an outcome—for instance, when the price of gold actually does climb to $2,000 per ounce—as confirmation of a prediction's accuracy, when in reality the outcome is merely the result of action motivated by a shared belief in an expectation. Expectations, in other words, can be performative (Callon 1998b, MacKenzie and Millo 2003), implying that they can be used as a means of pursuing interests in markets.

If it is possible to influence others' expectations and to gain from the decisions they make based on these expectations, it is rather naïve to assume that stories emerge through an experimental process in which they are open to revision and modification as new data and new interpretative insights become available. It seems more realistic to assert that fictional expectations may be used instrumentally and advocated even despite known flaws and incoherencies, in order to serve specific individual or organizational interests. Actors may express expectations that do not represent the best of their knowledge but rather aim to manipulate others' expectations for personal gain or political interests. Language and reasoning "serve the purposes of the speaker within the institution. For these purposes, it is important that one uses formulations that are effective—without necessarily being right" (Hellwig 1998: 721).

The deliberate shaping of expectations does not just take place in financial markets, however: it occurs in the shaping of investment decisions in general, the operation of the monetary system, in the structuring of consumer demand, and in innovation processes. This will be discussed in detail in the second part of the book; for the moment, it will suffice to turn to consumer markets as one further example.

Firms shape consumer expectations through marketing activities, which seek to make customers attached to their products and try to detach them from those of their competitors (Callon 1998b, Dubuisson-Quellier 2013). To do so, firms attempt to manipulate consumer expectations of products. Given that marketing expenses are growing as a part of total production costs, it is clear that shaping imaginaries of consumers plays an increasingly important role in market competition. The brand value of firms such as Gucci or Apple resides mainly in their power to motivate purchasing decisions by shaping the imagined futures of consumers. Firms, however, are not the only powerful players in the struggle over consumer expectations. Lobbying groups, economists, forecasters, consumer advocates, and social movements also participate in the struggle to influence expectations regarding the value of consumer goods.

To be sure, at any given moment there is a plurality of fictional expectations circulating in markets. But not all accounts have the same weight. From this perspective, power may be measured by the degree of influence an actor exercises over the expectations of others. Power in the economy is exercised to the extent an actor can make his own imaginary of the future become influential and mobilize others to turn it into the future present. This perspective also lends itself to social movement theories on mobilization and frame construction (Benford and Snow 2000, Fligstein and McAdam 2012, van Lente and Rip 1998). Frames legitimate specific interpretations of a given situation, fostering social mobilization and helping to align the decisions of independent decision-makers through a dominant imaginary. Max Weber's ([1922] 1978) concept of charismatic domination adds another interesting layer to this perspective (Kraemer 2010), as does Harrison White's (1992) concept of control projects. Both concepts speak to the issue of how actors or groups of actors gain authority over market expectations. The task consists of explaining the processes by which expectations are grouped and disseminated.

THE SOCIAL FOUNDATIONS OF FICTIONAL EXPECTATIONS

The American psychologist Thomas Ward (1994) conducted an experiment in which he asked participants to draw fantasy animals, which could be as "crazy" as the person wanted them to be.[17] There were no constraints to creativity. The images drawn by the participants had all kinds of strange features, but all of them followed certain physical rules of the animal world, such as symmetry and hierarchical ordering. The experiment demonstrated that even in our imaginations, we cannot avoid following certain kinds of rules and directions. Imagination cannot fully escape from the familiar. This experiment is highly relevant to the subject at hand, for fictional expectations, just like paintings of fantasy animals, are not simply subjective beliefs: they are necessarily connected to social context. Many authors have identified this: Castoriadis (1998), for instance, made it a core point of his theory, arguing that imaginaries are always connected to culture because they necessarily operate through language. Kendall Walton (1990: 52) asserted that "fictions are society relative. . . . An object may have a make-believe function for one social group but not for another." Karin Knorr Cetina (1999) coined the term "epistemic cultures" to show that the knowledge produced in different laboratories is shaped by the specific arrangements and mechanisms prevailing in scientific settings. And, in the tradition of Durkheim, François Simiand (1934: 38–39, own translation) posited that the belief in the value of money "is not a phenomenon arising from competent and well-informed individuals . . . but rather from groups, from collectives, from nations; it is social. Its role and nature are manifestly objective, because it is a *belief and a social creed,* and, as such, *a social reality.*"

While expectations are expressed by individuals, they cannot be understood without taking into account the historical, cultural, institutional, and political contexts in which they are formed, and in which the decisions they drive are made. It is, after all, only logical for a sociological theory of expectations to examine their social constitution (Mische 2009: 702) and to connect the future orientation of expectations to history and to the embeddedness of actors in social structures. We have touched on the relevance of social context in sections above, the experience of collective effervescence described by Durkheim, and the role of power in shaping expectations. Chapter 2 examined the changing temporal dispositions that emerged with the advance of capitalism, the role of competition, and of the monetary system. Future research would do well to examine in detail how expectations in the capitalist economy differ among historical periods and from a comparative perspective. There are at least seven kinds of social influences on expectations.

1. *Opportunity structures.* In his research on Kabyle peasants, Bourdieu (1979) showed that imaginaries of the future vary according to the social situation of the actor. The most socially deprived actors, who have few chances for upward social mobility, fantasize entirely unworkable scenarios for their future lives, while actors with higher socioeconomic status develop more true-to-life plans for elevating their social status through education and training or geographic mobility.[18] A similar point regarding opportunity structures can be made regarding entrepreneurial activities. The systematic entrepreneurial drive required to propel capitalist development could only develop within the context of a society that had started to eradicate traditional status barriers and thus make social status at least normatively the outcome of achievement rather than of ascription. It is only through the easing of individual mobility between classes that the motivation to engage in entrepreneurial activity for the sake of upward social mobility can expand (Deutschmann 2009). More broadly, it is "the vision of the different, of new and improved life chances, which turns resentment, or any kind of latent desire, in action, and thus into change" (Dahrendorf 1976: 13). Similarly, only when consumption is emancipated from the restrictions of traditional status orders can modern consumerism, which plays a significant part in capitalist dynamics, become possible. The dynamics of modern fashion, for instance, only came about once the traditional constraints of sumptuary law, which prescribed dress codes according to social status, had vanished (Deutschmann 2014; Sewell 2010).

When the constraints of traditional social structures are relaxed, cognitive dispositions to imaginaries of the economic future and economic aspirations find a more receptive social basis. In turn, these imaginaries can themselves become a force for detraditionalization. The "American dream" of achievement and upward social mobility through individual industriousness is probably the most powerful cultural representation of the orientation toward an open economic future where imaginaries inform decisions that create continuous restlessness on the individual and societal levels.

Similar observations have been made regarding firms. Empirical studies of technological imaginaries indicate that they depend on market structures (de Laat 2000). Technological imaginaries are often only weakly developed in monopolies, where future worlds must oppose a dominant existing world; in situations of pure competition, by contrast, future worlds proliferate. "All actors suggest different worlds of tomorrow, and different frames of reference correspond to each individual world. Positions are often unique and few elements are shared" (199).

2. *Cultural frames.* Talcott Parsons ([1959] 1964) has argued that the expectations of both adolescents and adults are the outcome of socialization processes in which they learn which aspirations their social position within the stratified social order allows them to have. On the macro level, Deirdre McCloskey (2011) argues that the extension of values of bourgeois dignity and freedom are among the most important preconditions for the acceleration of economic growth. Or, as Arjun Appadurai (2013: 292) argues, cultural systems "shape specific images of the good life as a map of the journey from here to there and from now to then, as part of the ethics of everyday life." Such cultural frames are at least partly learned through socializing institutions like the family, universities, business schools, and professional associations, and are thus also connected to the institutional shaping of expectations. Moreover, such frames are connected to and change with the life course.

3. *Institutions.* Institutions contribute to imaginaries of future states of the world by shaping expectations about the behavior of others, which they achieve by lowering the individual cost of compliance with prescribed behaviors while raising the cost of deviance from socially set expectations (Lepsius 1995: 394). Institutions stabilize actors' expectations by indicating what constitutes legitimate (and likely) behavior. By the same token, changing institutions are a source for changing expectations. The most obvious example for this are legal institutions such as contracts, property rights, bankruptcy laws, and antitrust regulations. Legal stipulations and their practical application shape an actor's expectations, for instance regarding a counterparty's trustworthiness when providing credit. Contracts specify in advance what will be expected of the counterparty and thus shape expectations. The connection between institutions and expectations can also be developed into a comparative political economy of expectations that proceeds from the notion that different imaginaries develop in different macroinstitutional contexts. Regional differences in innovation strategies are an example of this: imaginaries of radical innovations associated with high

levels of uncertainty are more likely to exist within the institutional configuration of the American economy, which has more flexible innovation systems, comprised of a "loose aggregation of people from widely diverse backgrounds" and higher tolerance for individual failure (Bronk 2009: 208). The Silicon Valley might be the epitome of this. Imaginaries of incremental innovations are more common within the institutional context of coordinated market economies, which feature "teamwork environments where engineers can build successfully on the collaborative mining of a deep seam of shared tacit knowledge of existing processes and customer requirements" (Bronk 2009: 208).

4. *Networks.*   Research on occupational aspirations finds that the career aspirations of adolescents are strongly influenced by their social surroundings (see Chapter 6). And network analysts (Uzzi 1997: 50) have shown for inter-firm relations that expectations regarding future cooperative behavior depends on network structures. More generally, it may be assumed that social networks play a role in the emergence of fictional expectations, since social ties lead to the diffusion of perceptions of the future and to converging interpretations of a given situation. Power relations are also manifested in the structure of social relations and the positioning of actors within fields, which in this way also influence the expectations actors hold (Bourdieu 2000).

5. *Cognitive devices.*   Economic theories such as the efficient market hypothesis are tools used by actors to assess how markets will develop, thus shaping their imagined futures (Miyazaki 2003). Expectations in the economy are more broadly anchored in prevailing cognitive models, which function as instruments for the construction of imagined futures (see Chapter 10). This connects to the notion of epistemic cultures and epistemic communities, social settings in which actors share specific interpretations of the economy. Convergence on specific calculative tools that allow for the (pretended) calculation of outcomes helps shape expectations.

Niklas Luhmann (1976) observed that an interest in chance, games of luck, and probability theory developed in conjunction with changes in perceptions of the temporal order in the seventeenth and eighteenth centuries. Especially in England, games of chance and the calculation of probabilities became a part of everyday culture, developing in parallel with the emerging capitalist economy (Kocka 2013: 72). In the face of decisions perceived as complex and risky, probability assessments, made possible by newly developing stochastic calculation (Daston 1988), tempered perceptions of the randomness of choice. Mathematical tools helped transform the open future into an object of calculation,[19] allowing decisions to be made *as if* the future were going to develop in a certain way. Rather than seeming random, expectations could appear rationally justifiable, encouraging exposure to risk. Stochastic calculation thus enlarged the time horizons of actors and encouraged planning, through which the future present is shaped. None of this, of course, means that expectations are entirely determined by cognitive devices. But such devices help shape imagined futures.

Like the stochastic calculation of future outcomes, utopias are another cognitive device that spread in conjunction with the unfolding of capitalism and shape expectations. Utopias may be optimistic or pessimistic; they "serve as a projection screen for hopes and fears" (Luhmann 1976: 142). By definition, utopias can never be reached: they are a kind of horizon, moving away as one approaches them. They do, however, offer socially shared images of a desired or feared future and thus orient decisions. Disappointments and new experiences chip away at utopias over time, and actors reach to new ones. As discussed in Chapter 7, the institutionalization and deinstutionalization of utopian imaginaries of technological and economic futures is an important cognitive device underpinning the dynamic restlessness of capitalism. Technologies of calculation and utopian imaginaries of future states of the world are both devices actors use to cope with their uncertainty about the open future, tools modern societies use to "colonize the future" (Giddens 1994: 74).

6. *The mass media.* The prominent role of mass media and popular culture in the articulation and dissemination of imagined futures must be recognized (Jasanoff and Kim 2009: 123). In his work on immigration, Arjun Appadurai points to the role of new communication patterns in the development of imaginaries of future changes in social status. Writing about the population of the global south, he argues that mass media in immigrant diasporas help to foster the emergence of imaginaries of a better future. "Electronic mediation and mass migration mark the world of the present not as technically new forces but as ones that seem to impel (and sometimes compel!) the work of the imagination" (Appadurai 1996: 4). Mass media disseminate scripts for possible lives. The crucial role they play in the diffusion of fictional expectations can also be seen in financial markets. The first

financial panics in the seventeenth century coincided with the spread of book printing, at that time a recent invention that for the first time made it possible for information to reach a large number of people across significant distances in a relatively short time (Shiller 2000). Today, television stations broadcast financial news nonstop and almost in real time, while providing a forum to financial market analysts. In this way, they help to constitute and maintain investors' expectations regarding the future value of financial securities (see Chapter 6).

7. *Past experiences.*   Expectations are, at least in part, built from historical experience; they are embedded in a specific horizon of the past and the present. In this sense, "the future is a daughter of the present" (Hölscher 1999: 44, own translation). Rational expectations theory, as explained in Chapter 3, sees expectations determined by past events that provide probabilistic information on future economic development. In financial markets, technical analysis is a forecasting method that builds imagined futures of price movements of stocks from the study of past market data. The phenomenological tradition argues, based on Husserl's notion of protention, that "people do not create and learn [the next steps to take] in the moment alone, but that they recognize the patterns from previous interactions that they consider 'similar.'" (Tavory and Eliasoph 2013: 924). As Arjun Appadurai asserts, "the personal archive of memories, both material and cognitive, is not only or primarily about the past, but is about providing a map negotiating and shaping new futures" (2013: 289). Imagined futures are also built from imaginaries of the past.

The relationship between experiences and expectations represents a historical development in and of itself. In traditional societies experiences can be translated into expectations almost seamlessly; this is much less the case in modern societies (Koselleck 2004: 264). When the future is not a repetition of the past, experiences necessarily lose some of their appeal and power in the formation of future expectations. This is one reason expectations vary over time: past experiences alone can never fully guide present action in a continuously changing economic order characterized by competition and an imperative to grow. Instead, imagined futures must restlessly point to a novel and hitherto unknown future horizon.

Although this list of sources of social influences on fictional expectations does not substitute for a theory of how expectations in the economy are influenced by social context and past experiences, it should at least make clear that it is awkward to see expectations as the result of individual choice alone and independent from history. There is room and need for a historical sociology of expectations, as well as for a comparative sociology of expectations. And yet, despite the social anchoring of fictional expectations, it would be as much of a fallacy to see fictional expectations as determined by actors' social circumstances alone, even though many social scientists have taken such a position.[20]

This too-limited understanding of the sources of expectations does not allow us to satisfactorily comprehend the role of imagined futures in the dynamics of capitalist development and actors' responses to situations characterized by uncertainty. Pragmatism may help in building an understanding of the action process that expresses the "creativity of action" (Joas 1996) much more prominently. John Dewey's ([1922] 1957) understanding of action as a dialogue between the actor and the situation, where the interruption of the action process leads to inquiry and creative responses that take conditions, means, and goals into account, may also help. This is a collective and power-laden process in which actors in the field present conflicting interpretations of their situation and produce a plurality of imaginaries of future development.[21] This "dissonance" (Stark 2009), however, is crucial for driving actors' creativity and the dynamics of capitalism. The "variety of competing tendencies enlarges the world" (Dewey [1922] 1957: 197).

CONCLUSION

This chapter develops the notion of fictional expectations, a concept juxtaposed with rational expectations, which are the lynchpin of the new classical economics. Fundamental uncertainty and the openness of the future make foreknowledge of the future impossible, which has powerful consequences for our understanding of how actors perceive the future. This has been recognized by leading founders of rational expectations theory such as Robert Lucas (1981: 224), who asserts that "in cases of uncertainty, economic reasoning will be of no value." The concept of fictional expectations offers a key to understanding the true nature of expectations under conditions of uncertainty. Considering what they have in common with literary fictions, expectations in the economy are assessments of a future reality that pretend to foreknow the future; they have the status of *as-if* statements. Such statements can be seen as placeholders, helping actors overlook the fact that the future is actually unpredictable. The most important trait fictional expectations in the economy share with literary fictions is that they create a world of their own. This "doubling of reality" in the imagination is crucial to understanding the creativity of actors in the economy and thus the dynamics of capitalism.

The parallels observed here do not imply that expectations under conditions of uncertainty are the same thing as literary fictions. They differ in significant ways: in the case of expectations in the economy, for example, actors seek to understand as fully as possible whether and how imagined futures can be realized. The way they scrutinize expectations is therefore very different from the ways readers scrutinize literary fictions. Fictional expectations may also be revised in light of new experiences and knowledge, while literary fiction is not revised based on new observations. The fictionality of literary texts, furthermore, is openly communicated, whereas it is hidden in the case of fictional expectations.

This chapter has in addition briefly explored some important questions regarding fictional expectations, including how fictional expectations may become a motivating force for action; how expectations are critical to power struggles in the economy; and how fictional expectations are anchored in political, institutional, cultural, and social structures. The chapters that comprise the second and the third part of the book return to these issues in greater detail.

The following four chapters discuss four central processes through which the dynamics of capitalism unfolds: the use of credit and money; investments; innovations; and consumption. The expansion of these four building blocks of capitalism underpins the growth of capitalist economies, and leads to profound crises.[22]

Work in the field of political economy has also focused on these elements. It is now time to focus on the level of social interaction, concentrating on the creation (and destruction) of actors' expectations and their role in the dynamics of capitalism. Viewed from the perspective of social interaction, the expansion of these four building blocks depends on fictional expectations. Capitalist growth, in other words, depends on actors who are convinced that it is worth making decisions whose outcome is unforeseeable. Just as positive imagined futures drive economic growth, bleak ones can trigger economic crises, causing actors to retreat into risk-averse, self-protective modes of behavior, even into inactivity, and thus bring the economy to a halt. Despite very consequential moments of crisis, capitalism has succeeded more than any other economic and social system in inspiring actors to believe that they should restlessly imagine and embark on new paths. Each of the following chapters discusses how this creativity and confidence is made possible. It should be borne in mind throughout that the willingness to act despite the uncertainty of outcomes also has social roots in pressures from competition, power, networks, institutional safeguards, cognitive devices, normative rules, the mass media, and past experiences.

Throughout these four chapters, the expectations actors hold is also discussed from the perspective of the valuation of economic goods. Whether those goods are financial securities whose future profit investors imagine, or consumer goods whose utility and impact on their social status customers imagine, actors assign value to goods based on the future they foresee. In either case, "valuation is expectation and expectation is imagination" (Shackle 1972: 2).

BUILDING BLOCKS
OF CAPITALISM

FIVE

MONEY AND CREDIT

The Promise of Future Value

> Monetary confidence helps to bring the future into existence.
>
> —ANDRÉ ORLÉAN, *The Empire of Value*

CAPITALIST MARKETS are markets in which commodities are exchanged against money. Simple exchange relations can be organized without the use of money, but they are greatly limited because they absorb little complexity. They play only a marginal role in the history of markets, and none at all in the development of capitalism. Scholars of capitalism may differ greatly in their approaches to it, but they all agree that money and credit are its backbone.[1] As Joseph Schumpeter so succinctly put it, money markets and the financial system are "the headquarters of the capitalist system" (1934: 126).

Money is indispensable to capitalist markets for several reasons. It is a means of payment that provides liquidity and frees economic transactions from the limitations of barter. Actors in the capitalist economy rely greatly on calculation and planning to contend with the uncertainty of outcomes, and money serves as a measure of value that provides a standardized unit of account for firms and households to calculate production, prices, loans, profits, and expenses. Money serves capitalism's orientation toward the future in two additional ways. First, money is inherently linked to credit, which provides access to goods for investment or consumption. The credit-money produced by banks finances future capitalist growth. Second, money stores value. It offers actors the possibility of keeping their wealth as abstract purchasing power for later use: provided it remains valued, money symbolizes a claim to whatever goods or services its owner may desire in the future. In this way, it is a representation of future value in the present.

By offering generalized purchasing power and storing value, money institutionalizes a utopian element in capitalism: it creates a cognitive horizon of potential access to goods, even to those still to be produced in the future, and of endlessly increasing wealth. Money is value in a completely abstract form, which is why Georg Simmel ([1907] 1978: 211) called it an "absolute means." There are natural limits to desires related to the use value of goods, whereas there are no such limits to the accumulation of monetary wealth: one can always strive for more money independent of any concrete needs.[2] The possibility of infinite desire for monetary wealth contributes to the open-endedness and restlessness of capitalism, as well as its orientation toward a future in which its actors imagine themselves as ever-richer, beyond all considerations of actual need.

This desirability of money, however, depends on its stability as a store and measure of value.[3] Capitalism's development is promoted by a stable monetary system; by the same token, economic crises can be triggered by crises of the monetary or the financial system. During such crises, confidence in the stability of money vanishes, or the solvency of banks is threatened through unredeemed credit claims. This chapter looks at money and credit as central building blocks of capitalism, and how fictional expectations are pivotal to their existence.

WHAT IS MONEY?

Money is one of our most puzzling social institutions. Why are we willing to give away valuable commodities or our labor in exchange for colored pieces of paper or numbers in a bank account, both of which are worthless in and of themselves? This question has perplexed economists for a long time. "It is obvious even to the most ordinary intelligence that a commodity should be given up by its owner for another more useful to him. But that every economic unit in a nation should be ready to exchange his goods for little metal disks apparently useless as such, or for documents representing the latter, is a procedure so opposed to the ordinary course of things, that we cannot wonder if even [distinguished thinkers find] it downright mysterious" (C. Menger 1892: 239).

Money is not valuable as such, but to operate it must be treated as if it were valuable. What is this game of make-believe? Some monetary theories explain the operation of money by naturalizing its value. These theories locate money's value in the intrinsic value of the object serving as money, or the commodity into which paper money can be exchanged at a fixed rate, such as gold or silver. Until the early 1970s, different versions of the gold standard bound the value of the dollar to gold reserves held by the U.S. Federal Reserve. The holders of banknotes were guaranteed to receive a fixed amount of gold upon presentation of those banknotes to their issuer. This, at least in theory, limited the money circulating by the relatively fixed amount of the precious metal available and thus bolstered belief in the stability of money (Carruthers and Babb 1996).

The international monetary system has not been tied to a valuable commodity since the 1970s, but even when it was, the value of money could not be explained in terms of the intrinsic value of the commodity it represented. This was true for two reasons. First, paper money was almost never fully covered by the gold reserves owned by its issuer, meaning that banks could never have redeemed all existing paper money with gold. The gold standard worked only as long as actors were confident that not all money holders (or even a significant portion of them) would simultaneously try to exchange their banknotes for the precious metal. They had to behave as if they could exchange their bank notes into gold. Second, the value of gold itself is not constant; it, too, varies with supply and demand. Inflation in sixteenth- and seventeenth-century Spain offers an intriguing historical example of the disconnect between "intrinsic" commodity value and purchasing power: large amounts of gold and silver were imported from the Americas during this time, and although it was thought to be a stable store of wealth, the increased availability of these precious metals actually raised prices in the Spanish economy, thereby diminishing their purchasing power (Ferguson 2008: 19ff.).

If we cannot explain money's worth as based on its guaranteed exchangeability against a valuable commodity, what does explain it? A more sociologically informed theory sees money as a representation of its holder's abstract claim on the commodities produced in an economy. Money "measures and stores the abstract value of general purchasing power and transports or transmits it through space and time" (Ingham 2008: 68). Its value is thus explained by the social and political recognition of its owner's claims to a share of the social product. From the perspective of the issuer, money is a "promise to pay." In other words, the possessor of money is owed goods. These claims to goods are expressed in a numeraire, or money of account (Ingham 2004: 12). The value of money is thus the result of a social relationship in which creditors act as if their claims are going to be honored.

This can be seen from an historical perspective: In a trade relationship, a merchant might not provide goods in direct exchange for the products he obtains; instead he promises to compensate the seller at a later point in time.

The seller then keeps a record of the debt in his books, or the debtor issues a promissory note, a kind of contract or token he hands to the seller of the goods stating that he owes the seller a certain amount. The promise made by the merchant creates a debt that he is obligated to honor by fulfilling his promise to pay, and the value of his promise lies in its credibility. It allowed traders to act as if the seller were to be compensated, even though this compensation had not yet taken place. The promissory note served as a prop that signaled the beginning of the transaction. For the holder of the promissory note, it was a placeholder, a claim on future compensation; for its issuer, it was an obligation, a concrete debt. Such promises were documented even before the existence of paper: in ancient Mesopotamia they were inscribed in clay.

Throughout much of history, credit has provided financial resources on the condition that these resources, or the principal, be repaid at a future point in time, with interest (Weber [1922] 1978: 80). Credit thus bridges a time gap by transferring expected future purchasing power to the present (Wray 1990: 11). At the same time, it creates debts, which are the obligation to repay a creditor. Monetary stability can exist only if the parties in an exchange believe that debts will be repaid through future economic success; these expectations remain unfulfilled if the production of credit-money outstrips the capacity of businesses or the state to produce the revenues for repayment (Ingham 2003: 303) and, in the contemporary economy, if consumers cannot repay their loans.

The process by which personal promises and individual debt were generalized into circulating legal tender is a historically observable phenomenon. So long as the issued promissory notes confirming rights and obligations could be redeemed only from the person who had issued them, they represented an interpersonal relationship, and could not be considered as money. Money emerged when the promises themselves began to circulate and were accepted to settle debts with third parties (Commons [1934] 1961: 392; Dodd 2014: 218), although it was still not yet legal tender.

In the middle ages, promissory notes circulated within networks of merchants and merchant banks. The exchange of these tokens, privately issued among traders, could take place as long as their recipients were confident that the original issuer of a claim would indeed redeem it. In trading networks, the use of the tokens as a means to cancel debt was ultimately anchored in personal trust, which limited the expansion of the monetary area. Such tokens were also issued by private banks, which promised to pay gold or silver bullion to anyone presenting them. So long as the promises they represented were credible, such tokens could circulate and provide liquidity in markets. A plethora of different and often unstable currencies emerged. Credit defaults frequently caused merchant banks to collapse, interrupting the flow of money and leading to recessions when the expectations associated with money were disappointed. Because it was not easy to assess the credibility of promises, tokens were not fully transferable. Nevertheless, these trading networks and merchant banks are the first steps in the historical process that extended the money economy as affirmations of debt became increasingly depersonalized and transferrable. Debt first became fully negotiable during the mid-sixteenth century in the Netherlands and in England. At this major juncture in financial history, a debt instrument became "payable to the bearer," whomever that bearer might be. For the first time, third parties could accept debt instruments as payment and then legally enforce their claim on the original debtor (Munro 2003: 545).

The stabilization of money and the extension of monetary spaces, however, was only achieved through the involvement of the state and its issue of legal tender. According to the chartalist theory of money (Knapp 1924), modern money was created when states began the issuing of tokens it then accepted to settle tax debts. The state's promise to accept these tokens as tax payments made them into a currency the state could then use to purchase goods or pay for services. Citizens were willing to surrender valuable commodities in order to obtain the tokens necessary to settle their tax debts. These tokens could also be used for payment in commercial transactions within a defined monetary space. The state underwrote these transactions using its power to levy taxes as a guarantee of the currency's value. Money functions because states promise to accept it "in payment of any debt owed to them, the form of money that they have issued and denominated in their declared money of account" (Ingham 2008: 69).

In the sense that its value depends on the credibility of the promise that it will ultimately secure access to valuable goods or settle debts, money issued by a state does not differ from a privately established bill of exchange or a clay tablet proffered by a merchant in ancient Mesopotamia. In all three cases, lenders must act as if the promissory token were valuable. This implies that the credibility of money issued by the state depends on the state's perceived ability to extract resources in the form of taxes as well as on the regulation of monetary supply to assure monetary stability. The value of state money is therefore directly linked to the coercive powers of the state as the money-issuing authority, a clear demonstration of the relationship of money to power. This can be seen in the negative, as well, for example, in situations of monetary crises such as those in Russia during the 1990s and in Argentina during the early 2000s (for Russia see Woodruff 1999). These monetary crises were directly connected to the loss of state authority and its perceived capacity to effectively extract tax revenues from its populations.

The coercive powers of the state are, however, not the only necessary conditions for a stable currency. The development of a stable monetary space also depends on the existence of a moral atmosphere that facilitates trust in the inherently worthless tokens that are used as money. If these tokens are to be treated as if they were valuable, a process of normative construction or "collective intentionality" (Searle 1995) must occur "in which the general quality of trustworthiness as a *public,* or *communal,* virtue replaced *personal* commitment" (Ingham 2004: 126; see also Polillo 2011). Money is also collective in nature from the perspective of money holders: as Georg Simmel put it, to hold money is to hold "a claim upon society" (Simmel [1907] 1978: 190). In this sense a bank note is far more than a piece of paper: it contains the completely invisible but very real power of the collective. Whenever money is used, whenever people surrender objects of value in exchange for it, the power of collective intentionality is experienced concretely.

The Creation of Money through Credit

Money exists today within a financial system that includes both the state and private banks. The integration of private banking and a public currency has allowed for greater monetary stability and, consequently, for faster economic growth (Ingham 2008: 72). Money is backed by the power of the state, which establishes the unit and standard of the numeraire, creates money through its central bank, influences money supply through its monetary policies, and acts as a lender of last resort. At the same time, most money is created by private banks, through the issuing of credit. The legal order regulates the creation of private money, thus linking the state and private banks.

The founding of the Bank of England in 1694 offers a particularly good example of how money is created through private banks. The bank, which was at the time a private institution, was financed with the issuing of bank stock worth £1.2 million provided by London merchants. The bank in turn loaned this money to the government for an indefinite term at an interest rate of 8 percent. In return for the permanent loan to the government, the bank was allowed to create paper money, which was accepted for the payment of taxes. The government paid interest using income from customs and excise revenues, which were specifically earmarked for this purpose, meaning that the loan was guaranteed by the government's ability to extract resources from its citizens. The government's promise of payment was at the same time considered as a bank asset, which in turn became the basis for the issuing of additional bank notes, up to the original deposit of £1.2 million. This money was then used in loans to private borrowers. In this way, £2.4 million in loans were issued from an original deposit of £1.2 million (Carruthers 1996: 77).

This mechanism for creating additional money from customer deposits is the cornerstone of modern capitalist banking; indeed, it is "one of the essential elements of modernity" (Kim 2012: 9). Banks issue credits that surpass the reserves they hold, based on the expectation that not all their depositors will reclaim their deposits at the same time. This system, known as fractional reserve banking, allows the money supply to grow beyond the money created by the central bank, and thus to finance capitalist growth. Banks are authorized to issue credit up to a certain multiple of the reserves they hold; these reserves depend in turn on the presumed default risks of the credits banks hold in their balance sheet. Banks' leveraging of deposits to create money is central to the financing of the capitalist economy, but it can also spark financial crises when demands for withdrawals and declines in the value of assets surpass the bank's liquidity (Admati and Hellwig 2013).

Essentially, as Joseph Schumpeter (1934) argues, capitalism is a system of indebtedness in which the creation of credit-money by banks creates purchasing power for entrepreneurs. Because entrepreneurial projects depend on banks' willingness to finance future production, an economic agent "can only become an entrepreneur by previously becoming a debtor" (101ff.). Credit allows entrepreneurs "to withdraw the producers' goods which he needs from their previous employments, by exercising a demand for them, and thereby force the economic system into new channels" (106). In today's economies, money is also created for the purpose of consumption, allowing for demand before consumers have actually earned the claim to the goods they purchase. New money created through credit generates new demand in the economy without creating new supply. Purchasing power is handed to an actor (either an entrepreneur or, in the case of consumer credit, a consumer) without being taken away from somebody else.

The "credit pyramid" created through credit-money exerts a structural force on the economy to grow. If principal and interest are to be repaid, the value of commodities produced by the entrepreneur in the future must be higher than the value of commodities purchased.[4] The entrepreneur must use his or her purchasing power to furnish new products whose value at least equals that of the credit, plus interest (Schumpeter 1934: 110). This expectation, however, is a fictional one: "By credit, entrepreneurs are given access to the social stream of goods before they have acquired a normal claim to it. It temporarily substitutes, as it were, a fiction of this claim for the claim itself" (107).

Only later market success can justify this fictive claim to goods. The fictional expectation entailed in credit, however, is favorable to capitalist growth because future productivity can be realized only if the means to produce this productivity are obtained in the present. The banking system may thus be seen as buying time for the economy (Esposito 2011: 73)—time that must be used to create additional value. The same holds in case of consumer credit, where the ability to repay depends on future income streams of the debtor. Lenders act as if their loans were going to be repaid. If too many borrowers fail to make good on their promises and default on their loans, the system then crumbles (Minsky 1982).

The Stability of Banks and of Money

It is evident that without "the foundation of borrowing and lending, the economic history of our world would scarcely have got off the ground" (Ferguson 2008: 31). But because the entrepreneurial success and repayment capacity of consumers is uncertain, banks take on risk by issuing loans. These risks can be limited by the regulation of banks' lending practices (Gorton 2009) and they may be calculated using risk assessment devices. Notwithstanding regulation and calculation, both banks and the stability of money are vulnerable to the actual economic success of debtors and to depositor sentiment.

For a bank to succeed, depositors must behave as if their deposits were always available for withdrawal and therefore abstain from actually doing this. The moment depositors lose trust in their bank's solvency, a bank run occurs and the bank collapses. Deposit insurance is an institutional countermeasure to reduce the risk of bank runs.

Similarly, currencies are threatened if their users believe their value will decline, in which case they will attempt to abandon them. This is why the promise of convertibility of a currency into a commodity such as gold, or into another convertible currency (one that actors believe will safely store value) can increase its acceptance and stability. In a system of flexible exchange rates, confidence in a currency is measured by the rate at which it can be exchanged against other currencies. The decline of a currency's value in relation to other currencies means a decline in confidence in that currency, and indeed in the collective force of the state as the money-issuing authority. States can attempt to stop such devaluation dynamics through capital controls, as well as through monetary policy and by trying to convince money holders of the currency's value with official communications.

Today, the scarcity of a commodity does not translate into a scarcity of money—what Schumpeter called the "golden brake" on the credit machine (Schumpeter [1927] 1952)—although demands for a return to the gold standard do occasionally resurface in the political arena. Rather, scarcity is the result of policy decisions by central banks, lending decisions of private banks, and the communicative strategies of central banks, economic analysts, and politicians. In other words, the stability of money is based on institutional and rhetorical commitments alone.

Here again, the history of the Bank of England is informative not only because it shows how private institutions create credit-money, but also as an example of how closely public and private interests are linked, and how they come together in the creation of a monetary system and the expansion of the credit base of the capitalist economy. When money began to be regulated by the state, and when it finally became legal tender, it left the confines of personalized trading networks, creating an incentive among the bourgeoisie to support taxes levied by the state. The formation of a system capable of creating credit-money at will means an "immense increase in infrastructural social power" (Ingham 2004: 132). It expands the capital available for investment and consumption, and, by creating expectations of stability and repayment, accelerates the dynamics of capitalism.

THE FICTIONALITY OF MONEY

Since modern credit-money is not directly linked to commodities that have exchange value in their own right, the question remains: why would anybody accept worthless tokens in exchange for valuable goods? The monetary system requires belief in three different fictions in order to function.

First, money relies on the fictional expectation that the collective will treat something of no value (bank notes or numbers on an account sheet) as if it did have value, and thus will accept it as a means of payment in the future.[5] As Mitchell Innes (2004: 56) writes: "The eye has never seen, nor the hand touched a dollar. All that we can touch or see is a promise to pay or satisfy a debt due for an amount called a dollar." For money to be valuable we must act as if it had value, even though it does not. A coin or a piece of paper is a prop, the representation of an abstract claim and the belief that this claim can be redeemed or exchanged for a valuable object. An actor will only accept such objects in exchange for goods if he expects that others will do the same: the functioning of money depends on its exchangeability, which is a collective belief, a game of make-believe that can only operate collectively. Confidence in money, Commons ([1934] 1961: 416) asserted, has its basis in a relationship between the individual money holder and the "rest of the world." Simmel stated the same when he wrote that money is a "bill of exchange from which the name of the drawee is lacking" (Simmel [1907] 1978: 177). Money is "socialized debt" and can only exist as a social institution (Dodd 2011: 6):[6] alone on his island, Robinson Crusoe could not have created money. "Each 'I' can play the money game only if 'we' play it" (Ganßmann 2012: 227, own translation).[7]

Second, capitalist credit-money can only function in the presence of the fictional expectation that its value is stable, and therefore that it is a secure means of storing wealth for future use. Economic development "depends on the stability of the value of money without which long-range calculations, large-scale enterprises and long-term credits would be impossible" (Simmel [1907] 1978: 125). Stability does not mean that money's value is invariant, but rather that its rise and fall is largely predictable. Monetary instability impedes economic growth: when it occurs, in the worst cases, markets lose their liquidity, and production and trade come to a halt. Keynes ([1936] 1964) assumed that money was essentially risk-free when he argued for the existence of a "liquidity premium" to which investors resort in times of high economic uncertainty. According to Keynes, investors can at least temporarily avoid the exposure to the risks associated with investment by holding their wealth in form of liquidity. In this sense, money absorbs uncertainty, buys time, and calms actors (Esposito 2011; Ganßmann 2012: 10; Shackle 1958: 195). The desire to hold money is thus "a barometer of the degree of our distrust of our own calculations and conventions regarding the future" (Keynes 1937: 216).[8] However, the frequency of monetary crises and the fluctuations of exchange rates show that money itself embodies risk (Bryan and Rafferty 2013; Reinhart and Rogoff 2009).

The credibility of the "fiction of a monetary invariant" (Mirowski 1991: 580) is thus itself contingent. The fact that money is not actually scarce is an inherent risk to monetary stability; after all, money tokens can be produced in unlimited quantity.[9] To maintain its value, however, actors must believe that it will be kept scarce *as if* it were a commodity. A particularly telling illustration of this was a proposal discussed among economists and politicians in 2012 to mint a coin with a declared value of one trillion dollars. This suggestion was made when a congressional majority refused to raise the country's borrowing limit. The U.S. treasury has the right to mint coins and could theoretically use this right to mint a coin with an astronomically high value, deposit that coin at the Federal Reserve, and then borrow an equal amount of dollars against it. The suggestion was ultimately rejected, not least because of inflationary fears. But it shows that the "invariance" of money is contingent.

Money may be devalued by inflation or even declared worthless in monetary reforms. The stability of money depends on the monetary policy of the state, on its central bank, on the lending practices of private banks, and on macroeconomic development, which are all unforeseeable. Given the fact that there is no natural limit to the creation of money, rules, norms, and the management of expectations must be used to limit the quantity of money available in an economy and to shape expectations of actors in order to maintain the fiction of its stability. The existence of this fiction is a social creation, depending on institutions but also on communicative processes in which the suspension of disbelief is established and reaffirmed. The speech acts of central banks and their forecasts are rhetorical devices used to shape expectations regarding the future value of money (see below).

Third, for fractional reserve banking to work, depositors must expect that they will be able to withdraw their money at any time, an expectation contingent on the repayment of loans issued by banks. This expectation is fictional in two senses: first, since the money created by banks through loans far exceeds the deposits they hold, depositors cannot all withdraw their money simultaneously. In the absence of asset securitization, the maturity mismatch between the long-term assets of banks, such as fixed-rate mortgages, and their short-term liabilities, such as deposits, makes it a constant challenge for banks to secure enough liquidity to repay depositors. A significant proportion of depositors trying to withdraw their money at the same time would render a bank insolvent. Since the possibility of withdrawing deposits depends on the repayment of the loans issued by a bank, the value of credit-money is based on the fictional expectation that loans will be repaid in the future, providing the bank with enough liquidity to remain solvent. In this sense, credit-money is a bet on the unknown future based on current expectations (Esposito 2011: 74). On the microlevel, whether borrowers can meet their obligations and repay their debts according to the terms stipulated in their contracts depends on entrepreneurial success; on the macrolevel, it depends on the growth of the economy—both of which are uncertain. Credit-money, in that it is used to initiate the production of as-yet-unknown products (Deutschmann 1999: 54), provides access to the future. At the same time, however, no one can know in advance whether an imagined future will indeed become the future present; it is always possible for credit-financed investments to fail. If too many loans in an economy turn out to be nonperforming, a financial crisis ensues.

The fictional expectations that make the monetary system possible suggest that money is essentially a relationship of trust, based on the perceived credibility of promises to pay. The value "of a unit of currency is not the measure of the value of an object, but the measure of one's trust in other human beings" (Graeber 2011: 47). If money is a relationship of trust, then the stability of money cannot be explained as the outcome of calculation alone. Georg Simmel, for instance, argued that a belief that money will retain its value "is only a weak form of inductive knowledge" (Simmel [1907] 1978: 179). Again, the unpredictability of the open future makes it impossible to have sufficient information to make fully rational calculations; in the case of money, this implies that monetary value contains an "element of social psychological quasi-religious faith" (179). Actors behave *as-if* money were stable. To create belief in the stability of money, its future value must be successfully feigned.[10] For François Simiand (1934), the uncertain nature of the future also makes beliefs regarding the stability of money crucially important. The future is "neither determined nor determinable by quantitative data, not even in the form of a greater or lesser mathematical probability coefficient, but a question of assessment. This . . . entails more or less distinct feelings more than it does reasoned and critical forecasting: in a phrase, it is a *matter of trust* (or of defiance)" (Simiand 1934: 36–37, own translation).

Indeed, one of capitalism's most remarkable achievements is the dissemination of the fictional expectations that make possible the operation of money and the expansion of credit. Markets could not operate if money were not accepted in exchange for goods; without it, different economic spaces could never have been integrated into a global economy. Moreover, the fractional reserve banking system provides the financial resources that firms use for investment and that consumers use to increase their demand at a time when they do not possess the necessary purchasing power to make the purchases with their own resources. Economic growth (and financial crises) are accelerated through credit-money.

Because it is not directly linked to any valuable commodity, money's value consists in nothing but the expectation that it will provide access to goods in the future. If this expectation vanishes, the value of money evaporates, and asset holders lose their wealth. *Ceteris paribus,* the higher levels of indebtedness are, the higher the risk that creditors will lose confidence. The importance of stable money for the operation of the economy, and, ultimately, for the integration of society as such—and the fragility of that stability—explains the strenuous efforts of governments and central banks to maintain confidence in the monetary system. The "production of a trusted currency, including an integrated banking network, and the stability of money's purchasing power are the primary concerns of all capitalist states" (Ingham 2008: 66). Belief in the stability of money, as in other institutions, is most effective if actors are unaware of the possibility of its faltering; that is, if its stability becomes naturalized (Carruthers and Babb 1996).

If monetary confidence prevails, money becomes a universal object of desire, and an inexhaustible source of energy in a market economy. "At the heart of the market mechanism is the general fascination with money and the overwhelming desire to possess it" (Orléan 2013: 53). Actors seek to acquire money because it offers purchasing power, and can be exchanged for any goods and services in the future. The fact that money is only attractive if actors believe in its future value and stability raises the question of how trust in money is created and maintained, and in what circumstances this trust is withdrawn.

BELIEF IN MONETARY STABILITY

If money itself is not valuable, but actors act as if it were, it is indispensable to establishing a microfoundation of capitalist dynamics to question the origins of their belief in it. Economists generally answer this question with reference to the money supply. According to the quantity theory of money, price levels depend directly on the quantity of money available in the economy. Price stability can be maintained by ensuring that the monetary supply corresponds strictly to the development of economic productivity.

This gives a prominent role to institutions that regulate the expansion of money circulating in the economy. Sociologists concur with economists on the importance of institutions for monetary stability.[11]

Governments deploy an institutional framework and policy resources, including central banks and financial market regulatory agencies, to maintain trust in the stability of the currency. They influence money supply by setting discount and Lombard rates, open market policies, repurchase agreements, and swap transactions, as well as regulating the reserves that private banks must hold. They also include institutional arrangements such as central bank independence (to shield monetary policy from short-term political interests) and the inscribed goals of central bank policy. Central banks hold cash reserves and gold reserves, encourage procedural correctness and transparency, and act as lenders of last resort (R. Hall 2008; Pelzer 2013). Monetary stability also relies on private institutions operating in financial markets. Rating agencies assess the credit risks associated with the debt of countries and private enterprises, contributing in this way to the assessment of financial risks and the channeling of credit flows. Private banks provide deposit guarantees to assure depositors that their money is secure. These banks are, for the most part, enmeshed in a dense network of regulatory rules.[12] All these institutional rules are intended to convince a currency's "users" of the soundness of monetary policy, the stability of the currency, and the safety of their deposits, encouraging them to act as if the tokens defined as money were actually valuable.

However, any theory of monetary stability that focuses only on the money supply overlooks something crucial: if the value of money is understood as a belief in the promise of future access to goods produced in the economy, then that value cannot only be explained "objectively" in terms of supply and institutionalized rules. Monetary stability should instead be understood as the outcome of a political and discursive process through which confidence is established. While the quantity of money available in the economy and monetary institutions plays a role in the existence of this confidence, so do interpretations of the different measures of the quantity of money and assessments of the power of monetary institutions. Confidence in monetary stability is created and maintained—or lost—through a constant flow of interpretations of the monetary situation, monetary policy measures, and goals. These communicative processes take place among influential actors in the field, particularly governments, central banks, private banks, companies, rating agencies, and economists, and create a narrative of the monetary situation. Confidence must exist among political and economic experts and at the same time extend to the users of a currency. Georg Simmel noted this in passing when he argued that money "becomes increasingly a public institution in the strict sense of the word; it consists more and more of what public authorities, public institutions and the various forms of intercourse and guarantees of the general public make of money, and the extent to which they legitimate it" (Simmel [1907] 1978: 184).

Belief in the future value of money is constituted through the narratives actors use to make sense of a monetary situation and the everyday experience of the use of money (Abolafia 2010). These discursive processes can be discussed in the context of primordial debt theory, which uses Durkheim's theory of religion to highlight the collective character of the valuation of money, and in the context of the communicative strategies of central banks.

Money as Totem

Although it may at first seem farfetched to turn to the sociology of religion for analytical tools to understand the interpretative processes that underlie the stability of money, there is in fact a long tradition of analyzing the operation of money in parallel with religious phenomena (Benjamin 1991; Deutschmann 1999; Mauss [1914] 1974; Simmel [1907] 1978; Yip 2010). One approach in this tradition uses Emile Durkheim's investigation of totemistic religions to examine the functioning of money (Aglietta and Orléan 1992; Théret 2008).

Durkheim asserted that totemistic societies assign a power to objects called "totems," which they revere and worship in religious ceremonies. A totem has power only in the context of a clan's belief system. This power is symbolically represented in the object, "yet the powers which are thus conferred, though purely ideal, act as though they were real; they determine the conduct of men with the same degree of necessity as physical forces" (Durkheim [1912] 1965: 260). In this sense, the specific quality attributed to the totem is simultaneously fictitious and real. The totem truly does exercise a power over individuals in a clan, even if the power of the object itself is imaginary. Money is highly comparable to these objects, since its value (or power) is not based on its material characteristics, but rather is produced through belief, and is, in this sense, fictional. The shared experience and belief in the (purchasing) power of signifiers of value is what makes money more than just "pieces of paper" or numbers on a balance sheet.[13] Money is treated as if it were valuable.

Durkheim argues that the power clan members perceive as originating from the totem is in fact the power of the social group over the individual. The totemistic societies whose religious belief systems he analyzed did not possess the cognitive means to understand the idea of group power, and thus ascribed the power they felt acting upon them to an object. This object plays a central role in religious ceremonies in which clan members assemble, and in which the power of the group is felt especially strongly. This power is then (falsely) attributed to the totem. The totem is treated as if it had power. Similarly, belief in the value (power) of money can be interpreted as the result of a collective attribution.

Seen in this light, confidence in the stability of money is confidence in its "magical" ability to prompt other members of society to surrender valuable goods in exchange for intrinsically worthless tokens sometime in the future. In large part, this expectation is anchored in communicative processes, most importantly in the "successful" use of money itself. Again, Durkheim is helpful in understanding this confidence: according to him, the power of the religious totem is reinforced through ritualistic practices and through its interpretation by authorized religious personnel. Quite similarly, the power of money is continuously reconfirmed through the practice of monetary exchange, in which users of money continuously experience its "mana"; at the same time, experts in the monetary field provide rhetorical confirmation of the future value of money.[14]

André Orléan's investigation of money (2014) combines Durkheim's insights from religion with Keynes's metaphor of a beauty contest to establish what he calls a "mimetic model" of money, which highlights the social character of its value. Actors in financial markets try to anticipate other actors' expectations regarding a currency's future exchange rates. The decision to hold money is thus conditioned by what other actors think about its development. Certain variations notwithstanding, the stability of money emerges from a collective consensus. If actors concur in their negative opinion about the value of a currency, a monetary crisis ensues in which the currency ceases to be liquid and loses its value.

Orientation toward the expectations of other market actors is not the only sense in which the stability of money is socially constituted. That actors will surrender goods in exchange for intrinsically valueless tokens indicates that money also expresses a relationship of power. The fact that money is described in terms of purchasing power bears testament to this on the semantic level, while the fact that it is declared legal tender shows this is also true at the legal level. But whose power is it? In Durkheimian terms, it is the power of the collective over the individual: money is valuable if it can effectively prompt the individual to submit to the collective will. As it is legal tender, a holder of goods is also legally obligated to accept the totems in exchange for goods. For money to be credible, the functioning of this power relationship must be assured; in the context of a market society this means that goods must reliably be surrendered upon the presentation of money. Confidence that money will be valuable in the future is also confidence in the power of the collective order and its ability to enforce the claims of the holders of money.

The users of money continuously experience the power of the collective order when they give and receive valuable objects in exchange for legal tender. This may explain the strong emotional relationships people develop to money: Georg Simmel stressed the association of money with emotions of great intensity (Simmel [1907] 1978: 269), recalling Durkheim's observation of the emotional force of totems. The strength of emotional relationships to money and the punishment of any form of disrespect for it can be seen in a "breaching experiment" conducted by the French singer Serge Gainsbourg in 1984. To protest against France's high taxation of his income, Gainsbourg burned a 500 franc note on live television. Thousands of angry viewers wrote to Gainsbourg to protest his act. What caused such strong reactions to the destruction of a piece of colored paper? From a Durkheimian perspective, Gainsbourg was attacking a symbolic representation of the social order itself. The colored piece of paper was a prop representing this order, and his attack on this prop was perceived as an attack on the authority of society (the state); as such, it was fiercely sanctioned.[15] Georg Simmel confirms this when he writes that the "feeling of personal security that the possession of money gives is perhaps the most concentrated and pointed form and manifestation of confidence in the socio-political organization and order" (Simmel [1907] 1978: 179). Gainsbourg sabotaged the make-believe game on which the possibility of money rests. Destroying money creates the emotions of an attack on the collective order.

Central Banks: The Economy of Words

The stability of the monetary system also relies on the rhetorical strategies financial market actors use to interpret the monetary situation. The expectation of future monetary stability is "a function of the *assessment* of both the government's fiscal practice and its central bank's monetary policy" (Ingham 2004: 145). Fantasies, fears, and hopes play a crucial role in this. Changes in the exchange rate of the dollar against the euro, for instance, cannot be explained simply by shifts in the money supply of their respective economies or by changed macroeconomic indicators. "Beliefs exert a far greater influence on economic behavior than any effect the money supply may indirectly bring to bear on prices" (Orléan 2014: 134). Given how important expectations are to investment decisions within financial markets, governments, central banks, and private investors try to influence these expectations and to govern markets this way. Rhetorical strategies have become increasingly important in recent years, especially in the monetary policy-making of central banks. Douglas Holmes speaks quite aptly of an "economy of words" (Holmes 2014).

For the past twenty years or so, the rhetorical strategies of central banks have attracted significant attention from scholars. The construction of credibility with regard to monetary stability through narratives uttered by central bank representatives has been investigated in economics (J. R. Campbell et al. 2012), in ethnographic studies (Abolafia 2010; Holmes 2009; Smart 1999; Tognato 2012), in political science (Braun 2015; Nelson and Katzenstein 2014), and by former employees of central banks (Blinder 2004; Issing 1997). In economics, central bank communication and policies of "forward guidance" now constitute a research field of their own.[16]

Studies of central bank communication all assume that today's central bank policy relies on more than just the application of established and legitimate tools of monetary policy. Instead, the expectations of "the economy" are seen as central to monetary policy. Central banks spend a great deal of time and energy observing and attempting to influence these expectations (González-Páramo 2007). Under conditions of uncertainty, the "challenge for central banks is to discipline expectations with persuasive narratives, informed by a continuous stream of data and analyses, articulated in measured and consistent fashion" (Holmes 2009: 385). Central banks attempt to "manage" market expectations regarding future interest rates and price stability. In economics, much of the literature on this topic follows rational expectations theory and sees the success of central banks' inflation policies as dependent on the banks' ability to credibly communicate its commitment to these policies. Actors in the economy should behave as if the narratives of central bank representatives regarding future inflation rates actually described the future present. The credibility of a central bank's commitment to price stability is measured by collecting and analyzing data on expectations.

Money markets "hang on every carefully chosen word uttered by the finance ministers and central bankers of the major economies" (Ingham 2008: 79). In this sense the communicative practices of central banks "underwrite a political economy" (Holmes 2009: 382) through a politics of expectation-building. Words construct "the economy itself as a communicative field and as an empirical fact" (Holmes 2009: 384). Such an economy of words operates under conditions of uncertainty "where the rational and the irrational coexist or may be entirely inseparable, where knowledge is imperfect, and where information is asymmetrical, and experience and intuition can or must inform judgment" (Holmes 2009: 385).

To influence expectations of future development in the direction intended, narratives must appear credible to economic actors whose decisions shape the future envisioned in the narrative. As Douglas Holmes shows, this credibility is achieved both through rules, such as those regarding the transparency of the decision-making process, as well as by including many different actors in the construction of assessments of the monetary situation communicated by central banks. Hence expectations are the outcome of a dialogical process. The Reserve Bank Governor of New Zealand, Holmes reports, travels across the country each month to visit a selection of companies chosen from a pool of about five hundred. "The governor and his or her staff communicate central bank policy during these visits but they also actively solicit stories—anecdotal data—from the employees, managers, and owners of these enterprises. . . . This complex network of interlocutors provides acute technical representations of the New Zealand economy imparting (or restoring) social mediation to economic analysis" (Holmes 2009: 399).

The Canadian central bank engages in a similar process of ongoing conversation with a wide range of economic and social groups as it goes about assessing the monetary situation (Smart 1999). Interpretations of the monetary situation and of policy measures are collective constructions made by actors in the economy, who are recruited to participate in the anchoring of expectations. They form an epistemic community that "fosters the assimilation of 'feelings,' 'intuition,' 'discretion,' and 'judgment' reaching into the reserves of 'experience' within these institutions sustaining the 'intersubjectivity—the grounds for shared understandings—that make possible the intellectual collaboration of the bank's economists'" (Holmes 2009: 401).

The anchoring of stories and predictions in the experiences and assessments of a broad community assembles the available knowledge of the economic field, distributes cognition, and supports these stories' credibility. In this sense, the senior officials of central banks "are not merely technocrats who fill a predefined institutional role; they are the architects of these institutions and the theorists of the conceptual issues and the pragmatic concerns at stake in monetary policy" (Holmes 2009: 392).

At the same time, stories are experimental, in the sense that they are open to revision and modification as new data and new interpretative insights become available (Holmes 2009: 401). The interpretations provided by central banks may be seen as an "unfolding experiment whereby skillfully composed narratives . . . serve as analytical bridges to the near future" (Holmes 2009: 386). This resembles John Dewey's depiction of the action process, where actors continually revise their interpretations of the situation based on new experiences and adjust their narratives and policy measures accordingly. This also resembles the collective convictions Durkheim observed constituting the power of religious objects in totemistic societies, where beliefs are reinforced through the ritualistic practices of clan members. At the same time, the "suggestion that economic value is a power that originates in the beliefs of a community of people, through the sharing of ideas and emotions, borders on heresy in a discipline where, with rare exceptions, only the willed actions of individuals are recognized" (Orléan 2014: 149).

The interpretations communicated are not merely projections of economic activity in the future, they are themselves instruments for shaping and defining that future (Holmes 2009: 386). In other words, they are part of the politics of expectations. The narrative construction observed here is performative to the extent that economic actors adjust their practices to fit the narrative. "If these statements are credible and persuasive, the public's expectations will themselves cleave over time to the (inflation) targets . . . thus aiding in the anchoring of prices and furthering economic stabilization, the overriding goal of this monetary regime" (402–3). If the behavior of prices is expectational, "then an anticipatory policy that projects central bank action into the future becomes a means to influence these sentiments" (395). The stability of money is shaped by the credibility of narratives and practices.

THE BELIEF IN THE REPAYMENT OF CREDIT

The observation that confidence is modeled linguistically and communicatively (Holmes 2009: 406) holds not only for the belief in monetary stability, but also for confidence about the repayment of debt. Credit relations are anchored in the credibility of a borrower's promise to repay a loan, which is based on an assessment of the borrower's trustworthiness (see also Carruthers and Stinchcombe 1999). The term "credit" comes from the Latin *credere*, meaning "to believe." The "belief" here is the expectation that the borrower will repay the loan, either voluntarily or by coercion. Credit, like money, is essentially a relationship of trust and confidence.[17]

As argued before, capitalist growth is intrinsically linked to credit. Credit provides investors and consumers with purchasing power, allowing for investments and higher demand in the present. At the same time, borrowing against future profits or future earning potential exerts pressure on the economic system to expand and may render the financial system fragile. Actors behave as if the outcomes they expect were the future present. "If the expectations are not sufficiently fulfilled the whole system becomes destabilized" (Ganßmann 2011: 14). Credit is a "risky temporal projection, based on the premise that debts will be repaid, that endows capitalism with its inextricably linked dynamism and fragility" (Ingham 2008: 91).[18]

If capitalist expansion depends on credit, capitalist societies must succeed in creating the expectation among capital owners that the promises at the center of credit relationships will be honored. For borrowers, the expansion of credit relations presupposes their willingness to take on debt in order to increase their monetary wealth or social status in the future, or their consumption level in the present. Credit must evoke imaginaries of a counterfactual future that involves entrepreneurial riches, economic survival, or an altered social status, such as through ownership of a company, a home, or consumer goods. This motivation, crucial as it may be for capitalist dynamics, cannot be taken for granted. Borrowing money for investment has social preconditions: it requires a social structure that allows for upward social mobility, individual life-plans directed toward upward social mobility, and a willingness among actors to engage in risks and speculation (Deutschmann 2009: 32). Imaginaries of economic progress such as the "American dream" or aspirations for home ownership culturally facilitate willingness to take on debt. This is true of an Austrian entrepreneur dreaming of founding his own dynasty (Schumpeter 1934), for an Indian woman applying for microcredit (Appadurai 2013: 244; Mader 2015), or a homeowner in Phoenix taking out a subprime mortgage to realize his version of the American dream. All these actors decide to borrow capital based on the assumption that the future they envision is desirable and will actually come about.

Once a person or firm is indebted—for investment or for consumption—credit has a disciplinary effect: it pressures the debtor to act in ways conducive to repaying the loan. Credit can therefore be seen also as a form of governmentality and domination (Bourdieu 2005; Calder 1999; Trumbull 2012). This is true of consumer credit, commercial credit, and sovereign debt. Private equity firms, for example, typically require the companies they buy to indebt themselves as much as possible, partly in order to exert control over the conduct of management and workers. The pressure thus exerted by credit helps generate further actions that drive capitalist dynamics, while at the same time increasing the risks of credit default.

Viewed from a historical perspective, the expansion of credit relations has been one of the most important hallmarks of the unfolding of capitalism. In 2010, the total credit market debt, which comprises private and public debt, was estimated at over USD 50 trillion for the United States alone, making it more than three times greater than the county's annual GDP (Figure 5.1). In 2014, total world debt was estimated at USD 199 trillion, or 269 percent of global GDP. Even since the financial crisis of 2007, global debt has increased by 17 percent of GDP (McKinsey Global Institute 2015). While these figures are usually viewed as showing the over-indebtedness of the global economy, they also raise an intriguing question: how was this unprecedented expansion of trust achieved?

Thinkers approaching the question of what the credit system requires to function have suggested a variety of factors. The foundations of trust in credit relations may be cultural; they may be rooted in a shared universalistic ethic (Weber [1930] 1992); they may stem from a commitment to rules of conduct by the "respectable merchant" (Braudel [1979] 1985); or they may result from classification schemes that categorize risks and guide lenders' expectations (Carruthers and Stinchcombe 1999: 356).[19] They may be based in social networks, such as have been observed in certain ethnic communities (Portes and Sensenbrenner 1993). For the most part, however, they are institutional (Carruthers and Ariovich 2010; Graeber 2011; Ferguson 2008) and depend on the existence of a legal system to effectively enforce property rights by punishing defaulting debtors (North 1990; Roehrkasse 2013), accounting and bankruptcy laws (Halliday and Carruthers 2009), an effective taxation system, the risk regulation of banks (Gorton 2009), and institutionalized forms of risk calculation (Carruthers 2013; Lazarus 2012; Rona-Tas and Hiss 2011). Without these institutional devices, the expansion of credit relations over the past two centuries would have been impossible.

Percent of GDP

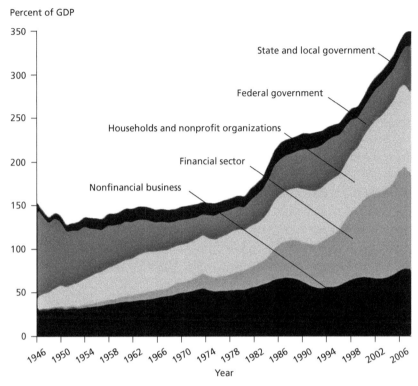

FIGURE 5.1. The components of U.S. public and private debt from 1945 to 2007 as a fraction of GDP. *Data source*: http://en.wikipedia.org/wiki/File:Components -of-total-US-debt.jpg.

Fraud and Unpredictability

Institutional safeguards and risk calculation have not, however, banished uncertainty from credit relations. Lenders must accept this uncertainty, which has two causes: fraud and unpredictability.

Despite institutional safeguards, fraud remains a threat to creditors, as may be observed in spectacular occurrences of malfeasance, such as the bankruptcy of Enron or the Ponzi scheme run by Bernard Madoff, or in banks' misrepresentations of the risks of credit derivatives prior to the financial crisis of 2008. Institutional structures allow for new forms of risk-taking associated with new profit opportunities; but they may also offer unforeseen opportunities for fraud. Expectations regarding the repayment of credit can therefore be a deliberately created fiction.

The second source of vulnerability is the unpredictability of a debtor's economic success. Even when borrowers are fully committed to repaying their loans, the market may turn against them, making them unable to repay. Future economic development cannot be fully foreseen by debtors or by investors. Creditors' expectations that they will be repaid are fictional in the sense that they are based on beliefs about an unknown future.[20] Viewed from the macro perspective, the trust entailed in credit is justified only if the economy grows and repayment of the credit can be enforced. Viewed from the perspective of actors, the promise to repay a commercial loan depends on the debtor being able to utilize the production factors purchased with the loan so that the value of the goods sold at t_1 is greater than the value of factor inputs at t_0. In consumer credit, future income streams must be sufficient to pay for interest, but future income cannot actually be known. Lenders can only act as if the borrower were going to repay the debt. The expectation is a placeholder until the debt is repaid—or not.

Credit decisions, like any other investment decision, are therefore based on what John Maynard Keynes called the state of confidence, which in this context is merely another term for creditors' expectations regarding debtors' creditworthiness. If entrepreneurs have pessimistic expectations about the economy, they will be less likely to embark on new investment projects. By the same token, the owners of financial wealth will develop a preference for liquidity and charge higher interest rates to borrowers. When capital is withheld from the production process, economic output is reduced. Expectations therefore determine investment levels and underpin business cycles and financial bubbles.

The financial and economic crisis of 2008 provides extensive evidence of the role of fictional expectations in credit relations. The expansion of credit in the American housing market—as well as in some European housing markets—was based on the expectation that housing prices would increase, which was the only way subprime mortgages could ever be repaid. It was also based on the social imaginary of a desirability for increased rates of homeownership. Lenders were, nevertheless, motivated by yet an additional consideration: they either planned to immediately resell the risk they had underwritten to other market actors—which many banks indeed did—or they simply followed the prevailing optimistic market opinion, believing they would "be first in line when the borrower gets into difficulties and a run takes place" (Hellwig 1998: 718). Assessments of market opinion are highly relevant to investment decisions, and asset overpricing, that may occur when actors imitate each other's decisions, causes market bubbles. Overpricing should not be explained psychologically, as a result of "overconfidence," but rather sociologically, as the outcome of collectively shared interpretations of a given situation.

The Politics of Expectations

Since credit is risky in addition to being a source of profit, and because expectations regarding a debtor's ability to repay a loan are contingent, the politics of expectations is a prime activity in debt relations. The credit economy is an economy of words. Through "impression management" (Goffman 1959), borrowers try to signal their trustworthiness (Bacharach and Gambetta 2001; Beckert 2005) in order to convince potential creditors of the prudence of investing in them. They use signals to persuade lenders of their honesty and to demonstrate the soundness of their business. Lenders in search of profitable investment opportunities must convince themselves— or their principals—of a deal's potential profitability. For this they must interpret and judge the signals provided by the borrowers and the market.

The politics of confidence is a strategic game of interested parties. A creditor already holding debt from a borrower will attempt to downplay any problems the borrower might have in order to avoid market depreciation of collateral assets. The creditor will do so by attempting to influence the expectations of other investors, while perhaps at the same time looking for an exit strategy. When Standard & Poor downgraded American government debt in the summer of 2011, the investor Warren Buffet went on television to express his conviction that American debt was fully secure for investors.

In contrast, doubt may be deliberately cast on a borrower's creditworthiness when investors speculate on the possibility of default. A notorious example of this occurred in a media interview with former Deutsche Bank CEO Rolf Breuer in 2002, in which Breuer publicly expressed doubt as to the creditworthiness of German media mogul Leo Kirch's company. Kirch, forced to declare bankruptcy shortly thereafter, sued Deutsche Bank for damages. At the end of a long trial, Deutsche Bank agreed to pay more than one billion dollars in compensation to Kirch's heirs.

If expectations are themselves a source of profit or loss, then the politics of expectations is a crucial power game in the capitalist economy. Creditors exercise "voice" by threatening "exit." This power of private business was described by Michal Kalecki in the 1940s (see Chapter 4) and can be observed in the acceleration of the sovereign debt crisis in the eurozone in 2010. Financial investors communicated their interests by threatening to remove trust in states—that is, to exit—effectively threatening them with unsustainable interest rates for further loans, or even blocking their access to capital markets. In order to bolster the confidence of financial markets, the governments of eurozone countries provided guarantees for the sovereign debt of countries that had already lost market confidence. These guarantees came on the condition that the countries comply with fierce austerity measures, which cut living standards and caused recessions in the countries affected. These policies satisfied the interests of financial investors (especially banks) by institutionalizing policies that would lower the risks associated with outstanding loans. More generally, power is expressed through the creation of visions of the future and beliefs in available options. This "shadow of the future" cast by fictional expectations shapes decisions.

Market intermediaries, especially analysts and rating agencies, play a crucial role in the rhetorical construction or destruction of this power. These experts assess the risks and opportunities associated with a security or a class of securities (such as American sovereign debt) thereby creating or destroying value. The work of these specialists cannot be considered as a market activity, but because it provides a cognitive frame for market actors, it has an immediate impact on markets. Financial analysts' reports provide a calculative frame for the assessment of risks, and provide models and categories of judgment, which transform market dynamics into seemingly calculable events for investors (Wansleben 2011: 498). Interpreting and categorizing helps to make uncertain situations seem calculable and thus to facilitate decisions. Rating agencies are also intermediaries in financial markets. Their function is to interpret borrowers' signals with regard to their creditworthiness (Carruthers 2013; Rona-Tas and Hiss 2011).[21] Rating agencies assess risks while framing situations through calculation and judgment (Beunza and Garud 2007). Such frames are contested, may be multiple, and change over time. They pretend a future state of the world, are part of the politics of expectations, and help to stabilize financial markets by providing points of reference. Assessments of risk in financial markets are themselves part of the governance of these markets.

As the history of the financial crisis of 2008 shows, credit ratings are not always accurate statements of the risks creditors are considering (MacKenzie 2011). The attempt to use credit ratings to shift uncertainty toward risk has never been fully successful: "Uncertainties might be hidden, but they did not cease to matter" (Carruthers 2013: 527). There are two explanations for this. First, in the case of ratings for collateralized debt obligations (CDOs), the financial vehicles that triggered much of the financial crisis, issuers and raters cooperated. Both sides worked to "game" ratings in order to obtain results that favored their interests, while at the same time vastly underestimating the risks involved. It is possible to employ rating algorithms so that they produce "counter-performativity"; that is, so that risk predictions measure less and less accurately the actual risks associated with a financial investment (MacKenzie 2006). Second, models measuring risk assumed normal distributions of risk based on incomplete statistical information, and underestimated correlation effects as well as systemic interdependencies, leading to unexpected outcomes known as "black swans" (Carruthers 2013: 545; MacKenzie 2011; Taleb 2010). Such rare events occur in financial markets far more frequently than the statistical assumptions of normal distributions imply. Like analysts' reports, the ratings of rating agencies should be understood as fictional expectations regarding future outcomes and seen as part of the politics of expectations.

Intermediaries' assessments are influential if they are found credible by a large and influential proportion of market actors. The mass media therefore has an important role in creating sentiments about risks and creditworthiness. Interviews, press releases, or comments in the financial press help to convince "the market" of a specific framing of the risks and opportunities of a situation. A good example of this is the interview with Deutsche Bank CEO Rolf Breuer cited above.[22]

MONETARY AND FINANCIAL CRISES

If the value of money and credit is based in fictional expectations, then it follows that financial crises are crises of confidence. Monetary crises are situations in which the promises on which the acceptance of money and the granting of loans were based have been broken, or are expected to be broken. Seen in this light, financial crises are linked to the time horizons of actors. In periods of high confidence, time horizons are enlarged. Credit brings expected future purchasing power into the present. At the same time, actors make commitments that expose them to the uncertainties of the future. During financial crises, time horizons shrink. The future contracts because it is perceived as too risky. Actors lack confidence in debtors, certain financial instruments, or in money as a store of value. In such situations uncertainty magnifies and markets can become illiquid and freeze, which is the principal manifestation of financial crises.[23] Investors attempt to clear their positions to reduce risks but they do not find buyers at a price level that keeps them from insolvency. The collapse of the market for mortgage-backed securities (MBS) in 2008 and of the interbank lending market are excellent examples of this illiquidity in financial crises: in 2008, the prices for MBSs tumbled and the Federal Reserve had to step in, providing liquidity to banks by buying the MBSs from them. In the interbank lending market, before the financial crisis, banks routinely borrowed money from other banks to assure their short-term liquidity. With the onset of the financial crisis, banks lost confidence in the solvency of their peers and stopped lending to them, whereupon central banks had to step in to provide the needed liquidity. In this sense, financial crises are credit booms gone bust (Schularick and Taylor 2012).

Keynes's metaphor of a beauty contest again provides a useful model for understanding how monetary and financial crises are triggered by changes in expectations. Keynes saw the value of financial assets as being anchored in actors' expectations about the expectations of other actors. As long as actors believe that other actors expect money to be stable or asset prices to rise, this is exactly what will happen. This is the case even if actors believe that a currency or asset's value is not justified by "fundamentals": optimism creates a self-accelerating process in which increasing values heighten optimism and encourage riskier strategies. Overly optimistic valuation of assets is possible because of the dynamic character of capitalist systems, which allows for imaginaries of future gains. An open future means that future returns are uncertain, but that uncertainty includes the possibility of speculation on still higher asset prices. Notwithstanding financial market regulation, expectations have no fixed boundaries, and in competitive financial markets actors have an incentive to use imaginaries of future value to justify higher and higher price levels. They act as if prices are going to rise even further. Speculation is an integral element of capitalism. Increase in financial risk, however, ultimately leads to what Schumpeter (1939: 635) calls reckless financing. The "reckless" creation of credit-money by private financial institutions or the state eventually undermines money as a stable store of value and a cushion against uncertainty; it also weakens financial institutions through higher and higher risks (Admati and Hellwig 2013; Boyer 2013; Schularick and Taylor 2012; Strange 1998). When expectations regarding the repayment of debt or the value of assets turn negative, financial crisis ensues: confidence in the hitherto expected future present vanishes.

Building on the work of Keynes, several economists developed models of monetary and financial crises that highlight the importance of actors' expectations. André Orléan, for example, observed that inflationary pressures are typically ignored at the beginning of currency crises. Most market actors react slowly at the onset of a crisis, remaining invested in a currency in the hope that the depreciation of its value is only a short-term phenomenon. The crisis is amplified when powerful economic groups abandon the existing currency in favor of a new emblem of liquidity that they believe to be better suited to their purposes. "In most cases the crisis begins with indexing, an expression of uncertainty with regard to the currency's capacity to correctly price commodities; it then becomes aggravated as doubts grow over the existing currency's suitability as a store of value . . . Finally, at the height of the crisis, an increasing number of producers and traders refuse to accept the currency in payment for their goods" (Orléan 2014: 123).

At this stage both the economically powerful and ordinary people have lost confidence in the currency as a store of value. The accumulation of doubt and dissatisfaction causes a new assessment of value to surface. During the period of hyperinflation in the early 1920s Germany, for example, farmers refused to accept marks in exchange for their goods, tax revenues fell, and investment ground to a halt.

The regaining of confidence in a currency is a political phenomenon, and reflects concerted action by the economic field's key players. Confidence in currency can only be restored once a stronger form of confidence asserts itself. Orléan shows that hyperinflation in Germany and in France in the 1920s both ended when the (new) currency was accepted, after leading forces in society aligned themselves to support it. In 1923, inflation and the falling exchange rate of the mark were stopped immediately with the introduction of the *Rentenmark,* without any other economic measure being taken. The sudden and seemingly miraculous restoration of confidence in the currency may be counted "as the effect of a spontaneous and collective expression of confidence" in which symbolic forces played just as crucial a role as economic policy choices (Orléan 2014: 169). The Rentenbank's action brought together politicians, farmers, industrialists, merchants, and bankers; the success of monetary reform, at least at the beginning, "was a matter of purely collective support, of the belief in the social collectivity" (Orléan 2013: 65). Actors returned to behaving as if the currency were stable.

Another example of this is the banking crisis in the United States during the Great Depression. An increasing number of bank failures in 1932 led to widespread uncertainty as to the soundness of banks, and then to panic as more and more depositors reclaimed their deposits, which in turn accelerated the crisis. As one of his first acts in office, President Roosevelt ordered a national bank holiday on March 12, 1933 and discussed the problem in a national radio address on that day (Buhite and Levy 1992). His message was an attempt to restore confidence in the banking system by changing expectations about the security of bank deposits.[24] To stop the bank run, Roosevelt had to convince the American public to behave as if their deposits were safe, which is exactly what he did.

Charles Kindleberger and Robert Aliber ([1978] 2005) and Hyman Minsky (1982) have put forward models of credit crises in which financial actors' expectations play a central role. Kindleberger and Aliber argue that financial crises result from the implosion of asset price bubbles, which have their roots in manias that spur spending and lending in the economy. These euphoric moments of mania, which are caused by overstated profit expectations, are interrupted when a pause occurs in the increase in asset prices and a number of investors are forced to sell assets under duress. At this point, a spiral sets in: investors change their expectations and sell their assets, leading to a crash, and possibly to panic. Kindleberger believes that these crises can be ended if the dominant country in the world financial system commits to the rescue of financial institutions.

Hyman Minsky also explained financial instability endogenously, as part of the normal functioning of a capitalist economy. He argued that the incentive structure of the financial system gives banks and companies an interest in making increasingly speculative investments during growth periods in the business cycle. Growing confidence among investors (see Chapter 6) may ultimately lead to increasingly speculative growth in credit, which, when it reaches its final stage, Minsky calls Ponzi finance. The progressively risky financial structure of banks and firms creates a situation in which small declines in expected profits or increases in interest rates make it impossible for firms and financial speculators to fulfill the payment obligations on their debts. For example, shortly before its collapse in 2007, the investment bank Bear Stearns had equity of USD 11.8 billion, and assets of USD 383.6 billion, giving it an equity ratio of 3 percent, which meant that the bank would become insolvent if its assets lost only 3 percent of their value.

Many other banks had similarly risky financial positions before the crisis began (Admati and Hellwig 2013). This created a conundrum for banks: the higher their leverage, the higher the profit opportunities—but with a greater risk of collapse from a sudden shift in confidence. While asset values were being supported by an imagined future of stable or increasing prices, these risky financial positions were sustainable. But once expectations about prices began to shift and asset market values declined, a downward spiral of bad loans, collapsing financial institutions, and restricted investments set in. Fictional expectations played a decisive role in this process, because anticipated profits "determine the willingness of bankers and businessmen to extend and to take on financial commitments" (Minsky 1982: 27).

Highlighting the importance of actors' expectations in no way denies the objective fact of insolvency, in which a firm's liabilities exceed its assets. But since the value of an asset depends on market expectations, so too does insolvency. A crisis is triggered once expectations regarding the ability of firms and financial institutions to fulfill their obligations turn negative. The as-if assumptions regarding future development on which credit had been extended fade away. In the financial crisis of 2008, this became known as the "Minsky moment."

In financial crises, depositors fear for the safety of their deposits and want to withdraw them, creating a bank run, a chain reaction capable of bringing down the financial system as well as the productive sector. In the financial crisis of 2008, governments and central banks reacted to the possibility of this scenario with rescue packages, monetary easing, and guarantees to financial institutions of unprecedented magnitude.[25] At the same time, they publicly assured depositors of the safety of their money. The state asserted itself as a stronger source of confidence by acting as an underwriter to payment obligations. This took place through bailout policies (Woll 2014) as well as through dramaturgy. German chancellor Angela Merkel and her finance minister Peer Steinbrück, for example, gave a joint press conference on October 5, 2008 in which they informed the German public that all private savings would be guaranteed by the state. Like the radio address of President Roosevelt seventy-five years before it, the statement was intended to calm the public, which was losing confidence in the solvency of banks in the wake of the bankruptcy of the Lehman Brothers investment bank a few weeks earlier. The guarantee covered EUR 568 billion in deposits—and how the German government would have paid such a sum had it become necessary to do so is a mystery. But the political authority's statement and the public's assessment of it shifted expectations, causing depositors to act as if their deposits were safe. This fictional expectation prevented German citizens from engaging in a bank run.

CONCLUSION

Capitalism is a system of indebtedness. One crucial source of capitalism's dynamism is the supply of credit-money, which is, at least in principle, unlimited; however, this unlimited supply is also the cause of the system's fragility (Ingham 2008: 66). Money is created through credit, which makes it possible to engage in economic activities that may or may not succeed in the future. Credit provides purchasing power to firms and consumers, thus stimulating demand. Money provides liquidity for markets, a numeraire for calculating transactions, purchasing power for investments, and a store of value. It is an indispensable precondition for the development of the impersonal market relations that connect economic transactions, as well as for the organization of the modern firm.

The institutionalization and expansion of money contributes to the extension of time horizons in capitalism by helping to absorb uncertainty (Ganßmann 2011: 2). Because money is a way of storing value, it promises access to goods in the future, reduces exposure to uncertainties the future holds, and secures against the indeterminacy of future wants. In other words, though I may not know what my future desires will be, I know I will be able to satisfy them (Esposito 2011: 30; Simiand 1934; Simmel [1907] 1978). Money is therefore "a tranquilizer against the effect of not knowing what to do" (Shackle 1958: 195), a way of gaining time. At the same time, financing investment through credit-money forces the system to expand without cease. Credit must be repaid with interest, which pushes firms to create a surplus from the production factors they employ. Consumers must strive to repay consumer loans. An economy increasingly dominated by finance requires behaviors and institutional forms in the economy that mirror the flexibility of the financial system, thus exerting pressure on the economy and society.

Money and credit are based on fictional expectations; belief in their value depends on imaginaries of uncertain future states of the world. Actors must act as if the value of money were going to remain stable, and as if they were going to be able to exchange intrinsically worthless tokens for commodities of value in the future. In order to entrust their savings to banks, they must also be convinced that they will be able to withdraw these deposits at any time. This conviction must exist despite the fact that banks hold only a fraction of their depositors' savings as reserves—claims of depositors could never all be repaid, at least not at the same time. Fictional expectations are just as necessary to the existence of credit relations. As Schumpeter explained, credit gives entrepreneurs access to goods before their claim to them is justified. Confidence in the outcome of the entrepreneurial activity is a kind of placeholder, since that confidence can only be justified in hindsight.

The expansion of monetary promises and the belief in their credibility must be considered a major development of modern society. Today's financial system's infrastructural, coercive, and rhetorical power is historically unparalleled, if in the contemporary world economy the value of three years of future world economic production is held as a claim against other actors. For this system to be maintained, creditors must believe that borrowers will respect their claims and have the means to settle them—and that borrowers believe they have an obligation to repay their debts.

However, money can only contribute positive connotations to imagined economic futures if its value is assumed to remain stable, and money's stability is itself a function of the trust actors have in the financial system. This trust depends partly on institutional frames, such as credible regimes of property rights, credit ratings, and the laws regulating central banks. It also depends on the institutional enforcement of the obligations of debtors—on the coercive power of lenders, in other words. The expansion of credit is only possible in the context of an institutional structure that leads lenders to develop a belief that the principal and the interest they are owed will mostly be repaid. Expanding trust in money despite recurrent monetary crises and defaults on loans must therefore be seen as a condition for keeping the present open to imagined futures.

Confidence in monetary stability and in financial institutions is, however, not objectively determined by the existence of specific institutional regulations. While there is no doubt that institutional features and technologies of risk assessment are crucial to the operation of the monetary system, they cannot by themselves explain confidence in money and the financial system. Confidence must also be created and maintained through discursive processes that take place among the actors in the field and the general public. These processes define situations and assess the riskiness of holding money and providing credit by means of interpretation; in this way, they set the value of money and inspire confidence in borrowers. The functioning of money and credit therefore depends on narrative constructions. Investigating the interpretative processes through which confidence in financial markets is created or shaken is a highly consequential field of research of capitalism (see Rona-Tas and Guseva 2014).

Expectations motivate actors to accept money and to make investments with uncertain outcomes. When these expectations turn bleak, they are the source of sudden contractions in economic activity. In these moments, when fictional expectations of monetary stability are revised and the value of financial assets is reevaluated, actors attempt to transfer their claims to the social product to different tokens (other currencies or commodities), sell financial assets, and refrain from extending credit. Monetary and financial crises may lead to the devaluation of money through inflation, or to prolonged periods of debt-deflation, accompanied by deep recessions and a loss of economic prosperity. As stated at the opening of this chapter, the centrality of the financial system as "the headquarters of the capitalist system" (Schumpeter 1934: 126) implies that financial crises are the most profound form of capitalist crisis. Just as the stability of the financial system is based on actors' confidence in it, crises in the system are triggered by the loss of that confidence. Since confidence is contingent, monetary and financial crises are an expression of the shifting interpretation of an open and uncertain future.

SIX

INVESTMENTS

Imaginaries of Profit

The varying expectations of business men . . . and not anything else, constitute the immediate and direct causes or antecedents of industrial fluctuations.

—ARTHUR PIGOU, *Industrial Fluctuations*

ECONOMIC GROWTH depends on investments, which keep resources from immediate consumption and use them to create future wealth. This broad definition of investment indicates that investment processes are not limited to capitalism but have a history as long as that of human settlement. But such processes can be motivated for very different reasons. The subsistence farmer who plants part of the past season's harvest instead of consuming it is investing in a future yield, with the goal of survival or economic reproduction. Investing capital in the construction of an automobile factory is an investment typical of modern capitalism and is fundamentally different from that of the subsistence farmer's, not just in nature but in motivation. In the latter case, the investor hopes that the sale of automobiles at a future point in time will generate revenues that exceed the costs associated with their production. This investment is not motivated by survival, but by the expectation of profit.

Investment into plant and equipment used for the production of goods or services is just one form of profit-seeking investment in capitalism. Two other distinct forms of investment exist. The first is investment into financial assets, which either provide the right to future income in the form of interest payments or dividends, or opportunities for profit in the event that the asset's price increases in the future. To obtain these opportunities for profit, the investor must make a commitment, which entails the risk of losses if the debtor does not repay the loan, the company does not pay dividends, or the market value of the financial product depreciates over time. A further

131

form of investment is investment in human capital, which may lead to higher income or access to more prestigious or more secure employment. Going to college, acquiring skills through professional training, or practicing an instrument or a sport with the intention of eventually generating income from these activities are all commitments undertaken with the hope of future gain.

Without exception, scholars of capitalism have identified investments as one of the pillars of capitalist dynamics. Karl Marx ([1867] 1977) believed investment was the starting point for the surplus production that takes place in the labor process. Max Weber ([1922] 1978) saw the capitalist economy as defined by rational investments through which the capitalist sought future profits. Joseph Schumpeter (1934) argued that investments in innovations break the circular flow of the stationary economy. For Keynes ([1936] 1964), total income in the economy was determined by effective demand, which consists of consumption and investments. Investments are determined by the expected marginal efficiency of capital, making the rate of investment dependent on expectations of profit. If these expectations are low, capital will not be invested and instead kept as liquidity, which leads to the underemployment of production factors. Given its importance for economic growth, an economy's investment rate is a closely watched macroeconomic indicator.

This chapter focuses on capital investments, financial investments, and human capital investments in order to advance the argument that all three types of investment converge in at least one way: they are all based on imaginaries of the future. Put another way, they are all anchored in fictional expectations. In an investment decision, the purchaser makes a commitment whose outcome will be known only in the future. As long as he is "invested," the purchaser hopes that the objects, rights, or qualifications acquired will generate profits, dividends, and a higher salary. The transaction is motivated by a future outcome that is desired, but by no means guaranteed.

The uncertainty of investment outcomes is revealed by the long history of disappointed investments. Worldwide, it is estimated that about 40 million businesses are launched each year, and that about the same number go bankrupt (Bosam et al. 2008, cited in Makridakis, Hogarth, and Gaba 2009: 800). To be sure, some investments have more predictable outcomes than others. But one can hypothesize that the investments mostly responsible for accelerating the dynamics of capitalism are generally the ones that have the most uncertain outcomes. In the field of venture capital, for instance, most companies in which venture capitalists invest never become profitable

(Shapin 2008: 274). Financial deals often end in losses, and while career goals motivate the choice to undertake education, education is no guarantee of professional success. While actors try to calculate future gains and the risks their investments entail, uncertainty about the open future often makes it impossible to know the outcome of an investment. To differing degrees, investments are choices "in face of a lack of sufficient knowledge" (Shackle 1970: 77). In this sense, investments are uncertain bets on the future. So how do actors decide on investments if they cannot know how successful they will be?

Investments are motivated by imaginaries of how the future will unfold. Actors express these imaginaries in the form of narratives that show their convictions, beliefs, fears, and hopes, supported by calculative tools. Because investment outcomes also depend on the contingent decisions of third parties, actors are attentive to the convictions of other actors and try to know or even influence their expectations. The politics of expectations thus plays a prominent role also in investment decisions.

INVESTING IN PRODUCTION

The idea that investment decisions are anchored in fictional expectations may initially seem counterintuitive, since entrepreneurs and financial investors carefully calculate the probable outcomes of their investments. Capital budgeting is a developed field of corporate finance, and it uses sophisticated methods to calculate investments and the risks involved (Demange and Laroque 2006; ter Horst 2009). Theories of capitalism emphasize the rational character of investment processes as one of the cornerstones of the development of modern capitalism (Weber [1922] 1978).

However, understanding investments as determined only by calculation misses a crucial point: while it is true that the calculative tools developed by corporate finance can help investors make optimal decisions in situations with predictable outcomes, such tools do not fulfill this function in situations whose outcome is uncertain. Max Weber ([1922] 1978: 91) saw capital accounting as crucial to the rational calculation of investments, but he also saw the possibility for this kind of calculation as dependent on sufficient knowledge of demand, supply of materials, costs, legal regulations, and technological conditions. The rational calculation of investments is impossible if this information is not available. This is still the case today. The models applied in capital accounting rely on many input parameters whose validity cannot be known in advance. The techniques used for capital budgeting, such as discounted cash flow (DCF), net present value (NPV), or internal rate of return (IRR) all require that the size and timing of the incremental cash flows from an investment be estimated in advance.[1] The calculated net present value—and thus the anticipated profitability of an investment—depends on the cash flows predicted, the risks assumed, and the discount rate chosen. And these, of course, are assumptions whose accuracy cannot be determined until future revenues, interest rates, and inflation are known.

Since investment decisions are often unique and directed toward an open future, the conditions spelled out by Weber and required by modern capital budgeting methods are rarely met. What are the costs of product development? When will production start? What will the sales volume be? At what price can the product be sold? What synergies can be realized after a merger? The answers to these questions cannot be known before the investment decision is made and the product developed and marketed. Firms can only make informed guesses about them, which enter mathematical models as assumptions. Though firms can reduce risks by building a portfolio of different investments or by hedging against certain risks within the investment (for instance, against currency risks), each investment needs to be justified by positive expectations regarding its profitability. Hedging against *all* risks would eliminate future profit.

It is no coincidence that Frank Knight ([1921] 2006) takes capital investments as a prime example for decision-making in conditions of uncertainty. As discussed in Chapter 3, Knight considers events characterized by their uniqueness as uncertain, and gives the example of a manufacturer considering expanding his plant's production capacity, a consideration for which only "judgments" and "estimates" are possible. The manufacturer "'figures' more or less on the proposition, taking account as well as possible of the various factors more or less susceptible of measurement, but the final result is an 'estimate' of the probable outcome of any proposed course of action" (226). This is necessarily the case because the situation in relation to which the entrepreneur acts "depends upon the behavior of an indefinitely large number of objects, and is influenced by so many factors that no real effort is made to take account of them all, much less estimate and summate their separate significances" (210). For Knight, such estimates and judgments are the dominant feature of the vast majority of investment decisions.

Investments made by venture capital investors are also a good illustration of the uncertainty associated with capital investments. Venture capitalists become either creditors or part owners of companies that normally do not yet have a fully developed and marketable product. Accurately assigning value to such a company—deciding whether it will succeed in the market, assessing the worth of a share in its equity, calculating its future earnings, and so on—is impossible, and not only because of moral hazard in the negotiation process: the uncertainty of the future makes this assessment challenging to an even greater degree (Giraudeau 2012: 213; Shapin 2008: 269ff.). Future cash flows simply cannot be known, which makes it nonsensical to sum them up and discount them to their present net value. Although investment professionals estimate the value of the firms as precisely as possible using reports, formal and informal meetings, and market analyses, "these numbers are subject to significant assumptions and judgment and so are inherently subjective" (Nama and Lowe 2013: 33). Successful investments in startups are far outnumbered by failures. But even established firms are often "unable to make very rational calculations about one project . . . because they lack the information necessary for rational behavior and because they lack the time and the inclination to get it or to use very complex methods of assessment" (Freeman 1974: 253). Uncertainties arise "both from the technical uncertainty inherent in innovation and from the possibility of misjudging the future market and the competition" (167).

Faced with this uncertainty, the techniques of capital budgeting order the factors deemed important for an investment decision and transform the decision into a mathematical procedure that produces a clear outcome. Once the input parameters for the investment decision have been estimated, the models "transform what looks like an impossible exercise (given the uncertainty that weighs upon each of these parameters) into a copy-paste-like task. . . . All one needs to do is to multiply, divide and sum" (Doganova 2011: 8–9). The decision situation is structured by calculation, producing the illusion that the calculated present value is anticipating the future, and that it is possible to clearly rank investment alternatives according to their future profitability and risk. Calculative tools are instruments that help create belief in future states of the world; they thus help actors to pretend that rational decisions are possible—to act *as if*.

It is clear that calculating future income streams is important, but it is difficult to argue that such calculations actually foretell the future present. Frank Knight ([1921] 2006: 227) casts doubt on this idea, arguing that investment decisions are not based on accurate calculations of the future as such, but rather "upon the amount of confidence in that opinion." Investors believe in the calculation and therefore act *as if* these calculations provide firm knowledge about outcomes. Keynes makes a similar claim: "Enterprise only pretends to itself to be mainly actuated by the statements in its own prospectus, however candid and sincere. Only a little more than an expedition to the South Pole, it is based on an exact calculation of benefits to come" (161–62).

The prevalent use of mathematical models in investment decisions should therefore also be understood in terms of the latent function they serve: they reassure actors and justify decisions despite the incalculability of their investment outcomes.[2] Moreover, one may point out, as Knight did, that the noncalculability of future yields is even a precondition for the possibility of profit, making fictional expectations an indispensable part of the capitalist economy.[3]

Investing in Imaginaries

If the future is unknowable, then how do actors decide whether to invest in new production capacity, innovative activities, or the replacement of existing means of production? Strikingly, authors who have set out to answer this question often point to the role of imagination in the investment process. For Shackle (1970: 111), the void created by the unknowability of the future "can be filled only by imagination, by the creation of figments." According to Frank Knight ([1921] 2006: 201), decisions are reactions "to the 'image' of a future state of affairs." André Orléan argues that the calculation of production "demands foresight and imagination" (Orléan 2014: 114). In other words, investment decisions, even if legitimated with reference to elaborate calculations, are based on imaginaries of the future, which are communicated as narratives.

Open at random any business magazine or newspaper business section and you will find myriad examples of the use of appeals to imaginaries of the future to justify firms' investment decisions. Decisions—from opening a new factory, to relocating production to another country, to investments in new technologies, to takeovers or cost-cutting through downsizing—are communicated with a story of the future prosperity that is the expected result of the decision.[4] Here are three examples:

1. In the summer of 2009, a consortium of European energy companies launched a coordinated effort to plan massive investments in the construc-

tion of solar energy plants in North Africa and the Middle East, with the goal of producing enough renewable energy to substitute for the current use of fossil fuels. The consortium, called Desertec Industrial Initiative (DIL), disseminated an imaginary of a solution to European energy problems: large fields of solar panels would be installed in desert areas in North Africa, and would produce enough clean energy to meet Europe's energy needs.[5] The project, in its presentation, referred to multiple utopias to give appeal to the imagined future they were touting. Most important among them was the integration of Northern Africa into a high-tech industry, creating new economic perspectives for a region otherwise known mostly for its developmental problems, religious conflicts, and nondemocratic political regimes.[6] The project was described as the largest infrastructure project in human history, creating up to EUR 2 trillion in estimated value by the year 2050, as well as more than 400,000 jobs. One of Desertec's later founders, the Trans-Mediterranean Renewable Energy Cooperation (TREC), stated in 2003 that it believed the project could "turn the formerly contradictory goals of climate protection and economic development into mutual reinforcing objectives by making clean energy production in NA/NE [North Africa/Near East] for both local and European markets a motor of industrial and socio-economic development in NA/NE countries [as well as] help transform the Mediterranean from a region of various divisions and conflicts into a region of harmonized socio-economic development, cooperation and good neighborhood" (TREC Development Group 2003: 2).

The project's advocates argued that Desertec would provide a solution to the coming energy crisis, help stop climate change, and fight poverty in Africa, all while showing that the Islamic and Christian worlds could work together as well as reducing emigration from Northern Africa to Europe. Since the energy produced by the project would also be used for seawater desalination, it further promised to remove the threat of wars over water supply in the region. Desertec was based on narratives that voiced promises of a utopian future (Gall 2012).

This story of a prosperous future was intended to consolidate support for the project among the general public and in political circles, as well as to convince energy firms to invest in the project. The actual feasibility of the project, however, was highly questionable. How would political instability in the producing countries affect energy security in Europe? Would the producing countries be at all interested in exporting the energy to Europe, given that they are undersupplied themselves? Could the energy be transported to Northern Europe? What would Europe's energy needs be in forty years' time? Would companies be willing to carry the investment risks? According to Schumpeter, the decisive characteristic of entrepreneurship is the ability to override such concerns. For this, the imaginaries of a desired future play a decisive role.

2. Investments in biotechnology are also closely tied to fictional expectations. Catherine Waldby's investigation (2002) of the therapeutic promises made in the context of stem cell research investments is an excellent example of this. She refers to the therapeutic hopes of regenerative biology as "dream biology" (Waldby 2002: 317), "based on the hope that the vitality, self-renewal and immortality of the biovaluable fragment can be scaled up to become the qualities of the macro-scale body" (Waldby 2002: 317). "Biovalue" describes the therapeutic use value of stem cells and the exchange value that will come from the commercialization of research findings in the future. Both are built upon promissory narratives: the use value depends on the success of the research, while the present economic value depends on the confidence investors have in the future scientific success described in the promissory stories. As contributors to the field have remarked, investments in biotechnology increasingly depend "on a promissory future of economic value and potential rather than present use" (Martin, Brown, and Turner 2008: 128).

3. Investments in the semiconductor industry are a third example of the role of fictionality in investment decisions. Guido Möllering (2010) studied the discursive processes underlying investments in the development of this technology by investigating a regularly held industry workshop called the Next Generation Lithography Workshop. The workshop, which takes place in California, brings competing firms from the semiconductor industry together to discuss their expectations with regard to industry development and their intended strategies for creating new technologies. Uncertainty over future technological developments is high in this field, and firms can easily err in their investment decisions, leading to significant losses. The workshop tries to help orientate firms by identifying prevailing sentiments among industry actors regarding the most important technological issues to be resolved, opinions on the most promising technologies, and insight into the timeframe in which certain technological developments are likely to occur. In other words, the workshop presents imaginaries of future states in the

form of a narrative, accompanied by calculations, which reveal participants' convictions, shape the expectations of industry actors, and provide rationales for investment decisions to be made in the present.

These narratives help constitute the market and the future by shaping the technological strategies pursued in the present. This also implies that investment strategies cannot be understood as rational calculations of optimal choice because the contexts of action in which they unfold are themselves endogenously constituted by actors' interpretations. As stories about possible developments are articulated, investment strategies are formed that eventually create the very developments the stories articulate (Sabel and Zeitlin 1997: 15).

The expected value (profitability) that creates the basis for investment decisions thus reflects assessments that form through the dissemination of narratives supported by techniques of capital budgeting. Studies on valuation show that the assignment of qualities to goods takes place through (hierarchically structured) communicative exchanges among actors in a field (Beckert and Musselin 2013; Callon, Méadel, and Rabeharisoa 2002). Similarly, we may understand the evaluation of investments as constructed through discursive processes. Take the example of venture capital: entrepreneurs pitch their business plan and company vision to venture capitalists during meetings in which they expose themselves to scrutiny and questions from their potential creditors. Assessments of firms' future profitability are based on narratives that must convince potential investors. These narratives must be supported by numbers. On their own, however, these numbers cannot inspire decisions. As Steven Shapin (2008) argues, the due diligence process is a far less decisive factor in establishing a narrative's credibility than are networks of familiarity and the entrepreneur's ability to convey an impression of personal virtue and passion. In pragmatist terms, the assessment of prospective returns on an investment can be understood as a process of inquiry and experimentation (Doganova and Karnoe 2012; Stark 2009; Troy 2012).

Viewed more broadly, an investment's profitability is calculated within an epistemic community that includes consultants, scientists, accountants, economists, analysts, investment bankers, managers, entrepreneurs, and capital owners, who assess an investment's value by articulating expectations of future development, generally supported by mathematical models for capital budgeting (Doganova 2011: 15). Expectations of future value emerge when imaginaries of future developments are combined with the results of mathematical calculations, accounting conventions, and available data.[7] In these power-laden practical processes, actors attempt to gain confidence in their imaginaries, revise their expectations as necessary, listen to the accounts of others, and convince others of their outlook on the future. Together, these assessments ultimately become the building blocks for judgments on which investment decisions are based. Value, in other words, is constituted in practical processes by means of the narrative staging of expected future returns on an investment, supported by calculative tools. The participants in these processes of valuation know that "value depends on how valuation is done, when, by whom and for what purpose; and that to value is a highly creative process. The value of an asset is, so to say, entirely in [the practitioners'] hands" (Muniesa 2011: 28); it is based on projected future earnings, which reflect the actors' optimism or pessimism about the venture. Depending on these sentiments, the "entire edifice of value is fundamentally a fiction that can work only as long as everyone is prepared to uphold that fiction" (Palan 2012). The expected futures influence profitability in that they shape the structure of competition through the decisions that follow from them.

The expectations of value underlying investment decisions are also the outcome of a social relationship, in that these decisions depend on the structural composition of the field; that is, on the relative economic power of its different actors. In a rare documentation of how an investment in a startup firm is determined in practice, the filmmaker Harun Farocki shows negotiations between the owners of the company and an interested investment bank, and the asymmetry of power between the two parties.[8] During the negotiation process, the bankers are able to substantially revise the owners' expectations about the firm's value, as they depend less on the deal and have greater knowledge of the instruments and conventions for calculating the investment.

Actors' expectations about outcomes are the object of interest-based contestation within firms or in the market: "Many different views may be held and the situation is typically one of advocacy and political debate in which project estimates are used by interest groups to buttress a particular point of view" (Freeman 1974: 251). Because imaginaries of the profitability of investments—generated through narratives and calculative devices—have distributive effects, interested actors may attempt to mobilize other actors around specific imaginaries—or to detach them from such imaginaries. Expectations regarding profitability may, for instance, have immediate economic effects by altering the costs of capital for firms: positive imaginaries may allow companies to borrow more cheaply, which, *ceteris paribus*, gives them greater chances at success (Soros 1998, cited in Bronk 2013: 344).

Models of corporate finance and procedures of due diligence help coordinate action not because they make it possible to foresee the future, but because they are considered to be legitimate tools within the community of experts charged with the valuation of investments. The unpredictability of investment decisions, however, is not dealt with solely by numerical operations; rather, expectations are set in the discursive processes described above, which are shaped by power relations, and may enter calculative devices as assumptions and parameter values. Conversely, numerical representations can be translated by experts into imaginaries of the signified economic object. Herbert Kalthoff illustrates this point with reference to financial markets by quoting a French merchant banker in Paris:

> One can say that figures do speak, that they provoke images. This means that we aren't like robots. Every time I see figures, they provoke images and a certain behavior. I'll give you an easy example. Let's say we have an enterprise: The margins are not particularly good, the cash flow is not very good, we also have liabilities. I see that immediately, I immediately imagine the workers doing their jobs. I also imagine the problems with the stock, which is very important. I imagine the clients who are not paying their debts on time. All this. I simply have a mechanism, a logic, which starts moving inside my head. What happens is that the figures are a pretext with which you can go further. Therefore, figures do speak. But the figures speak because they make other things speak. (Cited in Kalthoff 2005: 73–74)

Fictional expectations motivate investments in economic projects whose outcome is uncertain. Some of these projects succeed and help drive the dynamics of capitalism; others fail. The use of calculative devices such as discounted cash flow analyses plays an important role in assessments of the future profitability of an investment. Such techniques, however, rather than doing what they claim to do—that is, to calculate an unknown future—should be understood as instruments used to support the credibility of fictional expectations (see Chapter 10). Contrary to claims from the sociology of calculative practices, markets cannot be reduced to arenas of calculation. Investment decisions make use of a wide spectrum of imaginaries of future presents, and, under conditions of uncertainty, calculations themselves should be understood as a form of narrative.

INVESTING IN FINANCIAL ASSETS

Today, due to the increasingly dominant role of financial markets, interest in investments is often focused on financial investments, rather than on investments in plant and equipment.[9] The percentage of GDP produced by the financial sector in the United States has increased steadily in the postwar period, and earnings from financial investments have risen disproportionally since the 1980s (Figure 6.1). In 2010, approximately 35 percent of profits in the American economy came from the financial industry, although it accounted for only a little more than 8 percent of GDP. The expansion of the finance sector and its growing profits offer strong incentives to invest in financial markets, as well as eliciting wide interest in the topic of "financialization" in the social sciences (Fourcade-Gourinchas and Babb 2002; Froud et al. 2006; Knorr Cetina and Preda 2004, 2012; Strange 1998).

Financial markets are distinct from other markets in that they are not based on the relations of individuals to things, but rather on "individuals in their relation to time" (Orléan 2014: 175). A financial asset has no use value; it is nothing but a (speculative) claim on future profit or income, attained through a commitment in the present.[10] Financial investments are commitments to an expectation regarding the future. Expected future earnings

FIGURE 6.1. Finance profits as percentage of all domestic profits in the United States. *Data source*: U.S. Department of Commerce.

determine the value of a company on the stock market. With the possible exception of the most secure investments, such as German or U.S. government bonds, these expectations are fictional. Outcomes are unpredictable and the financial investment may lead to surprising results. As early as the nineteenth century, Marx had referred to financial markets as markets for fictitious capital (see Harvey 1982: 276).

Karin Knorr Cetina (2015: 105) points out that financial markets differ from consumer markets in that "the buying or selling of a financial instrument initiates an engagement or contract that lasts as long as you hold the instrument." When a consumer good is purchased—at least if it is paid for directly and not financed through an installment loan—the relationship among the parties involved ends as soon as the transaction has been completed. In financial markets, by contrast, the transaction starts a relationship with the counterparty that is only terminated once the asset is sold again. The investor becomes dependent on the counterparty's uncertain future.[11] Knorr Cetina uses the notion of promises to characterize relationships among contracting parties in financial markets. The party receiving funds—either as credit or as equity—does so through a promise of future profits, which will allow it to repay the loan with interest or will lead to an increase in the price of its shares.[12] The party granting the funds, who Knorr Cetina calls the promise receiver, "buys into" this promise. The notion of promises seems more helpful to understanding expectations regarding the payment of the coupon of a bond or of dividends as a share of profits (which are legal obligations) than it does to conceptualizing expectations regarding the future growth of asset prices. Still, similar to that of fictional expectations, the notion of promises highlights the future's noncalculability. Promises are based on imagination and persuasion, and are narrative in nature (107).

The uncertainty of an investment's future earnings is itself traded on financial markets. Economic actors may attempt to shield themselves from the economic consequences of an asset's possibly unfavorable price in the future by hedging, just as they may seek to gain from potential profit opportunities in the open future brought about by speculation. For hedgers and speculators, financial markets allow promise-takers to back out of their investment relationships and to transfer risks (including the opportunities entailed in the commitment) to someone else. Positions change rapidly as assessments of a situation change, or as new opportunities emerge. This is true even though not all investors in financial markets are oriented toward the short term; for example, pension funds and insurance companies are long-term investors that will remain invested as long as their imaginaries of future returns from their investments remain intact.

The possibility of quick exit, however, presents a striking contrast to capital investments and investments in skill formation. It keeps large segments of financial markets focused on the very short term: professional traders often hold positions for just a few seconds. Paradoxically, it is the possibility for individuals to limit their commitments to the immediate future (and avail themselves of the right to exit in the secondary market) that allows for plentiful supplies of long-term financing of the economy in the primary market—the possibility of exit is a way to remain liquid. It opens the way for actors to commit to an imaginary without the certainty of a return.

Efficient Markets?

How do expectations of the credibility of promises form in financial markets? How is the opportunity for profit (and the possibility of loss) assessed, and how do such assessments motivate actors to invest their money? Investigating the sources of credibility of expectations regarding the profitability of a financial investment can also be posed as an investigation into the sources of value of financial assets. This is because the value assigned to a security reflects beliefs in the credibility of imagined futures. In finance economics, the assessment of the value of financial assets is made by calculating future earnings and risks. In the capital asset pricing model (CAPM), for example, the price of a financial security is calculated based on expected return on investment and the risk associated with it. Risks are calculated as the standard deviation of the previous price of the stock. Rational demand for a financial security leads to an equilibrium with uniform returns for investors in proportion to the product's level of risk. This implies that securities have a fundamental value, which can be calculated as a function of the future income and risks associated with the asset, and be discounted to its present value (see Chapter 3).

According to the efficient market hypothesis, prices in financial markets reflect a security's intrinsic value. If the market price of a financial asset deviates from this value, profit-seeking investors will buy or sell it. Profit opportunities thus emerge from what this theoretical model perceives as mispricing. If undervalued assets are bought, their prices will vary until they correspond to their fundamental value: the "actions of the many competing participants should cause the actual price of a security to wander randomly about its intrinsic value" (Fama 1965b: 56), implying that in "an efficient market at any point in time the actual price of a security will be a good estimate of its intrinsic value" (56). The theory that financial markets are efficient has informed policy reform for financial markets since the 1980s, which have followed this theory's hypothesis that financial markets are self-regulating and operate best if left to their own devices, undistorted by political interference.

Unfortunately, the model world of finance economists often bears little resemblance to the real world of financial markets. If financial markets are efficient and asset prices wander randomly around the intrinsic value of an asset, how is it that capitalism has been rocked by financial crises since its beginnings? How is it possible that the volatility of share indices is so much greater than the volatility of company profits (Shiller 2000)? How can stock market prices deviate so significantly from the development of company earnings (Figure 6.2)? The assumption that financial markets are efficient leaves most price changes unexplained.

Deviations from fundamentals are characteristic of financial markets. In the dot-com boom of the late 1990s, the shares of newly founded Internet, computer, and telephone companies skyrocketed, reaching exorbitant price-earnings ratios. In most cases, these companies had never reported any

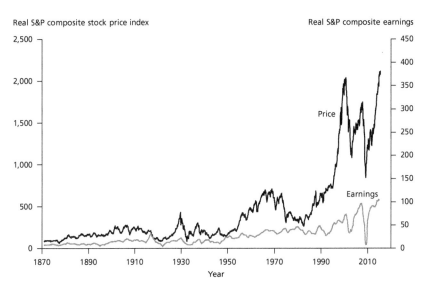

FIGURE 6.2. Real S&P composite earnings and stock market price index. *Data source*: www.irrationalexuberance.com/main.html?src=%2F#4,0.

profits: their value lay entirely in the imagined future profits they and market analysts were promising. Investors bought into these imaginaries. The dot-com euphoria is an extreme example of how far stock prices may deviate from companies' actual earnings based on fictional expectations. Actors behaved as if the imagined futures of the companies actually described the future present. The bubble burst in March 2000: investors revised their expectations, new capital became difficult to generate, and many high-flying companies were wiped out. When investors ceased expecting these companies ever to become profitable and withdrew their funds, the change was not in information about the companies' fundamentals; it was in the expectations of financial investors and the analysts advising them.

A similar pattern may be observed in the American real estate bubble, which, when it burst in 2007, led to the "great recession." Real estate prices in the United States increased dramatically in the early 2000s, peaked in 2006, and began spiraling downward in 2007. As a result, millions of American homeowners lost their houses, and the value of globally traded securitized mortgages imploded, causing a chain reaction which almost led to the collapse of the world financial system in the fall of 2008. What had changed were not the assets (houses) but the expectations of financial markets regarding future value increases in the American housing market. Book value had to be revised sharply. In both the dot-com bubble and the real estate bubble, financial markets incorrectly assessed the future value of financial assets. This completely contradicts the story of efficient financial markets as told by finance economics: in an efficient market, such mispricing of securities should not occur—and indeed, to this day, Eugene Fama insists that bubbles simply do not exist.[13]

The deviation of market prices from fundamental values may be explained at least in part by the fact that investors in financial markets do not necessarily seek to assess future earnings. Keynes distinguished two approaches to assessing the future price of a financial asset: "enterprise" and "speculation." The goal of enterprise is "forecasting the actual yield of assets over their whole life," while speculation is directed at "forecasting the psychology of the market" (Keynes [1936] 1964: 158). As long as a speculator expects that other investors will remain invested in an asset because they expect its price will continue to rise, it is rational for her to also stay invested in it even when she believes it is "fundamentally" overvalued. Consequently, a security's increase in price does not necessarily decrease demand; instead, demand may be reinforced as actors interpret the mounting price as a trend from which they may profit. New information regarding the fundamentals of an asset changes the intrinsic value of a security, but not necessarily the attitude of the speculator, who reacts to the "behavior of the group on which his wealth depends" (Orléan 2014: 236). The cause of price movements is social; they occur when there is a shift in expectations about the dominant expectations in the market. Price is thus not an intrinsic quality of the assets being traded; rather it is based on imagined futures. If decisions in financial markets are not oriented toward intrinsic values, then financial markets do not have the self-correcting properties assumed by the efficient market hypothesis. Instead, they are inherently unstable, because speculation triggers positive feedbacks that translate into cycles of boom and bust. That traders are highly attentive to market opinion has been confirmed empirically by studies in the sociology of finance, which have shown how hard traders work to find out what other traders think about how the market will move (Chong, Tuckett, and Ruatti 2013; Knorr Cetina and Bruegger 2002; C. W. Smith 2011; Stark 2009). Orléan (2014) speaks of "mimetic polarization," which drives financial markets in a certain direction based on the confidence actors have in a specific interpretation of market development.

Value from Collective Beliefs

In opposition to the efficient market hypothesis, Orléan has suggested we "abandon the idea that value enjoys some special sort of objectivity" (Orléan 2014: 189). In its place we may embrace the idea that prices in financial markets are the result of contingent expectations regarding their future value. This does not mean that assessments of future earnings of companies do not play a role: investors compare financial investments using expected earnings and assessed risks. But wrongly assessed and missing information means that investors may have lacked the very facts that, with the benefit of hindsight, would have provided accurate insights into the true situation of a firm. The fact "that there are no *known* fundamentals means that establishing definitive parameters of company strength is almost impossible. But this does not preclude attempts. It is standard [among fund managers] to try and value companies in the present, and calculate what they may be worth in the future" (Chong, Tuckett, and Ruatti 2013: 21).

Calculations of future earnings are abundant, but they have a different epistemological status from the one practitioners in the field perceive. They should be understood as props in discursive processes, providing justifiable accounts of value that help to create convictions about future price developments in the inherently uncertain conditions of financial markets. Fund managers do not actually know the fundamental value of a company, but rather "trade stories about the fundamentals thought likely to influence the prices" (Tuckett 2012: 1). Investments in financial markets are motivated by stories that "draw on unconscious phantasy and socially shared beliefs" (Chong, Tuckett, and Ruatti 2013: 9). Traders themselves describe such finance models as "*folk models* which do not reflect actual pricing mechanisms" (19). Chong and Tuckett (2015: 321) describe "conviction narratives," which consist of "'attractors'—elements that generate excitement and optimism often through associations with gain—and . . . 'doubt-repellers'— elements that manage doubts and anxiety often through associations with safety." Financial markets, in other words, are "markets in stories." Stories turn fundamental uncertainty into confidence, and thus function as placeholders that make it possible to act when outcomes cannot be known. If convinced, actors behave *as if* these stories were actual representations of the future present.

This assessment is a logical one if one considers the future to be open. Fundamental uncertainty rules out the very notion of intrinsic value, since an open future precludes the possibility of knowing a company's future earnings and fully understanding the risks it faces. Proof of this may be seen in market analysts' widely diverging assessments of firms' business prospects. Actors not only have access to different information, they also interpret the same information differently, and hold different views about the market opinions of other actors. In financial markets, there is "a bewildering diversity of individual estimates" (Orléan 2014: 195). Furthermore, it is impossible to forecast the development of market opinion because knowing that opinion ahead of time would have a direct impact on what that opinion would be: knowing when a bubble will end would effectively end the bubble, since the shadow of the future would immediately reorient actors' expectations. The analyses provided by financial market experts do not represent the future; instead, they are estimates and judgments that express imagined futures often by extrapolating from the past.

If prices in financial markets are not considered as anchored in fundamental value but rather as based on fictional expectations, a sociological theory of financial markets as outlined by André Orléan becomes possible. In such a theory, the assessment of the future price of a financial instrument "has the aspect of a collective belief. It rests on the confidence that the financial community places in it" (Orléan 2014: 209).[14] Actors gain confidence by assessing the future development of a firm and by observing the assessments of other market actors. The "justification for a price is its legitimacy" (209), its legitimacy being the belief in its accuracy. Price changes reflect a departure of at least some actors from existing beliefs.

The Narrative Construction of Value

If we understand the value of financial assets as being formed through collective beliefs, then it is only logical to explore the origin of these beliefs, and actors' confidence in them. Confidence in the future development of financial markets is the result of practical processes that are based on narrative. John Dewey (1915: 578) considers that value is "'objective,' but it is such in an active or practical situation, not apart from it." An estimation of fair value is a belief formed in discursive processes among investors and professional intermediaries.

In recent years, economists and sociologists alike have argued that expectations and confidence in financial markets depend on narratives (Bonus 1990; Kraemer 2010; Shiller 2000; Thrift 2001), sometimes known as motivating stories. The intentions of such stories can be seen starkly in certain particularly candid examples of this "genre." In their now ridiculed book *Dow 36,000: The New Strategy for Profiting from the Coming Rise in the Stock Market* (1999), journalist James Glassman and economist Kevin Hassett proclaimed that the Dow Jones Industrial Average (DJIA), then at 10,600 points, would rise to 36,000 points within the next six years. Their stated intention was to "convince you of the single most important fact about stocks at the dawn of the twenty-first century: They are cheap. . . . If you are worried about missing the market's big move upward, you will discover that it is not too late. Stocks are now in the midst of a one-time-only rise to much higher ground" (Glassman and Hassett 1999: 4). This projective imaginary was accompanied by a story of how the future development of the index would unfold: "A sensible target date for Dow 36,000 is early 2005, but it could be reached much earlier. After that, stocks will continue to rise, but at a slower pace. This means that stocks, right now, are an extraordinary investment. They are just as safe as bonds over long periods of time, and the returns are significantly higher" (140).

Other financial market prophets of the time predicted the DJIA would climb even higher, to 40,000 points (Elias 1999) or even to 100,000 (Kadlec 1999). The future, however, turned out very different: in 2005, the year

Glassman and Hasset expected the DJIA to reach 36,000 points, the highest value the stock index reached as it rebounded from a loss of 25 percent in the early 2000s was 10,700 points—not even one-third of the predicted level.

Narratives of how and why the prices of indexes, stocks, commodities, or bonds will develop are the main communicative tool in financial markets and exist in great abundance. Thousands of analysts of individual stocks or classes of financial assets write regular reports in which they assess the current situation and future outlook of companies or states, and draw conclusions about the future prospects of stocks and bonds. These reports are rarely pie-in-the-sky predictions like the ones cited above, which were published in an era of jubilance on Wall Street and were intended for amateur investors. Such reports usually offer a much subtler communicative net of calculations, estimations, interpretations, and judgments, from which individual investors gain an understanding of a market sentiment and are invited to make their own judgments and investment decisions. The idea, however, is the same: the stories pretend to provide foreknowledge of future value development. They offer projections of future earnings as basis for the valuation of companies in the market. An expected future is being traded, in other words, rather than the current or past performance of a firm.

Stories in financial markets sometimes do more than merely offer analyses of the earnings, risks, opportunities, or solvency of individual firms or states. They may also forecast social and economic trends that they predict will influence financial markets in the future. The "baby boomer" narrative in the stock market boom of the late 1990s was one of these forecasted social trends (Shiller 2000: 28). This narrative predicted that high birth rates in the 1950s and 1960s had created a cohort that would have strong purchasing power in the coming decades, leading to increasing company earnings and higher share prices. Another such narrative, this one recurring and typically circulated at times when stocks begin to be perceived as overvalued, predicts the dawn of a new era that will bring new economic laws (Shiller 2000: 96ff; Thrift 2001). During the dot-com bubble, for example, skeptics who pointed out that Internet stocks might be overpriced were informed that it was a "new economy," in which the rules of the "old economy" no longer counted: traditional indicators such as price/earnings ratios were useless for evaluating stock prices in the "new economy"; and business cycles were a thing of the past. Such stories seek to suppress experience-based knowledge (see also Reinhart and Rogoff 2009). When large numbers of financial investors believe in them, they become "valuation conventions" (Orléan 2014) that express collective beliefs about how to value a security or a class of securities. Such beliefs appear credible in the moment and create at least partial consensus, in that the financial community agrees on certain valuation principles. Such conventions are fictional in the sense that they pretend to actually anticipate future states of the world. This is impossible, but they still orient actors in the face of uncertainty, thus helping to create confidence and suspend disbelief. If actors are convinced, they behave as if these stories really did anticipate market developments. Stories are thus sometimes able to drive markets in the direction they predict.

This can only occur when a narrative has gained significant influence over investment decisions. Financial analysts contribute to collective imaginaries by telling tales of the market's future. These assessments need not be positive; negative assessments are also influential. For example, when rating agencies downgraded the sovereign debt of southern European countries in 2011, they sapped the confidence of investors and reduced the value of outstanding bonds.

This is not to suggest that investors blindly follow market stories; indeed, this would be impossible, since convictions about market developments are not and cannot be homogenous. In futures contracts the contracting parties have opposing expectations. Some investors hope to profit from financial market opportunities that other actors fail to recognize because they do not have access to the same information or because they interpret that information differently. Even traders in the same trading room of an investment bank do not necessarily hold the same expectations about future developments (Stark 2009). Individual traders are aware of different possible scenarios of how the market may develop. David Stark describes this as the "sense of dissonance." Nor are convictions stable over time. Nevertheless, the convictions they hold in the moment allow investors to position themselves within a cognitive space of alternatives deemed possible. David Tuckett (2012: 18) in his study of fund managers observes that they "constantly used judgment to make and update their decisions as matters unfolded through time in the absence of any secure knowledge about long-term outcomes and how they had to manage their subjective emotional experience while they waited. When they revised expectations it was not because they had any harder information than before. Revisions were based on experiences and estimations that were being updated and modified through review day by day." In pragmatist terms, investors' commitments can be conceptualized as a rapidly unfolding process of trial and error that takes place in a context of continuously revised interpretations of the situation.[15] Actors' choices depend on the way they imagine future development in the moment, a phenomenon that has, quite aptly, been called "conviction capitalism" (Thrift 2001: 414).

But where do actors derive their conviction that a specific narrative is accurate? Keynes ([1936] 1964) saw investor confidence as psychologically rooted in "animal spirits." In a study based on interviews with forty money managers at investment funds, Chong et al. (2013: 31) also emphasized the emotional impact of stories when they wrote that fund managers "make decisions under uncertainty through narratives which foreground the excitement of gain and deflect the anxieties of loss, so leading them to acquire conviction that their decision will lead to a successful outcome." From a more sociological standpoint, one may draw an analogy between the emotional sources of investors' convictions and Durkheim's description of the collective effervescence produced by religious rituals. Investment banks' trading rooms bring together large numbers of traders to work in an emotionally charged atmosphere loaded with anxiety, aspirations, suspense, and hope—a world clearly separate from the quotidian. In this community, and specifically in these emotionally charged situations, traders form convictions that embolden them to make decisions with unpredictable outcomes. Valuations may become mutually reinforced in a pro-cyclical manner, leading to speculative bubbles and, subsequently, to crises.

Belief in stories, as well as their social contagion, may also be explained in terms of being in thrall to authoritative sources. Robert Shiller (2000: 50) observes that predictions about stock market developments are "rarely offered in the abstract, but instead in the context of stories about successful and unsuccessful investors, and often with an undertone suggesting the moral superiority of those who invested well." Personal stories of successful investments enhance the confidence of their audience. Klaus Kraemer (2010) uses Max Weber's concept of charisma to argue that stock market analysts or investors may achieve prophet-like status and are able to mobilize followers who believe in their extraordinary powers.[16] The mass media plays a major role in this process, because it can disseminate narratives so effectively. The first financial bubbles occurred concurrently with the advent of newspapers in the seventeenth century. Ever since, the mass media has affected financial markets by propagating speculative price movements (Shiller 2000: 95). This is truer today than ever before. The process of financialization that began in the 1990s was accompanied by a boom in the financial press, as well as the arrival of investment and business television shows and channels that broadcast nonstop stories about the economy and the expected future development of financial markets. In addition to the mass media, economists, business schools, consultants, and governments all contribute to the propagation of such financial stories (Thrift 2001).[17]

Institutions and Categories

Valuation in uncertain markets is "necessarily an interpretative exercise" (Zuckerman 1999: 1431). If narrative references to authoritative figures help shape convictions about the future value of securities, they are not alone in doing so: institutions and categories are also devices used to shape expectations. Indeed, stories, institutions, and categories may not always be clearly distinguishable from one another. The "valuation conventions" André Orléan describes are narratives shared by authoritative actors in the market who continuously observe each other. Once they are detached from individual actors, these conventions may be seen as being institutionalized. Once they became a reference point for financial markets, the "Asian story" and the BRICS concept functioned both as authoritative narratives and as categorizations.

Finance economics itself can be understood as an institutionalized tool for the production of fictional expectations in financial markets (see Chapter 10). Financial investors and financial analysts use econometric models and mathematical formulae as calculative tools to estimate the profitability of an investment. While these models cannot anticipate the future, they reassure actors by justifying their decisions. Confidence is created by belief in the capacities of the risk assessment technology being used.

Accounting rules are also institutional devices that help shape expectations in financial markets. Rules institutionalizing ideals such as transparency, truth, accuracy, or completeness are not merely useful tools for calculating a firm's investment procedures (Weber [1922] 1978, [1930] 1992); they also affect expectations of investors. Accounting seeks to convince investors, in that it is rhetorical and not just technical (Carruthers and Espeland 1991). Investors' convictions are influenced by accounting rules and their practical application, which influence assessments of a company's financial soundness and the value of investing in it. Whether assets are valued according to their original price (book value), their current price (mark-to-market), or their discounted expected future price (mark-to-model) can make a tremendous difference in the valuation of a company and in the stories that are told about it. In mark-to-model accounting, the value of assets may only exist in the balance sheet without ever becoming a reality (Otte 2011: 37).[18]

Accounting rules and practices are part of the politics of expectations. They are not simply devices that objectively measure the value of a company and its financial risks. Instead, they are contingent conventions, and as such affect investment decisions. The at times dramatic impact of accounting rules and practices on the dissemination of fictional expectations can be identified empirically: before its bankruptcy in 2001, the energy company Enron made extensive use of mark-to-model accounting for derivatives, giving investors the impression that the company had much more valuable assets than was actually the case. Another example may be seen in the financial crisis of 2008. Banks at that time were required to value their assets according to their current market value, which, during the financial crisis, would have required them to report large losses from the securities they were holding. This would have revealed their failure to meet reserve requirements and would have resulted in their potential insolvency. To stabilize banks, the mark-to-market rule was suspended by political fiat (Admati and Hellwig 2013: 258). A mere change in accounting rules made these companies suddenly appear more stable.

Categorization also influences expectations regarding future value and thus contributes to the creation of imagined futures (Wansleben 2013; Zuckerman 1999). Market valuations are based on specific categorical frames. The most obvious example of this is that of rating agencies placing bonds in different risk categories (Rona-Tas and Hiss 2011). In assessing the failure risks of bonds issued by companies or states, rating agencies confirm or change existing outlooks about the riskiness of a given investment. This ordering of securities by risk category creates a common cognitive frame in the market. Institutional rules may reinforce the effects of categorization; for example, institutional investors may be required by law to invest only in bonds rated with a certain "investment grade." Although ratings do not provide foreknowledge of a bond's actual risks of failure (see Chapter 5), they offer justifications for investors' decisions and can create or destroy confidence.

Ratings are one important example of the effects of categorizations in financial markets, but such effects have also been demonstrated elsewhere. Ezra Zuckerman (1999), for instance, has shown that ambivalent categorical identities of stocks have a negative effect on stock prices. Because stock market analysts cannot unambiguously categorize firms that combine different product categories in their portfolios, they cover these firms much less, leading to discounted stock market prices. Categorization also had significant impact during the dot-com bubble of the late 1990s, when firms' stock prices depended largely on their categorization as "Internet firms" (Beunza and Garud 2007). Had amazon.com, for example, been categorized as a bookseller rather than as an Internet company, investors would have imagined a very different future for it.

Categorizations also count at the macrolevel, helping to channel global investment flows. The concept of BRIC countries mentioned above was developed by the investment bank Goldman Sachs in 2001 and became one of the most influential categorizations in financial markets over the next decade (Wansleben 2013). Later enlarged to BRICS (to include South Africa), this categorization defined a select group of countries as solid, stable destinations for long-term investment. Based on "calculative framings, narrative strategies, and metaphorical language" (1), the BRICS categorization had immense impact on the orientations of investors in financial globalization.

A category such as the BRICS concept is a cultural and political construct that cognitively orders complexity. Recategorization is a financial innovation in and of itself. The concept of BRICS was invented by the world's most powerful investment bank for commercial purposes, in a clear instance of the politics of expectations. The imaginary intentions of BRIC are highly visible: Goldman Sachs' second research report on the topic is titled "Dreaming with BRICs: The Path to 2050" (Wilson and Purushothaman 2003). Even the name of the concept connotes images of solidity and construction: "BRIC" and "brick" are homonyms. The BRIC classification uses neoclassical growth theory alongside stories and metaphors to credibly project a bright economic future for the four countries. The classification is intended to create imaginaries of a profoundly changed future world, and stimulates fictional expectations of how a single investor can profit from these changes. The effects of this categorization on investment flows has been empirically demonstrated (Wansleben 2013).

But the actual economic development of the countries in the BRICS categorization has been rather different from what was predicted: in 2013 Jim O'Neill, who created the category at Goldman Sachs, stated that he was "rather disappointed" (O'Neill 2013: 48). Today, all four countries in the

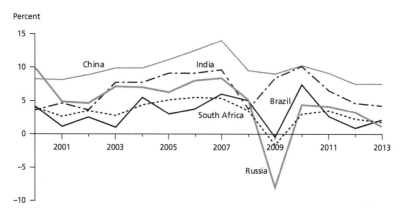

FIGURE 6.3. Annual real GDP growth rates of the BRICS economies (percent). *Data source*: IMF, World Economic Outlook.

original BRIC concept are struggling with profound difficulties in their development strategies. Their very different growth rates since 2001 have also shown that, in hindsight, their grouping in a single category was unjustified, suggestive of a homogeneity that simply does not exist. Despite the information now available, the concept was tremendously successful in motivating investment decisions by triggering an imaginary (Figure 6.3).[19]

Institutional rules and categories are collectively shared devices that help to orient assessments in financial markets and create confidence by providing images of the opportunities and risks associated with investments. These devices are not, however, deterministic. The institutional rules and categories used to assess an investment opportunity cannot relieve actors of the task of judging or estimating. Investment is a hermeneutic activity accomplished by the individual investor, but individual assessments are discursively, institutionally, and cognitively situated.[20]

The Politics of Expectations

If present investment decisions and future outcomes depend on the expectations of other actors, then expectations become a central element of the competitive struggle in which stories, institutions, categories, forecasts, and theories are tools. Those who successfully convince investors of a specific future are the victors in this struggle. The stories told are fictional in the sense that no serious truth claims can be made regarding events that lie in the future. At the same time, however, the expectations created by these tools, and the decisions they prompt, help to shape the future. Understanding the connection between expectations, stories, institutions, theories, categories, and outcomes is therefore crucial to building a microperspective on financial investments.

Companies use narratives as they attempt to convince financial investors of their financial soundness and future profitability. In "roadshows," conferences with important shareholders, and carefully worded public announcements, companies deploy discursive means to create and maintain investor confidence. Moreover, through aggressive accounting methods managers may "design" the bottom line in order to fulfill market expectations and prevent a loss in market value of the stock (and their bonuses). Financial analysts take up these narratives and numbers and tell stories to their audiences about how certain assets will develop in the future.

The aim of this politics of expectations is not necessarily to build company value on financial markets. Investors who take short positions can also benefit from the destruction of company value and may use narrative to pursue their goal. A particularly salient example of this is the case of the nutrition company Herbalife, which in 2012 found itself at the center of an unusual struggle between hedge fund managers.[21] In a press conference on December 20, 2012, Bill Ackman, the head of the hedge fund Pershing Square, claimed that Herbalife was a pyramid scheme, accusing it of pursuing an illegal and unsustainable business model. Following the press conference, Herbalife's stocks lost 40 percent of their market value. Prior to the press conference, Ackman had bet more than one billion dollars against the company by taking a short position. He thus stood to gain a huge profit from damaging the confidence of other investors in the company. The company denied these accusations. Moreover, it convinced Daniel Loeb, of the hedge fund Third Point, of the soundness of its business model, and Loeb bought stock in the company worth USD 350 million. In public appearances, the two hedge fund managers fought a battle to gain influence over the future expectations of investors in the market. But the politics of expectations did not stop there: Ackman, according to the *New York Times*, also lobbied public officials and contributed funds to anti-Herbalife advocacy groups to support his position and create further doubt over Herbalife (Partnoy 2014).

In the politics of expectations, categorizations play an important role. Investment banks that sold securitized mortgages before the meltdown of 2008, for example, used AAA ratings and partitioned securities into tranches to signal the allegedly low risks associated with these investments. The categorization of financial assets can itself create or destroy value (Beunza and Garud 2007; Zuckerman 1999): classifications that change the expectations of other market actors can produce desired outcomes if they are successfully used for "the re-creation of profit opportunities" (Wansleben 2013: 3).

One example of this is the restructuring of firms around shareholder value principles, which started in the 1980s. This shift began to take place under pressure from financial markets, which threatened to withdraw investments from companies that did not restructure their corporate governance with these principles in mind. Financial investors "lost confidence" in such companies, effectively depriving them of financial resources and reducing or destroying their ability to compete in the market. The resulting drop in share prices threatened to turn such companies into "sleeping beauties," a favored industry term for attractive takeover targets. The restructuring of corporate governance over the past thirty years, with its emphasis on increasing corporate profit and enlarged executive compensation, is deeply rooted in the narrative of agency theory (see also Chapter 10) and in the expectations regarding corporate behavior to which this line of economic reasoning has given rise (Dobbin and Jung 2010).

Similarly, financial investors have used narrative to force states to bow to their interests (Streeck 2014). States' increasing indebtedness over the last forty years has intensified their dependency on money controlled by private investors. By threatening states with higher interest rates or even the refusal of further loans, "the markets" effectively influence state policies. The level of confidence investors have in a borrower is, once again, determined by fictional expectations, which are communicated through stories and categorizations. Some of these stories derive from economics; for example, the assertion that states with a level of indebtedness above 90 percent of GDP will experience slower growth rates (Reinhart and Rogoff 2010). This analysis communicates to financial markets that loans to countries that have crossed the threshold of a 90 percent debt-to-GDP ratio are riskier investments, and sends a message to governments to reduce their spending in order to avoid punishment from financial markets. The narrative, if widely shared, reduces confidence in countries with higher debt levels, effectively pressuring governments into austerity policies or tax increases.

INVESTING IN SKILLS

Investments into material equipment and financial assets are not the only propellers of capitalist dynamism; it also relies on employees and entrepreneurs whose productivity depends on their skills. Levels of formal education and training have risen with the emergence of capitalism; indeed, the increase of formal qualification levels in the work force is one of the most striking economic and social changes to have taken place over the past 100 years. In 1900 only 6.5 percent of the American seventeen-year-old population had a high school diploma; by 2010, this number had increased to almost 80 percent. In 1920, only 4.2 percent of eighteen-to-twenty-four-year-old Americans were enrolled in institutions of higher education, while today almost 60 percent are (Figure 6.4).

A qualified labor force is a prerequisite for the performance and management of increasingly complex work processes, as well as for technological development. As entry requirements for jobs rise, training and education are becoming ever more important features of economic success. As children and young adults, and increasingly throughout their adult lives, people are investing significant time and financial resources to gain qualifications they hope will bring them income, economic security, and social status in the future. In the United States, the average college education now costs $20,000 per year and postpones gainful employment through work until the mid-twenties.[22] Investment in human capital formation is a joint effort between society and individuals. Tax money is spent on schools and universities, and parents make significant financial sacrifices based on imaginaries of the future well-being of their children. For the person in training, human capital formation is an investment of time and often of substantial amounts of money.

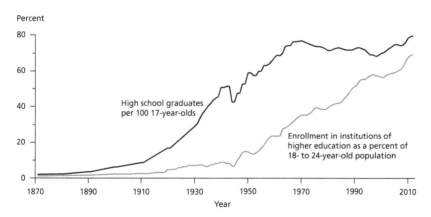

FIGURE 6.4. Educational participation in the United States, 1870–2012. *Data source*: U.S. Department of Education.

Though educational goals cannot be reduced to economic gains alone, it is a useful assumption to see investments in skill formation from the perspective of actors' hopes to gain marketable qualifications. We routinely expect future gains from the time and money we invest in education. If skill formation takes place against the backdrop of an uncertain future, then what role do fictional expectations play in it?

The notion of fiction in the analysis of capitalist labor markets is not new: Karl Polanyi ([1944] 1957) called labor a "fictitious commodity," by which he meant that labor power is not actually a commodity: it is neither produced for the market nor separable from its bearer, who as a human being was not born to satisfy market needs. And when there is no demand for it, labor does not, like a commodity, simply sit idle in a warehouse until it is needed; instead, actual people are deprived of their livelihoods. Market societies nevertheless treat labor *as if* it were a commodity, and Polanyi argues that this confusion was one of the causes of the economic and social crises of the nineteenth and twentieth centuries, eventually producing social counter-movements that destroyed the liberal political order in many countries.

Labor is also a fictitious commodity in a sense not discussed by Polanyi, but of central importance to the argument pursued here. This fictitiousness is related to the time dimension of investment processes. Investments in skill formation are usually made with an economic goal in mind, but the outcome of these investments is not predictable: career goals may change or remain unfulfilled, economic downturns may lead to periods of unemployment, shifts in technology may render acquired skills obsolete, the work experience may turn out to be less satisfying than hoped for, preferences may shift after a specific qualification has been attained. The outcome of investments in human capital is just as uncertain as for other types of investment.[23]

Fictional expectations therefore play as important a role in human capital investments as they do in other types of investment. Collective imaginaries justify educational expenditures on the societal level. In 1950s America, for example, the dire predictions of technological and economic inferiority that followed in the wake of the Sputnik launch led to a push for higher investments in human capital. Such collective imaginaries may also take the form of visions for the enrichment of a given region: the European Commission's plan to make Europe the world's most competitive and dynamic knowledge-based economy by 2020 is a good example of this. In both cases, public investments in the educational system were justified by imaginaries of the future. Currently, a global political imaginary sees future economic prosperity as requiring a more highly skilled workforce, one that engages in "lifelong learning."

Fictional expectations also play a significant role in the educational decisions of individuals. It would be nonsensical to assume that actors possess all the information they need to make an optimal choice when they decide to invest in their education (Foskett and Hemsley-Brown 2001). Inarguably, these decisions are strongly informed by imaginaries of the future: an actor's efforts in the present are motivated by the imagined future life they might make possible later on. These evocations are not only individually anchored: we live in a society that sees the future not as a repetition of the past, but as opening up uncharted territories and new horizons. Motivation for learning, delayed gratification, and expectations of upward social mobility through education are also all culturally inscribed.

Imagining Success

Human capital theory treats skill formation as an investment process (G. S. Becker 1964), and sees skills as similar to physical means of production, in that individuals' revenue-making potential depends on the utility of their labor power in the production process. Economists working with human capital theory therefore assume that decisions to obtain qualifications through education and training are an economic calculation that weighs current costs against expected future benefits. Benefits depend on the rate of return of one's human capital, as well as on the rate at which future benefits are discounted to their present value. The theory assumes that such calculations are indeed possible and has developed mathematical models actors are assumed to use.

Even if one does see decisions about education and training as based mainly on economic considerations, objections can be raised against human capital theory. The power relations in labor markets, mandatory schooling, unequal access to educational institutions, and preexisting cognitive frames all mean that human capital formation cannot be comprehensively understood as analogous to decisions to invest in material goods (Aynsley and Crossouard 2010: 134; Bowles and Gintis 1975). But it is necessary to ask to what extent actors are actually able to calculate future outcomes of investments in human capital. The answer to this question is rather disheartening:

empirically, purchasers of education "do not perceive labour markets sufficiently clearly to make efficient decisions about how much education to consume" (Johnes 1993: 51; see also Ball, MacRae, and Maguire 1999). Investment in human capital, like investment in material or financial assets, is riddled with uncertainty. Incomplete knowledge about jobs, changing labor market conditions, and changing preferences in the process of training and career development make the relationship between investments in human capital and outcomes highly unpredictable. "The success of a long education is as uncertain as the process of earning income during a long working life" (Bilkic, Gries, and Pilichowski 2012: 706).

This leads to the question of how expectations about the outcomes of investments into human capital formation take shape. Studies show that educational and career choices are at least partly shaped by idealizing imaginaries. These are fictional expectations that influence decisions about specific career paths and prompt the sacrifices necessary to complete training programs that actors expect will make possible the realization of the imaginary. Career choices are formed by "a complex set of internalized images" (Foskett and Hemsley-Brown 2001: 179) related to a person's identity, desires, and capabilities. Such career dreams "serve as a guiding and motivating force that help individuals to reach related, albeit less lofty, heights" (Kinnier et al. 2001: 25).[24]

Without a doubt, the most obvious examples of the role of career dreams may be found in expectations about artistic and athletic careers. These careers demand exceptionally disciplined training, often from a very young age, and offer stable incomes to only a fraction of those who embark upon them. Studies on the labor conditions of musicians, for instance, show that they often lack stable work, have no health or pension benefits, and must pursue commercial activities unrelated to their qualifications to earn a living (Devroop 2012: 394; P. Menger 2009, 2014). This is true also for other careers: art, acting, and athletics are winner-takes-all markets (Frank and Cook 1995; Lutter 2012a) in which a tiny number of people find high-paying and prestigious employment, while the overwhelming majority face unsteady, marginal work and often give up altogether after a few years (P. Menger 1999). Most movie actors appear in no more than one movie in the course of their "careers," and only about 20 percent of them play in more than two movies. After eight years in the business, about 50 percent of them have quit (Lutter 2012a: 442). Forty percent of all Hollywood movies are made by only 7 percent of its directors, while two-thirds of all directors make no more than one film in their careers (Faulkner and Anderson 1987: 894).

Despite these daunting figures, the cultural industries have a permanent oversupply of labor. In a study of British seventeen-year-olds, 20 percent of the respondents expressed aspirations to what the researchers called "lottery jobs" (Foskett and Hemsley-Brown 2001: 183), which they defined as jobs with high profiles but limited opportunities for entry, offering high salaries but demanding specialized talents and dependent on being "spotted." So what motivates young people to make investments in such careers? If human capital investments are motivated by rational considerations in which lifelong income, job security, and working conditions are priorities, then these career choices are inexplicable. Studies investigating career choices have shown that idealizing future projections of "winning" feature prominently in respondents' choices to invest in "lottery jobs": Ashley Mears's study of fashion models (2011) found that young women are attracted to the industry by imaginaries of high income, fame, and a privileged lifestyle. Model scouts, agencies, and the mass media encourage these dreams, along with investments in "bodily capital," distracting women from the slim chances of success, high levels of underemployment, and the actual working conditions in the industry.

It would be a mistake, however, to see the relevance of fictional expectations as limited to these outlying labor market segments. Students of management, for instance, project themselves into careers at the top of the managerial hierarchy, and these projections are encouraged by business school training methods, which portray firms from the perspective of top management. In the case method, students investigate strategic decision situations in companies by projecting themselves into the role of the company leaders—a role they will most likely never have a chance of filling in real life. Images communicated through the media are also highly influential in the development of career dreams, "amending the perceptual constructs young people have in relation to careers and the labour market" (Foskett and Hemsley-Brown 2001: 209).

The career dreams of adolescents and young adults and their parents—at least from middle- and upper-middle-class backgrounds—operate as a motivating force in the process of their skill formation, and research shows that occupational aspirations have a direct effect on occupational attainment (Sewell and Hauser 1975). Youth "with higher career aspirations tend to have higher job prestige and wages in adulthood, even after controlling for educational attainment, cognitive ability and other psychological factors" (Staff et al. 2010: 1). The projection of a "possible self" (Markus and Nurius 1986) is not just descriptive but also motivational, in the sense that it inspires behaviors focused on realizing the future state being imagined. Economists have also recognized the behavioral consequences of imaginaries of the future on educational investment decisions (Becker and Mulligan 1997; Borghans and Golsteyn 2004). Students with only low-quality images of their professional future discount this future more strongly, and are thus more likely to choose fields that do not maximize their utility and to put less effort into their study while taking longer to finish their degrees.

Career dreams remain active once actors are employed, taking the form of expectations of future promotions, higher salaries, or bonus payments. Such projections also influence motivation in the workplace (Chinoy 1955: 110ff.). From the perspective of the firm, the motivational effects of imagined futures help to "extract" labor power from the worker. Individuals realize the limits to their career advancement more clearly about mid-career, a subject that has been well researched in sociological and psychological studies. Time—that is, a person's specific position in their life trajectory—modifies career dreams (Carr 1999; Chinoy 1955; Zittoun et al. 2013). Unrealized expectations may then be experienced as deprivations and can lead to frustration, insecurity, and limited career development (Devroop 2012: 394).

Though many aspirations are ultimately disappointed, the capitalist economy is also propelled by imaginaries of the future rewards of investments in skill formation.[25] Similarly, to make investments, entrepreneurs must believe their investments will be profitable. Schumpeter was not choosing his words by chance when he described entrepreneurial motivation as anchored in a "dream and the will to found a private kingdom," rather than in rational calculation (1934: 93–94). Capitalist dynamics would slow if beliefs in opportunities for individual social mobility through strenuous effort, training, and hard work were to fade. Projections of future outcomes stimulate the efforts that underlie the dynamic changes that make capitalism so restless.[26]

The Social Anchoring of Imaginaries

In the context of this discussion of fictional expectations in the labor market, it is worthwhile to return once more to Pierre Bourdieu's study of the Kabyle in Algeria. Bourdieu paid detailed attention to the hopes and projections with which peasants saw their work-related future, and drew a connection between imaginaries and actors' social positions, thus relating imaginaries to social stratification. In the poorest social groups, actors who had little to no education and only unstable employment fantasized themselves into completely improbable positions. "The sub-proletarians are totally barred from establishing a rational hierarchy of goals . . . [They are] unable to work out a life-plan. . . . Totally overwhelmed by a world which denies them a realizable future (*avenir*), they can only accede to a 'future indefinite' (*un futur revé*) in which everything is possible, because there the economic and social laws which govern the universe of their daily existence are suspended" (Bourdieu 1979: 69).

Bourdieu later interpreted these observations as "evidence that, below a certain threshold of objective chances, the strategic disposition itself, which presupposes practical reference to a forthcoming, sometimes a very remote one, as in the case of family planning, cannot be constituted" (Bourdieu 2000: 221). Under such conditions, the link between the present and the future is broken.

By contrast, Algerian workers with some education and more stable employment had much more realistic views of possibilities they might have for advancement, as well as the steps they needed to take to achieve it. Aspirations, Bourdieu observed, tend to become more realistic and more strictly tailored to the possible as opportunities become greater (Bourdieu 1979: 51). He ascribed the differences between imaginaries of the future in the two groups to the differences in their objective conditions. Having "a permanent job and the associated security, is what provides such agents with the dispositions needed to confront the future actively, either by entering into the game with aspirations roughly adjusted to their chances, or even by trying to control it, on an individual level, with a life-plan, or on a collective level with a reformist or revolutionary project" (Bourdieu 2000: 225).

This social structural anchoring of future projections has been confirmed in research on educational aspirations (Aynsley and Crossouard 2010; Ball, MacRae, and Maguire 1999; Sewell, Haller, and Straus 1957; Yowell 2002). Bourdieu's explanation for the differences he observed, which he calls differences in habitus,[27] points to actual differences in the means to control the future available to the actors. "Outlooks on the future depend closely on the objective potentialities which are defined for each individual by his or her social status and material conditions of existence" (Bourdieu

1979: 53). In a similar vein, Arjun Appadurai (2013: 188) argues that the capacity to aspire is not evenly distributed in society. This is "because the better off, by definition, have a more complex experience of the relation between a wide range of ends and means, because they have a bigger stock of available experiences of the relationship of aspirations and outcomes, because they are in a better position to explore and harvest diverse experiences of goods and immediate opportunities to more general and generic possibilities and options" (Appadurai 2013: 188). At the same time, the different perceptions of the future help to reproduce social inequalities.[28]

Imaginaries of the results of skill formation are also institutionally and culturally anchored. Political economists (Hall and Soskice 2001a) argue that the specific skills actors seek vary from country to country because prevailing institutional structures differ. In countries with weak labor market institutions that provide limited job security, actors invest in general skills that are easily transportable from one employer to the next. In countries that have strong, protective market-regulating institutions, actors are more likely to invest in specific skills. Different institutions mediate uncertainty differently, and this affects workers' imagined futures.

Culturally, the "American dream" expresses the social promise and expectation that upward social mobility is possible through education and hard work. In many countries, the labor movement in the early twentieth century took up the cultural template of upward mobility through better education, and encouraged education and skill formation among workers as a means to improve living standards.[29] Another powerful motivation behind the sacrifices associated with human capital investments are imaginaries of the future that include the expectation of intergenerational mobility. Parents are willing to make sacrifices that benefit their child's education because they project their offspring's future well-being into them.

The downside of cultural templates that promise social mobility through skill formation is that they may raise individual expectations far beyond what structural conditions allow for. In the 1950s, Robert Merton (1957) argued that American institutions were leading everyone to strive for the same career goals. Since only some would succeed in those goals, status inconsistencies were inevitable, and would be expressed as frustration and sentiments of relative deprivation. This frustration, he speculated, might lead to apathy or baseless fantasizing. The extent to which the expectations societies create are unlikely to be fulfilled shows to what extent the cultural templates underlying them are mere ideologies.[30]

If aspirations are a force for social mobility, and if they are at least partially linked to actors' objective opportunities, then capitalist dynamics depend on the opportunities available to actors. Realistic hope is crucial; such hope is "not about the ultimate stretch of the human imagination, but about the visible potential of human life-chances, about things which can happen, because they do happen" (Dahrendorf 1976: 14). Such hope depends on structural conditions such as access to education, legal equality, social rights, and citizenship rights. To maintain their momentum, capitalist societies must maintain real possibilities for social mobility. If actors perceive the avenues to personal advancement as blocked, social apathy and anomie may ensue.[31] Both are detrimental to capitalist growth.

CONCLUSION

Investments are a core element of capitalist dynamics. In line with theories of corporate finance, financial investment, and human capital, theories of capitalism perceive the rational calculation of investment decisions as a cornerstone of modern capitalism. While there is no doubt that, at least for capital investments and financial investments, calculative tools play a major role in investment decisions and have grown more and more sophisticated over the past two centuries, the uncertainty of investment outcomes makes it impossible to conceive of investment decisions merely as mathematical exercises. Instead, investments must also be understood as relying on decision-makers' contingent imaginaries about future states of the world, fictional expectations. Fictional expectations are constructed as narratives that circulate in the relevant market field, and may be shaped by mathematical models and influenced by categories, institutionalized rules, cultural templates, and social position. Investment decisions are based on the credibility of such narratives, convincing actors to invest their resources.

If imaginaries of future states of the world become credible through narratives, then it follows that investment decisions are the outcome of a communicative process in which decision-makers seek understandings of a given situation that are convincing enough to make the risks of their investment seem worthwhile. Forming the convictions actors need to invest takes place through practical processes that include entrepreneurs and investors, analysts, rating agencies, the media, consultants, the government, educational institutions, families, and the calculative tools legitimated in the market field.

Investments are inherently connected to the issue of valuation. To invest in plant and equipment, in a financial security, or in skill formation means to assign a certain current value to the objects purchased based on expectations of future profits or utility. At the moment of investment, this value is merely a belief, which may be disappointed as time unfolds. The multitude of failed investments confirms the uncertainty associated with investment decisions.

Perceptions of the value of investments are inter-subjective in character, not only because they stem from communicative processes and legitimated calculative devices, but also because actual investment outcomes depend on the decisions of other market actors. This is particularly visible in financial markets, where the collective assessment of future value is at the heart of the market process. Moving asset prices in the direction of the future present currently being imagined requires shared belief in that imaginary. The confidence of powerful market actors in a future value of an asset matters far more than what is known as its intrinsic value. Once actors lose confidence in an asset's future, it loses its value. The same is true of investments in plant and equipment, which can only be profitable if consumers value the goods produced. The collective assessment of value and the stratified character of this assessment are the bedrock of a sociological theory of investment.

SEVEN

INNOVATION

Imaginaries of Technological Futures

For future events, the truth is undetermined.

—ARISTOTLE, cited by Guicciardini

INNOVATIONS are another cornerstone of capitalist dynamics. Capitalist growth is driven by the introduction of new products, more efficient production methods, and the expansion of the realm of market exchange. From the steam engine and the railroad to microelectronics and nanotechnology, technological progress propels capitalism, and vice versa: while technologies tended to remain constant for centuries in precapitalist social formations, they began changing rapidly with the advent of capitalism. Innovations satisfy previously unmet needs and create new ones, make the production process more efficient, and provide firms with opportunities for profit. The rate of innovation has an immense impact on the economic performance of firms, regions, and countries; were it to slow significantly, the economy would become stationary. As the Italian sociologist Carlo Trigilia notes, the "'high road' to development passes through innovation" (Trigilia 2006: 9).

While there is no doubt that the desire to earn profit propels innovations in capitalism, decisions made by entrepreneurs and firms cannot be explained in terms of optimization, since there is no way to determine what an optimal investment in innovation would be. Nor can innovations be understood as simple continuations of trajectories from the past, since innovation's "creative destruction" implies a departure from existing paths. Especially in the early phases of the innovation process, decisions about innovations are informed by actors' fictional expectations. Utopian visions of a pretended future reality—imagined futures—are an impetus for innovative activity. Because decisions about innovative activities are themselves

169

creating the future, competition in capitalist economies is in no small measure a struggle over imaginaries of future technologies.

INNOVATION AND UNCERTAINTY

For much of the twentieth century, economists had great difficulty conceptualizing technological change. This is surprising, given that in the eighteenth and nineteenth centuries, the connection between innovation and the market was broadly discussed by political economists: Adam Smith wrote about the increasing specialization of research as well as the connection between science and the progress of the machine-building industry, and examined the possible effects of what is now known as the learning curve. Karl Marx's economic theory described technological innovations as driving economic and social development. Even in the 1920s, certain economists remained interested in the role of innovation, generally as a means of explaining profit and economic growth (Kirzner 1985: 2ff.). Most important among them was Joseph Schumpeter (1934), who saw innovation as the seed of capitalism; in his theory of economic development, entrepreneurs are creative, innovative actors, the very linchpin of capitalist development.

Neoclassical economics, however, which formed the mainstream of twentieth-century economic theory, assumes technology to be constant, meaning it does not account for dynamic processes of change, a weakness Schumpeter (1934) criticized in his work. This shift toward a static model of technological development was one result of neoclassical economic theorists' attempts to give economic theory a mathematical foundation (Kirzner 1985; Nelson and Winter 1982: 195).

A systematic and detailed discussion of the many attempts made by economists since the 1930s to integrate technological progress into neoclassical economics does not fall within the scope of this book (see Beckert 2002: 52–65). Even a brief overview, however, reveals just how necessary it is to identify a different approach. One strand of this research, for example, focuses on shifts in the production function caused by technological change (Solow 1957), arguing that new technologies lead to changes in the allocation equilibrium, and thus to new prices. These changes are described as a process of adaptation from one equilibrium to another. In other words, this approach focuses on the effects of technological change on the production function, while failing to examine the endogenous causes of technological progress.

The idea of investment-induced progress was introduced into general equilibrium theory to explain the causes of technological progress. Later on, this idea led to the development of endogenous growth theory, which is based on the notion that an investment in new capital goods is always accompanied by technological progress or learning effects (Arrow 1985; Kaldor 1957). Kenneth Arrow's model of learning-by-doing employs this idea, starting from the assumption that new capital investments increase present production capacity while producing new technological knowledge, which together increase future productivity.

Models of investment-induced learning axiomatically assume a rate of technological progress without explaining how this progress comes about, despite the fact that, considered empirically, innovation processes are anything but routine, and rarely—if ever—have fully predictable outcomes. Models of induced innovation sidestep this unpredictability entirely (Freeman 1987: 859). Endogenous growth theory (Roemer 1990) focuses on innovation processes as central to growth, which it claims is achieved through an extension of the knowledge base of an economy as a side effect of activities in research and development. It sees knowledge as a collective good and as an external effect of research activities; it grows with use. But this raises the question of how to incorporate increasing returns into a theoretical model that assumes decreasing marginal productivity of production factors.

Another limiting condition for neoclassical theory applied to innovation processes relates to uncertainty. How is it possible to determine an optimal rate of investment in innovation under conditions of uncertainty? "What markets cannot do is to deliver information about or discount the possibility of future states-of-the-world whose occurrence is, to different degrees, the unintentional result of present decisions taken by heterogeneous agents characterized by different competences, beliefs, and expectations" (Dosi and Orsenigo 1988: 18).

The future value of an innovation can only be determined if it is known in advance what the innovation will be—a kind of knowledge no one possesses. The innovation process is unpredictable because it is nonlinear; no one knows its precise outcome when it begins. Even initial conditions are only partly known; the ends are not fully clear and the means are open (Eckersley 1988: 87). Innovation studies all demonstrate the "messiness" of innovation processes. A developer "does not keep means and ends separate, but defines them interactively as he frames the problematic situation" (Schön

1983: 68). Objects achieve their meaning through an interpretative process. As a result, initial expectations may be disappointed, although this does not necessarily imply that investment in the innovation process was useless. Indeed, many development processes lead to discoveries completely different from those intended by their planners. Particularly well-known examples of this include the inventions of the Viagra pill and Post-it notes. In the latter case, 3M's engineers did not at first realize they had innovated anything: they were aiming for a new glue recipe, and discovered the ultimate use of the substance they had made only by accident (Garud and Karnoe 2001). Pragmatically, a "problem to the solution" was found through a process of experimentation that led to the discovery of a use for 3M's new substance. The original goal led to an unintended invention; the innovation's "overflow" (Callon 1998a) was followed by a phase of experimentation. All this took place in a "community of practice," in which rationales for action were not based on abstract models but emerged as "situational rationality" (Ansell 2005: 14).

Outside the neoclassical mainstream, and following in the footsteps of Schumpeter, institutional and evolutionary approaches have acknowledged this unpredictability, using empirical investigations of technological change from a microperspective and examining their historical and sociological conditions (see Dosi and Orsenigo 1988).[1] These approaches abandon the central assumptions of neoclassical theory, such as the use of uniform technology, seamless and immediate adoption of new technologies, and the possibility of optimized decisions in uncertain situations, replacing them with empirical observations of innovation processes and the diffusion of new technologies. They use these observations to explain phenomena such as differing rates of profit, the perpetuation of inefficient technologies, and disequilibria.

Proceeding from the assumption that optimizing decisions about innovations is impossible because no outcomes can be determined ahead of time, institutionalists argue that actors rely on institutionalized rules of decision-making, world views, beliefs, and social practices to orient their decisions in the face of uncertainty. As a result, "technologies develop along relatively ordered paths shaped by the technical properties, the problem-solving heuristics and the cumulative expertise embodied in technological paradigms" (Dosi and Orsenigo 1988: 16). Paradigms lead to "lock-in" effects, which make adjustment to market changes more difficult. Institutionalists therefore see technological change as relatively independent of market signals; they link it much more strongly to endogenous historical factors. Furthermore, institutional and evolutionary approaches focus on structural indicators such as company size, scale, and capacity for innovation. Selection mechanisms for new technologies within technological paradigms thus operate through the "evolutionary hand" of the institutional and cognitive order in the economy more than they do through the "invisible hand" of the market.

From the perspective of this book, evolutionary and institutional approaches, though much closer to the approach pursued here, are also lacking; while they are right to let go of the assumptions of equilibrium and rationality used in neoclassical approaches to innovation, they focus too much on structural context and path dependencies in their assessment of technological development, neglecting the significance of contingent, creative action in innovation processes (Brown, Rappert, and Webster 2000: 5).[2]

FICTIONAL EXPECTATIONS IN INNOVATION

Certain economic approaches connect innovation rates to actors' expectations. Nathan Rosenberg (1976) observes that when entrepreneurs expect an existing technology to improve quickly, they are less likely to invest in it out of fear that it will become obsolete too soon. An excellent empirical example of this is the American solar industry during the 1980s. To reduce the production costs of solar cells, the industry needed to invest in large production facilities, something companies were hesitant to do because they expected rapid advances in basic research that would make the production facilities technologically obsolete before they could become profitable (Ergen 2015: 226ff.). In such cases, waiting may be the most sensible decision: the expectation of a "rapid rate of technological change may lead to a seemingly slow rate of adoption and diffusion" (Rosenberg 1976: 534). Rosenberg's model highlights the importance of expectations, but does not answer the question of how actors assess the future rate of technological change.

Decisions about innovation, like the other kinds of investment decisions, are motivated by imaginaries of the future. This is part of the creative aspect of innovative processes, as imaginaries allow actors to move beyond inherited thought patterns and categories and into an *as-if* world different from the present reality—a fiction, in other words (Bronk 2009: 201; Tappenbeck 1999: 53). These imaginaries take the form of predictions, forecasts, visions, and projections and are communicated as narratives: "Technolog-ical predictions and forecasts are in essence little narratives about the future. They are not full-scale narratives of utopia, but they are usually presented as stories about a better world to come. The most successful of these little narratives are those that present an innovation as not just desirable, but inevitable" (Nye 2004: 160).

Joseph Schumpeter (1934) saw the central role of imaginaries in innova-tion, which he claimed could not be rationally deduced from existing knowl-edge. Instead, contingent imaginaries of future states of the world motivate and guide actors to engage in inherently incalculable activities. While most actors are caught up in routines, some "with more acute intelligence and a more active imagination envisage countless new combinations" (Schumpeter [1912] 2006: 163).[3] These imaginaries lead the entrepreneur to "adapt his economic activities accordingly" (Schumpeter [1912] 2006: 165). Based on his imaginary of a new factor combination, an entrepreneur changes product demand. To return to the terms used in this book's earlier chapters, the en-trepreneur "pretends" that new combinations in the future actually exist, and structures her present behavior accordingly, *as if* the new combinations were the future present.

Schumpeter is not the only thinker to have connected innovation and imagination: many theorists working in the Keynesian and Austrian tradi-tions, as well as the Carnegie School, have given imaginaries a great deal of attention in their thinking about innovation. George Shackle (1979), for ex-ample, posits that the uncertainty of expectations gives actors the freedom to create hitherto unexplored visions of the future; to him, choices are made "amongst imagined experiences" (Shackle 1964: 12). According to James Buchanan and Victor Vanberg (1991), entrepreneurs do not choose among possibilities that already exist; rather, "the reality of the future must be made by choices yet to be made, and this reality has no existence independent of these choices" (386). Knowledge of the future can only be a matter of spec-ulation: it is not foreknowledge. Following this line of reasoning, lack of foreknowledge spurs innovation in a market economy; indeed, markets institutionalize the "creative-inventive-imaginative element in choice" (389). From an organizational perspective, James March claims that fictionality is a nonrational decision device that encourages actors to innovate: "Sooth-sayers create sheltered worlds of ignorance, ideology and faith. Within the shell that they provide, craziness is protected long enough to elaborate its challenge to orthodoxy" (1995: 437).

The concept of fictional expectations assigns action a much greater degree of freedom than does rational actor theory (Schütz 2003: 148–49). Imagination, because it makes possible "conceptual jumps which allow us to generate new hypotheses and see things differently" (Bronk 2009: 203), is a building block of economic transformations. Using imaginaries to creatively rethink the factors entering into a decision makes it possible to reorganize parameters in a "new narrative texture" (Patalano 2003: 4), which can be "subversive of established order" (Bronk 2009: 201). Images of the future may be wild speculations; conversely, they may pretend to be a determinate representation of a future state,[4] but they are not determined by the situation at hand and are therefore not predictable. To ignore the imaginaries of the actors engaging in innovative activity is to ignore an essential element of the dynamic character of the capitalist economy. And to understand that expectations of *future presents* are indeterminate is to understand that it is impossible "to predict the actual direction of future logics" (Sewell 2008: 523).

Fictional expectations associated with new technologies are not necessarily positive: in firms, they may take the form of perceived threats to existing business models or to competitive edge. At the social level, imaginaries of technological development may express fears of social and cultural decay or existential anxiety (Nye 2004: 171; Turkle 2004). When associated with future catastrophes, or with uncontrollable side effects, technological progress is seen as morally and politically objectionable[5] (van Lente 2000: 49). Positive and negative technological imaginaries often exist simultaneously, but the judgments they engender are always based on fictional expectations about an unknown future.

TECHNOLOGICAL VISIONS

In the field of innovation studies, expectations and their role in shaping scientific and technological developments have become a research field in their own right.[6] This is hardly surprising, given that innovative processes are oriented toward the future, and as such are necessarily based on expectations. Innovation studies do not, however, use the term "fictional expectations"; instead, researchers speak of visions, imaginaries, promises, regimes of hope, sociotechnical imaginaries, narrative infrastructures, beliefs, or future-oriented abstractions. These terms, despite their different nuances, all express the idea that technological innovations "preexist" only in actors' imaginations, and that actors must act *as if* their projections were the future present. Harro van Lente and Arie Rip use the term "prospective structures" to describe "expectations about possible [technological] developments, especially as these are put forward and taken up in statements, brief stories or scenarios" (1998: 205). These prospective stories are a "forceful fiction" that has the power to open up space for action. "Expectations, and stories about the future in general, reduce essential contingency in a non-deterministic sense, by providing blueprints that can be used in action" (217).

Narratives about technological futures are thus also make-believe games in Kendall Walton's (1990) sense of that term. Beyond their technological implications, sociotechnical imaginaries describe imagined forms of social life and social order associated with the development of novel technological projects. Such imaginaries also play an important part in political decisions on innovation policies: they "at once describe attainable futures and prescribe futures that states believe ought to be attained. . . . Such visions, and the policies built upon them, have the power to influence technological design, channel public expenditures, and justify the inclusion or exclusion of citizens with respect to the benefits of technological progress" (Jasanoff and Kim 2009: 121).[7]

Empirical studies of innovation processes show how expectations about future technologies influence outcomes. Particularly in the early stages of a technology's development, fictional expectations reduce uncertainty by orienting decisions and channeling resources to projects (Borup et al. 2006: 289; Deuten and Rip 2000). Different actor groups align their actions based on overlapping expectations, which allow them to bridge boundaries among otherwise separate individuals and organizations, thereby increasing coordination. Resources are reallocated, new institutions founded, and new networks built (Borup et al. 2006: 286), all based on promissory stories.

Promissory stories may be described as narratives that assign roles to actors and objects and develop a plot around the anticipated innovation (Deuten and Rip 2000). By containing a script for the future, promissory stories "position the relevant actors, explicitly or implicitly, exactly as characters in a story are positioned" (van Lente and Rip 1998: 218). The stories create shared worldviews among industry actors, compelling them to follow the path envisioned in a certain imaginary (Ansari and Garud 2009: 389). Actors' activities become intertwined based on what they expect one another to do in the future according to the script. Expectations that a given technology will bring future profits and open up research horizons cause interests to emerge and resources to be mobilized, leading to investments, research, and training (Pieri 2009: 1105). Promissory stories evolve continually as new actors appear, new information becomes available, and new interpretations unfold, leading to a "multi-authored and always heterogeneous mosaic of stories" (Deuten and Rip 2000: 68).

Since promissory stories influence the allocation of resources by altering expectations and changing the behaviors of firms, research institutions, and government agencies, they cannot be understood as mere representations of a future path. The extent to which anticipated futures occur as predicted must also be attributed to the imaginaries themselves. Fictional expectations "generate and perform distinctive distributions of value, power and agency" (Moreira and Palladino 2005: 67). They set agendas, create relationships, define roles, and influence the allocation of resources. Through the creation of convictions, they shape a protected space, securing resources for actors to engage in activities intended to bring about what a story has anticipated. Whether imaginary and outcome actually correspond must be answered empirically. By the same token, expectations collapse if promissory stories cease to be convincing. Before it proves itself through success, a project's strength lies only in its promises, and may tumble like a house of cards (Deuten and Rip 2000: 69).[8]

The development of sociotechnical imaginaries can be described in a dynamic model. Technological expectations go through a "hype cycle" (Figure 7.1), in which enthusiasm about a new technological vision waxes and then wanes over time (Fenn and Raskino 2008). Technological developments are born from utopias and high hopes, which then give way to more realistic assessments, which ultimately lead to the initial utopian vision being replaced by another one. Deutschmann (1999: 145ff; 2009) has aptly described this dynamic movement as a "spiral of myths." The early phase of invention is particularly prone to imaginaries, since "coincidences, playful dispositions, and fantasies are much more important for the generation of the decisive idea than rational or even 'economic' motifs" (Deutschmann 2009: 147, own translation).

According to van Lente and Rip (1998: 222) expectations in innovation processes evolve in a three-step process: at the beginning, the voicing of promises shows the way to collective projections of the future, helping actors form a shared mind-set. This observation aligns with the pragmatist understanding of deliberation and the intermingling of means and ends in the tradition of John Dewey, who defines ends not as fixed ideals outside the

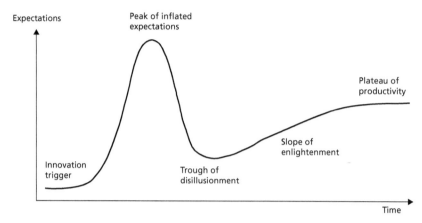

FIGURE 7.1. The "hype cycle" in technological innovations. *Source*: Reproduced from Fenn and Raskino 2008.

realm of activity, but as "foreseen consequences which influence present deliberation" (Dewey [1922] 1957: 223). During the action process, existing views "are enhanced, recombined, modified in imagination. Invention operates" (225). Dewey describes this process in terms of impulses: "The elaborate systems of science are born not of reason but of impulses at first slight and flickering; impulses to handle, move about, to hunt, to uncover, to mix things separated and divide things combined, to talk and to listen" (196).

In a next step, these promises form, as van Lente and Rip put it, an agenda, which is subsequently interpreted by agents as a requirement. Agenda-setting and the definition of requirements protect new ideas from disbelief, allowing them to be cultivated and pursued. "Once technological promises are shared, they demand action and it appears necessary for technologists to develop them, and for others to support them" (van Lente and Rip 1998: 216). In other words, the evocations produced by imagined technological futures make it possible for new technologies to become real. Technological visions define new technologies and are causally influencing their construction (Sturken and Thomas 2004: 7).

Early hopes, however, rarely reflect actual outcomes. Because disappointments are "accompanied by serious costs in terms of reputations, misallocated resources and investment" (Borup et al. 2006: 290), the hype generated by early hopes may be perceived later on by actors in the field as a waste of time and resources; it may also, however, be interpreted as a necessary condition to protect ideas that do not yet have any hard evidence to support them. Imaginations "are justified by their potential not for predicting the future ... but for nurturing the uncritical commitment and preserving madness required for sustained organizational and individual rigidity in a selective environment" (March 1995: 437). In capitalism, actors typically do not look backward to disappointed utopias; they direct their gaze forward, to new possibilities they hope to realize through new innovation.[9] New imaginaries must develop independently of earlier failures and motivate the channeling of resources into new projects, thus propelling the dynamism of capitalism.

Making fictional expectations credible and obtaining support sufficient to even begin the task of attempting to transform them into concrete reality is a formidable challenge: firms and policy-makers "are confronted, even bombarded, with technological promises (and their attended risks) creating new decision-making demands based on the interpretation and analysis of the expectations environment. Just as often, such actors are confronted with disappointing outcomes and with promises that do not seem to hold" (Borup et al. 2006: 287).

Empirical findings from case studies show that confidence in technological visions is much more likely when there is a certain "detachment or distance from the acute uncertainties more usually experienced by researchers at the 'coalface'" of research (Borup et al. 2006: 292). Because ignorance of the difficulties presented by the innovation process increases the likelihood that a promissory story will be seen as credible, a researcher may express different degrees of confidence in interactions with peers in the research lab than when presenting an idea to politicians or investors.

THE SOCIAL AND HISTORICAL ROOTS OF TECHNOLOGICAL IMAGINARIES

Schumpeter has been criticized, and rightly so, for providing an overly individualistic account of the motivations behind entrepreneurs' engagement in innovative activities: their expectations are also socially and historically motivated. As studies of innovation processes show, technological promises are often collective projections, even though the utopias associated with new technologies may ignore these cultural and social roots and portray these technologies as possessing a force seemingly outside of social and political influences (Sturken and Thomas 2004: 4; van Lente and Rip 1998: 222).

Scholars in the field of innovation studies have shown the social and cultural anchoring of expectations by demonstrating the historical roots of promissory stories (Lyman 2004). Futures have a history: technological imaginations are socially influenced by the cultural norms of the social contexts in which they arise as well as by "promissory pasts,"[10] the term frequently used to describe past futures. These imaginaries, sometimes long forgotten, guided decisions in the past and shaped the path to the futures imagined today. A study investigating the trajectory of different promissory stories in the history of stem cell research is an excellent example of this: Brown, Kraft, and Martin (2006) show that current expectations associated with human stem cells emerged in a field structured by earlier expectations and their disappointments, reaching back to the 1950s. Each new promissory story makes reference to the preceding one and builds its own credibility by distancing itself from the disappointed hopes of the past.

Scholars of innovation processes also observe what has been called "cognitive path dependence." References to the past shape perceptions of and serve to legitimate plans for the future, which endorses institutional and evolutionary approaches to innovation that stress path dependencies (Nelson and Winter 1982). Portraying new fictional expectations regarding future technological developments as part of a longer historical trajectory of technological progress helps to justify them. As an example of this rhetorical strategy, van Lente cites a report arguing for investments in the development of high-definition television (HDTV) in the United States in the 1990s. HDTV was developed to introduce substantially higher screen resolution for televisions and was thought to be a technological revolution. It was promoted with imaginaries of a technological trajectory that reached from the nineteenth century into the future. A report stated, "As early as 1883 inventors dreamed of transmitting visual images. By the 1920s, significant efforts were under way to scan and project images. . . . TV was still futuristic at the time of the New York World's Fair in 1939 but finally erupted into widespread commercial use in the 1950s. . . . Television technology is now on the threshold of a new evolution. We are on the verge of combining digital based computer technology with television. The impacts of the development of HDTV will ripple through the US economy" (Office of Technology Assessment 1990, p. iii, quoted in van Lente 2000: 47). The innovation is presented as the historical trajectory's logical "next step." Justifications for technological investments that use the "next generation" metaphor legitimate activities by making them appear to be part of a logical succession of events. Departing from the trajectory would "kill" the "next generation."

Expectations associated with new technologies also refer to history by drawing analogies to earlier technological developments in the same field (Briggs 2004). In Western societies, one such recurring utopian comparison is with transportation: in the nineteenth century, the railroad was the source of important narratives of cultural and social transformation (Sturken and Thomas 2004: 7). When airplanes were invented in the early twentieth century, railways were replaced by the "aerial man," which in turn was succeeded by visions of individual mobility through the automobile. In the 1990s this was supplanted by the idea of the "information superhighway." Metaphors of transportation are remarkable for their religious connotations; they "imply that new modes of transportation will provide transcendence and that they will lift people out of their worlds and their selves, and take them to new spiritual heights—they are inevitably religious in their implications. The transportation metaphor is finally about the idea that we have a destination, that we are going somewhere, that movement has meaning—that, indeed, is its attraction" (Sturken and Thomas 2004: 8).

Reference to history and culture can also take the form of analogies to technological success in other fields, which is seen as proof that developments believed to be impossible can actually be realized. One example of this is the expectations regarding the commercial use of solar energy at the turn of the twentieth century. In 1907 the solar energy entrepreneur Frank Shuman attempted to draw investors with the promise of how sound their investments would be by making an analogy with the invention of airplanes: "You will at once admit that any businessman approached several years ago with a view of purchasing stock in a flying machine company would have feared the sanity of the proposer. After it has been shown conclusively that it can be done, there is now no difficulty in securing all the money which is wanted, and very rapid progress in aviation is from now on assured. We will have to go through this same course" (Schuman, cited in Ergen 2015: 47). As Richard Bronk (2009: 246) has emphasized, new ideas must make connections to the socially given world. To be enacted they must suit their cognitive and social environment; otherwise they will just remain ineffective dreams.

Opponents to a specific technological development may also support their arguments with references to the past. In a study on neurotransplants—a medical procedure in which patients diagnosed with Parkinson's disease had fetal cells transplanted into their brains—Moreira and Palladino (2005: 65) found that opponents to this medical procedure sought to delegitimize research by comparing it to neurosurgical interventions from the mid-twentieth century such as lobotomies and lobectomies, which have been widely discredited because they alter patients' personal identities. In this case too, the images associated with a future technological development are informed by historical, political, and cultural contexts.

Imaginaries associated with innovations are also part of a national "cultural repertoire" (Lamont and Thévenot 2000), as has been shown through comparative studies of national differences in how technological progress is valued, both in general and with regard to specific technologies. There are "distinctive national visions of desirable futures driven by science and technology against fears of either not realizing those futures or causing unintended harm in the pursuit of technological advances" (Jasanoff and Kim 2009: 121). In Germany, nuclear energy is associated with the bleak outlook of catastrophe, while in France it is widely perceived as efficiently securing the energy needs of an industrial society. At the same time, French political culture has portrayed genetically modified food as an uncontrollable threat, while in the United States it has been broadly accepted as a technological development based on the notion that no threat to health has been proven scientifically.

Fictional expectations about technological innovations are also anchored in the protected niche modern societies have carved out for "technologists," who are mandated to be the legitimate overseers of technological progress and are counted as experts within a "mandated territory." Experts "are the ones who are allowed to speak first, they can in the first instance determine what is to happen. That they are allowed to have this space can be legitimated by a claim referring to the ideograph of technological progress" (van Lente 2000: 53). The authority attributed to experts helps to shield their promissory stories from the lay public. This indicates the institutionalization of innovation processes as a precondition for leaving the past through innovations. Innovations are also social products, and not the outcome of lone individuals. They are organized through research universities, research and development departments in firms, funding agencies, and state-run structures such as the Food and Drug Administration or the Pentagon (see Bronk 2009: 246).

Perceived "imbalances" in the application of existing technologies to different products also lend credibility to promissory stories. For example, after the successful market introduction of the compact disc, audio engineers set out to develop a television with the same sound quality as a CD. The recognition of a possible development goal was not stimulated by consumer complaints about poor sound quality in televisions but rather by another technological development. Research activities, in other words, are defined "in terms of what is missing compared with what is projected as technologically feasible" (van Lente and Rip 1998: 214). Consumption studies have identified a similar phenomenon called the "Diderot effect," which states that purchases give rise to new desires because objects already possessed lose their value when compared with new acquisitions. (See Chapter 8.)

In addition, the imaginaries that motivate actors to pursue innovations have social-structural preconditions: "capitalist entrepreneurs do not fall from heaven but can grow only in a particular structural, institutional, and cultural environment" (Deutschmann 2011: 4). Robert Merton (1957) suggests that innovative activities are anchored in the normative structures of modern societies that value inner-worldly transcendence through success-seeking by risk-taking. These imaginaries are also affected by demography: young people are more likely to take risks, which implies that societies lose a portion of their innovative capabilities as their members age. Entrepreneurial motivations can only emerge if merit-based social inequality is legitimated and social classes are not polarized in a way that makes upward mobility practically impossible: in such societies, individual expectations of upward mobility cannot prevail. Although there are very real barriers to social mobility in capitalist society, and despite the fact that throughout its history, large social groups have been excluded from exercising entrepreneurial activities, capitalism is nevertheless historically unique as an economic formation in which social status is legitimated not by social origin but based on market success ascribed to effort. The enlarged possibilities for social mobility that emerged with capitalism make actors more likely to project futures for themselves in which they fulfill their dreams.

A critical number of individual actors and firms must believe that engaging in innovative activities fosters new opportunities for technological imaginaries to move beyond the realm of fantasy and be made into effective forces for economic development. Creating these beliefs, at least among a certain proportion of relevant actors, is necessary if innovations and the dynamics created by them are to be maintained. Failure to do so would deprive capitalism of one of its main sources of growth. Institutions, networks, and cultural factors play a crucial role in orienting actors toward a distant and abstract future: a society's education system must allow for upward mobility; family and community networks must encourage, or at least tolerate, individual success-seeking (Portes and Sensenbrenner 1993; Trigilia 2006); cultural or religious traditions must support entrepreneurial orientations (see Deutschmann 2011: 4–5). Beyond these structural conditions, the market and the credit system push entrepreneurs and firms to seek opportunities that open up through innovation.

THE POLITICS OF EXPECTATIONS

If resources for innovation are allocated based on promissory stories whose future success is uncertain, then actors will inevitably contest not just the distribution of these resources, but also the imaginaries surrounding innovations. Competition for resources for innovation is to a great extent a power struggle over the credibility of imaginary futures. Reinhart Koselleck, in his discussion of the development of techniques for political prognoses in early modernity, describes how imaginaries of future developments are instrumentalized politically: prognoses are "part of the political situation, so much so that making a prognosis already means changing the situation. The prognosis is a conscious element of political action" (Koselleck 1979: 29, own translation).[11]

Sophie Mützel (2010) offers an insightful empirical example in her study of innovation processes in a cluster of biotechnology firms seeking to develop a genetically engineered medication for treating breast cancer. In this highly uncertain environment, the success of firms' research strategies cannot be foreseen, and hopes for successful product development are often disappointed. Mützel observed how actors try to influence others' expectations—and the decisions to which they lead—by communicating accounts of the innovative strategy they expect will lead to successful product development. These imaginaries of a future present send signals to competitors and the financial community. As decisions hinge on expectations, actors attempt to manipulate them as they vie for resources and seek to influence the research strategies pursued in the field. This power struggle shapes present decisions and affects the field's future development.

Studies on innovation that examine the role of fictional expectations often recognize the political dimension of imaginaries. Brown, Rappert, and Webster (2000) speak of "contested futures," arguing that the future "is constituted through an unstable field of language, practice and materiality in which various disciplines, capacities and actors compete for the right to represent near and far term developments" (5). Struggles over how the future present should be conceived have real consequences because dominant discourses affect the distribution of resources and can thus prevent or marginalize alternative futures. The power of the actors advocating a given imaginary has an impact on whether or not it becomes relevant. Steve Jobs is perhaps the best such example of the link between entrepreneurial success and the communication of imaginaries. Apple captivated the computer industry and large consumer groups; it shaped technological futures partly because of its strategic positioning in the market, but also thanks to the charismatic appeal of its CEO.

When "spin" is given to certain imaginaries, they become political as the complex effects of technology are transformed into simple narratives in order to provide legitimating support or delegitimizing criticism to technological developments (Turkle 2004: 19). "Expectation work" (van Lente and Rip 1998: 222) is always a struggle between the advocates of existing expectational structures and those contesting it, where opportunities to proliferate expectations reflect inequities of power and authority.

The connection between the politics of imaginaries and material or ideal interests can also be deduced indirectly by observing how actors are associated with stories. In their work on biomedical research, Moreira and Palladino (2005: 68) found that different narratives regarding a new technology—to which they refer as a regime of hope and a regime of truth—are associated with different actor groups, which align according to the gains and losses the envisioned future present is expected to bring about. Unsurprisingly, actors seek to dispel any impression that the expectations they hold are tied to their (material) interests. Portraying technologies as "a force seemingly outside of social and political influences" (Sturken and Thomas 2004: 4) may be interpreted as a strategy to counter skepticism employed in cases where choices about technology are suspected to be politically motivated. Just as Mary Douglas (1986) saw the stability of institutions as based in their naturalization, the proclaimed ahistoricity of technologies creates an aura of unavoidability and can be used to shield a technological vision from critical scrutiny.

CONCLUSION

Actors innovate under conditions of uncertainty. Before an innovation takes place and a product is successfully introduced to the market, it is impossible to say whether it will be profitable to invest resources to pursue it. Investments in innovation cannot therefore be based on reliable calculations of the future present. While levels of uncertainty differ among innovations, growth dynamics and high profits tend to come from the most radical ones, which are generally also the ones with the highest levels of uncertainty (Shapin 2008; Verganti 2009: 3). Particularly in the early phases of the innovation process, actors resort to fictional expectations—that is, imaginaries of the future state of the world—to decide which strategies to pursue and to obtain resources. From the investor's perspective, the value of investing in an innovative activity depends entirely on the perceived credibility of the envisioned future present.

Imaginaries of the future state of the world coordinate activities, thereby helping to create structures that are made possible by the very fictional expectations that anticipate them. By behaving *as if* their projections would come into existence in the future, actors are provoked into making decisions that move reality toward the future situation they envision. This practical role of imaginaries offers interesting insights into the relationship between structure and agency, showing, at least in part, that structures are built with actors' expectations and would vanish without them. As Charles Sabel and Jonathan Zeitlin write:

> Actors' choices depend on their articulation of stories about possible developments and these stories may contain models of those various possibilities and assessment of their probability. In that case, there is no clear distinction between choosing a strategy and thinking about the actors' strategic choices. Where many outcomes are possible, it may simply be impossible to deduce the actors' motives from the outcome, for among those motives there were intentions to construct worlds which did not succeed. If you believe that the failed intentions had to fail because they did not capture some essential feature of the local or global logic in progress, then it is natural to consider these strivings as confusions without consequences except insofar as their origins pique sociological curiosity. But if you believe . . . that such logics are only loosely defined at any given moment and are constantly being redefined by the intended and unintended consequences of pursuing them, then analysis of the actors' intentions provides an indispensable independent source of information about the range and robustness of the constraints that they faced and created. (Sabel and Zeitlin 1997: 15)

The observation that structures are represented in agency should not lead to the assumption of one-sided voluntarism. As this chapter shows, the

promissory stories associated with technological development are themselves anchored in economic power structures and cultural repertoires
prevalent among "technologists" or in political cultures. Moreover, the motivation to engage in the "creative destruction" characteristic of innovation
has cultural and social preconditions. Once again, history matters. Given,
the extent, however, of how expectations are integral to decision-making, it is
clear that these structures only become relevant through interpretation, and
that interpretation is necessarily contingent. In innovation processes, interpretation takes place through imaginaries of novel future technologies.
The term "prospective structure" tidily expresses this synthesis of structure
and agency in its future-oriented time dimension.

Finally, promissory stories regarding technological developments influence more than the economy: they are just as important at the societal
level. Utopian visions of collectively desired lifestyles are projected onto new
technologies. In the early 1990s, for example, the Internet was used to express many utopian visions of societal progress: "The Internet, prognosti-
cators stated, would solve the long-standing problems of education, make
bureaucracies function better, create the global community through increased connectivity, empower the disenfranchised, and forever alter the
roles of consumer and producer" (Sturken and Thomas 2004: 3).

All of these were fictional expectations. Some of them are more easily
recognized as such today than others, but when they were first articulated,
they all motivated actors, coordinated their activities, and mobilized resources. As Ann Mische (2009: 694) observes, "hope is both constituted
and constitutive; it provides the emotional substratum, so to speak, of the
dialectic between the old and the new, between the reproduction and the
transformation of social structures as these figure in thinking and acting
individuals."

EIGHT

CONSUMPTION

Value from Meaning

Consumption is the sole end and purpose of all production.

—ADAM SMITH, *The Wealth of Nations*

ECONOMIC THEORIES differ widely in their assessment of the importance of the demand side of the economy. Neoclassical theory follows Say's theorem that aggregate production creates an equal quantity of aggregate demand. Keynes, on the other hand, saw the demand side as the Achilles heel of the capitalist economy. Indeed, demand is precarious and cannot be taken for granted. However, while Keynes believed that the pessimistic sentiments of investors and insufficient purchasing power of consumers were the main causes of low demand, consumer motivation must also be taken into account. What attracts consumers to products and why, even in affluent consumer societies, does demand continue to exist for a seemingly endless proliferation of new products? Fictional expectations are crucial to understanding the expansion and dynamics of consumer demand.

For most people in modern consumer societies, the desire to consume appears quite natural, and warrants no further inquiry. A closer look, however, reveals that demand for products is far from spontaneous. For most of history, societies maintained levels of wealth defined by custom rather than by the striving to maximize consumption levels as they now do (Sahlins 1972). Such a traditional way of life still dominated societies at the time of the industrial revolution. As Chapter 2 mentions, when industrialization first encountered traditional social lifestyle, entrepreneurs were recurrently confronted with workers who would end their workday when they had earned whatever they defined as sufficient (Thompson 1967). They would rather save surpluses than spend them. Some entrepreneurs would even sell their firms once they had made enough profit to live on. The possibility of earning additional resources to consume beyond these perceived needs was not attractive enough to motivate further work.

Unsurprisingly, given the poor standard of living at the time, once these traditional attitudes loosened, the desire to acquire additional consumer goods followed. At this point, at least for the lower classes, consumption served mainly to fulfill very basic needs. A first movement toward the expansion of consumption with a focus on cultural and social needs can be found among the European nobility in the sixteenth century. Only in the eighteenth century, though, did modern consumption, centered on the cultural and social meaning of goods, begin to develop more broadly. Actual consumer societies developed only in the first decades of the twentieth century, with the United States leading the way (C. Campbell 1987; McCracken 1988). Consumption became a pillar of modern life and was fundamental in expanding capitalist growth. Detraditionalization, the development of bourgeois consumer ethics, expanding purchasing power, and the activities of an ever-more refined advertising industry were all factors that made this expansion of consumerism possible.

Capitalism depends on the expansion of consumption to create the aggregate demand that allows for the selling of expanding supply (Bell [1976] 1978; Galbraith [1958] 1998). For this it needs willing and confident consumers. The rise of living standards during the twentieth century has meant that more and more people in affluent countries are able to satisfy their fundamental needs. One hundred years ago, the average household in an OECD country spent 80 percent of its income on food, clothing, and housing. This figure has dropped to 30 to 40 percent today (Adolf and Stehr 2010: 3). From this perspective the question of why affluent people continue to purchase more goods instead of saving their money or simply working less is an intriguing one. Sociologists of consumption emphasize that "consumers do not automatically use surplus income to satisfy new wants" (C. Campbell 1987: 18). Market saturation and decline of demand are constant threats to markets (Fligstein 2001: 17).

Why is there scarcity in the midst of abundance? The answer to this lies in understanding what attracts customers to the goods they purchase.[1] George Shackle defines a commodity as an object that "promises performance" (Shackle 1972). To be willing to "sacrifice" money to purchase a consumer good, a buyer must have a positive view of that performance and the "difference" it will make to his or her life. Consumption is thus always associated with imaginaries of the future. Departing from the view that recognizing these promises and desiring such future performances is "natural" or spontaneous, it is clear that the expansiveness of capitalism does not depend on the supply side and available purchasing power alone: the creation of positive expectations in consumers regarding the performance of the goods to be purchased is just as crucial. What are the performance promises that engender expectations strong enough to motivate actors to make the sacrifices necessary to purchase ever more products?

Buyers' attractions to goods brings us back to the question of valuation.[2] This is a valid connection since the promise a product makes in the eye of the consumer is nothing but the outcome of an evaluation of it. Many studies of valuation in economic sociology focus, however, primarily on issues of the classification of goods, leaving unattended the question of why actors feel attracted to goods in the first place as well as any serious discussion of the macroeconomic significance of consumption in the operation of capitalism (Streeck 2012: 11). Examining the role of fictional expectations in motivating consumption and their significance to capitalist dynamics can close these gaps.

Fictional expectations about consumer goods revolve around the images evoked by these goods and the desires prompted by imagining their possession. These imaginaries in turn revolve around the meaning a buyer ascribes to a given product: consumer markets, in other words, are markets for meaning.

Fictional expectations play two roles in the purchasing of consumer goods. The first parallels their roles in investments and innovation, as already discussed in earlier chapters. Imaginaries associated with consumer goods are placeholders that help actors deal with uncertainty. Consumers considering new consumer goods have no clear idea of the satisfaction they will obtain from these products. From a rationalistic perspective, it is therefore difficult to explain how demand for novel products develops. Given the uncertainty associated with new products, a "rational" consumer "would simply not strive to obtain new products or services as this would . . . be more in the nature of an adventure or a gamble than 'calculation'" (C. Campbell 1987: 41).

Imaginaries can close this gap. Imaginaries associated with a good before it is purchased inspire consumers to project a desirable life situation that its acquisition will help them to achieve. Imagined new experiences can be an intrinsic motivation for consumers' experimentations with novelty (Andreozzi and Bianchi 2007). In their imaginations, consumers act *as if* they already possess the product whose purchase they are considering and thus "test" whether the product would bring the desired satisfaction. To refer once more to Alfred Schütz's (1962: 20) theory of action, the possession of goods can be imagined in the future perfect tense. The evocation of future satisfaction itself creates desire. Following John Dewey ([1922] 1957), "anticipatory consumption" forms an obstacle, in that the goods are desired as an end in view but not yet owned, which itself reinforces the desire to purchase, thus motivating demand. The same idea was also expressed by Georg Simmel, who postulated that the "possibility of enjoyment must be separated, as an image of the future, from our present condition in order for us to desire things that now stand at a distance from us" ([1907] 1978: 71). By creating desires in the present, imagined future satisfaction drives consumer demand.

The second role fictional expectations play in consumption is not related to the future per se, but rather to the symbolic representation of transcending qualities in consumer goods. Goods can be desired for the symbolic meanings they carry that have nothing to do with their material qualities.[3] Desire for the symbolic qualities of goods does not depend on an individual's physical needs, implying that in principle, there is no limit to the expansion of demand based on symbolic value. Goods desired for their symbolic value therefore entail a much greater potential for growth than goods that are desired for their physical performance alone (Hutter 2011; Reisch 2002: 227).[4] It is not by chance that the economies of affluent societies are increasingly built around expectations about the symbolic performance of goods. If aggregate demand depends on consumers' desires for symbolic value, the production of consumer dreams is itself a productive force in the economy. As the increasing growth of marketing costs as a percentage of overall production costs shows, more and more extensive efforts must be made to create the socially enshrined symbolic meanings that make goods valuable (Hirschle 2012: 138). Without giving attention to the fictional expectations associated with symbolic value, it is impossible to understand the markets for most of the products that create growth in modern economies: not only cars, tourism, mobile telephones, computers, fashion items, and real estate, but also antiques, wine, lotteries, and fair-trade products, to give just a few examples.

From this perspective, the precariousness of current-day capitalist growth is also clear. The fictional expectations associated with consumer goods are particularly unstable, even evanescent, since they are largely anchored in the inter-subjective recognition of symbolic qualities attached to them, not in the material qualities of the goods themselves. The success of products "goes together with quick failure, as when the space for dreams associated with a particular brand no longer resonates with the symbolic needs of a large enough group of customers" (Djelic and Ainamo 1999: 628). Declining growth rates in affluent consumer societies over the past forty years may also indicate that new products being introduced to the market are less effective at inspiring consumers' imaginaries, and that established products such as cars are losing their imaginary attraction.

The work of Emile Durkheim, who has dealt with symbolic value in the economy in several of his works (Durkheim [1893] 1984, [1911] 1974, [1957] 1992), can shed light on the role of imagined futures in consumption. Although Durkheim's sociology of religion does not deal explicitly with the valuation of economic goods (Durkheim [1912] 1965), it offers a particularly informative perspective for understanding the role of fictional expectations in decisions about consumption.[5] Indeed, *The Elementary Forms of the Religious Life* can be read not only as a sociology of religion, but as a sociology of valuation, in which fictional expectations are paramount. Durkheim's analysis of totemistic religions is the ideal tool for exploring how the value of consumer goods is created and maintained. Kendall Walton's (1990) theory of make-believe games, introduced in Chapter 4, is also useful in this regard. Together these theoretical foundations support the idea that the symbolic value of consumer goods depends on an implicit agreement among consumers regarding the meaning of a brand or product, which is a form of make-believe.

The symbolic connections between goods and the social position of their owners are a key source of demand, as are socially rooted values and aesthetic ideals. If the economic value of goods is closely linked to social values, then the desire for goods cannot be understood as the mere expression of hedonistic individualism (see Bell [1976] 1978). The fictional expectations associated with consumer goods connect them to the social and moral order of society (Fischer 2014; Fischer and Benson 2006; Richins 1994; Stehr, Henning, and Weiler 2006), which is expressed, reinforced, and challenged through the meaning of goods.

Expectations related to consumer goods are subject to the politics of expectations. To attract consumers, firms use marketing to tell stories that link their products to specific meanings. The struggle over the meaning of consumer goods is therefore a crucial aspect of the competitive struggle among firms; the final part of this chapter discusses the mechanisms that demolish the fictional expectations associated with specific consumer goods. While the demolishing of the value of sacred objects is not a frequent phenomenon in religions, it is vital to understanding the dynamics of capitalism. Cognitive space can be opened up to foster desires for new products especially if products already possessed lose their attraction over time.

THE FICTIONALITY OF THE VALUE OF CONSUMER GOODS

One crucial consideration in a consumer's motivation to purchase a good is the functionality of the product. Goods can alter physical states of their owners in many ways: a shirt covers the body and keeps it warm; a car brings its owner from point A to point B; a house provides shelter from the weather. Considerations of this kind can be expanded to take into account differences in quality within a given product category, in order to distinguish among goods of the same type. One shirt can be warmer or more durable than another; one car can be faster, safer, or more comfortable than another; and so on.

This physical performance of a good is objective in the sense that it is a quality of the object itself.[6] The valuation of its physical qualities, on the other hand, depends on its user's cognitive understanding of the good (C. Menger [1883] 1963; Witt 2001: 27). Since a potential purchaser values a good based on her knowledge of it, valuations differ depending on which of its physical qualities a potential user recognizes. There is no value without knowledge, and value differs among actors with different knowledge—a point famously analyzed by George Akerlof (1970) for the case of used cars.[7]

When it comes to understanding fictional expectations in consumer demand, the physical performance of goods is secondary to two other types of value. A product's positional value expresses its capacity to position its owner within a differentiated social world. Products that co-occur among certain types of people and social occasions make it possible to infer the social status of their owners (Ravasi, Rindova, and Stigliani 2011). Demand for this positional value is explained by desire for status. Preferences for these goods are not exogenous; rather, they emerge endogenously, as actors observe the behavior of other market actors. In other words, "scarcity is fundamentally a social relationship" (Orléan 2014: 96).

Judging the positional performance of goods requires agreement about their meaning among the group in which the judgment takes place (Miller

1998; Reisch 2002: 232; Witt 2001). In this sense, it is a make-believe game in which many actors agree that a specific good signifies a specific social position and identity—that possession of a given commodity stands for being rich, fashionable, sophisticated, competent, and so on. Although some variation may exist in the way an object is interpreted, a complete lack of agreement among the members of the social group would make it impossible for the object to be used as a signifier of social status and social belonging. Positional value does have an objective basis, but this objectivity is not anchored in a product's material qualities. Instead, it depends upon what meaning is ascribed to the product in the actor's social environment. This should not, however, be understood as a form of contractual agreement: it is the outcome of an ongoing and power-laden communicative process by which objects are classified and defined (Bourdieu 1984).

The positional value of goods has been meticulously described in sociological and anthropological accounts, notably by Thorstein Veblen ([1899] 1973), Georg Simmel ([1904] 1971), and Pierre Bourdieu (1984). The early sociology of consumption emphasized the hierarchical stratification that occurs through the possession and exhibition of luxury goods, the social dynamics that develop out of attempts by lower social classes to imitate the consumption patterns of the upper classes, and the reactions to these imitations by the upper classes. More recent accounts of the social performance of goods place focus less on the element of status and class differentiation and more on the multilateral constitution of heterogeneous lifestyles through different patterns of consumption (Arnould and Thompson 2005). Differentiated lifestyles are expressed in specific consumption patterns, and constitute and convey various aspects of actors' social identities. Consumers construct a wide range of identity narratives associated with certain kinds of products offered in the market, a process that may be seen as the democratization of symbolic value creation (Djelic and Ainamo 2005: 48).

Like its positional performance, a good's imaginative performance is based in its symbolic qualities.[8] In both cases, the good is valued based on qualities that transcend material reality. In this sense they are fictional: "People buy things not only for what they can do, but also for what they mean" (Levy 1959: 118). Imaginative performance refers to the images commodities evoke.[9] These may be based on symbolic associations with desired events, people, places, or values (d'Astous and Deschênes 2005; C. Campbell 1987; Holbrook and Hirschman 1982; McCracken 1988: 104ff; Ullrich 2006: 45ff.) and thus express desired futures that become "attainable" through the purchase of a specific product. In this way, a good functions as a link between a subject and her desired but intangible ideals. Imaginative performance does not need recognition by anyone but the imaginer to exist. It relies only on the cognitive and emotional assessments of the purchaser, who seeks a "connection" to the spaces, times, people, or ideals the object she is purchasing embodies in her eyes.[10] Figure 8.1 depicts the differences between the types of value explained above.

An unlimited number of instances may be identified in which demand for consumer goods is constituted through the symbolic associations and images their symbolic connotations evoke. The imaginary power of consumer goods occurs in several dimensions: it occurs through time, by associating their owners with a desired future state or a distant past; through *space*, by connecting their owners to desired but distant or unreachable places; socially, by linking their owners to out-of-reach people; and through values, by linking their owners to values they espouse. All four dimensions transcend the "here and now," allowing a good's owner to mentally associate

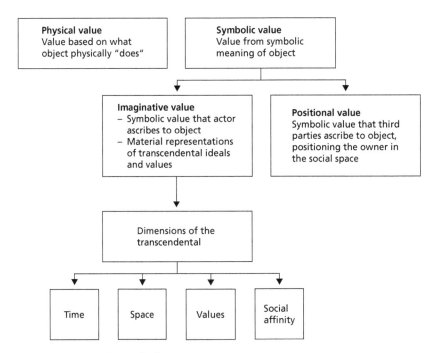

FIGURE 8.1. Typology of value.

herself with otherwise intangible things. These associations are fictional in the sense that they add qualities to the good that exist only through ascriptions of meaning.

Associations with the future are particularly evident in the purchase of lottery tickets (Beckert and Lutter 2009, 2013; Lutter 2012b): two-thirds of German lottery players state that they daydream about what they would do with their future wealth.[11] Lottery players picture a wealth-filled future based on the slim hope that the numbers on their tickets will be drawn. The global market for this product exceeds USD 200 billion and is fueled entirely by players' imaginaries of a future in abundant wealth.

Blood banks that store babies' umbilical cord blood for use in stem-cell therapy later in life constitute a medical consumer market also built on imaginaries of the future (Brown, Kraft, and Martin 2006; Martin, Brown, and Turner 2008). This market is being developed on the claim that stem cells can only be collected at birth, and is built on imaginaries of future medical needs and the fears of parents seeking to provide their children with the best possible care. This is a striking instance of the "capitalization of hope," in which value is based on fictional expectations of an uncertain future. "The biomedical imaginary refers to the speculative, propositional fabric of medical thought, the generally disavowed dream work performed by biomedical theory and innovation . . . the fictitious, the connotative . . . desire" (Waldby 2002, quoted in Martin, Brown, and Turner 2008: 128). In a similar vein, direct-to-consumer genetic testing provides "customers" with personalized genetic reports containing information about the possible genetic risks they carry. Although its practitioners present their service as a medical, not a commercial one, their business has located a marketable commodity in people's fears about their future health (Almeling 2014).

The purchase of old wines, and, more generally, the purchase of antiques, are examples of how objects allow their owners to transcend time toward the past. Owning such objects creates a symbolic connection to the cultural or political values of specific periods or historic people. Marie-France Garcia (2011) offers a particularly illuminating example, quoting from a book written by a collector of fine wines. The collector, François Audouze, describes the experience of drinking aged wine: "The oldest red wine I have drunk was an 1811 Chambertin. Imagine what this evokes: you're at the height of the Napoleonic era, this becomes a heavy symbol, and moreover, it's the year of Halley's Comet, which isn't even yet called Halley's Comet. To have a comet in your cup, that's straight from the history books!"

(Audouze, 2004, cited in Garcia-Parpet 2011: 140). The value of the—very expensive—bottle of wine Audouze consumed comes from the year it was produced, not just from its rarity, and certainly not from its taste. The wine creates an imaginary bridge to events that took place long ago, connecting the person who consumes it to a distant time. Its power to evoke Napoleon's rule and the passing of Halley's Comet confer a kind of sacredness on the product.

Elena Bogdanova (2013) offers other examples of associations with the past in her research on Russian antiques markets, where vendors create value by telling stories about the provenance of antique pieces. Auction house catalogues contain highly evocative information associating objects with historically important individuals and events. An especially graphic example is from a 2011 Sotheby's catalogue concerning the auction of a table by Gioacchino Barberi from the early nineteenth century. It is a painstaking description of the table, the historical circumstances under which it was produced, and its provenance. The analysis by a team of art historians comes to the conclusion "that the original, intended owner of this table could only have been Nicholas I, Emperor of Russia from 1825–1855" (Sotheby's 2011). The value of the table is not only justified by the craftsmanship of its creator but also by its association with the Russian czar and the historical event of the Russo-Turkish War of 1828–1829. The table, estimated at $400,000–$600,000, sold for close to $2 million.

Products that are marketed based on their geographic origin reveal the spatial dimension of the imaginative value of goods. These products are valued because they connote a specific place, evoking images of proximity that allow the consumer to imagine himself in a specific environment or participating in a particular way of life. The French AOC label, for example, ties products to images of locality and tradition. These images and narratives provide value that can be used to market products and regions and thus constitute the "cultural wealth of nations" (Bandelj and Wherry 2011). Symbolically charged products allow their consumers to transcend place in the same way they do time, thereby connecting them to the ideals they associate with that particular location.[12]

The "contact charisma" of certain objects reveals the social dimension of fictional expectations about consumer goods. When a handbag is carried by an idealized celebrity such as Madonna, it becomes "infected" with her charisma. The desire for the same handbag is motivated by its capacity to create a link to the idealized person, a way of partaking in her identity. The singer's aura is transferred to the handbag's purchaser, and becomes a symbolic quality that creates value in its own right.[13] The parallel to religious phenomena is very direct here, since value is created in the same way that sacredness is conferred on any object that comes into contact with a prophet (Durkheim [1912] 1965: 254). The handbag becomes a relic: something touched and carried by the idealized person, a symbolic representation of their charismatic power.

The transcendent qualities of goods may finally also create symbolic associations to the values their owners espouse. Fair trade products, for example, connect purchasers to a geographically and socially distant world, allowing them to imagine they are "doing good" for people far away. The additional value of these products lies not in their physical qualities but rather in the opportunity they offer consumers to put their value convictions into practice by purchasing them. Whale watching is another such example (Lawrence and Phillips 2004): to a contemporary of Herman Melville, paying money to board a ship for the sole purpose of observing whales swimming in the ocean would have seemed an act of utter madness. But symbolic connotations of whales have changed since his time, and whales are now seen as representing freedom and untrammeled nature rather than as frightening wild creatures. The cultural shift from "Moby Dick" to "Free Willy" has made it possible for whale watching to be commercialized. Its value stems from contemporary Western culture's symbolic associations with whales.

As the examples cited above show, the imaginary performance of goods has a transcending quality to it: it offers access to past historical events, distant regions, unreachable social positions, or aesthetic or moral values by making the object a symbolic representation of something that is otherwise intangible. A recent and particularly striking example of the power of this magic was a blind test of the sound qualities of Stradivari violins. Although these violins are considered the best in the music world, the test showed that professional violinists could not distinguish the sound of a Stradivari from that of a new violin (Fritz et al. 2012). The fact that a Stradivari sells for several million euros when a new violin of superior quality may be purchased for a few thousand cannot be explained by the former's superior physical value (its sound, in other words). Rather, the Stradivari's value is driven up by its aura, which is generated in the discursive communities of the music world.

It would be a mistake, however, to describe the symbolic value of goods as purely illusory. As discussed in Chapter 4, imagining future states of the world can provoke sensations similar to those associated with the actual experience of them. In their role as material representations of otherwise abstract or distant events, values, and ideals, goods offer a way to mentally experience something that is desired, similar to what is experienced by readers of fiction. As may be seen in the discussion of consumer goods above, this is true not only of future states—as is the case with investments—but of the past and of socially and geographically distant places, connecting consumers with the transcendent through what Kendall Walton (1990) calls "quasi emotions." Sipping an 1811 Chambertin allows the drinker to feel as if he is actually experiencing that era. Holding a lottery ticket summons fantasies of being rich, triggering emotions that make the experience of wealth mentally accessible in the present. "Consumers entertain dreams of yet unacquired products and experiences for purposes of anticipatory consumption and purchase prioritization, as well as for speculation and intrinsic enjoyment of the experience" (Fournier and Guiry 1993: 357).[14] Symbolically charged objects are more than just representations of desired events, values, or ideals: because they allow their purchasers to participate in the reality they are perceived to represent, they are an essential part of that reality (see Tillich 1986: 5). These imaginaries incite consumers to purchase symbolically charged consumer goods.

GOODS AS TOTEMS

The work of Emile Durkheim is particularly helpful to understanding how expectations are derived from symbolic meanings. From this perspective, the consumer's attraction to goods is not merely a hedonistic urge whose psychological cause may be located "in a desire for the pleasure which it brings" (C. Campbell 1987: 80). Rather, it may be interpreted as a specific form of orientation toward the realization of shared values and as confirmation of membership in a moral community. This follows Durkheim's intuition that secularization does not imply the extinction of the sacred in society, but instead leads to the emergence of secular forms of the sacred. While Durkheim demonstrated this social transformation primarily with regard to the expansion of rights granted to the individual (Joas 2000), it also provides a model to analyze the imaginaries associated with consumption of goods in the economy (see Belk, Wallendorf, and Sherry 1989). Again, this indicates a parallel between contemporary capitalism and religious classifications.

Durkheim's central insight in his sociology of religion is that the moral influence of a society over its members is not based primarily on felt obliga-tions and fear of sanctions, but on a positive binding of clan members to its values. In other words, people feel attracted to religious regulations (Durk-heim [1912] 1965: 240–41). The notion of attraction is crucial because ex-change is voluntary, meaning that demand for goods will only exist if the goods have a positive appeal, that is, if they provoke a desire to own them.

Durkheim uses this insight to explore the origins of the attraction to so-cial values, investigating the ritualistic practices of Australian clans and the role of sacred objects in these practices, starting with the observation that the world of tribal society is strictly divided into two spheres, the sacred and the profane. Objects that symbolically represent the clan—its totems—are separated from other objects through a strict set of rules on how to en-gage with them, which are based on belief in the power—or *mana*—of these objects. As discussed earlier on in this book, the power of the totem is not inherent in the object itself, but attributed to it by the believers. Durk-heim insists, however, that the power emanating from these sacred objects and felt by the clan members is not purely illusory, but may be seen as the power of the moral community of the clan ([1912] 1965: 236). The symbolic qualities of sacred objects are "imaginative bridges to the transcendental" (Tappenbeck 1999: 50), in which the moral community finds a collective representation.

The human capacity Durkheim identifies at the core of religious beliefs is the same one present in the fictional expectations identified by this book, that of attributing qualities to objects that exist only in the imagination and have no objective material correlate in the objects themselves. "Collective representations very frequently attribute to the things to which they are at-tached qualities which do not exist under any form or to any degree" (Durk-heim [1912] 1965: 259–60).

Though fictitious, qualities symbolically represented in an object are experienced as if they were real. An object's fictitious qualities are not determined by the objects themselves, nor by the brain's neurological struc-tures. This does not, however, imply that they are arbitrary: they emerge from cultural and social worlds of the community; the imaginative attributes of an object only have "power" to the extent that they are perceived col-lectively by a social group (Durkheim [1912] 1965: 238). By the same token, the positional and imaginative value of goods, though individually experi-enced, is a social phenomenon. Sociologists of consumption concur: "Our taste for luxuries, for goods beyond our conventional buying power, is not simply greed, not only self-indulgence. It is also attributable to our need, as groups and as individuals, to re-establish access to the ideals we have displaced to distant locations in time or space" (McCracken 1988: 116).

The capacity to attribute qualities to things that exist only in the imagination forms the bedrock of the symbolic value of goods in the economy, making positional and imaginative value possible. First, a product's power to position its owner in the social space may be seen as an instance of the totemic power identified by Durkheim: actors are recognized in a specific way by associating with specific objects. Goods bestow identities and signal membership in a social group much as totems do for clan members. Consequently, a change in consumption patterns also leads to a change in social identity. A person is categorized based on classifications of the objects he consumes. In this way objects exercise power over individuals.[15] If a (potential) owner desires the social identity associated with the good, the good exercises an attraction independent from its physical performance, based purely on its symbolic meanings.

Second, collective symbolic representations in objects also help constitute imaginative value. Just as a totem is the symbolic representation of a clan's moral rules (values), goods can become symbolic representations of a moral community's secular values. Durkheim ([1912] 1965: 251) offers the example of a flag, which is a material representation of a nation that is revered (or valued, for the purposes of this discussion) as a symbol of that nation's values. In this sense it is a sacred object: it both represents a moral community and is the community. As Durkheim observes, this phenomenon causes soldiers to risk their lives to defend flags, which, in purely material terms, are nothing more than fungible bits of fabric (251–52).[16]

Durkheim's analogy between religious phenomena and military or political actions can be extended to the valuation of material goods exchanged in markets, provided we show that the sacred can also be symbolically represented in commodities and can serve as a "bridge" to the transcendental. Just as a totem stands for the moral community of the clan and a flag stands for the nation, a bottle of wine can symbolize a cherished historical event to which it links its purchaser. This connection presupposes the exercise of the imagination, because the object and its meaning are discontinuous: their unity exists only as a mental construction (Tappenbeck 1999: 104).

Objects can be inscribed with meanings that conjure up mental images. In the case of religious symbols, these meanings remind the believer of the force of the community, while in the case of the consumer, they allow for an association with intangible ideals. Symbolic meaning transforms an object into an intermediary, provoking sensations in its owner that connect him to his ideals. The object becomes "the medium through which the ideal becomes capable to be understood" (Durkheim [1911] 1974: 96). This magical power of objects is a source of attraction because it provides the experience of pleasurable or even intoxicating sensations.[17] At the same time it is a form of "doubling of reality" and creates fictional expectations in the sense of a belief in something that is semiotically added to the object.

The Role of Practices

Though an objective part of reality, the symbolic meanings that constitute the positional and imaginary value of goods are not material qualities, which raises the question of how these transcendent qualities become attached to the objects that represent them. Answering this question requires special attention to practices in the market field (Warde 2005). In general terms, a good's meaning is constituted through the marketing activities of firms, socialization, repeated interaction with the good, and participation in group activities (Richins 1994).

Here again, Durkheim's work on ritualistic religious and secular practices is illuminating. Durkheim observed that social life in tribal communities could be divided into periods of everyday activity and periods of ritualistic festivity, during which a clan's members would assemble. Ritualistic festivities would usually take place in physical proximity to the clan's totem. The passion and exaltation experienced through dance, music, fires, the darkness of the night, and the use of drugs would provoke a collective effervescence in which clan members experienced a state in which they transcended their own consciousness. Since the totem was the center of these festivities, clan members attributed this experience of self-transcendence to the power of the totem (Durkheim [1912] 1965: 252).

It is possible to observe similar—albeit less dramatic—phenomena in consumers' relationships to consumer goods in contemporary economies. The positive aura surrounding an object associated with a charismatic celebrity such as Madonna may derive from experiences of collective effervescence at, for example, her concerts. The transcendent power of such "extraordinary" experiences may also be associated with places, as would be the case with a regional product that evokes treasured memories of a place where one has lived or vacationed. Particularly large lottery jackpots often lead to mass public excitement that resembles the intoxication Durkheim describes and increases demand for tickets. New car models and consumer electronics are presented to the public in theatrical performances at fairs that are similar in many respects to the ritualistic practices Durkheim describes. The late Steve Jobs could easily have been confused for a guru or religious leader, right down to his clothing choices. As Alfred Marshall has pointed out, these are all instances of practices generating wants, rather than wants generating products ([1920] 1961).

Durkheim mentions a second practice necessary to keep the *mana* of religious symbols alive: the passions created in moments of collective effervescence lose their impact on individual clan members over time. To avoid this deterioration, religious groups and political movements regularly assemble their members in meetings to revitalize communal values and beliefs (Durkheim [1911] 1974: 92; [1912] 1965: 240). Church services and party conventions both bring together communities of believers and use ritualistic practices to remind them to cherish the values of the community.

Similar connections between the stabilization of goods' symbolic value and group practices can be observed in markets. Markets in which the symbolic value of products plays an important role typically have a social organization that fosters communication among consumers and experts in the field. In the art market, for example, galleries host openings at the beginnings of shows that bring together potential buyers, the seller, the artist, other artists, and art experts in a ritualistic affirmation of the quality of the objects to be sold. Museums and art critics participate in the art world's discursive community, helping to reaffirm the value of an artist and setting standards for the assessment of quality through communicative practices (H. S. Becker 1982; Beckert and Rössel 2013; Velthuis 2005). In the lottery market, syndicate play leads to higher participation rates (Garvía 2007). In the car market, the symbolic value of a car is established and reaffirmed through advertisements and car magazines, visits to car dealerships, car races, and private communications among lay "believers" who have faith in the qualities of the object. Post-sale advertising then reminds customers of the transcendent qualities of their cars, shielding them from the danger of disillusionment. Vintage car owners form clubs and assemble in ritualistic club meetings to admire the old cars they possess, thereby reconfirming their value. Consumer electronics firms—Apple is probably the most prominent example—organize the release of new products by creating scarcities that bring the most dedicated customers together to wait (sometimes overnight) to be among the first to buy the product once stores open, creating a group experience of like-minded people. Group experiences can also be organized virtually, leading to para-social interaction, the illusion of face-to-face interaction through mass media (Horton and Wohl 1956). Nespresso, for instance, seeks to create an "imagined community" among purchasers of its beverage machines by making them members of a "Nespresso Club," which includes a subscription to a magazine with regular updates about the product and its users. Magazine ads and television commercials remind potential customers of the symbolic qualities of products being advertised, which would otherwise fade from consumer consciousness.[18] In the terms used by Kendall Walton (1990) in his make-believe theory, advertisements can generally be understood as props that spark imaginative games that constitute or reinforce the symbolic value of commodities.

Imaginative value is fragile and requires constant reaffirmation through communicative practices to be maintained. As Hirschman (1986) observed in his analysis of the utopian element experienced in idealistic political practices (see Chapter 4), the value an actor assigns to an object will increase with the intensity of his personal engagement with that object. To a person ignorant about wine (or about history), an 1811 Chambertin might have no specific significance and therefore evoke no specific imagined future. Only an aficionado or an expert deeply committed to the product and engaged in the communicative processes of wine appreciation may perceive its symbolically intoxicating quality. And even among such people, this intoxication must be constantly revitalized through social practices that reaffirm the wine's symbolic "content."

THE DYNAMICS OF SYMBOLIC VALUE

The observation that fictional expectations regarding the performance of consumer goods must be established and maintained raises the question of why they fluctuate. Innovations that change a product's physical qualities or add new and superior functions may render other products obsolete. In this context, changes in value are easy to understand. But the symbolic value of goods changes too. Why can't their meaning, once established, remain constant? Durkheim's sociology of religion is not useful to understand changes in symbolic value, since, as he observes, religious symbols remain stable over time: "While the generations change, [the totemic emblem] remains the same; it is the permanent element of the social life" ([1912] 1965: 252). Although the significance and meaning of specific sacred objects in monotheistic religions has changed over the course of history and may remain theologically contested, religions do not continuously change their sacred objects.

Consumer goods in capitalist economies, by contrast, exist in a constant cycle of valuation and devaluation. This is not an ephemeral difference between consumer goods and religious objects: without this flux, capitalist growth would not be possible. As the products already owned by consumers lose value, new sales opportunities are created. Aside from products that are used up in the consumption process, space for new products emerges mainly as products that have already been purchased are devalued and discarded. This open space may then be occupied by new products associated with symbolic qualities that create desires to purchase them. To understand the microfoundations of capitalist dynamics on the demand side, it is necessary to identify the mechanisms underlying the devaluation of consumption goods.

Three such mechanisms should be discussed here, for which fictional expectations about future states of the world are crucial in motivating actors to engage in behaviors that preserve or intensify the capitalist economy's momentum. The first mechanism operates on the logic of differentiation described by Georg Simmel ([1904] 1971), and is connected to the positional value of goods. If the purpose of consumption is to signal social status, then goods lose value once they become available outside a defined social group and diffuse into the mainstream. As a result, new objects must constantly be defined as symbolic representations of distinction, a mechanism expressed in continuous processes of valuation and devaluation, whose effects Georg Simmel described using fashion as an example. As members of the lower classes imitate the fashions worn by members of the upper classes, that attire is devalued, forcing the upper classes to change fashions in order to retain their mark of social distinction. The possibility of such a dynamic is a distinctive trait of modern societies, as in traditional societies sumptuary laws dictated what clothes were to be worn by different social groups, effectively ruling out the possibility of devaluation through mimicry. As early as the nineteenth century, Tocqueville described how detraditionalization processes were opening an imaginary horizon through which "people begin to hope for material things that they never could have hoped for in the old class society" (Swedberg 2007: 10). Again, this points to the social anchoring of fictional expectations.[19]

The second mechanism has been called the "Diderot effect" after a story by the French philosopher in which he describes receiving a dressing gown as a gift, which drove him to change his home's décor to match his new garment, one object at a time (McCracken 1988). Each time, in the narrator's imaginary, a new object promised to eliminate the painful discrepancy between his current belongings and the ideal established by the dressing gown. Consumers experience this effect when they feel compelled to make a purchase they perceive as advancing them toward an overall ideal or impression. Purchasing a new object may thus devalue other objects, and foster a desire to substitute them for new ones (Deutschmann 2014; McCracken 1988: 120).

The third mechanism is connected to the process of appropriation itself, which leads to the devaluation of the acquired object. This process is rooted in Georg Simmel's understanding of fictional expectations as a means of mentally inhabiting future states of the world. The imaginary expresses a distance between subject and object which at the same time creates the value of the object: "Only the repulsions that we experience, the difficulties of attaining an object, the waiting and the labor that stand between a wish and its fulfillment, drive the Ego and the object apart; otherwise they remain undeveloped and undifferentiated in the propinquity of need and satisfaction" (Simmel [1907] 1978: 71–72). The object cannot, however, be too far removed from a person's actual purchasing possibilities: "The distance between the self and the object of demand could become so large—through the difficulties of procuring it, through its exorbitant price, through moral or other misgivings that counter the striving after it—that the act of volition does not develop, and the desire is extinguished or becomes only a vague wish" (Simmel [1907] 1978: 72).

Consumer credit (see Chapter 5) is a possible means to close this gap. Desired products that are unattainable due to the current purchasing power of the consumer can be brought within reach by credit. Consumer credit can turn vague wishes into actual desires that materialize in demand by bringing future purchasing power into the present. The financialization of consumption thus adds another layer of future orientation to it. In sociological terms, status inconsistency deriving from a sense of falling behind consumption standards set by the relevant peer group is counteracted by consumer credit that allows consumers to "catch up."[20] For this to occur, consumers must feel attracted to higher consumption levels and financial institutions must develop the technologies of risk calculation that make consumer lending a profitable business. If this is achieved, it creates an alignment of interests among businesses seeking to sell their products, consumers seeking to "keep up," and the financial industry wanting to sell credit. Credit makes the expansion of consumption possible, as consumer demand makes the consumer credit industry possible.

Studies show that consumers value products that do not yet exist, simply because of their expectations of future satisfaction (see Dahlén 2013). Companies recognize the future orientation of consumer desires and exploit it profitably in marketing campaigns, creating expectations by, for example, announcing the introduction of new technological devices. Marketing is mostly a technology of imagination applied to create expectations that lead to purchases. Again, in recent years, Apple has probably succeeded the most in deploying marketing campaigns that create fictional expectations regarding future consumption opportunities. The film industry uses this technique to great effect as well, creating expectation-based desires by releasing film trailers, sometimes more than a year in advance of the actual film. Products appear especially attractive to consumers when their exact features are still unknown and the openness of the future can be filled by their imaginaries.

At the same time the expectations of consumers are often disappointed once they are confronted with actually purchased products. The value of the product is higher in imagination than when it is actually experienced. This has to do with the nature of value. "We desire objects . . . in terms of [their] distance as something not-yet-enjoyed, the subjective aspect of this condition being desire. . . . The object thus formed, which is characterized by its separation from the subject, who at the same time establishes it and seeks to overcome it by his desire, is for us a value" (Simmel [1907] 1978: 66).

Similarly, outside of economic processes, John Dewey analyzes desire as emerging from obstacles to the action process. Without such obstacles, "there is nothing which we call desire" (Dewey [1922] 1957: 249). If value comes from desiring an object that is not yet possessed, and whose nonpossession is a kind of obstacle, it follows that purchasing and enjoying the object will also devalue it: "The moment of enjoyment itself, when the separation of subject and object is effaced, consumes the value. Value is only reinstated as contrast, as an object separated from the subject. Such trivial experiences as that we appreciate the value of our possessions only after we have lost them" (Simmel [1907] 1978: 66).

Disillusionment

In economics, the idea of devaluation through appropriation has been taken up by Albert Hirschman (1982) and Micael Dahlén (2013). In the sociology of consumption, Colin Campbell (1987)—contrary to Simmel—argues that devaluation does not arise from a loss of distance between subject and object, but rather from the discrepancy between the object's imagined perfection before it is owned and the imperfections that become visible once it is in the owner's possession. "Since reality can never provide the perfected pleasures encountered in day-dreams . . . each purchase leads to literal disillusionment, something which explains why wanting is extinguished so quickly" (C. Campbell 1987: 90). Closing the distance between owner and object itself does not produce disillusionment, but closing the distance between the object and the imaginary does (see also Hirschman 1982: 631–32).

Simmel and Campbell are both correct in their assessment of the process of disillusionment associated with the appropriation of goods, but the causes for this disillusionment can be described more precisely by comparing economic goods to totemic objects once again. The pivotal difference between the two may be found in their relationship to the sacred. Goods sold in the market hold the promise that possessing them will give the possessor access to the dimensions these goods symbolically represent. A (potential) purchaser sees the object as embodying the transcendent, which can be appropriated through the purchase. This reifying illusion both constitutes the object's attraction as a commodity and is the source of its devaluation once it is actually possessed.

This stands in contrast to religious symbols: because religious ideals are always physically unattainable, they maintain their distance from the faithful. Proximity to a totem thus allows a follower to achieve spiritual closeness to the sacred, while in no way being taken as a realization or appropriation of the religious ideals it embodies. The significance of religious objects is limited to representation; their possession serves only to remind community members of the values the community stands for and of their membership in it. This difference is visible in the way access to sacred objects is strictly regulated and even restricted. Followers may not be allowed to touch or even to see a totem outside specific dates in the religious calendar.

There are no such restrictions on secular goods, which are distanced from the consumer only until they have been purchased. The sacrifice made with the purchase allows the object to be appropriated and used, or carried into the world of the profane, to return to religious terminology. Possession reduces a consumer object's imaginative value, as it "is now an incipient part of the 'here and now' and to this extent vulnerable to contradiction" (McCracken 1988: 112). While the object appears to be part of the transcendental quality it represents, this is logically and empirically impossible, a realization that is experienced once the object has been purchased and appropriated: this kind of disillusionment is specific to commodities.

If a purchaser is to be persuaded to pay for a commodity, he must have the expectation that its transcendental qualities can be appropriated with the purchase. But this fictional expectation is at the root of the disillusionment that follows: as soon as the object comes into his possession, the imaginative space in which it existed shrinks, and the purchaser attains only its immanent (profane) qualities. After it has been drunk, the 1811 Chambertin becomes nothing but a wine—and a presumably bad one at that. Indeed, this is the limit of the reification of values in commodities and also an entry point of political resistance against the commodification of imaginaries. In the words of a French advocacy group: *"Le rêve ne s'achète pas"* [The dream cannot be bought] (*Métro*, October 19, 2012, p. 8). Such resistances, if successful in demystifying the symbolic meanings of consumer goods, are in effect undermining the growth of capitalism by reducing the motivation to buy products whose value rests mostly on imaginaries.

As described in the previous section, the producers of consumer goods try to reduce and defer this disappointment by reconfirming the transcendental qualities of the good, generally through post-sale communications. Consumers can also postpone disillusionment by postponing their consumption of a good (not drinking the 1811 Chambertin, for example) or by restricting their use of it (wearing a new suit only for special occasions) to keep it within the realm of the sacred.[21]

This process of disappointment and devaluation is specific to consumer goods. Fictional expectations relating to investment in plants and equipment, in financial markets, or in human capital may be disappointed, but not at the moment of appropriation. Disappointment occurs over time, if the profit expectations associated with the investment go unfulfilled (see Chapter 6).

The only "purchase" to which the process of disillusionment does not apply at all is the accumulation of money, since money is both devoid of any concrete characteristics and at the same time offers the freedom to buy any good with it (Parsons 1963). In a way, it is the most perfect material representation of an unbound imagined future, in that it withstands the disillusionment of appropriation. The only threat to the imaginative force of money is its devaluation (see Chapter 5). One can see the special attraction of money in this duality: having no concrete qualities itself, money still allows for the potential to obtain any quality desired. Money cannot be contradicted by experience, because money is an abstraction (Deutschmann 2009; Parsons 1963; Simmel [1907] 1978). At the same time, it makes the question of why actors purchase "unnecessary" consumer goods even more puzzling, since the value of any specific consumer good must be higher than the perceived value of the money not spent (Ullrich 2006: 59ff.).

THE POLITICS OF EXPECTATIONS

The limits of the representation of time, space, position, and values in goods described above drive the dynamics of symbolic value, opening a path to understanding a central mechanism of capitalist dynamics on the microlevel. Once a consumer has been disillusioned with regard to the symbolic qualities of a specific good, imaginaries must be projected onto new objects. Future possibilities direct desire. However disappointed a purchaser may be with the promised value of an object once the object has been purchased, that promise remains in other objects she does not yet possess. Once goods are appropriated, "the individual must swiftly transfer [or] 'bridge' status from the purchased object to one that is not now owned" (McCracken 1988: 115). This specifically human vulnerability would appear to stem from our ability to create fiction, as well as from our "need for fiction" (Iser 1993).[22] In an economic system that depends on consumers' willingness to desire more and newer products, human fictionability is the source of the demand for products that are "relative" in Keynes's sense of the word ([1931] 1972). In advanced economies, this is an ever more important source of economic growth, and it remains for most of us a source of motivation, even if products, once consumed, do not lead to heightened levels of satisfaction (Frank 1999: 64ff.). The paradoxical conclusion may be that it is "absolutely essential for us never to receive what it is we want" (McCracken 1988: 116).

Here, the supply side of production comes together with the demand side. Producers depend on the marketability of their products and therefore invest in associating their products with consumers' ideals, attempting to shape what consumers value and then communicate those values through advertisements and other marketing activities in association with their products. As André Orléan (2014: 104) writes, "No better description of the contingency of commodity valuation can be imagined: norms of social recognition are created, and then enforced, by persons who are able to make others wish for what they wish them to wish for." The advertising industry was created for this purpose: it can be described as an instrument for the creation of fictional expectations. Over the course of the twentieth century, firms have made increasingly intensive efforts to manufacture consumer dreams. The sale of their products depends on these dreams, which are therefore an indispensable productive force within capitalism. Inciting consumers to identify with the created imaginary qualities of goods instrumentalizes the archaic mechanisms of totemistic identification.

The identification with imaginary value is a necessarily dynamic process for two reasons. First, as discussed above, the unrelenting disappointments that follow the purchase of goods create a continuous renewal of demand for new products. This occurs through a shift in imaginative associations that Durkheim argues is possible because symbolic qualities can, in principle, be attached to any object. Second, competing producers contest the attribution of symbolic value attributed to products, vying to create fictional expectations that induce consumers to choose their products over those of their competitors (Callon, Méadel, and Rabeharisoa 2002). Firms expend enormous effort and funds to create, maintain, and shift goods' symbolic qualities, and to convince customers of their performance. These efforts have created a vast industry as the marketing departments of firms and firms specializing in marketing services strive to shape consumers' expectations (Dubuisson-Quellier 2013). The mass media also plays a central role in the creation of symbolic qualities of goods by disseminating lifestyles and associating them with consumer products.

This politics of expectations also takes place through "judgment devices" (Karpik 2010) produced and applied not only by firms but also by state regulation and the many intermediaries active in the economic field. Classification systems, critics, guidebooks, product rankings, product tests, opinion leaders, certificates of authenticity, and fair-trade labels are all used to shape consumer expectations about goods' functional and symbolic qualities. Furthermore, consumers themselves contribute to the dynamics of changing value with their constantly revised definitions of what is "in" and what is "out." The wants that help create demand and economic growth exist because of the fictional expectations created as actors emit and receive communications about the qualities of the goods. Because they are not based on a product's material qualities but on communicatively constructed meanings that are created and shifted by powerful market actors, the expectations that constitute the symbolic value of goods are contingent and fragile. If value is created through the contingent definitions of the performance of goods, then economic growth cannot be understood as based on "the necessaries of life" (Smith [1776] 1976: 368): it must be seen as a social and cultural process through which meaning is constructed. This meaning is particularly relevant to the dynamics of capitalism, for capitalism "is the world of make-believe in which one lives for expectations, for what will come rather than what is" (Bell [1976] 1978: 70).

CONCLUSION

Investigations of the economy in the field of political economy have focused primarily on the supply side of markets. Market sociology, too, places much more emphasis on firms and their coordination in competition than it does on the demand side. This productionist bias fails to offer a comprehensive account of contemporary economies in which there is a dependency on consumption but where many consumer needs have already been satisfied and consumers' motivation to buy products cannot be taken for granted. If markets are to function and the dynamics of capitalism are to continue, consumers must value the products on offer and be willing to make sacrifices in order to possess them. What are the origins of this willingness? Distinguishing among the physical, positional, and imaginative value of goods helps to explain the different sources of value for consumer goods in the economy.

Durkheim's sociology of religion, read here as a sociology of valuation, provides important insights into the construction of fictional expectations in consumption: his claim that totem emblems are respected as the symbolic representation of a social group's values can be transposed to the valuation of secular goods in contemporary capitalism. While the role of imaginative value has been investigated in studies of consumption (C. Campbell 1987; McCracken 1988; d'Astous and Deschênes 2005; Ullrich 2006), these studies are often limited in their focus on the psychological desire for newness or other individual traits to explain imaginative value (d'Astous and Deschênes 2005). On the contrary, the imaginative performance of goods comes from the way values and ideals are attributed to them. These ideals may be aesthetic or normative, relating to distant times and places; either way, their symbolic representation in consumer objects is a social construction.

In light of this claim, markets can no longer be seen as expressing unbounded individualism. In modern economies, as the basis of valuation shifts increasingly to goods' positional and imaginative performances, demand must instead be understood as a part of the cultural fabric of society. This corresponds to claims of scholars of consumption that we are currently witnessing the "moralization" (Stehr 2007) and "aesthetization" (Rössel 2007) of markets. Furthermore, the increasing importance of positional and imaginative value is evidence in the economic sphere that supports Emile Durkheim's claim that processes of secularization do not lead to the elimination of the sacred, but rather to the emergence of secularized forms of it. In modern societies, values are also expressed through consumption practices, which requires fictional expectations. Rather than an object's sacredness becoming contaminated when the object is brought into the sphere of market exchange, the symbolically charged goods become representations of value—not just in the economic sense, but also in the moral sense of the term (Fourcade 2009; Zelizer 2004).

Emile Durkheim's social theory may also be used to conceptualize the social practices through which goods become charged with fictional expectations, and through which actors in the field attempt to maintain (or destroy) these expectations. Experiences of collective effervescence are one source of expectations, and communications among consumers, experts, producers, and critics are meant to keep them alive and shield them from the disappointment that sets in once a product is actually possessed. Indeed, an entire industry has developed to market products, and in conjunction with mass media, shapes the symbolic meaning of consumer goods. The communicative practices surrounding the construction of imaginative value are part of sociation *(Vergesellschaftung)* and thus part of the fabric of society. At the same time, there is a utopian element to the mental representation of intangible ideals in objects and the striving to realize these ideals through their purchase. Understanding this helps advance our comprehension of economic dynamics far beyond the sphere of consumption. Investment decisions, as discussed in Chapter 6, are characterized by a very similar form of striving for a utopian state (Schumpeter [1912] 2006: 164ff.). Charging products with imaginative value requires manipulation and reifies actors' desires to "appropriate" transcendent values, but it also promises imaginative salvation by providing access to intangible ideals. Because of the mechanisms described above, this salvation is never fully achieved. But producers' needs to sell their products correspond to consumers' aspirations to find symbolic representations of their transcending desires, and the manner in which they do so shows the significant contribution fictional expectations can make to the system integration of the economy and the social integration of actors.

The final part of this book continues to investigate fictional expectations, but on a more abstract level by discussing the instruments used to create them. The term "instruments" is used to describe the cognitive technologies through which social reality is perceived. These technologies help to create imaginaries of the future and give rise to specific interpretations of the causal relations leading to this future. The instruments of imagination contribute to constituting reality as they interpret it, and thus play a role in the way decisions are made and social interactions are coordinated. They shape the present by providing descriptions of possible futures, which in turn can guide decisions and thus shape future outcomes. In this sense, the instruments of imagination are influential: they are crystal balls creating present futures that provide justifications for decisions.

In economic sociology, and in the sociology of finance in particular, the role of cognitive instruments in the operation of the economy has been the subject of a great deal of work. Mathematical formulas are central to the sociology of finance (MacKenzie and Millo 2003; MacKenzie 2011), as are technological apparatuses (Knorr Cetina and Bruegger 2002; Preda 2006) that guide calculations and communications and thus influence market outcomes. This interest has also recently expanded beyond financial markets (Muniesa 2014). The following chapters discuss forecasts and economic theories. They build on crucial insights from the sociology of finance, while focusing on expectation building. Forecasts and economic theories are part of the cognitive infrastructure underlying capitalist dynamics. They provide cognitive support for risky decisions by creating convictions of certain future developments, and support innovations by producing imaginaries of new possibilities. At the same time, because they influence expectations, forecasts and theories are also instruments of power and governance.[23]

INSTRUMENTS
OF IMAGINATION

NINE

FORECASTING

Creating the Present

So in summary, Your Majesty, the failure to foresee the timing and
severity of the crisis and to head it off, while it had many causes, was
principally a failure of the collective imagination of many bright
people, both in the country and internationally, to understand the
risks to the system as a whole.

—Letter of the British Academy to Her Majesty the Queen, 2009

MANY OF THE fictional expectations described in the second part of this
book can be interpreted as forms of prognosis and forecasting, although
those terms are used only occasionally: an entrepreneur's expectations about
an investment are based on forecasts of market development and anticipations of competitors' strategies. Financial investors build their investment
strategies using prognoses of how the prices of financial assets will evolve
within a given time span. Before purchasing a good, consumers project the
satisfaction it will bring them.

The techniques used to systematically build expectations about future developments include macroeconomic forecasting and technological foresight.
These "techniques of prospection" (Mallard and Lakoff 2011) are employed
to envision an unknown future.[1] Economic and technological forecasts
play a role in economic decision-making and in the dynamics of capitalism. Forecasting technologies are instruments used to create fictional
expectations and as such are coordinating, performative, inventive, and political. Forecasts coordinate by pretending probabilistic foreknowledge of
the future to help orient actors seeking to act rationally in the face of its unknowability. Actors use forecasts to help them behave *as if* they know the
future present, or at least important elements of it. Forecasts also help to coordinate action by creating shared expectations about the future and justifications for decisions made in uncertain conditions. Forecasts are performative

in the sense that predictions of future developments influence decision-making and may have direct impact on the future. They are inventive in the sense that they open new cognitive horizons for action by depicting counterfactual states of the world, and thus contribute to the innovation dynamics of capitalism. They are political because of their impact on decisions, which makes them and their assessment the locus of power struggles within the economy. Forecasts are an instrument of the politics of expectations. Identifying the role of forecasts in the creation, stabilization, and influencing of expectations helps address the puzzling question of why forecasts are so widely used despite the fact that their high failure rate is well known.

While the economy relies on forecasts to operate, the correctness of these forecasts is ironically of only secondary importance. Much more crucial is their credibility in the present; that is, whether they convince actors and inspire them to make decisions whose outcomes they cannot know. Since actors focus on forecasts' credibility, not their correctness, inaccurate predictions merely impel them to seek new forecasts, rather than disregarding the genre altogether. This raises the question of the origin of forecasts' credibility: what leads actors to be convinced of specific forecasts? An answer to this question must highlight the practices of forecasting, the authority of forecasters, and the need to justify decisions in the face of uncertainty. Ethnographic studies show that forecasts are embedded in discursive processes that involve legitimate technologies and a multiplicity of actors from "the economy," which together create and disseminate a shared cognitive field. Through "epistemic participation" (Reichmann 2013) actors in the field form convictions regarding the future and influence others' convictions. The relative economic and political power of actors plays a crucial role in this process. As perspectives on future developments are at least partially shared, they operate as conventions, which provide cognitive anchors for actors in the form of expectations of other actors' behavior or attitudes. Once they are seen as credible, forecasts and technological projections become crucial instruments in the creation of fictional expectations.

FORETELLING THE FUTURE

Though the exact definition of forecasting is contested, it is clear that forecasting is a form of expectation building (Reichmann 2013: 854). Forecasts may be defined as calculations of the future before it happens, or as predictions of future events that are arrived at through formal modeling and expert opinion (de Laat 2000: 178; W. Friedman 2014: xi). Techniques for anticipating the future are probably as old as humanity. Oracles, prophecies, divination, and other techniques have existed since the beginning of recorded history, although today they are largely dismissed as nonrational and based on superstition (Bronner 2011, chap. 1).

Modern macroeconomic forecasting techniques became a specialized field of applied economic research only in the early twentieth century.[2] Predictions that used statistical and econometric methods were first developed during that time for private purposes: they were intended to help investors make better investment decisions by attempting to anticipate the evolution of the business cycle. These forecasts of future macroeconomic development were sold to investors.

Economic forecasting did not maintain this exclusive focus on private business for very long. Most forecasting institutes founded in the United States and Europe following World War I were assigned the task of providing statistical information to the state.[3] As the state intervened more and more in the business cycle, and as macroeconomic indicators such as GDP, inflation rates, unemployment rates, and foreign trade balances were developed, macroeconomic forecasts became crucial instruments for policy-making. The institutionalization and enlargement of statistical offices and institutes dedicated to the observation of macroeconomic development must be seen in the context of the state's growing role in steering economic processes, the organization of war production, and a turn toward the idea of social and political planning in the twentieth century (Wagner 2003).

Macroeconomic forecasting institutes were further institutionalized after World War II, when formal modeling techniques were introduced; they became increasingly sophisticated throughout the postwar era, which also saw a renewed emphasis on social and political planning. Today, macroeconomic forecasting has become a veritable industry. Alongside national forecasting institutions, other public institutions such as federal banks and ministries provide forecasts. International organizations such as the OECD, the IMF, and the European Commission also have forecasting departments, which predict the macroeconomic development of their member states, groups of countries, and even the world as a whole. Public institutions are not the only ones making economic forecasts: private banks, rating agencies, and investment funds do, too. Indeed, economic forecasting has developed into a major subfield of applied economics and statistics, into which substantial public and private funds are invested.

One form of forecast is the point prediction. A report may announce, for example, that the output of the American economy will grow by 2.3 percent next year. Such a precise figure pretends accuracy, helping actors build expectations regarding the future economic situation—to act *as if* the economy were going to grow by 2.3 percent. Reichmann (2011: 8–9) argues that the use of numbers and graphs in economic forecasting makes them function as what Karin Knorr Cetina calls "scopic systems." "Like an array of crystals acting as lenses that collect light, focusing it on one point, such mechanisms collect and focus activities, interests, and events on one surface, from whence the result may then be projected again in different directions" (Knorr Cetina 2003: 8). In other words, forecasters use the unambiguous mathematical phrasing of numbers and graphs as prisms, drawing together the macroeconomic indicators of the past to create projections of the future. In so doing, they reduce the economy to a manageable, orderly set of unambiguous numbers that can readily be put into a spreadsheet.

Point predictions, however, are always accompanied by narratives of how the economy will develop in the near future. These stories support the scopic system of numbers and graphs by telling how the present will be transformed into the anticipated future state. They provide an account of the mechanisms that will bring about this transformation, offering readers plausible causal links that bridge the gap from the past to the present and onto the predicted future. The authority of the experts and institutions telling these stories helps make them credible to their audience. The following is an example of such storytelling in a forecasting report published by the International Monetary Fund in early 2013:

> Global growth is projected to increase during 2013, as the factors underlying soft global activity are expected to subside. However, this upturn is projected to be more gradual than in the October 2012 World Economic Outlook (WEO) projections. Policy actions have lowered acute crisis risks in the euro area and the United States. But in the euro area, the return to recovery after a protracted contraction is delayed. While Japan has slid into recession, stimulus is expected to boost growth in the near term. At the same time, policies have supported a modest growth pickup in some emerging market economies, although others continue to struggle with weak external demand and domestic bottlenecks. If crisis risks do not materialize and financial conditions continue to improve, global growth could be stronger than projected. However, downside risks remain significant, including renewed

setbacks in the euro area and risks of excessive near-term fiscal consolida-
tion in the United States. Policy action must urgently address these risks.
(International Monetary Fund 2013: 1)

Technological forecasts are a second field of forecasting in the economy,
most often created by specialized departments in firms or private research
institutions. These forecasts attempt to anticipate technological developments and their market potential. Firms use the information such forecasts
provide for investment decisions, for the allocation of research funds, and for
marketing. Venture capitalists and public agencies that finance research on
the development of new technologies also use such technological forecasts.

Systematic technological forecasting started after World War II, using
techniques first developed in the military to understand the impact of new
technological developments on warfare (Andersson 2013). Technological
forecasts now use a wide variety of techniques, including the Delphi method,
scenario analysis, forecast by analogy, extrapolation, growth curves, relevance
trees, and morphological models (Andersson 2013; Martino 1983; Makridakis, Wheelwright, and Hyndman 1998). Technological forecasting
techniques, though they do include quantitative analysis, are often more
qualitative than those used in macroeconomic forecasting. Scenario analysis,
for instance, replaces fact and scientific rationality with imaginative storytelling, while the Delphi method uses structured communication with
panels of experts in a given field (Andersson 2013: 13).

Despite their more qualitative approach, these techniques resemble macroeconomic forecasting in that they attempt to craft plausible narratives to
explain how technological development will move from its present state into
the future. Put simply, they tell stories about what has not happened yet and
thus serve as props for decision-making. Firms, financial investors, and
research funding agencies use these "fictive scripts" (de Laat 2000: 176) to
make decisions about which research projects, investments, or start-up firms
they will fund. By extension, their decisions promote different future worlds
that depend not only on structural constraints and factual information, but
also on discursively constructed and culturally ingrained convictions.

THE FAILURE OF FORECASTS

Few macroeconomic and technological forecasts are accurate. The future
they anticipate rarely comes to pass. More often than not, they neglect or

fail to notice the developments that actually end up changing the world. Indeed, with hindsight, all too many predictions seem outright ludicrous.

The observation that forecasts fail is as old as economic forecasting itself. In December 1929, just weeks after the stock market crash, the Harvard Economic Society, one of the first American forecasting institutes, predicted a quick economic recovery: "Today a depression seems improbable, and continuance of business recession is all that is in prospect. . . . This justifies a forecast of recovery of business next spring, with further improvement in the fall, so that 1930, as a whole, should prove at least a fairly good year" (cited in W. Friedman 2009: 82). It goes without saying, of course, that the worst of the depression was still to come.

One might object that macroeconomic forecasting was still in its infancy in the 1920s, that econometric methods and the data available for statistical analyses were still rudimentary, and that today's macroeconomic forecasts are more reliable. This, however, is not the case. Today's forecasts are just as inaccurate. An analysis of transcripts of the Federal Open Market Committee, the Federal Reserve's main decision-making body, shows that as late as December 2007 the Federal Reserve had taken almost no notice of the impending financial crisis (Fligstein, Brundage, and Schultz 2014). Other macroeconomic forecasts made on the eve of the financial crisis of 2008 fall just as far from the mark. In 2008, none of the five leading forecasting institutes in Germany predicted the deep recession that hit the German economy in 2009, for example. In a series of papers, Wieland (2012) tested different econometric models and expert judgments with regard to their ability to foresee the slump of 2009 and the subsequent recovery in 2010. Figure 9.1 shows forecasts of real output growth for the U.S. economy made in the third quarter of 2008 using six different models and two expert forecasts from the Federal Reserve's Greenbook and the Survey of Professional Forecasters. All forecasts "failed to foresee the downturn as late as the third quarter of 2008" (17). By the second quarter of 2009, the models were correctly predicting the recovery, but not the renewed slowdown.

Looking at the forecasts of five German macroeconomic forecasting institutes over a longer time period leads us to the same conclusion: forecasts are not terribly accurate. Figure 9.2 depicts the predictions made at the end of a given year for GDP growth of the German economy in the year to come. For all but three years (2001, 2004, 2008) actual economic growth lies outside or on the margin of the range of GDP growth predicted by the

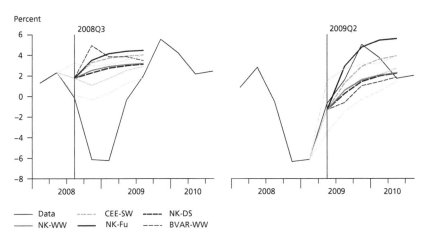

FIGURE 9.1. Real output growth forecasts during the 2007–2009 recession.
Source: Reproduced from Wieland 2012.

forecasting institutes. Predictions of other macroeconomic indicators such as unemployment rates and inflation rates paint a similar picture.

It should be noted that macroeconomic forecasts are probability statements, meaning they only predict outcomes within a range determined by the confidence level. Though confidence levels are not always explicitly stated in forecasts, forecasting institutes defend their work by pointing to the probabilistic nature of forecasts. Though methodologically correct, this is merely a sophisticated way of saying that such forecasts cannot tell us very much. Predicting GDP growth of 2.5 percent with a confidence level of 95 percent, for example, means that growth as low as 1.2 percent or as high as 3.8 percent is considered to confirm the estimate (R. Evans 1997: 421). But such variations have tremendous implications for economic policy-making and investment decisions, making the figure a very imprecise statement about economic development. Intriguingly, when point predictions are communicated or used in economic and policy decisions, error margins are given very little scrutiny. Point predictions divert attention from the true uncertainty of the economic future; proclaimed precision creates the illusion of accuracy when correct forecasts are impossible.

The predictions of banks are just as unreliable. Gerd Gigerenzer (2013) analyzed predictions made by twenty-two international banks between 2001 and 2010 for the dollar-euro exchange rate in a given year for the following year. The range of predictions made by the banks, the average of these

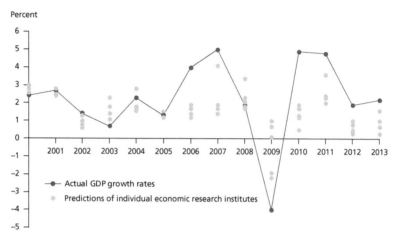

FIGURE 9.2. GDP growth in Germany, 2000–2013. *Note*: Forecasts are made at the end of each preceeding year. *Data sources*: German Federal Statistic Office; DIW Berlin; IWH Halle; ifw Kiel; RWI Essen; ifo Munich.

predictions, and the actual exchange rate make clear that in most years the variation between predictions and actual exchange rates was great. Often, the actual exchange rate lay outside the range of predictions. Whether the euro is worth one dollar or one dollar and thirty cents is of immense importance to export-oriented companies hedging against currency risk. And yet bank predictions were unable to tell them what the exchange rate would be. The only accurate conclusion that could be drawn from them was that almost anything could happen. In fact, tossing a coin would have been just as effective, since only half of the forecasts the study examined were even able to correctly predict general trends. As Gigerenzer (2013) observes, the banks' prognoses were usually trend extrapolations: they simply predicted that the previous year's trend would continue.

Technological forecasts are equally unreliable. More often than not, their predictions never materialize, and they fail to anticipate important techno-logical developments. Examples of their inability to foresee the future are myriad. In the early twentieth century, the success of the automobile was unimaginable. Gottlieb Daimler believed the car market was limited by the number of available chauffeurs and predicted that it would be limited to one million cars (presumably in Germany). Some of his contemporaries were convinced that the high price of the car would limit the market. Not one of them anticipated the invention of the assembly line in car manufacturing and its impact on automobile prices, and few believed that chauffeurs would become the exception and not the rule for personal motor vehicles (Nye 2004: 162). In 1954, the head of the American Atomic Energy Commission declared that electricity would be too cheap to meter by the end of the twentieth century (Nye 2004: 162). Even though this prediction was more a sales pitch by an industry lobbyist than it was an actual forecast, it created an imagined future intended to influence choices in energy technology. Since the early 1970s, the International Atomic Energy Organization (IAEO) started predicting global nuclear power capacity by the year 2000 in its annual reports (see Figure 9.3). In the early 1970s, it set this number at 4450 gigawatts, correcting downward every year. By 1986, the IAEO had reduced its original estimate by a factor of ten (Traube 1999). When the year 2000 arrived, the actual installed capacity came in at even less than that, at around 350 gigawatts.[4]

Forecasting in the computer industry has been no more successful. In the 1950s, IBM chairman Thomas J. Watson famously estimated the world market for computers at about a dozen. Watson was referring to supercomputers; the idea of a mass market for personal computers had yet to be imagined. Bill Gates, whose company went on to play a crucial role in developing the mass market for personal computers, made another legendarily erroneous declaration when he stated that 640K of memory ought to be enough for anyone (Sturken and Thomas 2004: 6). And in 1991, MIT Press published *Technology 2001: The Future of Computing and Communications,* a collection of fourteen articles by leading figures in the field, none of which discussed the Internet—indeed, it is not even listed in the index (Nye 2004: 163). It is perhaps only appropriate that the Internet is awash in websites that feature erroneous technological predictions for the amusement of their readers.[5]

The accuracy of predictions has also been scrutinized systematically by economists (Antholz 2006; Elliott and Timmermann 2008: 31ff.; Taleb 2010), and their findings confirm the illustrative examples given above. Macroeconomic and technological forecasts are highly inaccurate (Billeter-Frey 1984; Kholodilin and Siliverstovs 2009; Wieland 2012). As Elliott and Timmermann (2008: 4) state succinctly in their review of evaluation studies on economic forecasting, "the result of the feedback from forecasts has been disheartening."[6] Technological predictions are just as disappointing: "Many methods were used, including intuition, analogy, extrapolation, studying leading indicators, and deduction, but all were of roughly equal value. In short, technological predictions by any methods proved not more accurate than flipping a coin" (Nye 2004: 161).[7]

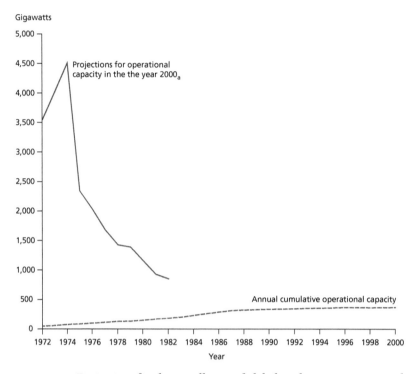

FIGURE 9.3. Projections for the installment of global nuclear power capacity by the year 2000 and actual capacity. *Note:* "a" is the mean for the range of estimates in each year. *Data sources:* projections, IAEA Annual Reports (1973–1981) and IAEA Reference Data Series 1 (1982); operational capacity, IAEA Reference Data Series 2 (2011). See also Traube (1999).

It is interesting to note that the sophistication of the econometric models used in forecasts does not improve their accuracy; indeed, simple heuristics often lead to better outcomes than more complicated computation methods. In part, it is difficult to outperform simple approaches because they are less subject to parameter estimation errors (Elliott and Timmermann 2008: 49; Gigerenzer and Brighton 2009; Makridakis and Hibon 2000).

That macroeconomic and technological forecasts are frequently wrong is an indisputable fact. This critique is in no way limited to the field of economics: political scientists and sociologists fail in exactly the same way. Political scientists did not foresee the fall of the Iron Curtain in 1989, nor did they predict the Arab Spring in 2011. Sociologists in the 1950s had no clue that family structures would change the way they did in the half-century to come, and descriptions of future social and cultural developments recorded in the 1960s are as bounded by their times as technological forecasts. This is not because any one forecasting method is faulty. Rather, the lesson forecasts teach us is that it is impossible to predict the future. Anyone claiming that the social sciences should be able to do so is, at the very best, laboring under an illusion. Society and the economy are endlessly complex, and the future is open: truly, hardly anything can be foreseen. The failure of forecasts only reveals the hubris of those who claim it is possible to predict future states of the social and economic world.

WHY PREDICTIONS FAIL

Forecasting institutes are not blind to this problem, and they analyze their own predictions after the fact in order to gain insight into the differences between those predictions and what really happened. They often defend their track records by referring to the statistical error margins mentioned above. Forecasts, they remind the world, "are no prophecies, they are conditional statements on probabilities" (Nierhaus 2011: 25) and should be read as such. Some scholars, however, object strongly to this line of argument. Their response to high failure rates is more radical: they question the very legitimacy of macroeconomic forecasts and even contend that they should be done away with entirely (Antholz 2006: 26).

Research on the causes of the high failure rates of economic forecasts emerged almost at the same time as forecasting itself, in the early twentieth century. Austrian economists and philosophers took a particularly strong interest in this topic, and as early as 1928, Oskar Morgenstern argued that economic forecasting was naïve. Morgenstern declared it impossible to predict economic development, in part because forecasts create expectations that alter the conditions they assume, which renders them meaningless (Morgenstern 1928: 111). Morgenstern also observed that information regarding the causal factors affecting the economy is always necessarily incomplete, since economic processes are irregular and historically unique. The economic models that underlie forecasts inevitably lack complexity, ignoring or overlooking important causal factors. Later, Morgenstern argued that general equilibrium theory is based on the assumption of perfect foresight, meaning foresight up to the end of the world, including every economic event to come. An individual must "not only know exactly the influence of his own transactions on process but also the influence of every other individual and of his own future behavior on that of others" (Morgenstern [1935] 1976: 173). Such assumptions are not only unrealistic, according to Morgenstern: they also imply that the economy is absolutely static.

Fifteen years later, another Austrian, Karl Popper ([1949] 1963: 339) expanded on Morgenstern's observation that forecasting is only possible in isolated, static, and cyclic systems. Popper pointed out that such conditions are rare in nature and nonexistent in modern societies, and that contemporary economic systems are dynamic, interdependent, stochastically multidimensional, and nonlinear. Popper's lecture was directed against Marxist historical prophecies, which he saw as the "relic of an ancient superstition" (336).[8] Today, it reads more like a manifesto against the hubris of social scientists who claim it is possible to predict the economic future.

Yet another Austrian, Friedrich von Hayek (1974), accepted the Nobel Prize in Economics with a speech that also rejected the idea that the future could be foretold. Specifically, he critiqued Keynesian macroeconomics, arguing that the social sciences should not shape society using "scientific" predictions, since such predictions were impossible. This, for Hayek, justified the institutionalization of unfettered markets, but his critique can also be read as an objection to macroeconomic forecasting. To Hayek, predictions "happily proceed on the fiction that the factors which they can measure are the only ones that are relevant" (Hayek 1974: 1).

The literature evaluating the failures of macroeconomic forecasts identifies two types of causes. The first is endogenous; that is, factors related to the forecasting process itself. The second is exogenous; that is, factors related to features of the economy that make its future impossible to foresee.

Data problems are a key endogenous factor identified as a cause of erroneous forecasts. Data are often outdated, since there is necessarily a time lapse between the moment data are gathered and the moment a forecast is made (Hinze 2005: 118). Data may also be misleading or insufficient: GDP may simply miss many economic activities in today's economies, meaning that trying to foresee changes in it may be an unreliable guide for decision-making. Then again, data may be missing, and there "may not even be a consensus about the type of data required for determining the best choice or about the method which should provide such data" (de Laat 2000: 180). This cannot be corrected with more and more timely data, however. The social and economic worlds are so complex and indeterminate that it is impossible to establish models capable of taking all factors into account

(Arrow 2013; Priddat 2013: 10; Priddat 2014)—which is, according to Morgenstern, the condition for accurate forecasts.

Another key endogenous cause of the failure of predictions may be identified in the technical shortcomings of the instruments and methods used, which lead to incorrect assumptions in econometric models. The equations used in these models are very sensitive to changes in the sample period being used; furthermore, the models themselves do not contain a "correct" sample of the historical data (R. Evans 1997: 404). Macroeconomic models also vary greatly in how they take external causal effects into account, such as the impact of public spending on economic growth, known as the multiplier effect. Keynesian models use a factor of 1.6 to account for the multiplier effect, while dynamic stochastic general equilibrium models (DSGE) use a factor of 0.3. The Ricardian equivalence hypothesis assumes that there will be no effect at all, except in the case of a severe financial crisis, when it assumes over-indebtedness will trigger highly pessimistic expectations and uses a negative multiplier (Boyer 2012: charts). It goes without saying that each of these models believes its own assumptions are correct and the others are not. Only historical data can prove any of them right or wrong, and then only if the effect itself can be isolated at all.

The behavior of forecasters is another endogenous factor. Herd behavior is common in the field, as forecasters seek to enhance their credibility by aligning their predictions with those of other research institutes, creating "consensus forecasts." The reason for this may be found in the homogenous intellectual background of forecasters: they work within a shared economic paradigm (R. Evans 2014). In addition, forecasters tend to overestimate the importance of the current moment and shy away from excessively gloomy prognostications, meaning that most forecasts turn out to have been too optimistic (Antholz 2006: 21). Signals that seem obvious in hindsight are ignored, and economic downturns are recognized too late (Kholodilin and Siliverstovs 2009: 213). The failure to recognize the financial crisis of 2008 is the most obvious example of this.

Exogenous factors that help to explain the failure of forecasts include external shocks, such as earthquakes or terror attacks, as well as unexpected political decisions. Most notably in recent years, Nassim Taleb (2010) has argued that the social sciences are not able to predict what he calls black swans: rare and even unique events that have a decisive impact on the world. Predictions, as Morgenstern pointed out, can only be accurate if the world functions as a closed system, or, at the very least, if the future resembles the past to a significant degree. Forecasts that "base their studies on the nonrepeatable past have an expert problem" (Taleb 2010: 147).

The economy is not a mechanistic system. Unlike the material world, it is not governed by physical laws. Models that assume otherwise, for instance, by predicting the future as a continuation of the past and its variations, are inevitably "surprised" by the new behavior of whatever they attempt to predict. Thus, the "efficacy of any probability framework to make accurate predictions is precluded by the uncertainty of whether the future will follow historical precedent" (Chong, Tuckett, and Ruatti 2013: 8). The openness of the future means that probability calculations are a form of fiction in that they are as-if assumptions. Economists like Oskar Morgenstern were aware of this. Keynes, too, was fully alert to the impossibility of scientifically forecasting economic development, along with the fundamental uncertainty of future events, as discussed in Chapter 3. Econometric models that calculate risks cannot account for this uncertainty. They cannot take all influencing factors into account, and may overlook the most important ones. Moreover, in the social world, actors react to the actions of others, and base their own actions on their expectations regarding others' reactions. Effects from such interaction between actors cannot be predicted.

In the field of technological projections there has also been much discussion about what causes these predictions to fail. David Nye (2004) points to unforeseeable changes in technology and the social environment. Consumers also prove technological forecasts inaccurate by finding uses for products very different from the ones innovators imagine. When Thomas Edison invented the phonograph, he intended it as a device for businessmen to record dictations for their secretaries to type. It did not occur to him that its ability to play music would make it far more popular as an entertainment device (Nye 2004: 168). If the actual future uses of a product cannot be predicted, neither can market volume. Additionally, as described in Chapter 8, the symbolic value consumers ascribe to an object may differ greatly from its functional value, and symbolic value is entirely unpredictable. Often, it only emerges once a product is available for purchase and customers are able to interact with it. Technological predictions may also fail because the technologies themselves do not work, as can be observed in the field of medical research, which continually promises breakthroughs in the treatment of major diseases. And as studies on technological path dependencies have shown (David 1985), technological forecasts can also fail because the functional superiority of a product is no guarantee of market success.

Finally, technological predictions fail to imagine actual future technological innovations in part because current conceptions of technological utility lead us to perceive the future simply as a fancier version of the present (Borup et al. 2006: 288; Sturken and Thomas 2004: 7). For this reason, predictions say more about the fears and hopes of the present time than they do about the future. Correctly envisioning the future requires "knowing about technologies that will be discovered in the future. But that very knowledge would almost automatically allow us to start developing those technologies right away. Ergo, we do not know what we will know" (Taleb 2010: 173).[9] From the perspective of organization studies, James March (1995: 436–37) reflects that "organizational futurology is a profession in which reputations are crafted from the excitements of novelty, fear and hope. They are destroyed by the unfolding of experience."

DOING FORECASTING

Throughout the twentieth century, the evolution of economic forecasting technologies has led to ever more complex and refined econometric models. These models have recourse to seemingly endless sources of statistical data, whose availability has grown as national statistical offices and many other organizations conduct longitudinal surveys tracking macroeconomic indicators. Despite the increasing methodological sophistication of forecasts and the substantial resources spent on them, their accuracy has not systematically increased over time (Makridakis and Hibon 2000).

This observation raises a number of questions: if forecasts are not accurate or very general, what makes them credible? And what do they actually accomplish? Why do we continue to fund research institutes that forecast economic and technological developments when we know these forecasts will mostly turn out to be wrong? Finally, given the poor track record of macroeconomic and technological forecasting, how should it be categorized analytically?

Forecasting should be considered as an instrument for the construction of fictional expectations. Forecasts are imaginaries of a future state of the world that help actors pretend the future will be a certain way and thus to find direction in unpredictable situations—to make sense of the world. These imaginaries do not need to be correct to set actors' minds at ease or to help them make decisions—they merely need to be convincing. The credible claim for correctness is a substitute for actual accuracy.

To understand the processes making actors in the economy believe in and use forecasts, it is necessary to examine the actual practices of forecasting, as well as the way forecasts are used in decision-making. A small number of analyses, mostly in the field of science and technology studies, have investigated the epistemic practices of macroeconomic forecasters (R. Evans 1997, 1999, 2007; Holmes 2009, 2014; Reichmann 2011, 2013; Smart 1999). Robert Evans (1997, 1999) and Werner Reichmann (2011, 2013) studied the question of how macroeconomic forecasts are produced through ethnographic observations and interviews with staff researchers at British, German, and Austrian macroeconomic forecasting institutes. Both scholars showed that forecasting is a multilayered process. Macroeconomic forecasts are not an objective and purely mathematical procedure in which a small group of experts applies an econometric model to a set of data. Instead, forecasts are embedded in a discursive process of judgment and interpretation that takes place among a set of diverse actors in the economy.

Forecasters begin by producing "draft forecasts" that run an econometric model on various indicators such as GDP, inflation, and unemployment. "Draft forecasts" are produced in specialized departments, then brought together and subjected to a series of discursive exchanges among researchers with different expertise, and are subsequently taken through multiple revisions. Initially, these exchanges take place within the forecasting institute: department heads meet to discuss their results and adjust them to one another, a process called fine-tuning. The term itself neatly describes "how economic forecasters adjust, readjust, and re-re-adjust their results until the overall-forecast is a 'round image'" (Reichmann 2013: 869–70). If a calculated result appears wrong, parameters are readjusted until the outcomes appear plausible. It is interesting to note that this "calibration" of models means that implausible outcomes from econometric models do not lead experts to change the model; instead, they change the parameters they enter into the model. This differs from physics, in which parameters are a given and cannot be changed to fit outcomes (Fourcade 2009).

The calibration of a forecast is an inter-subjective process that takes place through exchanges among forecasters as well as through intense communication with representatives of the object being studied (the economy), as well as with policy-makers. Once they have met with one another, economic forecasters meet with actors in the economic field, such as representatives of federal banks and ministries, the managers of big corporations, and policymakers. They exchange ideas, share new insights, and discuss problems

(Reichmann 2013: 863). About a week before its publication, forecasters meet with policy-makers to discuss the forecast they are working on and check its plausibility and assumptions. More broadly, the work of forecasting is "characterized by extensive participation in a wide range of professional networks" (R. Evans 2007: 691). Forecasters, politicians, and representatives of firms come together at talks, meetings, and conferences; in their formal and informal exchanges, they collect information, trade assessments, swap stories, present plans and ideas, and gauge one another's emotions. The world of macroeconomic foresight can be seen as a complex meshing of different but overlapping communities. In these communities, forecasters "foretalk" (Gibson 2012) the results of their forecasts.

Observing the practices of forecasters reveals that their work is divided between a "front stage" and a "backstage." "Whereas the front stage of the forecasters is mainly dominated by quantitative data and numerical results, the epistemic process itself is dominated by discursive action between forecasters and 'the economy'" (Reichmann 2011: 8). Technically, the discursive process is necessary because econometric models are inconclusive: the performance of most econometric models cannot be determined ahead of time, so it is impossible to know which model will produce the most accurate forecast. Not only that, different forecasters using the same models produce different predictions. In the face of all this inconclusiveness, professional networks are a source of expertise that helps "overcome the uncertainties of econometric models and help people judge between models" (Reichmann 2013: 863). Forecasters, by participating in these networks, gain access to evaluations that bring in a "judgmental component which, in the final analysis, determines what the forecast will be" (R. Evans 1997: 426).[10]

Given the indeterminacy of their models, it is the insights forecasters gain from their discursive exchanges that ultimately give them confidence in their own forecasts. It is therefore most accurate to say that macroeconomic models *support* rather than produce forecasting (R. Evans 1997: 426). This observation should also serve as a caution against the claim that econometric models are performative.

Since forecasts cannot be reliably accurate, the obvious justification for the process of "epistemic participation" described above—that it is a way to increase their accuracy—makes little sense. After all, the addition of more and more varied sources of information and expertise does not make the future any less open. By including many economic actors in the production of forecasts does, however, increase their credibility. If nothing else, forecasts include assessments by the very practitioners who use them to make decisions. Exchanges with politicians and representatives of firms inform these actors about the ambiguities and uncertainties in forecasts, and keep them apprised of why forecasters are predicting certain future developments. What interests actors in the economic field "is not so much the specific forecast numbers . . . but the narrative that surrounds them and the policy analysis that informs the narrative" (R. Evans 2007: 695).

The exchange of information, opinions, and expectations has a stabilizing effect. It distributes knowledge, aligns expectations within the field, and raises awareness of assessments made by respected members of the community. Nobody can know what will actually happen in the economy, but the distribution of assessments helps to anchor expectations in judgments that take others' considerations into account. The "ecology of discourses fosters the assimilation of 'feelings,' 'intuition,' 'discretion,' and 'judgment' reaching into the reserves of 'experience'" (Holmes 2009: 401). As John Dewey maintains (Dewey [1922] 1957: 205–6), "the object of foresight is . . . to ascertain the meaning of present activities and to secure, so far as possible, a present activity with a unified meaning." When different assessments are confronted with one another, opinions and evaluations form, eventually contributing the confidence necessary to make decisions in conditions of uncertainty. A parallel can be drawn with Harrison White's (1981) market theory, according to which producers track each other's product prices and volumes, and use this information to adjust their production schedules. Just as producers cannot foresee consumer demand, economic actors cannot foresee the future. Just like producers, however, they can orient their decisions to the expectations of the other actors in their field.

Participating in the discursive process of the epistemic community is thus useful for forecasters and economic decision-makers alike: for forecasters, anchoring their predictions in expectations that already exist "in the economy" makes their forecasts more legitimate. For decision-makers, heads of companies, and politicians alike, knowing about assessments of the state of the economy and predictions of how it will develop provides tools for imagining a specific future as a setting for their decisions while increasing their confidence and the legitimacy of their decisions.

In this sense, epistemic participation is itself a coordinating device in the economy and an instrument of imagination: when shared among economic actors and justified through narratives, forecasts can become focal points for expectations upon which decisions can be based. By reciprocally affirming which expectations should be given credence, uncertainty is communicatively and communally suspended. By continuously telling stories about the future toward which they are headed, economic actors constitute the present future, and cognitive orientation is produced (Lane and Maxfield 2005: 12; Priddat 2012: 259; Tavory and Eliasoph 2013: 909).

A similar conclusion can be drawn with regard to technological projections, whose methods share the same emphasis on consensus building. The Delphi method, for example, is an exercise in consensus creation, while scenario analyses foster cognitive alignment by providing an overview of the range of possibilities imaginable for technological futures (Andersson 2013). The direct aim of such methods is to create joint cognitive perspectives, at least of the spectrum of alternatives seen as possible within a technological field. This does not mean that there is one perspective upon which all actors converge; rather, it implies that actors can locate and build their own perspective in a structured field of expectations. Though the future cannot be known, it is possible to know what other actors think about it, in particular which outcomes they deem plausible. This awareness brings some measure of serenity to actors who must make decisions in conditions of uncertainty.[11] From a broader sociological perspective, as noted earlier in this book with regard to other aspects of the economy, Emile Durkheim's analysis of the beliefs that emerge in totemistic societies from ritualized clan assemblies can serve as an informative analogy. As clan members—or, in this case, members of the professional network in which forecasters operate—come into contact with one other, their social interactions shape and reinforce their beliefs.[12]

THE ROLE OF FORECASTS

Although forecasts gain their credibility from the communicative structures in which they are produced, why forecasts are taken at all seriously remains a puzzle, especially given their disappointing record. The status of forecasters seems to stem in part from singular predictions of important economic developments that turn out to be correct. One example of this is the economist Nouriel Roubini, who predicted the financial crash in 2007. Ever since, Roubini's predictions have enjoyed special authority. Another source of status is the presentation style of analyst reports (Giorgi and Weber 2015). As Reichmann (2015) shows for German and Austrian forecasting institutes, the reputation of forecasting institutes has its roots either in the academic reputation of its founders or in a close connection to the state during the founding period.

Understanding the authority of forecasts in a more general sense must take their function within the economy into account: unreliable as forecasts may be, they are also indispensable to economic decision-making. Actors need them because they need to act in ways that appear nonrandom, despite the future's uncertainty. Forecasts "are impossible because the future is uncertain and non-transparent and they are indispensable because many of our actions are future-oriented and thus cannot be conducted without any assumptions about the future" (Rothschild 2005: 125, own translation). This implies that when economic and political decision-makers act based on forecasts, they are playing a kind of make-believe: they are pretending that forecasts depict the future present.[13] In the terminology of Pierre Bourdieu, the credibility of forecasts is based on an *illusio:* namely, a belief in the meaning of the explicit and implicit rules governing the social field of the economy. For this *illusio* to work, the inaccuracy of forecasts must be overlooked. What is relevant here is not actual accuracy, but the momentary belief in accuracy.

Forecasts help actors make sense of seemingly chaotic or incomprehensibly complex situations. And they do more than simply orient actors: they also lend legitimacy, allowing for what is known as defensive decision-making. If a decision has been made based on a widely shared forecast, its potential failure can be justified by pointing to the expectations that prevailed at the time it was made. Responsibility for the decision's outcome is delegated to the forecast, effectively insuring the decision-maker against the personal consequences of a decision that turns out to be wrong. In this way, widely agreed-upon forecasts encourage isomorphism in economic fields, operating as conventions that homogenize decisions.

In addition to providing a consensus from which decision-makers can safely operate, forecasts at the same time support novelty and thus contribute directly to the dynamics of capitalist economies. This is especially true of technological projections, which can help open minds, raising possibilities that might otherwise have gone undetected. "Scenarios provide a means of distancing oneself from present arrangements and thus in some circumstances enabling a space for criticism" (Brown, Rappert, and Webster 2000: 12). From this perspective, technological projections are discovery and innovation tools, providing "fictive scripts" that help motivate actors and mobilize resources to learn whether these scripts will come true

(March 1995). By the same token, econometric forecasting models open up the future by helping to detect presumed causalities, which make it possible to evaluate the impact of possible change, revealing deviations from which actors can recognize opportunities and alter their strategies.[14]

Finally, forecasts influence the future directly because they shape strategies. Macroeconomic and technological forecasts influence investment decisions. After all, their claim to legitimacy lies "in the claim to represent a basis for action and influence" (Andersson 2013: 7). Foresight exercises in innovation processes "are collective processes of future thinking toward the definition of priorities" (de Laat 2000: 181). And because they suggest trajectories for decision-makers to choose, forecasts are political.

THE POLITICS OF EXPECTATIONS: FORECASTS AS POLITICS

It is commonly accepted among macroeconomic forecasters that their predictions affect market behavior, although they do not necessarily know how (Reichmann 2011: 4). Outwardly, at least, they often perceive this influence as a problem or an embarrassment, one that poses a threat to their legitimacy. By contrast, influencing the future is one of the stated intentions of technological forecasters. Typically, they see the future "as a quasi object, as something that could be known, controlled and engineered" (Andersson 2013: 4). Technological forecasts are often cast as helping to build the future: "The best way to invent the future is to predict it—if you can get enough people to believe your prediction, that is" (Barlow 2004: 177).

The influence of projections and knowledge on social processes is an established topic in sociology. Robert Merton's (1957) notion of self-fulfilling and self-defeating prophecies, as well as the concept of performativity (Callon 1998b; MacKenzie 2006), are ways of describing this influence. The self-fulfilling or performative effects of technological forecasts are often demonstrated with the example of "Moore's law." This "law" is named after the engineer and entrepreneur Gordon Moore, who predicted in 1965 that the processor speed of semiconductors would double every twenty-four months. That his prediction has been confirmed by technological advances over the past fifty years does not prove that Moore could foresee the future, but rather that belief in his prediction organized activity in the semiconductor industry, which directed its efforts toward achieving the progress he predicted. Firms setting goals in the semiconductor industry have taken Moore's law as a benchmark, while industries downstream plan for the future with the expectation that processor speed will indeed increase at the rate Moore predicted.

This is one example among many of the practical effects of technological forecasting: the fictional expectations they support may mobilize investments in the development of certain technologies while causing actors to abandon potential alternatives. Prophecies do not need to be right or wrong to affect the future: it is sufficient for them to inspire belief and action by a powerful actor (Reichmann 2011: 4). This opens the way to using forecasts to deliberately influence expectations. Politicians and firms can make strategic use of the effects of forecasts by advocating forecasts that inspire decisions from which they expect to benefit. As discussed in Chapter 7, researchers show different levels of confidence with regard to an innovation's potential for success when speaking to the general public and when communicating with peers in their research community. To gain access to funding, which is an important practical outcome of technological projections, researchers may deliberately overstate their case in the public arena.

Macroeconomic forecasts, on the other hand, while they can influence the future, should not be seen as performing it. A performative macroeconomic model would be one whose predictive capacity increased with its use, meaning forecasts based on it would become more and more accurate over time. As we have seen, this is not the case. Because of the economy's uncertainty, the effects of economic forecasts on it are largely unpredictable. However, forecasts can influence and legitimate decisions, meaning that they can have an impact. This implies that they can also become politicized. This leads to what might be called reflexive behavior among forecasters, who may try to anticipate the practical consequences of their projections and adjust them accordingly. As Kholodilin and Siliverstovs (2009: 213) remark, "forecasters have a significant responsibility" because their assessments may influence the economy—and this "responsibility" may in turn influence forecasts. As shown above, forecasts are never "blind" applications of an econometric model; they are always mixed with judgments. The fact that macroeconomic forecasts are consistently overoptimistic may not be attributable to forecasters' inability to foresee economic downturns—at least not exclusively. Their tendency to look on the bright side may also be due to their expectation that predicting a downturn makes it more likely one will occur, and should thus be avoided.

Rating agencies, which provide forecasts in the form of predictions of how likely a borrower is to default on a debt, hesitate to publish negative outlooks in bullish markets. As we now know, on the eve of the financial crisis of 2008, the ratings of important classes of financial products were far too optimistic (MacKenzie 2012; Rona-Tas and Hiss 2011). In an effort to gain them broader acceptance as investment vehicles, CDOs were given triple-A ratings despite the fact that they included many highly risky mortgages. The actual risks they carried were vastly underestimated. Shortly before their collapse, though, rating agencies may have continued rating these derivatives with high investment grades to hedge against the potential negative effects of a downgrading, as well. These ratings may have been too optimistic from the beginning, but in financial markets in which value depends chiefly on expectations, downgrading comes with the risk of product dumping, which creates the very scenario being predicted (Pénet and Mallard 2014).

Macroeconomic forecasts are also political in that they are a key source of information for economic policy-makers and for the legitimation of political decisions. Although they do not predict an unalterable future that will unfold like a weather event, they offer indicators that can be used to put together economic policies, which influence the business cycle. For this reason, Keynes objected to the idea that the future of the business cycle could be determined by investigating the past. "I do not regard [the business cycle] as something unalterable in its broad outlines and independent of policy. I think it could be largely eliminated and that it certainly depends on such things as the policy of the Federal Reserve Board more than anything else" (Keynes 1925, quoted in W. Friedman 2009: 71).

If this is the case, forecasts can be used as instruments that direct economic policy decisions; their influence on the future is therefore to be located in the political actions they trigger. In a decentralized market economy, however, their influence may be even more direct. In his *General Theory,* Keynes ([1936] 1964) argued that macroeconomic outcomes depend on the contingent optimism or pessimism of the business community. In other words, forecasts themselves can be a kind of economic policy in that by influencing expectations about the economy's future, they influence decisions about investment and consumption.

If forecasts cannot objectively predict the future and the projections articulated in forecasts help to shape that future, then it is clear that forecasts are inherently political. Even without intending to deceive (Harrington 2009),[15] firms may promote certain visions of the future in an attempt to gain from the decisions their projections encourage.[16] Projections, if believed, may shape the future. There is clear empirical evidence that fictional expectations are used this way in technological forecasting. Forecasts are used to achieve goals, such as obtaining venture capital (de Laat 2000: 182). The forecasts employed to obtain funding for technological development often take the form of promissory stories, as Sophie Mützel (2010) shows in her study of narrative competition among biotech companies (see Chapter 7). Companies tell positive stories about the future prospects of technologies in which they have a stake. The decisions prompted by these stories promote certain trajectories "and reduce the 'value' of trajectories of others" (de Laat 2000: 192). Clearly the dynamic of the capitalist economy is (also) driven by the deliberate influencing of macroeconomic forecasts and technological projections. Capitalism is, in important ways, a struggle over whose expectations are the most credible.

That macroeconomic forecasts take political interests into account has also been confirmed empirically. Political interests can usually be easily identified: economic actors and policy-makers, who fund forecasters, seek high growth rates, low inflation, and low unemployment. By the same token, forecasters understandably try to avoid provoking negative reactions from their financial backers by interfering with their "expectation governance." Several studies of the International Monetary Fund (IMF), for example, have concluded that its forecasts are systematically overoptimistic: they overestimate output growth and underestimate inflation. The error term increases with the size of the IMF loan a country receives—predictably, in a way that justifies the IMF's lending decision (Dreher, Marchesi, and Vreeland 2007: 3). The more heavily a country is indebted to the IMF, the more pronounced the underestimation of inflation rates is likely to be. Furthermore, these empirical studies show that the closer a country's ties to the United States and other G-7 countries that dominate the IMF, the more positive the IMF's forecast is likely to be. Moreover, countries voting in line with the United States in the UN General Assembly receive lower inflation forecasts (6). Direct political influence has been documented, too: in the 1990s, when the Republicans controlled the U.S. House of Representatives, the annual budget forecasts of the Congressional Budget Office (CBO) predicted that if taxes were cut, budget deficits would grow. The Republicans, outraged by this projection, demanded to know whether the budget office had factored in the stimulus to investments that tax cuts would produce, which would improve growth enough to offset revenue lost by the state through the tax cuts. The CBO had not; they had used "static" modelling, and the Republicans insisted that they go back and redo the models with dynamic assumptions built into them—in other words, they forced the Congressional Budget Office to change its methodology and reimagine the future (J. L. Campbell and Pedersen 2014: 252). Forecasts are thus part of the governmentality (Foucault) of modern societies.

States and state agencies are not the only institutions pursuing political agendas through forecasts. Private interests pursue profit goals through projections that seek to shape expectations about future economic and technological development. Indeed, one might contend that "the nature of the political contexts is a far more significant explaining factor [for the way in which scenarios are built] than the substance of the models themselves" (de Man 1987: 119, cited in de Laat 2000: 183). This kind of influence is possible because forecasts cannot anticipate the future present, which also explains why so many plausible econometric models exist, each predicting different outcomes. As shown above, this requires that forecasts be "adjusted" and leaves much leeway for political influence and discretion. At the same time, however, organizations such as the IMF and economic forecasting institutes maintain public and professional credibility through scientific integrity. Forecasters "call themselves and feel like scientists . . . and do all to ensure their scientific independence" (Reichmann 2011: 2). Forecasts are taken seriously only if they appear to be free of corrupting influences. The importance of maintaining credibility under public and professional scrutiny helps to counterbalance the temptation to misuse economic expertise for the sake of political interests, although one might argue that all this really implies is that any attempts to influence forecasts for political reasons will be hidden.

Forecasts are also part of the governmentality of modern societies in that they may contribute to the shaping of social life forms. As discussed in Chapter 7, technological development ensures economic competitiveness in a dynamic context. More than that, though, technical choices implicitly involve a hypothesis on how, socio-technically, the future will be organized. Technological projections "define radically different worlds for which neither science (including economics) nor future studies is able to propose selection criteria" (de Laat 2000: 202). Fictional expectations in the economy must therefore also be evaluated in terms of the normative ideals they convey. In a democratic polity, such evaluation should take place in the public sphere.

CONCLUSION

Each year, a great deal of money is spent to predict economic and technological futures. But most predictions fail. A century of econometric forecasting of macroeconomic indicators and the development of many quantitative and qualitative techniques to predict technological progress has not brought us any closer to predicting the future.

So much is invested in an activity that regularly fails to deliver what it promises because forecasts serve functions that are different from the ones they proclaim to fulfill. Forecasts are only failures if we define them as attempts to predict the future. As an "expectation technology" (van Lente 1993) they are highly successful, helping to coordinate the economy by orienting and justifying decisions that must be made despite the future's inescapable uncertainty, and protecting decision-makers when they make choices that, in hindsight, turn out to be wrong. In this way, forecasts are coordination devices for the actions that produce the future. Furthermore, they open spaces in which new possibilities may be imagined, painting counterfactual realities and telling stories of the future that contribute to the process of creative destruction underlying the dynamics of capitalist economies. Just as important, because they may be used to justify decisions in the present, they participate in the politics of expectations. In short, the latent function of forecasts is to help build credible fictional expectations.

Forecasts are instruments that help create imaginaries of future states of the world; they are narratives that describe imagined futures. As such, they instill confidence in conditions of uncertainty. By making claims about a future that does not yet exist, they help actors make decisions about it. Although they do so with much more caution and scrutiny than the average reader of a novel, "readers" of forecasts suspend disbelief and treat forecasts as (probabilistic) representations of a future present. The narratives laid out in forecasts transform uncertainty into a fictitious certainty contributing to decision-making. A successful forecast is therefore a convincing one—not necessarily an accurate one. Convincing narratives of the future in the form of forecasts and technological projections are the tools actors need to make decisions that would otherwise seem random (Priddat 2014: 260). By engaging in this willing suspension of disbelief, actors make forecasts part of their reality; the judgment that forecasts make possible has tangible effects in the economy.

Credible forecasts are created through an interactive process that involves sophisticated calculations, as well as multiple individual judgments from a diverse group of actors, and the observation of other forecasts. This process of mutual observation helps to coordinate economic activities by at least partially aligning expectations.

Because neither the future nor the effect forecasts have on it can be known ahead of time, forecasts can become an instrument in the competitive struggle that characterizes capitalist markets—in other words, they play an important part in the politics of expectations. To maintain their competitive edge, firms build technological visions in an effort to develop investment strategies and to vie for the attention and trust of other economic or political actors. To strengthen trends from which they will profit, financial investors use forecasts in their battle to convince other investors that their outlook on the stock market is the right one. Politicians seeking reelection have an interest in optimistic macroeconomic outlooks, if only because they hope favorable forecasts will exert a positive influence on the economy, or at least on the sentiment of future economic development, and thus increase their chances at reelection. Forecasts shape expectations and determine decisions; inevitably then, they play an important role in struggles for profit and power.

Economists' awareness of the limits of their predictions tends to vary. Economists in the early twentieth century, especially those in the Austrian and Keynesian traditions, deemed it impossible to predict the future of the economy. But while many economists are still conscious of the limits of predictions, these early objections to forecasting have largely faded into the background. Today, a great deal of attention and money is devoted to improving technique, distracting us from the early insight that predicting the social world is impossible. The proliferation and honing of techniques makes accurate forecasting seem just one step away.

Within the field of economics, a few dissenting voices have called for more moderation in claims about how possible it is to predict the future. "The very failure of most predictions in the area of macroeconomics and finance theory over the last decade should itself prompt questions and render attractive this downgrading of the status of apparently precise predictive models" (Bronk, forthcoming). More realism seems advisable: if the social world cannot be predicted, perhaps social scientists should refrain from attempting to do so. At the same time, however, forecasts, together with the general claim—however outlandish—that the social world is predictable, serve important functions in the operation of the economy. We need projections to justify decisions; if economic actions are to be coordinated, projections about them must at least in part be shared. By setting actors at ease about the uncertainty of their decisions, and by creating imaginaries of novelty, forecasts contribute in significant ways to the dynamics of capitalist economies. Seen in this light, their accuracy or lack thereof is of little, or at least secondary, concern. An inaccurate forecast will merely be replaced by a new one.

This, of course, leaves economists with the thankless task of defending the claim that economic events are predictable against immense empirical and theoretical evidence to the contrary. They must dispel all doubt and disbelief, even in the wake of financial crises such as the crash of 2008, which made blatantly clear just how wrong the expectations of experts could be. And they must field embarrassing questions from world leaders. In 2009, the Queen of England asked, "Why had nobody noticed that the credit crunch was on its way?" An honest reply would have been "because nobody can predict the future, but we must pretend that we can." That answer, of course, was never given: if forecasts are to serve their true purpose, their fictional character must remain hidden. In audiences with Her Majesty, and when communicating with the public at large, most economists chose to suspend disbelief and continue behaving as if it were possible to predict the future, to claim that truly precise forecasting instruments are just over the horizon. The failure of prediction is rarely taken as an opportunity to reflect upon whether or not it is actually possible, but instead as a justification for building even more sophisticated models. Karl Popper ([1949] 1963) was right when he declared that prediction of the future is prophecy, not science. But in a world characterized by uncertainty, it would have been even more germane to ask why we need prophecy and just how we use it.

TEN

ECONOMIC THEORY

The Crystal Ball of Calculative Devices

> The model is a self-contained construct, which can be interpreted as
> a description of an imaginary but credible world.
>
> —ROBERT SUGDEN

ACTORS MUST THINK imaginaries of the future are credible if they are
to use them to make decisions. Credible imaginaries must not only paint a
realistic-seeming picture of the future state of the world, they must also assess the causal mechanisms that lead from the present into the future they
depict. Economic theories are a crucial instrument for building expectations
of the future, because they designate causal relationships and measure the
suitability of different paths to achieving desired goals. Theories break the
unreachable, intangible future into seemingly calculable, accessible units:
result R is caused by the properties $A_1 \ldots A_n$; the relationship between R
and $A_1 \ldots A_n$ is established by a causal mechanism through which the two
interact. Theories that claim to predict the future based on the identification of causalities shape and justify actors' expectations about future developments. Just like forecasts, economic theories are instruments used to
create expectations.

Theories may be more or less general: the most general of them proclaim
that universal laws underlie natural or social events, and identify those laws;
some are models that state causalities in specialized circumstances; and some
are paradigms, sets of beliefs that are used as lenses for viewing reality and
justifying certain responses to a situation. The natural sciences progressed
through the discovery of general scientific laws and along the way became a
model for the social sciences. Particularly in the nineteenth century, it was a
widely held belief that social laws analogous to natural laws could be identified, and that once identified, these laws could be a means for the rational
organization of society, leading to scientific and social progress. Auguste

Comte's law of the three stages of human development or Karl Marx's scientific laws of historical evolution are examples of this positivism.

Today, most disciplines in the social sciences are much more cautious about the existence of general laws in the social world, and most advocate more limited and historically specific claims. These are often expressed through concepts such as "ideal types," "mechanisms," "middle range theories," "processes," or "analytical narratives." The discipline of economics remains the great exception: it continues to embrace an epistemological model proceeding from the idea that general laws govern the economy. Since the eighteenth century, economists have referred to generalized statements about behavioral traits and causal factors as "economic laws," which they assume hold universally true. That the discipline refers to the "law" of supply and demand, the "law" of decreasing marginal utility, or Say's "law" is indicative of the way it perceives itself and its observations about the world. Historians of science have observed that the field of economics has modeled itself on the field of physics: its notion of equilibrium is borrowed from Newtonian physics, for example (Mirowski 1989: 17). Not without Freudian undertones, Albert Hirschman (1991: 155) described the "physics envy" of economists.

But while the discipline perceives its theories and models as positivist, is this perception an accurate one? In recent years, economists and their use of theories and models have been examined by sociologists, historians, philosophers, and anthropologists, as well as by economists themselves (Backhouse 2010; Fourcade 2009; Mäki 2002; Mirowski 1989). To borrow Niklas Luhmann's terminology, these analyses provide a second-order perspective, observing and analyzing the theories and epistemologies economists use. Sociological and historical studies have found cultural and historical variance among economic approaches (Fourcade 2009; Steiner 2006), as well as the intermingling of economic theories with politics (Blyth 2002; Hall 1993; Mirowski and Plehwe 2009). Anthropologists and scholars from the sociology of science have also scrutinized the practices of economists (R. Evans 1999; Holmes 2009; Knorr Cetina and Bruegger 2002; Muniesa 2014) and found effects of economic theories on the reality they describe (Callon 1998b; MacKenzie and Millo 2003; Steiner 2006).[1] Although they do so from quite different perspectives, each of these analyses questions the existence of objective economic laws.

The question of how theories, models and paradigms contribute to actors' expectations regarding future states of the world has received only limited attention in contemporary discussions of economic knowledge. Like forecasts, predictive theories can be understood as instruments for the formation of expectations. Applied to concrete decision-making situations, they prompt actors to form imaginaries of future states that will be reached through their decisions. In doing so, actors identify "good reasons" and gain the confidence they need to make decisions despite the unknowability of the future.

As with forecasts, the expectations created by theories are fictional: rather than depicting a future present, they help actors pretend they can foresee future outcomes. The expectations created through economic theories are fictional for four reasons. First, in epistemological terms, theories and models are analogical apperceptions; they are a means of mentally assimilating ideas about the world by ordering them analogically with other ideas a person already possesses, but they can never reach the world of "things-in-themselves" (Kant [1787] 1911). Second, and relatedly, theories and models necessarily reduce the complexity of the factual world, meaning that the accuracy of predictions derived from them depends on the assumptions they make and the parameters they use, which simply cannot exhaustively account for all of reality, and whose degree of validity can only be assessed after the fact. Third, predictive theories are fictional in an ontological sense. They are built by observing past events. Economic processes, however, are open and nonlinear, meaning that future outcomes are not already entailed in information from the past. Finally, theories and models are reflexive: they influence the behavior of their objects, thus changing the causality of the situation they intend to project—but not predictably so.[2] Predictive theories can be compared to crystal balls, not in the sense that they show us the future, but in the sense that we gaze into them in the hopes of catching a glimpse of the future, and instead see a vision of ourselves reflected back at us.

THEORIES AS FICTIONS

The idea that scientific theories are a kind of fiction is not new and stems from a problem in the philosophy of science.[3] As Immanuel Kant so famously observed, it is impossible to obtain direct knowledge of the world because knowledge is an a priori conception the human mind applied to its sense impressions, and is acquired only through analogical apperceptions. Since no impressions can be pure or fundamental, no impression can exist unmediated by cognitive structuring. Ideas and concepts are imaginaries constructed in the mind, based on the sensual perception of the empirical world and expressed by analogy.[4] Knowledge cannot extend to things-in-themselves. Kant was not being fanciful when he spoke of "heuristic fictions" ([1787] 1911: 503) in his reflections on the theoretical concepts guiding our perception of empirical reality. For Kant, this is true of all concepts, not only scientific ones: according to his understanding, the organic body, God, freedom, and eternity are all fictions as well. Since there can be no direct access to things-in-themselves, we can only behave *as if* concepts were faithful representations of reality.

Kant's idea that the world as it appears to us is a creation of our own minds was taken up by many philosophers in the Kantian tradition, including Hans Vaihinger, whose work was especially influential in the early twentieth century. In his *The Philosophy of As-If* (1924), Vaihinger proceeded from the Kantian notion that no direct access to the object of investigation is possible. This makes it necessary to generate categories that are used *as if* they faithfully mirrored the phenomena observed. For Vaihinger, categories are "simple representational constructions for the purpose of apperceiving what is given" (31). He calls these constructions "fictions." Categories do not capture reality in any direct way; indeed, "as analogical fictions they cannot provide us with any true knowledge" (30).[5] Thus, we "can only say that objective phenomena can be regarded *as if* they behaved in such and such a way, and there is absolutely no justification for assuming any dogmatic attitude and changing the 'as if' into a 'that'" (31). For Vaihinger, as for Kant, as-if constructions are not limited to scientific theory: when we act, we must proceed *as if* ethical certainty were possible; in religious practice, we must behave *as if* there were a God.

Theoretical constructs use "consciously false assumptions"; that is, theoretical terms that are known to be wrong. Their use in science is justified because they have proven to be useful instruments in the scientific discovery process, crucial to ordering empirical phenomena.[6] At the same time, the use of categories brings an element of creativity into the scientific discovery process (Bronk, forthcoming: 7; Ricoeur 2002).

Vaihinger takes an instrumentalist approach to epistemology, pointing to the use of consciously false assumptions in the natural sciences.[7] His theory of the *as-if* is not limited to the natural sciences, however, and he discusses the use of scientific fictions in psychology, political science, economics, and law as well. In economics, he uses the example of Adam Smith's assumption that all action is dictated by egoism. This is not a hypothesis that can be examined empirically (it would be invalidated immediately, since examples of actors behaving unselfishly abound). Rather, it is a heuristic conceptual proposition, a fiction many have found useful for advancing scientific progress. By proceeding from the fiction that all action is egoistic, Smith "succeeded in bringing the whole of political economy into an ordered system" (Vaihinger 1924: 20).

Following Vaihinger, scientific fictions allow us to treat an object of scientific inquiry *as if* it had certain properties. Theories both simplify reality and create imaginary properties of the objects they describe. No theory can take into account all the relevant causal factors present in reality—they can only pretend to represent it. This does not prevent actors from using theories *as if* they did fully represent reality, however. The behavioral assumptions used in game theory models, for example, do not hold true when it comes to the actual decisions of actors in the economy: in reality, actors' behaviors are much more varied. But by making assumptions about others' behavior and the strategic options available, and by acting on the assumption of predictability, these models nonetheless orient decisions in the economy. The behavioral assumptions of game theory are "legitimated errors" (Vaihinger 1924: 100) that help us build convictions about the future effects of present decisions.

Vaihinger's suggestion that scientific theories, concepts, and classifications should be understood as fictions expresses what Niklas Luhmann has called a "doubling of reality" (see Chapter 4). Reality exists both as the real world, which is not directly accessible to human cognition, and through categories in scientific theories. This means that the "model world is not so much an abstraction from reality as a parallel reality" (Sugden 2000: 25).[8] In their doubling of reality, scientific theories are comparable to literary fiction, which also constructs a new reality that does not (fully) correspond to the real world. Economic models and theories, like literary fiction, have a broken relationship to reality (see Chapter 4).

The concept of heuristic fictions resembles other conceptualizations used earlier in this book to express the bifurcation between the objective world and our perception of it. To return to the theory of Kendall Walton (1990) discussed in Chapter 4, heuristic fictions can also be understood as make-believe games. Walton sees readers' reception of fictional texts as analogous to a game of make-believe in which participants act *as if* their game were real (Walton 1990: 37). Economists' concepts about the economy can thus be understood as an agreement among themselves to conceptualize it *as if* certain assumptions were valid. For Walton, a proposition is fictional if it is "true in some fictional world or other" (35). In economics, the assumption that actors act egoistically (strive to maximize expected utility) is one such fiction. Other rules can easily be added to this game of make-believe: the idea of equilibrium, the assumption of fixed preferences, or the conjecture that actors use all available information. To be part of the game of economics, one must agree to the rules; in other words, one must agree to reason *as if* the economy worked in the ways economic theory assumes it will.

Although economists make and maintain the rules of economics, anyone who perceives reality through the prism of these rules can take part in the "game," including consultants, managers, politicians, or lobbyists. A network of fictional truths emerges from these assumptions to constitute a universe that cognitively frames the field of the economy to the extent actors in the economy share it (Bareis 2008: 33; Burgdorf 2011: 111; Walton 1990: 17). Under these conditions, fictional truths stimulate the actions of the players of the game, as well as their expectations regarding the actions of other players, their perception of causal relations, and their images of future states of the world. This, of course, does not imply that all actors in the field of the economy agree on the fictional truths advocated by the discipline of economics. It should also be borne in mind that economics is not a homogenous field and that different fictional truths exist at the same time within it.

The notion that predictions are based on fictional assumptions exists in both the economic and the sociological traditions. Milton Friedman (1953) argues in "The Methodology of Positive Economics" that hypotheses in economics, if they are to develop a predictive and in this sense an objective theory, must be based on assumptions "that are widely inaccurate descriptive representations of reality" (14). The notion of *as-if* is central to Friedman's approach, even if he does not specifically refer to Vaihinger's work. Like Vaihinger, he argues that economic theory is correct to use as-if assumptions: it is useful, for example, to assume that firms behave *as if* they were rationally maximizing their expected returns and *as if* they knew all relevant functions of cost and demand. That these assumptions are empirically false and thus fictional—no businessman can make all the calculations necessary to arrive at the optimal decision—does not alter their utility in the development of economic theory. Economic theory is thus based on consciously false assumptions about empirical reality, which are justified as long as they "work"; that is, as long as the predictions about the economy derived from them are sufficiently accurate.[9] To paraphrase Friedman, economists must theorize as if rationality and competitive markets existed. And if these assumptions do not lead to sufficiently accurate predictions, then new—and just as fictional—assumptions should be applied.[10]

The idea that theories are fictions, make-believe games, or as-if assumptions also exists in the sociological tradition, which describes them as forms of collective representations. As discussed earlier, Emile Durkheim ([1912] 1965) describes how totemistic societies organize their identities and social lives by dividing the world into the strictly separate spheres of the sacred and the profane. They ascribe characteristics from one or the other sphere to the objects they use—for example, of purity or impurity—and then behave as if these objects actually possessed these characteristics. Interestingly enough, Durkheim takes the idea that the sociology of knowledge should be based on the notion of classification from Kant (Lukes 1973).[11] Depending on its categorization, an object may take on radically different qualities, affecting how it can be used, how it is valued, and how it can influence the real world. Objects do not determine theoretical representations: classification systems determine objects.

As discussed earlier in the book, theories about the social world are also not simply representations of an underlying objective reality, for the reason that human actors, in contrast to the objects observed in the natural sciences, change their behavior based on their knowledge of the observations made of them. This influences the causal relations theories claim to identify. In other words, theories are transformative. The social world changes with the theories used to describe it. This phenomenon, known as reflexivity (Giddens 1984), is paramount in the social world. In the 1930s, Oskar Morgenstern observed that "atoms [do not] need to make assumptions about the behavior and conditions of other atoms" ([1935] 1976: 175). Nor do they change their behavior based on the insights of theoretical physicists. Humans, on the other hand, are spurred to action by theories. For Morgenstern, reflexivity meant that economic forecasts were impossible to make. It also implies that theories cannot predict the future.[12]

THE CREDIBILITY OF THEORIES

The epistemological approach discussed above sees scientific theories as a type of fiction, as cognitive constructions rather than mirrors of the empirical world they conceptualize. So long as one assumes, as Vaihinger does, that these conceptualizations are open to revision once more useful heuristic fictions are envisioned, this does not in any way constitute an argument for scientific relativism. From a realist perspective, theories can be "regarded as conjectural and evolving through competition and learning" (Mäki 1989: 196). Pragmatists share this perspective and see method as the organization of knowledge "into continuous dispositions of inquiry, development and testing" (Dewey [1922] 1957: 196). This process can lead to new theories, but never to the thing-in-itself, nor to fully accurate predictions of the future.

But if theories are so distant from empirical reality, why do they have any authority? As with forecasts, theories and models gain influence in the scientific community when they appear credible. But what makes an economic theory credible?

For Milton Friedman, the answer to this question lies in the predictive accuracy of a theory, but there are other approaches. British economist Robert Sugden (2000, 2009) begins with the assertion that theoretical models in economics are fictional in the sense that models are a kind of parallel or counterfactual world set up by economists, and are neither realistic nor the outcome of empirical observations. Sugden argues that the real world and the model world are connected through inductive inferences. These are conclusions about the real world that use likelihoods to push beyond available evidence. Economists are able to convince their readers that their general propositions are credible because, to a certain degree, they seem to resemble aspects of the real world. There can be no proof that correspondences exist between the real world and the model because the model contains no proof that the causal claims it makes are actually true. But economists "can ask for credibility in the sense that the fictional world of the model is one that *could* be real" (Sugden 2009: 10). Perceived connections between models and the real world are based on confidence that specific real-world phenomena are caused by mechanisms similar to those described as causes in the model world. "We perceive a model world as credible by being able to think of it as a world that *could be* real—not in the sense of assigning positive subjective probability to the event that it *is* real, but in the sense that it is compatible with what we know, or think we know, about the general laws governing events in the real world" (18).[13]

The gap between the model and the real world is closed through inductive inference. When we observe an outcome in the real world that resembles an outcome in the model world, we conclude through abductive reasoning that the causes of the outcome described in the model are also the causes of the real-world outcome. The model world is not a real world stripped of its complicating factors, but rather a parallel reality constructed by the theorist.

For this reason, Sugden (2000: 25ff.) compares theoretical economic models to realistic novels. Even though the places and characters in a work of fiction are figments of its author's imagination, the author must convince us that they are credible, that there could be places and characters like the ones she describes. The reader then makes the connection between the imaginary world described by the author and the real world in which he lives. By the same token, a theoretical model is taken as credible if the audience suspends disbelief and follows the author in his (implicit) claim that important aspects of the real world are just like his model world. Audience and author must agree that it is *as if* the model were truly reflecting the real world. Sugden does not say much about the sources of this credibility, but he mentions the coherence of the different elements and the causal mechanisms described in the model (2000: 26) as one such source.

Mäki (2009a: 40) adds conceivability, plausibility, and persuasiveness as three further conditions for the credibility of economic models. These abstract criteria, however, do not yet show how the credibility of a model is actually achieved. For this, as in the case of forecasts, it is informative to look at the actual practices of economists, as American economist Deirdre McCloskey (2011) and historian Mary Morgan (2002, 2012) have done.

Like Sugden, McCloskey compares economic models with fictional texts, and like Sugden, she argues that the assertions made by economists rely on more than statistical tests or empirical and experimental data. McCloskey claims that economists are storytellers, and that the credibility of economic theories depends at least partly on their effective use of narrative techniques, through which they convince their peers and a lay public of these assertions. "Plainly and routinely, ninety per cent of what economists do is such storytelling. Yet even in the other ten per cent, in the part more obviously dominated by models and metaphors, the economist tells stories" (McCloskey 1990: 9).

Economists persuade their readers with appeals to introspection or to authority, by relaxing assumptions, constructing hypothetical thought experiments, proposing definitions, appealing to symmetry, or making analogies (McCloskey 1985: 58ff.). Certainly, the narratives told in economics are based on theoretical models, but these models participate in the production of knowledge only when combined with compelling stories. Stories connect models to the specifics of the world, and help define a model's potential, as well as its limits (Morgan 2002, 2012). Narratives "provide the possible correspondence link between the demonstrations made with the model and the events, processes and behavior of the world that the model represents" (Morgan 2012: 243). Just as in the case of forecasts, this is true because the meaning of a model does not come from its mathematical formulae, but from interpretation. Narratives give models concrete form by linking them to the real world.

McCloskey and Morgan's main point is that although economists claim their methodology is based on logical positivism, and that all their conclusions follow logically from a theory or model, analyzing the actual practices of economic reasoning shows this is not the case. McCloskey (1990) and Morgan (2012) use narrative analysis to examine some of the most influential writings in modern economics. Employing the terms of literary analysis, such as character, plot, beginning, and ending, they show how economists use rhetorical figures such as metaphors and analogies. The defamiliarization *(Verfremdung)* of economic texts reveals the discrepancy between the way economists perceive themselves and their actual narrative practices.

This approach shows how economists deploy model-based storytelling to tell other economists, policy-makers, and the lay public how economic phenomena should be perceived. Alongside statistics, claims about causal relations, graphical representations, and reference to empirical facts, they deploy rhetorical devices that make their "stories" ring true. This in no way means that their intent is to deceive. Like actors from other fields, economists seek to persuade each other and the wider public by using concepts that are consciously false in Vaihinger's sense of that term, and then use narrative devices to produce credibility.

Although McCloskey's assessment of economics is often polemical in tone, she is not critiquing the practices she observes, but rather the profession's mistaken perception of itself, which is rooted in a methodology that demands the fictional character of assumptions and the narrative strategies of persuasion be concealed. Economics uses fiction without acknowledging it. In literary fiction, reader and author agree that the reality presented is different from "real reality," but economists do not recognize their own fictions as such (Esposito 2007: 88).[14] As Philip Mirowski (1991: 578) asserts, "economists seem to think that 'models' exist to capture the reality of the situation in which the economic actor finds himself embedded. This unobtrusive postulate of a fixed reality, independent of the interpretative engagement of human beings, has undoubtedly been fostered by the persistent tendency of economists to imitate physicists and their models."

Economists who insist that it is a mistake to equate mathematical descriptions with reality (von Mises), or who recommend that economists use models only as a foils for the real world (Akerlof), are rather exceptional. Perhaps this is because it feels subversive to reveal that scientific concepts are not mirrors of empirical reality and its causal structure, to the extent that such a revelation contradicts familiar understandings of science and threatens scientific authority. In the field of historiography, Hayden White (1980: 20) writes that the "plot of a historical narrative is always an embarrassment and has to be presented as 'found' in the events rather than put there by narrative technique." Likewise, making categories appear natural is a stabilizing mechanism of the social order, because it distracts from their contingent character (Douglas 1986).

As Vaihinger does for heuristic fictions, McCloskey sees the rhetorical character of economists' work as helping the process of scientific discovery. She calls on economists to improve their narrative capabilities, not abandon them. Economists should write more persuasively, improve their teaching methods, and make better arguments. Just like readers of fiction, readers of scientific articles must be convinced. In "a well-done novel or a well-done scientific paper we agree to submit to the authorial intentions, so far as we can make them out," (McCloskey 1990: 12). If a narrative is unconvincing, readers will refuse to enter the author's imaginative world. The goal of the scientific process is to evoke this submission to authorial intentions. As they do in novels, convincing narratives make scientific articles credible.

The model of scientific progress advocated by McCloskey—taken from the philosopher Richard Rorty (1980)—is to see the social sciences as a conversation (McCloskey 1985: 174) in which the participants use an array of rhetorical tools to persuade competent members of the scientific community. Defining them as a "conversation" rejects the positivist understanding of the social sciences as achieving progress through tests that produce objectively verified general results. Instead, it anchors the social sciences in the discursive practices of the scientific community,[15] much in the same way that forecasts are anchored in the discursive practices of an epistemic community and its exchanges with "the economy." From this perspective, beliefs in economic models are established through collective practices— harkening back, once again, to Emile Durkheim's account of the practices through which religious belief systems are created and reinforced. The credibility of theories is necessarily relational.

This is not to say that scientific knowledge is detached from reality. Instead, as Robert Sugden (2013: 242) emphasizes, we "can ask of any particular community of researchers, with its given history and its evolving pattern of characteristic modes of enquiry, theoretical preferences and similarity judgments, how far it has been successful in discovering unexpected but predictable regularities in its domain of enquiry. To the extent that a research community can show such success, that is its claim to credence and authority—not its compliance with principles of reasoning laid down by philosophers of science, logicians or decision theorists."

PRACTICAL EFFECTS OF HEURISTIC FICTIONS

Highlighting the "fictional" character of the predictions provided by theories is part of a broader attempt to gain insight into how theoretical knowledge shapes the economy on a practical level. The fact that theoretical concepts are not representations of an underlying reality does not mean they do not influence decisions, and in this way affect the future. It does imply, however, that theories are necessarily contingent, and that different theoretical perceptions of reality are possible. It is because scientific theories and models do not mirror reality that they can lead to the formation of different expectations and play an effective role in the practical construction and dynamics of the economy. "We use models for envisioning the future and influencing it" (Derman 2011: 43).

Like forecasting, economic theories have several kinds of practical impact on economic decision-making: they affect the coordination of decisions, they affect the creation of novelty, and they are used to shape expectations of other actors in the economy. In this way, they can become, like forecasts, part of the politics of expectations.

Coordination and Performativity

Economic theories and models have practical effects when they influence action by proposing causal relationships for actors to presume, inspiring imaginaries in which perceptions regarding future developments and strategies can form. Theories "frame sets of possibilities within which the actors develop different strategies in order to position themselves" (Ortiz 2009: 38), and in this way orient decisions; if a theory is accepted by many, it can become a coordinating force in the economy. Theories do more than suggest decisions: they also make claims on how other actors will decide, creating beliefs in the predictability of outcomes. The fact that theories do not simply represent reality and that actual future developments are uncertain does not prevent them from having this coordinative effect. Actors must merely believe in specific theories, paradigms, or economic "laws." This does not preclude actors experiencing disappointment in their decisions if the future unfolds differently from what the theory they followed led them to expect, but it does inspire action.

The following two examples highlight how the imaginaries created by economic theories and concepts end up coordinating decisions. The anthropologist Hirokazu Miyazaki (2003) argues, based on ethnographic observation, that the trading strategies used by arbitrage traders on the Tokyo stock exchange are based on their "faith" in the efficient-market hypothesis. Arbitrage trading seeks to identify financial assets that are mispriced relative to their theoretical value as defined by the efficient market hypothesis. This mispricing opens up arbitrage opportunities to traders, which are expected to disappear in the future as the market price aligns with the theoretical price of the security. Miyazaki's study of these traders shows how they use the efficient market hypothesis to categorize current prices, and how it shapes expectations regarding the future development of the prices of the financial assets they are trading. These expectations in turn prompt decisions. Traders, in other words, act *as if* the efficient-market hypothesis were true.[16] Miyazaki (2003: 259) observes that traders' temporal orientation is an "anticipation of retrospection," which parallels Alfred Schütz's (1962: 20) observation that projects are "anticipated in the Future Perfect Tense." The efficient market hypothesis carries a utopian vision that "anticipates the eschatological moment of market efficiency" (Miyazaki 2003: 261). In other words, the efficient market hypothesis gives rise to the conviction that prices will evolve in the future toward what the theory defines as efficient—which then may actually move them in the direction anticipated by the theory. This, however, does not necessarily occur. The history of the Long-Term Capital Management (LTCM) hedge fund is an excellent example of just how little the future present resembles the future projected by the efficient market hypothesis: its managers made investments based on theoretically determined deviations of securities from their assumed equilibrium prices, and, in 1997, LTCM went spectacularly bankrupt.

The second example is the Phillips curve, an economic model that emerged in the 1950s, which states a correlation between changes in prices and unemployment. In the 1960s, the model created the expectation among economists and policy-makers that it was possible to make the macroeconomic choice to reduce unemployment by increasing the inflation rate, and vice versa. This model-generated expectation shaped policies at first but disappointed in the 1970s when high inflation rates were accompanied by growing unemployment. The monetarist critique of the Phillips curve offered a model that raised very different expectations: it assumed the neutrality of money and predicted that an increase in the monetary supply would lead to inflation without any effects on unemployment, because workers would anticipate inflation correctly and adapt their wage demands accordingly (see Figure 10.1). As the monetarist Phillips curve was increasingly accepted in economics and among policy makers, a change in expectations took place. It was now assumed that an expansionary monetary policy would be unable to stimulate economic growth and that monetary policy should therefore focus exclusively on the goal of price stability. The ongoing controversies about the Phillips curve between monetarist and Keynesian economists are a struggle over expectations regarding the consequences of specific economic policy measures. They show how economic models are a crucial component of the coordination of economic action.

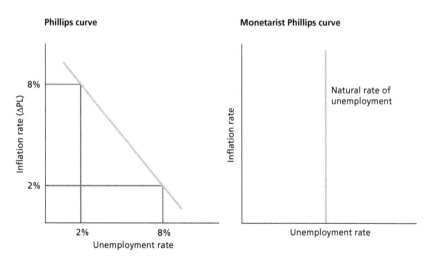

FIGURE 10.1. The Phillips curve and the monetarist Phillips curve, assuming no effect on unemployment from higher price levels in the long run.

Understood this way, theories, models, and paradigms are scripts or conventions that embed actors in a network of "fictional truths." This creates expectations, informs decisions, helps to coordinate economic activity, and influences economic outcomes.

Novelty

While theories provoke imaginaries of the future and inspire decisions that actors perceive as helping them reach that future, they are not determined by any underlying reality. At least in the realm of the social sciences, basing actions on scientific theories implies that the theories may also be instruments for producing a new reality. In this way, theories can have effects not only as devices that help actors to suspend disbelief, but also as a creative force in the economy. Theories' seemingly contradictory role is crucial to understanding their place in the dynamics of capitalism. While actors need devices such as theories and models to coordinate, they can never rely on the stability of established forms. In the search for new profit opportunities, existing forms are also undermined with the help of new theoretical models, offering different ways to grasp causalities. This leads to new imaginaries of profit opportunities and possible threats, and, subsequently, to different decisions.

In his treatment of imagination, Paul Ricoeur (1991, 2002) characterizes scientific models as one form of productive imagination in that they are not duplicative; that is, not determined by an original (see J. Evans 1995; Taylor 2006). Ricoeur argues that, like fiction, scientific models provide a new description of reality, which opens up a hitherto unknown imaginary space and may in this way redirect economic activities. Models allow actors to play with new possibilities and to assign new meaning to reality. For Ricoeur, the productive imagination expressed in scientific models is not irrational: it does not express unbound fantasies, it simply explores possible options more fully, meaning that the distance between a new scientific model and existing reality cannot be too large. However, productive imagination does introduce a fiction, an image without an original, something from nowhere. By opening new imaginative horizons, scientific models are heuristics that inform decisions about the unknown, and therefore contribute to the dynamics of the capitalist economy.

Yet another aspect of their use causes theories to foster creative responses: credible theories or models do not determine actors' decisions, but rather provide evaluation schemes for actors to apply to their particular situations. If, like John Dewey, one characterizes uncertain situations as "disturbed, troubled, ambiguous, confused, full of conflicting tendencies, obscure, etc." (Dewey [1938] 1998: 171), then effective theories cannot be mere scripts that tell actors exactly how to respond to a specific set of circumstances. Instead, actors interpret theories and models to hone new solutions to complex problems.

In their ethnographic study of the decision-making processes of financial traders in the trading room of a Wall Street investment bank, David Stark and Daniel Beunza (Stark 2009) examine how traders convince themselves they are making the right deals, thus shedding light on how traders in a highly competitive market identify what they believe to be an opportunity for profit. On the surface, it would seem adequate to reply that traders simply follow the prescriptions of the dominant financial model, but further examination reveals a tricky question: "If everyone is using the same formulas, how can anyone profit?" (Stark 2009: 124). While the mathematical formulas used in finance theory do play a crucial role in traders' practices, Stark and Beunza demonstrate that traders' interpretations of their situations are much more critical. This interpretive process is not determined by financial theories and models, as traders must "find new types of associations among the abstracted qualities of the securities they were trading" (Stark 2009: 186). They do so by referring to multiple evaluation schemes (in their case, financial models), instead of dwelling on any one assessment of the future present and the causal mechanisms leading up to it. They keep "multiple evaluative principles in play . . . to exploit the resulting friction of their interplay," which Stark defines as a key trait of entrepreneurship (Stark 2009: 15).

This very much resembles the findings from ethnographic studies of central bank policies and the practices of macroeconomic forecasting presented in Chapters 5 and 9. In the case of central banks, their work and the discussions of policy-makers are informed by the theoretical macroeconomic framework. However, the theoretical frameworks do not determine policy action in any rigid or mechanical fashion. The "paradigms are open to vigorous contestation and, importantly, they each rest on an explicit gap between theory and practice that personnel of central banks must negotiate prospectively" (Holmes 2009: 392). Central banks and forecasting institutes achieve the co-presence of various evaluative schemes through intensive discursive exchanges within the epistemic community and "the economy."

The traders in the Wall Street investment bank studied by Stark and Beunza negotiate a similar evaluative heterogeneity through the spatial configuration of the trading room. Because trading desks are organized so that traders using different trading strategies can easily communicate with each other, they are able to exchange information and interpretations and "test" their ideas. The facilitation of "reflexive cognition" (Stark 2009: 184) fosters new types of association, which lead to "re-cognition"; that is, seeing a situation from a new perspective.

This, of course, implies that financial traders at least tacitly understand that the models they are using do not simply represent an underlying reality. No matter what the model, they must be alert that the expectations it generates are fictional, both because models cannot be more than analogical apperceptions, and because the future is indeterminate and unforeseeable. Indeed, ethnographic evidence shows that traders do not assume that the models they use can tell them unambiguously about future developments in the markets; they develop a reflexive relationship to these models instead. For example, Chong, Tuckett, and Ruatti (2013: 21) show that fund managers see economic models as tools for interpreting the situation at hand. Managers build trust in their own and others' assessments by testing their theories against alternative models, making a specific model "one of many folk models that fund managers may deploy" (20). This, however, casts doubt on the claim that economic theory can ever "perform" the economy.

Politics of Expectations

The contingency of theories also makes them political. In strategic social interactions, an actor's success depends on the behavior of other actors. Since decisions are at least partly shaped by beliefs in certain theories or models, actors have an interest in shaping a third party's decision by persuading them of the validity of the theories and models that suggest policies advantageous to themselves. Although this may sound quite abstract, the point is very concrete: if theories influence outcomes, then defining new theories or paradigms and influencing the credibility of existing ones is a crucial element in actors' struggles in the market. Often, rival theories do not participate in a struggle over competing goals so much as they offer competing visions of how goals can best be reached. Which is the most effective way to reduce unemployment, improve supply-side conditions, or stimulate demand? Will introducing a minimum wage increase or decrease social inequality?

Will tax advantages for the rich benefit also the poor? Can markets regulate themselves? Theories are politically contested because no one theory can provide uncontestable answers to these questions. Competing theories provide alternative responses, often proposing opposing policies with different distributional consequences.

Shaping the way actors interpret the world is a central aspect of the exercise of power. Economic theories thus are part of the governmentality (Foucault) of modern societies. They exercise social control in the form of knowledge. Power, Foucault maintains, can be exercised through knowledge and discourses that become internalized. Establishing and ensuring the influence of specific theories and paradigms expresses power, which is applied through institutions such as universities, think tanks, and the media. It would be naïve to analyze the development and prevalence of economic theories and paradigms as a mere sharpening of the scientific instruments through which causal relations are depicted. Economic theories are themselves instruments with which actors pursue material and ideological goals.[17]

In general, these goals are carefully hidden, usually behind claims of "accuracy" and "objectivity"—or behind methodological debates. The latter can be observed in a close examination of Milton Friedman's famous essay on the methodology of positive economics, already mentioned above. As Marion Fourcade (2009: 93ff.) demonstrates, Milton Friedman's suggestion that economic theory should be based on as-if assumptions cannot be understood as purely methodological. Friedman himself claimed that the as-if assumptions used in economics would allow accurate predictions—the goal of positive economics. Why is Friedman's assertion not only a methodological proposition? In his essay's extensive arguments against the theory of monopolistic competition, Friedman (1953: 35) objected vehemently to the idea that more realistic assumptions had any kind of scientific utility. He believed that more realistic assumptions were a danger because they would cause economics to create a descriptive, photographic representation of the economy, with little analytical leverage. Fourcade shows that Friedman saw much more than simple epistemological questions at stake in his argument. In demands to be "more realistic," he perceived a critique of the fundamental beliefs of economic theory, chief among them the assumptions of perfect competition and constrained optimization. To follow the critique of these assumptions, Friedman believed, was to threaten the credo of free markets, the very core of neoclassical economics. Friedman's intention was to maintain these core assumptions of economic theory despite empirical observations that they were not valid, arrived at by the theory of monopolistic competition. Friedman's essay participated in the politics of expectations: by defending specific heuristic fictions, Friedman was defending a specific set of ideas about how the economy works and which forms of its organization are legitimate. Ultimately Friedman's methodological essay was defending an ideological position, that of the laissez-faire approach to the economy.

THE DYNAMICS OF THEORIES

If economic decisions are influenced by economic theories, then investigating the dynamic character of their credibility can shed new light on the dynamics of capitalism as a whole. But what causes them to change? Hans Vaihinger's view that heuristic fictions change with scientific progress seems rather naïve, at least in the case of theories in the social sciences: as demonstrated above, theoretical depictions of the economy are highly contingent. Furthermore, the fact that theories influence the legitimation of decisions with widely different distributional consequences means that interest in them can be expected to be vested.

One point is highly germane to the thesis of this book: theories lose credibility if they cease to produce convincing imaginaries of a desired future. In macroeconomics, these imaginaries usually include the goals of strong growth, low inflation, low unemployment, and increased profitability. While theories, to be credible, must present themselves as strongly tied to imaginaries of a desired future, they may compete with alternative theories that generate different proposals as to how institutions regulating the economy and the firm should be structured to achieve desired goals.

This is especially evident in the evolution of economic policy paradigms. Several studies have investigated the evolution of the economic paradigms that informed macroeconomic policy-making and the managerial theories that motivated managers' decisions regarding the organization of firm structures, both in context of the transformation of capitalism during the 1970s.

Peter Hall (1993) was at the vanguard of historical institutionalists investigating the role of policy paradigms in economic policy-making, as well as the evolution of such paradigms.[18] Paradigms provide interpretative frameworks that operate as sets of beliefs. They comprise several elements: policy goals (for example, to increase growth or to lower inflation), the instruments to be used (for example, fiscal changes, regulation), and the legitimate settings for these instruments (for example, lowering taxes, deregulating industries). Hall investigated British macroeconomic policies during the 1970s, studying the paradigm shift from Keynesianism to monetarism occurring at the time. The two paradigms had different views of the macroeconomic effects of specific policy tools, and motivated utterly different policy decisions. The paradigm shift toward monetarism led to policies that facilitated industry deregulation, as well as the privatization of firms, tax cuts, market liberalization, and the reform of the welfare state.

Hall's main interest was in explaining this paradigm shift, which he argued was triggered by a crisis in the old paradigm. When anomalies were observed in the old paradigm, confidence in the policies it inspired was lost.[19] Keynesian policy instruments, which sought to stimulate demand and control inflation, were perceived as less and less effective as a means of keeping unemployment low and encouraging growth. As the paradigm ceased to create imaginaries of a future people actually desired, monetarism, with its fundamentally different assumptions about the effects of macroeconomic instruments, began to replace it, stimulating new, more persuasive imaginaries. Monetarism gained credibility; eventually, it replaced Keynesianism as a paradigm to achieving policy goals.

Taking up where Peter Hall left off, Marion Fourcade and Sarah Babb (2002) investigated this policy shift more broadly. They followed the transition from Keynesian policies to neoliberal ones in four countries, focusing on the way economic theories, transformations of the economy, and domestic institutional factors interacted with one another. They not only confirmed that cognitive reorientations lead to shifts in economic policy (Blyth 2002; Campbell and Pedersen 2014; Mirowski and Plehwe 2009), they discovered that the inverse was true, as well: "deep transformations in the structure of domestic and international economies contributed to change the cognitive categories with which economic and political actors come to apprehend the world" (Fourcade-Gourinchas and Babb 2002: 534).

Like Hall, Fourcade and Babb observed that as markets globalized, states became increasingly vulnerable to international capital movements, and that the collapse of the Bretton Woods system had made supply-side interpretations of the economy appear much more credible to political actors in the 1970s. They noted, however, that altered economic conditions do not automatically lead to ideological shifts: these must be proliferated through an institutional infrastructure. In this case, the IMF, the OECD, and the World

Bank all exercised institutional pressure on countries to change their policies. Other institutional factors, such as the evolving role of the business press, also contributed to the proliferation of market-oriented ideas. When "faced with the choice between yielding to the neoliberal discipline supported by international financial markets and constituencies, and attempting a more protectionist, domestically centered, economic strategy, political decision-makers in all four countries resolved in favor of the former, legitimating market reforms as an inevitable course imposed upon them by an increasingly globalized economy" (Fourcade-Gourinchas and Babb 2002: 569).

Economic theories not only create imaginaries at the level of macroeconomic policies; they also shape imaginaries of how to structure firms. The role agency theory has played in the transformation of American companies and the emergence of shareholder capitalism since the 1970s is an excellent example of this (Dobbin and Jung 2010). In the United States the economic recession of the 1970s was generally perceived as caused by a profound crisis of American industry, which was losing ground to international competitors, particularly in Japan.

In the mid-1970s, agency theory (Jensen and Meckling 1976) offered a diagnosis of these problems and proposed solutions that stimulated new imaginaries of how the future profitability of ailing American firms could be improved. The narrative of agency theory describes a causal relationship between the profitability of firms and their governance structure. Agency theory attributed the malaise of the American firm to managers who were more interested in the stability and enlargement of their companies than in maximizing profits. Managers, the theory argued, were too focused on making acquisitions and forming multidivisional conglomerates that would consolidate their power and give them critical mass to protect them from bankruptcy. The theory asserted that such conglomerates could not be very profitable, which went against their owners' interests. According to agency theory, executives (agents) were serving their own interests, rather than those of their firms' owners (principals).

Agency theory offered solutions to this perceived problem that gave rise to imaginaries of a future present in which firm profitability rose again. It proposed that managers be provided with incentives that encourage them to serve the interests of their firm's owners—that is, to increase the firm's profitability. These included stock options, dediversification, and debt-leveraged equity, as well as increased board oversight to monitor the risks taken by management. From a sample of almost 800 American firms, Dobbin and Jung (2010) showed that companies had embraced the first three of these recommendations, demonstrating how the expectations derived from agency theory had shaped corporate governance.

Today, in the wake of the financial crisis of 2007 and the public bailouts that followed, agency theory is much more controversial, and much of its utopian content has evaporated. Indeed, many now see it as going against public interest by encouraging managers to take unsustainable risks in order to maximize their bonus payments, and by emphasizing short-term priorities that ultimately undermine firms and the orientation toward the future that drives capitalist dynamics. Whether and when agency theory will be replaced by another managerial theory with new imaginaries is now an open question.[20]

Both of the above examples show how a perceived crisis caused an existing paradigm to shift and led to the emergence of a new heuristic fiction, offering new imaginaries and new measures to reach economic goals. Theories, by alleging causal relationships, create credible reasons for advocating specific policies or corporate reforms. If put in place, these reforms alter the structure of the economy and its firms. Theories gain influence when they shift the decision-making orientations of elites and produce (temporary) cognitive lock-ins that limit the range of political, organizational, or individual choices envisioned (J. L. Campbell 2004: 107).

These examples also demonstrate the three effects of heuristic fictions discussed before: first, these theories contributed to the coordination of action in the economy. As Fourcade and Babb (2002: 569) write, as "an ideological force, the neoliberal creed was self-reinforcing, in the sense that there 'were no alternatives' simply because everybody believed this, and acted upon this belief." Second, these theories stimulated imaginaries and provided conceptual tools for the reorganization of the economy, thereby contributing to newness and spurring the dynamics of the capitalist economy. Third, these theories were political in the sense that their advocates expected to gain from the institutional changes they suggested. The goal of agency theory was to increase the value of shareholders' portfolios.

To systematize our understanding of the dynamics of theories and models, it may be helpful to look at them—in analogy to technological paradigms— as following a life cycle consisting of several phases (Deutschmann 1999). Economic paradigms often start with the publication of a new theoretical approach in a scientific journal, which may go unnoticed for many years. This was the case with the John Muth (1961) article that launched rational expectations theory: it received almost no attention for nearly a decade. The theory is then taken up and made more applicable to concrete policy or governance issues. At this point, imaginaries of a desired future state of the world become associated with the theory. The theory is then institutionalized—for example through policy reforms, or through a change in firm governance structures. Finally, the theory loses its imaginary appeal and is perceived as incapable of resolving contemporary challenges. As this decay takes place, a new theory is "discovered" and creates new imaginaries.

Deutschmann (1999: 145) describes this cycle as a "spiral of myths." In each case, the theory is naturalized as economists "prescribe behavior and explain those prescriptions not in terms of human-made norms, but in terms of the way nature made the universe" (Dobbin 2001: 3). Economic policy paradigms are not the only such myths: the idea of the self-regulating market, the idea of sustainability, the notion of equilibrium, or the BRICS concept are all examples, as well, because they are all forms of classification that create imaginaries of a desirable future. They all, to the extent that they are followed, lead to cognitive mobilization in the economy, help shape decisions, and influence the future.

CONCLUSION

Theories are a force in the dynamics of capitalism. By creating imaginaries of future states of the world, as well as of causal relations, and helping orient actors' decisions as they attempt to achieve goals, they influence events and mobilize resources. Theories and models may support existing practices, or may subvert established economic practices by constructing counterfactual futures. Either way, they contribute to the dynamic restlessness of capitalism. Theories and models affect actors' perceptions of a situation and influence their decisions by prompting imaginaries of the future, while at the same time offering directions on how to achieve it. Theories can also make claims about the conditions for rupture and crisis in the future. They offer visions of actual and possible worlds, and generate expectations. If credible, they persuade actors and become reference points for economic decision-making.

To characterize theories as instruments that generate fictional expectations may at first seem fanciful. In the philosophy of science, however, theoretical concepts have long been characterized as fictions, though this categorization remains controversial. On one level, as Immanuel Kant and then Hans Vaihinger argued, the model world and the real world are separate, meaning that theory is fiction: theoretical concepts cannot be direct representations of things-in-themselves. Debates in the philosophy of science do not question this assertion; rather, they focus on the issue of which theoretical constructs should be characterized as fictions, of how models and reality are connected, and of whether fiction is the appropriate term to describe the phenomenon (Bar-Hillel 1966; Mäki 2002; Ströker 1983). Not only must theories necessarily use abstractions to describe the future, they also cannot be mirrors of the real world because they change the behavior of actors and thus depict an uncertain and hence unforeseeable future. Predictive theories are thus also fictional in an ontological sense.

To influence behavior, theories do not need to be "true" or "false," they must be credible. The credibility of economic theories has an institutional basis, and stems from a social process of power-infused interactions in which the legitimated participants of the scientific community and expert elites persuade one another and the broader public of a given theory and the way to apply it. To gain influence, theories and paradigms require the institutional basis of economics departments, business schools, think tanks, political interest groups, and the media (Campbell and Pedersen 2014; Fourcade-Gourinchas and Babb 2002; Mirowski and Plehwe 2009). The scientific community, politicians, the media, and the wider public adopt certain theories as credible because they assess that these theories describe worlds that could be true. Credibility is established in a thought collective (Fleck [1935] 1979), and epistemological beliefs are established and destroyed in collective practices. Economic theories use formalized models to convince their audiences, but narrative and storytelling play an equally important role. Once convinced, actors act *as if* the theories they believe in were true. At the same time, the fact that decisions made based on a specific theory or model have distributional consequences makes theories and models politically contested and part of the governmentality of modern societies. Actors may advocate theories because they believe them to be beneficial, rather than accurate.

No matter how comprehensive the theory, it can never account for the uncertainty of the future. As the sociology of economic practices shows, competent actors are aware of this. They know that theories or models are nothing more than instruments that help to make sense of a situation—to suspend disbelief or to envision counterfactual futures—crystal balls reflecting not the future, but visions of ourselves.

ELEVEN

CONCLUSION

The Enchanted World of Capitalism

> "And are you happy, Velina, with our life here? Have you stopped
> hoping for anything better?"
>
> —KAREN RUSSELL, *St. Lucy's Home for Girls Raised by Wolves*

CAPITALISM is a socioeconomic system oriented toward the future. With
the expansion of competitive markets and the extension of the credit
system, actors in the economy are required to shift their attention to the
future, which cannot be imagined as a repetitive pattern of events known
from the past. To survive in the competitive world of the capitalist economy,
producers and investors must seek new products, higher productivity, lower
costs, new forms of production, and new domains of investment to create
ever more value. Freed from the confines of an enforced social hierarchy,
consumers feel continuous pressure to assert their social status by acquiring
new products and increasing their consumption. Stasis is deadly: it wipes
economic actors out of the market and robs consumers of their social position. However it unfolds, the unknown future inevitably involves restless
striving. Attempting to create new value is seen as an opportunity to excel,
to make profit, and to maintain or improve social status. At the same time,
it comes with the risk of economic failure, which is attributed not to fate
but to actors' own decisions. The disposition to create novelty, which plays
at most a marginal role in traditional societies, is indispensable in capitalism.
The historical perspective shows that action oriented toward a future experienced as open and different from the past and the present is not inherent
to human nature: it has emerged as a feature of the institutional and cultural development of capitalist modernity.

To understand the dynamics of capitalism we must understand the role
expectations play in economic decision-making, how these expectations are
formed, and how they affect actors' decisions. Perhaps more than anything

else, the future—or, more precisely, images of the future formed by actors—informs decisions and thus explains outcomes. Such a revision to our understanding of the economy demands that the social sciences adjust their approach to include assessments of the future as a causal factor in economic outcomes. The future matters!

If actors had some way of knowing how the future would unfold and what impact their choices had on it, it would not be difficult for them to foresee their fate or predict the consequences of their decisions. All cultures possess "technologies" that they believe help them foresee the future (Rescher 1998). In the past, these took the form of oracles, prophecies, and astrological signs, among others. These lost legitimacy in the enlightened world of modernity. By the seventeenth century a new set of technologies began to develop that used probability theory and other rational devices to anticipate the future. These technologies laid the groundwork for economic forecasting and rational planning methods. But these technologies also failed to achieve what their magical forerunners had failed at: foreknowing the future.

If uncertainty is real and the future is open and cannot be known ahead of time, in capitalist modernity anything claiming to predict the future is making an essential error. The recent financial crisis has made it abundantly clear that rational expectations theory's claim of prices reflecting intrinsic value cannot be trusted. For an understanding of the economy, then, the question of how expectations form needs to be reassessed—expectations under conditions of uncertainty should be characterized as *fictional*. Although this term has been associated with pure fantasy, it can accurately describe the status of expectations in situations where uncertainty prevents actors from calculating outcomes, and thus from anticipating future states of the world. When outcomes are uncertain, actors are required to pretend they can anticipate outcomes in order to make justifiable decisions—to act *as if* the future were going to develop in a given way. Fictional expectations build a kind of parallel reality—an *imagined future*. Imagined futures in the economy include assumptions about the profitability of investments, projections about technological developments, assessments of the default risk for financial securities, and the anticipation of satisfaction derived from a consumer good that has yet to be purchased. Although fictional, these imagined futures—if deemed credible—justify, inform, and legitimate decisions, thus influencing the unfolding of economic processes.

Fictional expectations help actors to find direction in an uncertain economic world. Decisions about the main buttresses of the capitalist economy—money and credit, investments, innovation, and consumption—would be impossible without contingent imaginaries of perceived futures. Indeed, imaginaries have been and still are a necessary condition for the operation and spectacular growth of the capitalist economy over the past two centuries. The creation of credible imagined futures, *despite* and *because of* awareness of the future's contingency, is a major accomplishment, necessary for the operation of the capitalist economy. No monetary system could function without the expectation that money will remain largely stable. No loans would be granted without the expectation of repayment. No serious research and development activities would be undertaken without the expectation of successful innovation. No investment—in equipment, financial assets, or human capital—would be made without the expectation of future benefits. No consumer society would be possible without the continuous construction of imaginaries associated with cars, computers, or traveling, and their operation in the motivation of future purchases. By downplaying at least momentarily the possibility of failure and disappointment, imaginaries of the future allow risks to be taken and growth to be sustained. They open the door to the unknowable future.

Often enough, these imaginaries crumble as the future actually unfolds: hyperinflation evaporates the value of money; loans go unpaid; innovations are not accepted in the market; investments fail; the car, once purchased, disappoints the driver. Far less often, the future outshines the imaginary: when they were founded, no one expected the spectacular successes of Amazon, Google, Apple, or Facebook. For the actors involved, whether or not individual outcomes actually correspond with expectations is crucially important: failed investments, hyperinflation, bankruptcies, unemployment, and disillusioned consumers are all instances of disappointed expectations with important individual and social consequences. But at the macrolevel, these are mere episodes, and while they may affect whole societies, they are an integral part to the continuation of the capitalist system. All that really matters to the dynamism of capitalism is that we continue to pursue risky activities. For each success there can be many failures. But for capitalism to flourish, hope for new profits must spring eternal, nourished by the development of ever new imaginaries.

Fictional expectations in the economy have become increasingly important as capitalist modernity has unfolded. The historical expansion of credit relations, the increasing abstraction of money as it became unbound from scarce commodities that once gave it its underlying value, the disembedding

of investments from particularistic networks, and the increasing significance of symbolic value in consumer goods all bear witness to this. But
expectations may also stop capitalism dead in its tracks: crises in capitalism
occur when expectations shift suddenly, and the future in which actors once
believed vanishes, sharply reducing the timeframe to which actors are
willing to commit. In no time at all, the promises embodied in financial
products can be infected with doubt. Loan sources dry up, currencies are
abandoned, investments are postponed, shares are sold. The future becomes
devalued. The same thing may occur with consumer products: the dreams
of satisfaction promised in the purchase seem unattainable, unreasonable,
or outmoded; the products lose their appeal and demand disappears. In
2001, investors lost confidence in the imagined futures reported by Enron's
executives, accountants, and stock market analysts. In an instant, the giant
energy company collapsed. In 2008, the value of the securitized mortgages
of American homeowners plummeted when investors' expectations about
whether they would be repaid suddenly shifted. The latter crisis is a particularly salient illustration of how fundamental a role fictional expectations
and imagined futures play in the dynamics of capitalism: one cannot even
say that the value of these assets declined with regard to their *actual value*
at the moment of crisis, because, like any other commodity, they never had
any "intrinsic" value to begin with, given the openness of future events. Expected future value, which is the starting point for the calculation of current value, is always anchored in fictional expectations.

Indeed, there is no fundamental economic value, in the ontological sense
of that term, that can exist independent from actors' imagined futures.
Imaginaries of the future are imaginary above all things; they reflect contingent and shifting assessments of what may or may not transpire. This does
not make them any less important: if they are credible, imagined futures
are able to provoke action in the economy, and in this way drive capitalist
dynamics. But this dynamism cannot be taken for granted. As may be increasingly observed in financial markets, in corporate governance, and in
investments, our current obsession with the short term may deplete capitalist modernity of its central source of growth, which is the patient willingness to engage in economic activities with uncertain outcomes (Haldane
2015). Imagined futures may also be deflated by social structural changes
in the economy, such as growing job insecurity, decreasing opportunities
for upward social mobility, aging populations, or a diminished desire for consumer products. Mounting debt caused by economic crises can also "colo-

nize" the present and block out the future by preventing investment into new imaginaries. The dynamics of capitalism continue virtually uninterrupted when faced with alternative utopias, because they are easy to assimilate. But diminished attractiveness, vanishing structural preconditions or the colonizing of the present by former commitments may bar the way to an economic future that realizes new economic forms, and result in a slowing of growth and economic crisis.

CREDIBILITY, INTERPRETATION, INVENTIVENESS, AND POLITICS

The observation that expectations in the economy are fictional raises several questions that demand closer scrutiny. Most important, perhaps, is that of the origins of credibility: what makes actors hold certain expectations and not others? In literary fiction, readers are not looking for reality when they open a novel, and submit easily to the fictional worlds created by authors, so long as they are internally coherent and suspenseful. In the economy, however, fictional expectations require a great deal of careful management to achieve credibility: actors examine potential expectations by gathering as much information about them as they can, as well as information about competing projections of the future. Sources of credibility for expectations in the economy are manifold: they may be institutional, social, emotional, conventional, arise from practical processes, and reflect the power structures of the economy.

Two points should be taken from this discussion. First, the credibility of expectations is unthinkable without the structures provided by institutions, conventions, and social power. Credit systems, for example, require formal and/or informal rules that enforce the repayment of loans; they must rely on conventions, such as credit ratings or accounting methods; and they are based on the (sometimes coercive) assertion of political and economic power—for example, the enforcement of austerity measures in countries in danger of defaulting on their sovereign debt. Second, the credibility of expectations is rooted in the practices of economic actors. As I have argued throughout this book, an expectation's credibility—that is, its capacity to inspire belief in a specific future—comes in large part from actors' observations of and interactions with one another, as well as their proclamations about and justifications for their assessments of a given situation. Firms, consumers, and economists form convictions and coordinate their assessments in communicative processes. These processes may take place through exposure to a multitude of different perspectives, but dominant players attempt to create alliances around their worldviews. Beliefs, as Emile Durkheim and John Dewey both argue, are formed from collective practices. Once the structural and practical roots of expectations have been exposed, it becomes clear that while expectations may be held by individuals, they can only be explained when the social world in which these individuals operate is taken into account. In this sense, expectations are not individual, and must be examined from a sociological perspective if they are to be understood.

Meaning and interpretation are central to a rigorous examination of economic decisions and outcomes. This is predicated on the premise that the economy is a social system. As such, it operates based on the meaning actors assign to the phenomena they observe. Meaning and interpretations of situations emerge and change through communicative processes in which shared perspectives develop and prevailing interpretations are confirmed or contested. If the future is open, expectations of the future, and the actions taken based on those expectations, are the result of contingent interpretations. These interpretations take narrative form. Economic action should therefore be understood as anchored in narrative constructions, implying that no empirical inquiry of the economy can detach itself from the investigation of the hermeneutics of economic action. Narratives are built around past experiences and formed from imaginaries of future states and assessments of how decisions will affect future outcomes. In this, economic theories play an important role. Theories give weight and body to imaginaries by offering a detailed perspective on a problem and the causality of events; assembling, selecting, and ranking circumstances, evidence, or criteria; defining possible alternatives; naming participants; and, if specific actions are to be undertaken, telling how they will unfold. Because the economic future is uncertain, economic theory is actually a narrative—a commitment to a specific interpretation of the economy. To be sure, this narrative construction of the economy always takes place against a backdrop of known facts, rules, institutional structures, economic and political power, and social networks. Their relevance in the action process depends, however, on the meaning they obtain in the specific situation. Fictional expectations are oriented toward the future, but because of their institutional and social anchoring, "history matters" just as much in their construction.

Fictional expectations also play a crucial role in the inventiveness of capitalism. Shared expectations have a coordinating function because they align actors' decisions in the economy, making them more predictable. That is not to say that actors' expectations in the economy must converge. In this sense, social processes in modernity are not necessarily a trajectory of increasing homogenization, as has been argued by sociological institutionalism. The very uncertainty of the future, the differentiation of products and markets, and differences in social position imply that actors will differ in how they assess the future: some see opportunities where others do not; perceived risks are prohibitive to some and acceptable to others; the indeterminacy of the future opens up the possibility of myriad counterfactual worlds. Perhaps counterintuitively, uncertainty is not—or at least not only—an obstacle to the sustained momentum of the economy: it is also one of its preconditions. As proponents of general equilibrium theory, as well as Frank Knight and Joseph Schumpeter demonstrate, an economy with perfect information and fully rational actors would be a static one without time or inventiveness: the future would be known in the present and all exchanges could take place at once. In such an economy, however, no dynamism could take place; no profit would be made. Under conditions of uncertainty, this is not the case.

Time matters; uncertainty makes newness possible, and expectations of the future drive the dynamism of the economy. No one can know whether a counterfactual imaginary of the future present is "correct," and the only way to discover whether it is, is to move toward it. At the same time, any attempt to realize an imaginary influences the conditions for its success. Most innovations fail, but because the world is indeterminate, actors are free to imagine theirs will not. Their capacity to generate or adopt fictional expectations inspires them to seize imagined opportunities. When successful, the innovations that result add new value to the economy.

The final sociologically salient issue that emerges from the notion of fictional expectations is the politics of expectations. If the future is unforeseeable, then expectations are necessarily contingent; since no one can know what the future will look like, the number of possible scenarios to be imagined is infinite. At the same time, the future that *does* unfold depends on the decisions actors make in the present and will affect different actors in different ways. It is only logical, then, to conclude that actors in the economy have an interest in influencing other actors' expectations. By doing so, actors hope to orient others' decisions in directions they believe are favorable to their interests. This makes expectations a central element in the governance of capitalist markets.

The deliberate influencing of expectations is a key feature in all the empirical realms discussed in this book. In the realm of technological innovations, firms try to convince investors and other firms of the technological futures they envision in order to secure the financial means to learn whether their technological projections are technologically and economically viable. They may, in the process, weaken the positions of competitors pursuing other technological futures. In financial markets, investors attempt to convince other investors of their market predictions; when powerful investors announce their expectations, they do so in the hope that their assessments will generate enough momentum in the market to actually create the market prices they predict. The Keynesian beauty contest is not a struggle over the definition of beauty but an attempt to understand other actors' concepts of it. When banks hold equity in or grant loans to firms or states, they may forecast their debtors' futures in a positive light (sometimes too positively) in order to stabilize other investors' confidence in their assets. Increasingly, central banks have been using expectation management as a form of monetary policy. By shaping expectations about products, marketing strategists seek to convince consumers that a given product will satisfy their desires more than any other product can.

The futures projected in all of the above cases have profound implications for the development of the economy. It follows, then, that competition in capitalist modernity is in crucial ways a struggle over imagined futures. This contradicts rational expectations theory in its claim that attempting to manipulate expectations is vain because actors cannot be fooled. If we are to understand competition in the capitalist economy, we must ask why certain imagined futures prevail over others. And to answer this question, we must pay close attention to struggles over expectations, as well as to the power of the actors involved in these struggles. Competition, over economic theories and paradigms, over technological projections, or over the proclaimed symbolic features of a product, always takes place through the shaping of beliefs, ideas, hopes, fears, and promises. If a given imaginary of the future is to have credence, an actor must successfully influence others' expectations; being able to exercise that influence is one of the prime expressions of power in the economy.

This leads to another key observation. The performativity approach has been one of the most influential paradigms in economic sociology in recent years, Given that economic models, if widely shared, can have influence on the economy, and even give rise to a reality that mimics their assumptions, the conclusion that the economy increasingly resembles the representations of it made by economic models is still dubious. While this effect has been demonstrated in some carefully chosen cases, the broader empirical observations covered in this book point to a different conclusion: the models actors apply have a variety of real world effects, which constantly surprise players, forcing them to continuously readjust the assumptions of their models and generate new interpretations of the situations they face. Whether one hopes for it or fears it, there is little evidence that the future economy will ever come to resemble the world described in economic textbooks.

In addition, economic and financial models comprise only a few of the cognitive and normative influences on expectations and decisions in the economy. The scope of the investigation of the impact of cognitive structures on economic outcomes needs to be broadened significantly. Economic paradigms like Keynesianism and neoliberalism, technological projections, moral evaluations of consumer products, and beliefs in monetary stability are all part of the cognitive and normative base of economic decision-making, and they influence economic outcomes in often conflicting ways. If economic sociology is to focus on the role of cognition and norms, it must take into account all the classifications and categorizations that shape economic action, not just economic theories. Furthermore, a cognitive approach can explain economic outcomes partially only because cognitive devices are not the only factor behind economic processes: any comprehensive sociological theory of the economy must also take into account how expectations are shaped by emotions, social position, institutions, and the distribution of power in the economic field.

FUTURE RESEARCH

The significance of expectations to economic outcomes opens up an intriguing empirical and theoretical research agenda for economic sociology and political economy.[1] Imagined futures are part of the present assessment of a situation by actors and can thus be studied empirically. One finds them documented in the reports of analysts and forecasters, in company documents crafted to justify specific strategy decisions, and in reports in the mass media. Research may be qualitative as well as quantitative, including analysis of written documents or databases as well as interviews regarding stock market analysts' or rating agencies' expectations of the future performance of financial securities. Fictional expectations could be analyzed as the independent variable in research into their effects; they could be used as a dependent variable in research into how they are developed. Further empirical investigations of economic decisions in the fields discussed in Part 2 of this book could provide deeper insights into how certain imagined futures develop, and how they affect economic decisions.

Possible research topics are manifold: mergers and acquisitions, venture capital investments, decisions related to technology development, career aspirations, consumers' hopes surrounding the purchase of goods, the imaginaries associated with the introduction of the euro, the technological imaginaries of Silicon Valley entrepreneurs, or the strenuous efforts of central banks to establish monetary confidence, to name just a few. Another empirical field could investigate what Part 3 of this book calls "instruments of imagination." This includes not only forecasts and economic theories, but also business plans, accounting, strategies, and marketing. What is the role of these instruments in the creation of imagined futures and in the dynamics of capitalism? A detailed investigation of the role of the mass media in the emergence and diffusion of imagined futures is another possibility. Research in the social sciences on some of these topics already exists, but this book has sought to contribute something new: a unifying research perspective that focuses on how imagined economic futures can help explain the restless dynamics of capitalism. This provides a fresh perspective and an integrated agenda that draws together and extends many of the different angles from which some of these phenomena have been examined before.

The theoretical side of the research agenda suggested here would focus on the emergence and dynamics of imagined futures in the economy. Actors' expectations should not be understood in individualistic terms—neither as utility maximization, nor as hardwired cognitive distortions that prevent actors from maximizing returns. Instead, actors' expectations are shaped by their social, cultural, institutional, historical, and political backgrounds. How these expectations emerge, and how they are socially anchored, should be examined in far more detail than has been possible in this book. Topics remaining to be explored include historical and comparative research into how expectations develop over time, how they differ among countries, and their connections to actors' social positions and macrosocial conditions. From a historical perspective, how understandings were developed into the predictability of economic affairs, as well as the development of instruments of prediction are both rich fields of inquiry.

The influencing and shaping of expectations through the exercise of power is another theoretical issue discussed in this book that requires further exploration. To what extent can others' expectations be manipulated or even "steered"? Is it possible to "manage" expectations? If so, who can do so, and what are the counterforces to such efforts? Who constructs imaginaries, and what role do experts and intermediaries play in that process? How do imaginaries of the future become credible? Who are the "enchanters" of the economy? How are imagined futures used politically in the governance of economic affairs?

The question of the dynamics of imagined futures also requires further exploration. Evocations of the future are cyclical, and existing expectations are continuously being replaced by new ones that evoke new imaginaries. But the whole process of diffusion and collapse of imaginaries would need much more systematic scrutiny than it has been possible to exercise here.

It is equally important to learn more about how the future orientation of capitalism interacts with experience-based traditional temporal orientations in the economy, which do not simply vanish with the unfolding of capitalist modernity, but reemerge persistently in ever-changing forms. A much more detailed understanding of the distinction between risk and uncertainty is also necessary. Which situations are incalculable because of their uniqueness? Does calculation in such situations allow for better decisions or is it nothing more than a way to give actors enough confidence to make decisions? To what extent do institutional developments such as the enforcement of the market mechanism lead to more uncertainty, thus encouraging the evocation of imagined futures?

Finally, it would be fruitful to further investigate the way the explanation advanced in this book can be related to existing explanations for the dynamics of capitalism, such as theories of functional differentiation, evolutionary theories, and institutional theories. The emphasis on expectations here is not intended to exclude these well-established approaches; rather, it demands exploration of their relationship to the role of imagined futures in the economy.

The macrohistorical side of the research agenda would attempt to periodize the historical development of capitalism with regard to changes in its dominant imaginaries. Approaches in political economy have identified different control concepts of capitalism and different production regimes that show the evolution of capitalism as an economic and social form. Such a historical classification should also be attempted to describe different periods of capitalist development using the development of imaginaries as the demarcating aspect. During the spread of entrepreneurial capitalism in the nineteenth century, the production of new products and technologies occupied imaginaries and propelled growth. From around the 1920s on, imaginaries of consumption—supported by the developing marketing industry—provoked consumer motivation that drove aggregate demand. The making of consumer dreams became a force of production in and of itself. Since the 1990s, imagined futures have focused on financial markets, causing a further reconfiguration of capitalism, albeit one much less able to generate significant levels of growth. Such a *historical economic sociology of imagined futures* could also center on different actor groups such as workers, entrepreneurs, managers, consumers, or economists, in order to understand the trajectory of imagined futures with more specific reference to social groups. Research should demonstrate the immense effort dedicated to the creation of fictional expectations in the unfolding of capitalism and the different forms this effort has taken.

SECULAR ENCHANTMENT

Imagined futures help to explain capitalist dynamics and contribute to a microfoundation of political economy that reaches beyond rational actor theory. The social sciences have sought to explain the dynamics of the capitalist economy and the radical social transformations associated with it since the late eighteenth century. Many of these explanations point to structural changes on the macrolevel, such as new sets of institutions or the division of labor. But the capitalist economy, like any social formation, unfolds through actions by individuals that take place within the confines of a historically emerging social context. Any sociological theory of capitalist dynamics must demonstrate how the macrolevel and the microlevel are linked in the production of observed outcomes. Max Weber examined this question in his thesis on Protestantism, as did other major theorists of capitalism. Schumpeter drew attention to the role of entrepreneurs who attempt to force their visions of the future on the economic system. Similarly, Karl Marx's historical work paid close attention to the conflict between the moral economy of workers and the structural demands of the emerging capitalist system. Pierre Bourdieu's studies on Algeria in the 1950s explored how actors dealt with the new logics of an economy driven by money, bringing the changing temporal orientations of actors in capitalist modernity to the foreground.

Ultimately, however, these eminent theorists of capitalism have a tendency to see the role of agency as secondary or insignificant when compared with the self-propelling forces of the structures of the capitalist economy. Weber and Schumpeter both postulate a specific historical trajectory for the capitalist economy. Weber describes how the motivations generated by Calvinist religious doctrines were the driving forces behind the emergence of modern capitalism, but these doctrines became superfluous once modern capitalism was set in motion. Weber used the famous metaphor of the "iron cage" to describe how actors become mere objects of the systemic powers of capitalism, once it is fully in place. Weber emphasized that the outcome of the capitalist economy might conflict deeply with the ethical demands of "material rationality," but he was convinced that modern capitalism would create a completely disenchanted world. Schumpeter ([1942] 2014) specified in his later work that entrepreneurs would ultimately be replaced by the dominant power of large bureaucracies, implying that capitalism as he defined it would ultimately come to an end. Marx, in his later writing, became increasingly committed to a reading of capitalist dynamics that saw the forces of production as the true determinants of history. Bourdieu, though his work places strong accent on agents, emphasizes habitus to explain action and thus downplays the contingency of agency.

By introducing the idea of fictional expectations, this book also intends to contribute to the reexamination of Weberian assertions about the disenchantment of capitalist modernity and the "iron cage" in which actors are confined. The book's investigation into the microfoundations of the dynamics of capitalism has sought to draw attention back to the impact of agents and to highlight the ways in which their behavior cannot be confined to structural forces, hardwired cognitive regularities, or rational calculation. In crucial ways, capitalism is animated by expressions of agency that are non-rational in the economic sense of the term. Imaginaries of counterfactual futures, pursued with non-rational inspirations such as fantasies, hope, fear, and desire, are a constitutive element of capitalist dynamics, but are only rarely given any serious attention.

Fictional expectations are assessments of the future that pretend the future will unfold in a specific way. Cognitive frames, norms, and emotions are crucial for motivating action based on these imaginaries. As numerous ethnographic and behavioral studies have confirmed, economic decisions, even in modern financial markets, are invariably made with hope, greed, fear, tradition, and familiarity. Modern consumerism reinvigorates the archaic when it produces brand fetishism that resembles the worship of totems described by Durkheim. Innovators indulge in utopian imaginaries of technological futures and pursue them against all odds. With the exception of fully automated decision-making processes, decisions in the economy cannot be detached from the evocation of imaginaries, nor from emotions and tradition. To use Weber's own vocabulary, the modern economy is not exclusively a realm of instrumental rational action; it is also a realm of affective, charismatic, and traditional action.

The concept of fictional expectations accounts for the role of hope and fear, as well as that of fantasy, newness, creativity, judgment, familiarity, and tradition in economic decision-making. Rationalistic approaches to the economy contend that such features are either inconsequential or relics of bygone eras that will vanish as capitalist modernity marches on. But the enchantment Weber believed would evaporate with the unfolding of capitalist modernity is still integral to the operation of the capitalist economy. At the microlevel, one observes "the presence of 'meaning' and 'tradition,' of the 'body,' of 'intimacy,' 'local knowledge' and everything else that is often thought to have been bred out of 'abstract' and 'rationalized' systems" (Knorr Cetina 1994: 6). If economic action is so closely interwoven with life-worlds, then the economy, like other social spheres, is made up of interpretations that are informed by social and normative contexts and shape imaginaries and expectations as to how the future will unfold.

The "hermeneutic construction of the economy" is also animated by the social structures of local environments and by the imaginaries they inform. This is particularly true in situations characterized by high levels of uncertainty, such as the profit-driven world of venture capital. Even there, where one might reasonably assume that desire for profit trumps everything else,

> people matter; their personal constitutions matter; their virtues matter. And the reason they matter has to do with the radical uncertainty of these future-making practices. You need to know about the virtues of people because there is little else you can rely on that is so durable and salient. While there is a clear link with the premodern modes of familiarity that some social historians and social theorists assure us is 'lost,' the reliance on familiarity and the personal virtues is no mere 'survival' of premodernity.

Such things don't belong just, or even naturally, to the premodern 'world we have lost'; they belong equally, or even especially, to the world of making the worlds to come. (Shapin 2008: 303)

Modern capitalism, in other words, is also animated by extra-technical, non-calculative assessments expressed as imagined futures.

The very term "fictional expectations" hints that under conditions of uncertainty nonrationality contributes to all economic action, even that which seeks to be purely rational. The idea of fiction can be used to locate the non-rational core of economic action in the investors, innovators, and consumers who enchant the market through their projections, rather than in religious doctrines driving individuals to fulfill their religious fates. Actors' practices and beliefs are a kind of *secular enchantment* of the world, which dovetails with Durkheim's hypothesis that modern society develops secular forms of the sacred. But while Durkheim's primary focus was on what he called the "cult of the individual" in political and social affairs, the focus here is on the role that secular forms of the sacred play *in the economy*. Credible fictional expectations are deeply held convictions. And, as is the case with religious classifications, fictional expectations in the economy are social projections upheld through collective practices.

Weber did not see the iron cage he predicted modernity would become in a particularly positive light. Indeed, he warned that it would lead to a loss of freedom. Representatives of the Austrian School agreed with him that modernity, with its large bureaucratic structures, was a potential threat to freedom, and argued that organizing the economy around markets was the only way to counter this threat. They believed that given the future's uncertainty and human fallibility, the market should be society's core institution, unfettered by regulatory interventions, since no central agency or forecaster can be capable of grasping the open future's many possibilities well enough to allocate resources efficiently. The market, in their minds, ensured not only economic efficiency but—far more importantly—protected human freedom, because in it, all individual initiatives were possible. This claim became the touchstone of economists in the Chicago School and of German Ordoliberals, and it informs much of economic policy implemented over the past thirty years.

Of course, the argument set out in this book is not the first to object to Weber's vision of the rationalization of the world by modern capitalism, nor to subsequent attempts by the Austrian School and others to institutionalize unfettered markets to preserve the freedom Weber predicted rational-bureaucratic capitalism would threaten. As Bruno Latour (1993) so famously put it, "we have never been modern." Gérald Bronner (2011: 4ff.) points out that the idea that the advancement of knowledge will lead to the elimination of beliefs is itself only a belief, which has its roots in the Enlightenment. The epistemological, institutional, and normative conclusions to be drawn from the observation that Enlightenment descriptions of modernity were inaccurate vary greatly, however.

A small group of social scientists and philosophers argue that the capacity to imagine is central to human freedom. These scholars, however, do not link this capacity to the market. Cornelius Castoriadis (1998), for example, shares Weber's normative concern with protecting freedom, but disagrees with his vision (as well as Marx's) of how modern capitalism will develop, arguing that assertions about rationalization and modernization as unifying processes are themselves attempts to silence history. Such assertions assume a kind of historic predestination, implying that the future cannot be altered through political action based on social imaginaries. This is, Castoriadis contends, a totalitarian understanding of history that falsely portrays complete control over social change as a credible possibility (Joas and Knöbl 2009: 416). Other social theorists plead in favor of the idea that imaginaries have the potential to emancipate by providing new horizons of possible action. Ernst Bloch (1995) makes one such argument in *The Principle of Hope,* and Albert Hirschman and Paul Ricoeur have written along similar lines. More recently, Arjun Appadurai (2013) identified aspirations and the orientation toward the future as a vital cultural capacity that allows actors to detect and navigate new opportunities. Unlike the economists of the Austrian School, Appadurai does not limit the ability to detect new paths to a small group of heroic entrepreneurs and the market; for him, the realization of aspirations does not depend on the operation of the market. Very much in resonance with Bourdieu, Appadurai points to the negative impact of the unequal distribution of resources through market mechanisms on the capacity to aspire in society. Developing this capacity is, for him, a highly desirable goal of social and political mobilization beyond the market.

The work of these thinkers raises the question of whether actors' creative responses to capitalism's uncertainty—imagined futures—can also be understood as a potentially emancipating force. With this question in mind, this book ends on a note of caution. Bill Sewell (2008) observes that capitalism is an economic and social formation that continuously changes its concrete historical form while at the same time remaining perpetually the same. Capitalism is both hyper-eventful and invariable. New products are developed, new features of social life are commodified, and capitalism expands its geographic reach and widens the time horizons it brings under its control. But all this restless creativity is provoked by and perpetually repeats investments into new profit opportunities and the purchase of ever more goods—nothing more. For the most part, the fictional expectations that are pursued in the capitalist economy express no utopian aspirations for individuals or for society, nothing that reaches beyond the demands of capitalist accumulation. Capitalism's imagined futures reflect an endless striving to renew the capitalist principle of gain. Even the utopias that offered alternatives to capitalism, such as certain currents in the labor movement or the protest movements of the 1960s, have seen their imaginaries, as well as the practical activities they inspired, historically reincorporated into the capitalist logic. Capitalism, to maintain the stamina required for its dynamism, must be continuously "animated" by novelty. It thus depends on the creativity and imaginary power of actors, which sometimes articulates itself as resistance to capitalism itself. But in the end, none of that creativity ever sweeps away the principle of accumulation itself. Ultimately, imagined futures are all reincorporated into the inner logic of capitalism. What started as the hippie counter culture in California developed into the hyper-capitalism of Silicon Valley. As detached and even opposed as they may initially seem, imagined futures are in reality an integral part of capitalist reproduction. By including the creative potential of human imagination in the capitalist circuit, capitalist modernity draws it into the iron cage. But the cage of contemporary capitalism is more complex than the ideal type Max Weber once described. Modern capitalism entails much more than instrumentally rational actors and calculative devices—it includes the creativity expressed in imagined futures. The infinite new paths they propose are an indispensable part of the eternal process of capitalist renewal, which is fully contingent in its content, and is sporadically interrupted by crisis. This mixture of creativity and destructiveness was described many decades ago by the German-American theologist Paul Tillich in a single word: demonic.

NOTES

1. See, for instance, Baumol (2002), C. Campbell (1987), Landes (1969), Luhmann (1995), Marx ([1867] 1977), Deirdre McCloskey (2011), North (1990), A. Smith ([1776] 1976), Solow (1957), and Weber ([1930] 1992, [1927] 2003).
2. See, for instance, Hayek (1973), Keynes ([1936] 1964), Kindleberger and Aliber ([1978] 2005), MacKenzie (2011), Marx ([1867] 1977), and Minsky (1982).
3. It should be noted that issues of agency play a stronger role in sociological institutionalism, particularly in notions of the "institutional entrepreneur" (DiMaggio 1988) and "institutional work" (Lawrence and Suddaby 2006).
4. Political science is another field in which there is increasing attention being paid to the role that imaginaries of the future play in political decision-making. See, for instance, Cameron and Palan (2004), Ezrahi (2012), Mallard (2013), Mallard and Lakoff (2011), and Gibson (2012). In psychological research, the role of imaginaries is also significant. For a discussion of imaginaries from the perspective of life course analysis, see Zittoun et al. (2013).
5. See also Tavory and Eliasoph (2013) and C. Taylor (2004).
6. It should be clear that the emphasis on the dynamics of capitalism is not intended to affirm this dynamic normatively. While the capitalist economy has produced unprecedented levels of wealth, it has also led to the detraditionalization of life forms, alienation, recurrent crises, and environmental destruction. The purpose of this book is to contribute to our empirical understanding of the unique and puzzling development of capitalist dynamics and the "restlessness" (Sewell 2008) of capitalism as a social formation.
7. For economics, see Bronk (2009), Davidson (2011), Dequech (1999), Dupuy et al. (1989), Keynes ([1936] 1964), and Orléan (2014). For sociology, see

Beckert (1996), DiMaggio and Powell (1983), Ganßmann (2011), Karpik (2010), P. Menger (2009, 2014), Podolny (2005), and H. C. White (1981). Different forms of uncertainty have been distinguished in the long debates on uncertainty that followed Knight's seminal contribution on the topic. The different typologies are discussed in Chapter 3.

8. The term "future present" was coined by Niklas Luhmann (1976).

2. THE TEMPORAL ORDER OF CAPITALISM

1. See, for instance, Braudel ([1979] 1985), Polanyi ([1944] 1957), and Weber ([1922] 1978).

2. The change of temporal orientations is not just a characteristic of capitalism but of modernity in general. Because the focus of this book is capitalist modernity, other modern economic systems, especially socialism, are not discussed. Another approach to the temporal changes of modern societies has been pursued by Hartmut Rosa (2005). Rosa identifies the acceleration of events as central to the time structures of modernity, rather than the openness of the future. This acceleration can be observed in social practices, institutions, and the attitudes of individuals to the world.

3. Richard Biernacki (1995), for instance, shows that German and British workers also "acquired their understanding of labor as a commodity and their expectations for its use" (383) from devices used to connect time and labor output.

3. EXPECTATIONS AND UNCERTAINTY

1. A similar observation has been made by Arjun Appadurai (2013: 285) regarding the discipline of anthropology. The "intellectual infrastructure of anthropology, and of the culture concept itself, remains substantially shaped by the lens of pastness." This is confirmed by the social anthropologist Mary Douglas (1986: 48), who explains that "past experience is encapsulated in an institution's rules, so that it acts as a guide to what to expect from the future."

2. "Future matters" is also the title of an interesting book by Barbara Adam and Chris Groves (2007). The authors, however, do not focus on how imaginaries of the future influence present decision-making, but rather on the normative question of how we should include future outcomes in the decisions we make today.

3. For a similar assessment, see Joas and Knöbl (2009: 417): "The creative potential of individuals and societies . . . most schools of social theory, with the exception of pragmatism, have either ignored or given only marginal consideration."

4. Irving Fisher (1930) played an especially important role in this when he introduced the notion of "time preference" to explain interest and how to cal-

culate the profitability of investment opportunities. The current value of an investment is calculated through discounted future earnings, making the future the reference point for present decisions. John Commons ([1934] 1961) wrote more than 200 pages in his main work "Institutional Economics" on what he called "Futurity." The chapters, dealing mainly with credit and debt relations, make clear that if economics deals with property rights "plainly it deals only with expectations of income" (418). The notion of expectations regarding future outcomes and discounting future value to the present has been crucial in economics ever since. See also Muniesa and Doganova (2015) and Palan (2012).

5. For a summary of general equilibrium theory, see Hahn (1980) and Weintraub (1974).

6. A similar point has been made by Bill Maurer (2002). Maurer argues that although economic theory has detached itself from deterministic models, the stochastic models used in financial market theories assume a normal distribution of events. This makes it impossible for stochastic models "to deal with radical contingency—the flow of temporality unwritten by divine hand, the accident of luck non-personified. The fetishization of the bell curve and equilibrium supposedly renders predictable the unpredictable, but just as often fails" (29). The models show what ought to be, not the way things are. Rational expectations theory is thus a normative argument, not a factual statement about the future.

7. Another critique points to the impact of the economic model itself on price development as a source of the inaccuracy of economic predictions. It is impossible to determine the intrinsic price of a security because prices "depend at least as much on the models (or the theories) in investor's minds as on outside information" (Guerrien and Gun 2011: 28).

8. This is also the case with subjective expected utility theory (Savage 1954), in which uncertainty is conceptualized as a state in which actors do not know which outcome will happen. Based on their past experiences, however, they can assess the likelihood of each outcome's occurrence. They use Bayesian probability updating to keep account of changes, and are thus able to calculate the optimal choice. Subjective expected utility theory is an example of an economic attempt to do away with uncertainty in the Knightian sense of the term, which assumes the uniqueness and unpredictability of events in the future.

9. More recent discussions in sociology and heterodox economics have further refined the analysis of situations Knight characterizes as uncertain. Giovanni Dosi and Massimo Egidi (1991), for example, distinguished between substantive and procedural uncertainty. The former arises when it is not possible to access all the information necessary to make decisions

leading to certain outcomes, while the latter is attributed to limitations to agents' computational and cognitive capabilities, given the information available, to pursue their objectives in a complex environment. Jon Elster (2009: 4ff.) distinguishes between brute uncertainty, information-gathering uncertainty, and strategic uncertainty. "Brute uncertainty" refers to situations in which appeal to uniform distribution is unwarranted because Bayesian updating does not work; "information gathering uncertainty" refers to search situations in which it is not possible to rationally decide when to stop the search process; and "strategic uncertainty" refers to the infinite regress of the expectations one holds with regard to the expectations of other strategic actors. Davidson (1996: 491–92) distinguishes between "epistemological uncertainty" in complex situations where agents are confronted with a great deal of information they can only incompletely compute; and "ontological uncertainty," which refers to the indeterminate nature of creativity and innovation—in other words, to the openness of the future. Finally, David Dequech (2000) distinguishes between ambiguity and fundamental uncertainty. Ambiguity is uncertainty about probability that arises due to missing—but potentially knowable—relevant information; in an ambiguous situation, the decision-maker does not possess fully reliable knowledge of the probability of the possible outcomes. Fundamental uncertainty, on the other hand, is characterized by the possibility of creativity and nonpredetermined structural change. Since the future is yet to be created, there is no list of predetermined or knowable outcomes to which actors may refer to make decisions. In cases of fundamental uncertainty, decisions must be made despite some relevant information being unknowable, even in principle (see also Beckert and Dequech 2006). In still another definition, a distinction is made among truth uncertainty, semantic uncertainty, and ontological uncertainty (Lane and Maxfield 2005). While there is no consensus on any of the typologies of uncertainty, it seems useful to me to distinguish among three types of uncertainty: first, uncertainty stemming from the complexity of a situation, which makes it practically impossible for actors to choose a course of action that maximizes utility. This form of uncertainty, however, does not undermine theoretical models that assume actors to be perfect calculating machines. Second, uncertainty may stem from the unpredictability of an open future, leading to what has been called "fundamental uncertainty" (Dequech 1999). It is not possible to know in the present what innovations the future holds, and how these innovations will influence considerations relevant to present decisions. Third, uncertainty may stem from social interactions, in which outcomes depend on the actions of third parties, which would need to be accurately predicted in order to choose the optimal course of action. However, even game theory models, with their restricted assumptions, do not make it possible to model unequivocally the choices actors should make to maximize utility.

10. For an insightful discussion of the notion of fundamental value that shares the position that fundamental value cannot be determined, see Bryan and Rafferty (2013). The authors make the intriguing claim that the impossibility of determining the fundamental value of assets is only secondary to the need for measurement, no matter how inexact. See Chapter 9 for more about fundamental value and economic forecasts.

11. This is true despite the fact that individual actors attempt to minimize the uncertainty they face (Knight [1921] 2006: 238). Indeed, one argument often made is that firms try to turn uncertainty into (calculable) risk through calculative devices such as credit rating, due diligence, and capital budgeting. This claim only holds in situations where the law of large numbers applies. Life insurance or credit scoring agencies, for instance, cannot predict the outcome for each individual case but can assume a normal distribution of events over the whole population of insurance buyers or borrowers. Most economic decisions, however, are not of this variety, and in many of them actors are exposed to unpredictable outcomes.

12. Later, in a similar vein, Keynes wrote, ". . . human decisions affecting the future, whether personal or political or economic, cannot depend on strict mathematical expectation, since the basis for making such calculations does not exist" (Keynes [1936] 1964: 162–63).

13. Post-Keynesian economists like Paul Davidson as well as economists from the French *école des conventions* such as André Orléan have also used Keynes's analysis to understand expectations under conditions of uncertainty. Davidson (2010: 21) argues that decision-makers cannot merely assume "that the future can be reduced to quantifiable risks calculated from already existing market data," while Orléan takes up the idea of mimetic imitation as the dominant response to uncertainty.

14. It is striking that Max Weber had relatively little to say about the role of expectations. He touches on them when he defines instrumentally rational action as "determined by expectations as to the behavior of objects in the environment and of other human beings; these expectations are used as 'conditions' or 'means' for the attainment of the actor's own rationally pursued and calculated ends" (Weber [1922] 1978: 24). In a passage from the essay "Some Categories of Interpretative Sociology" (1981: 159–60), Weber explains that action is future-oriented and that expectations with regard to a desired outcome are *reasons for action*. He sees expectations as rooted in the objective probability of an event occurring, as well as in subjective beliefs in the chances that expectations will be realized. Such subjective expectations are at least partly rooted in "agreements" actors *believe* will be

fulfilled. Weber uses the term "agreements" to allude to the institutional backing of expectations that may lead to risky (economic) decisions, thereby pointing to the social context in which expectations are formed. Although the passage does not explicitly mention the concept of uncertainty, it is an implicit part of Weber's deliberation. Instrumentally rational action must confront the problem of uncertain outcomes, and actors obtain reasons to assume the risks related to a given action through expectations. Weber's understanding of expectations, particularly his emphasis on probabilities, is closely related to conventional economic thinking on the subject. At the same time, in his writing on the stock exchange ([1894] 1988a), Weber observes that in speculative transactions, objective chances and subjective expectations fall apart unpredictably, resulting in the speculator's acceptance of "'accidental' factors" (159). Moreover, in his methodological essays, Weber sees imaginaries as epistemological tools. He explains the logic of "singular causal attribution" as based on the construction of alternative courses of events in imagination. In order to understand the causal relationships leading to events that did take place, the historian imagines the consequences of alternative courses of events that did not occur (Weber [1906] 1988b).

15. By referring to order as based on rules that are taken for granted, Garfinkel also connects to the phenomenology of Alfred Schütz. Schütz contends that actors' projections of the future focus on the typicality of situations, and not on novelty. Although they make no explicit reference to Garfinkel or Schütz, Lane and Maxfield (2005) take a similar position when they explain action under conditions of uncertainty through its embeddedness in narrative structure. Social action, they argue, can be conceptualized as a story in which context and past events show each character how she is to act: the story, in other words, "sweeps the actor-narrator along with it" (14). As in the phenomenological approach, scripts or taken-for-grantedness explain action. Such approaches thus underestimate actors' capacity to respond creatively to a situation. Lane and Maxfield emphasize that actors may change stories, but it remains unclear how this claim may be related to the idea that action is "generated by narrative logic" (14).

16. Bourdieu (2000: 234) also speaks of a "relative autonomy of the symbolic order, which, in all circumstances and especially in periods in which expectations and chances fall out of line, can leave a margin of freedom for political action aimed at reopening the space of possibles. Symbolic power, which can manipulate hopes and expectations, especially through more or less inspired and uplifting performative evocation of the future—prophesy, forecast, or prediction—can introduce a degree of play into the correspondence between expectations and chances and open up a space of freedom through the more or less voluntaristic positioning of more or less improb-

able possibles—utopia, project, programme, or plan—which the pure logic of probabilities would lead one to regard as practically excluded." Though Bourdieu sees this possibility of voluntarism as based on imagined futures, it is clearly of secondary importance in his analysis. The dominant thread of his assessment of expectations is that of their being determined by actors' objective life situations.

17. In certain ways, "expectations state theory" in social psychology takes up this research by investigating how "widely held cultural beliefs that link greater social significance and general competence, as well as specific positive and negative skills, with one category of a social distinction compared to another" (Ridgeway 2001) lead to nonmerit-based status orderings in social groups. Inequality is explained by evaluative assumptions made with regard to different social groups. Critics of this explanation of stratification, Pierre Bourdieu (1973) among them, argue that models of educational attainment should focus not on attitudes but on structural constraints stemming from the opportunity structure of society.

18. This corresponds closely to Kendall Walton's (1990) theory of make-believe, which is discussed in Chapter 4. Make-believe, according to Walton (68) provides experience "for free. . . . We realize some of the benefits of hard experience without having to undergo it." Also Paul Ricoeur (1979: 134) writes with regard to the productive role of fiction in creating reality that "in the state of non-engagement we try new ideas, new values, new ways of being-in-the-world. Imagination is this free play of possibilities."

19. This section on Castoriadis relies on Joas and Knöbl (2009).

20. More recently, Mustafa Emirbayer and Ann Mische (1998) have taken the openness of the future into account in their assessment of imagined futures. They distinguish between three components of agency, which they call iterational, projective, and practical-evaluative. Emirbayer and Mische use the term "projectivity" to describe "the imaginative generation by actors of possible future trajectories of action, in which received structures of thought and action may be creatively reconfigured in relation to actors' hopes, fears, and desires for the future" (971). Following Dewey and Ricoeur's lead, Emirbayer and Mische emphasize that actors "reconfigure perceived schemes by generating alternative possible responses" (984). In social processes, these imagined futures are created through narrative construction, symbolic recomposition, and hypothetical resolution. Narratives are tools actors can use to move forward (and backward) in time; they also provide a group-specific cultural frame for imagining the future. Symbolic recomposition is the process by which units of meaning are taken apart and reconfigured in unexpected ways. This overview of the role of expectations in the dynamic and the openness of the social process is only partial; other important contributions

have been made, notable among them George Herbert Mead ([1932] 2002), Ernst Bloch (1995), Hans Joas (1996), Charles Taylor (2004), and Raymond Boudon (2012). Some of these works are discussed in later chapters.

4. FICTIONAL EXPECTATIONS

1. Such fictional worlds can also emerge spontaneously, without props, as, for instance, in dreams and in daydreams. It should also be noted that not all imaginations are fictional, and that real things can be imagined, for example, a spouse who is at home uttering the sentence, "I imagine my spouse is at work." For a highly interesting treatment of the more general role of make-believe games and play in the development of imaginaries of the future from a psychological perspective, see Zittoun et al. (2013), especially pp. 259ff.

2. See also the section in this chapter headed "Fictional Expectations as a Motivating Force for Action."

3. This is also Hayden White's (1973) main argument, that historical facts do not speak for themselves, only through historians' interpretations of them, which involve selecting and weighting facts and then ordering them into a coherent story.

4. The notion of legal fiction has additional meanings in legal philosophy, which are not discussed here.

5. Literary theorists have also argued that fictions are not merely a literary phenomenon, but also part of the larger social world. Wolfgang Iser (1993: 12), for instance, argues that fictions "play vital roles in the activities of cognition and behavior, as in the founding of institutions, societies and world pictures." Philosopher Kendall Walton (1990: 7) argued that "make-believe" is critical to more than just fiction: it "may be crucially involved as well in certain religious practices, in the role of sports in our culture, in the institutions of morality, in the postulation of 'theoretical entities' in science and in other areas."

6. One might indeed ask why the notion of fiction is used here, rather than another term that expresses the difference between depictions of the future and the assessment of facts. Such terms include "beliefs" (Arrow 2013; Bronner 2011), "myths" (Deutschmann 1999), "hopes" (Miyazaki 2004; Swedberg 2007), "imaginaries, stories, narratives, scripts, and ideas" (Blyth 2002; Münnich 2011), "ideologies" (Marx and Engels [1846] 1976), and "ideals and promises" (Knorr Cetina 2015). While these concepts overlap, they each have a different emphasis, none as suitable for my purposes as "fiction," which avoids connotations of false consciousness ("ideology"), is not biased toward optimistic scenarios of the future ("hope, promises"), includes the notions of story and narrative, and in connection to the notion of expectations is directed toward the future (unlike "beliefs"). "Fiction" also connotes creativity but is at the same time more concrete than "imaginaries." Moreover,

it allows parallels to be drawn between the literary fiction and expectations under conditions of uncertainty.

7. Stories are a topic in economic sociology (Diaz-Bone and Krell 2009; Mützel 2010; H. C. White 1992), economics (Akerlof and Shiller 2009; McCloskey 1990), political sociology (Tilly 2006), historiography (H. V. White 1973, 1978) organization studies (Boje 1995; Brown et al. 2005; Czarniawska 1997; Gabriel 2000), economic anthropology (Holmes 2009), and political science (Salmon 2007).

8. Scholars also noted that new forms of fiction, especially the modern novel, developed in historical parallel with the advance of modern capitalism. The development of the novel and the expansion of a fiction-reading middle class have been linked to the advent of modern consumerism, as well as the modern credit economy (C. Campbell 1987: 24ff; Poovey 2008). Similarly, Elena Esposito (2007: 13ff.) has highlighted parallels between the development of probability calculus and the expansion of the theater as an art form in the seventeenth century. Both developments may be seen as an attempt to come to grips with a social situation experienced as increasingly contingent. Both the fictional worlds created in the arts and probability calculus contributed to a general awareness of the contingency of social reality and offered rules for dealing with this newfound contingency.

9. An example, the expectation that the money deposited at a bank can be liquidated any time is a fictional expectation. It holds true only if it is not tested by all customers of the bank simultaneously. For customers to remain willing to deposit money in a bank and to refrain from bank runs, they must be distracted from the fictionality of the expectation that it is possible for them to liquidate their assets at any time.

10. This points to the investigation of the instruments of concealment as a research field in its own right, and at the same time reveals the subversiveness of such investigations. Identifying expectations as fictions returns the contingency and uncertainty of the future to the foreground.

11. In some ways, this resembles the notion of wishful thinking, defined as "the tendency to believe the facts are as one would like them to be" (Elster 1989: 37). However, under conditions of an open future, what the facts actually are is ontologically undetermined. This makes it impossible to say which thinking is wishful and which is not.

12. This is also supported by studies in neuroscience showing that the brain regions activated when imagining pleasurable events are the same as the ones activated when actually experiencing these events (Costa et al. 2010; Speer et al. 2009).

13. See also Appadurai (2013: 289–90) for a similar observation: "I see the capacity to aspire as a navigational capacity, through which poor people can effectively change the 'terms of recognition' within which they are generally

trapped, terms which severely limit their capacity to exercise voice and to debate the economic conditions to which they are confined."

14. For investigations in economic sociology on the role of emotions see Bandelj (2009), Barbalet (1998), Beckert (2006), Berezin (2005), DiMaggio (2002), and Pixley (2004).

15. Niklas Luhmann puts it succinctly: "In the course of the observation of observations true assumptions are made regarding false assumptions and false assumptions regarding true assumptions" (Luhmann 1988: 119). As early as the 1950s John Sawyer (1952: 199) made the observation that there are "instances in which entrepreneurial error or misinformation not only is massively present but where it appears to have been a condition of successful enterprise."

16. This focus on coordination and convention is also prominent in the French school of the *économie des conventions,* which relies strongly on Keynes's discussion of uncertainty and work on coordination by the analytical philosopher David Lewis.

17. I would like to thank Gérald Bronner for pointing out this experiment to me.

18. This is also confirmed by research on lottery ticket purchases. Demand for lottery tickets, which enable daydreams of completely changed lives, is skewed toward the lower middle classes, a social group whose desire for upward mobility contrasts starkly with their actual socioeconomic opportunities. See Beckert and Lutter (2013).

19. In a similar vein, in the seventeenth century infinitesimal calculus was developed by Leibniz, and Newton introduced the concept of infinity to mathematical thinking. This occurred just as capitalism, with its never-ending expansion of wealth, was being developed. I thank Wolfgang Streeck for pointing this out to me.

20. Karl Marx for instance, saw belief systems as ideologies—that is, socially necessary false consciousness—that reflected objective class positions. This deterministic view also strongly influenced the work of Pierre Bourdieu ([1972] 1977), who sees the *habitus* of actors as essentially determined by their position in the field. Though Bourdieu acknowledges that reactions to concrete situations are not fully determined by the position in the field, the notion of habitus leaves very little room for creative responses.

21. This reveals a further difference between the stories in an economy and the stories told in novels: novels are written by individual authors while the stories in an economy emerge from social practices. Stories transporting fictional expectations are sometimes deliberately disseminated by individuals and organizations, but often emerge unintentionally through the discursive processes within a specific field. Fictional expectations in an economy are in this sense based on stories written by author-collectives.

22. The four building blocks discussed are not a complete list of elements crucial to the dynamics of capitalism. Production could also have been discussed. Such a chapter would involve discussion of production models and organizational models, as well as an analysis of the role of fictional expectations in employee motivation and the role of imaginaries in the work process.

5. MONEY AND CREDIT

1. Early on, Max Weber ([1922] 1978: 104) pointed out that money was a precondition for universalizing exchange relations and rational economic calculation. For the centrality of money and credit in the development of capitalism see also Carruthers and Ariovich (2010), Commons ([1934] 1961), Deutschmann (1999), Ganßmann (2011), Ingham (2004), Pollilo (2013), and (Simmel [1907] 1978).

2. This assessment differs from economic accounts of money, which view money as having declining marginal utility, as is the case in all other goods. For a recent analysis of the desire for money for its own sake as central economic motivation see Yuran (2014).

3. By "value of money" I mean actors' expectations that they will receive goods in exchange for the tokens they use as money.

4. Companies can also raise capital through the issuing of equity, and, particularly since the 1980s, companies have increasingly relied on self-financing. The logic, however, remains the same: equity is provided on the expectation of future profit and will be withdrawn if profit goals are disappointed.

5. See Mary Poovey (2008) for an outstanding historical assessment of this "problem of representation." In it, she explains that the expansion of monetary economies based on fiat money shows how the expectation of the value of valueless tokens has grown as a social conviction, allowing for the extension of orientations toward the future in the economy. As can be seen from the increase in debts, the capability of the monetary system to maintain trust has continued to increase despite recurrent monetary crises.

6. Simmel writes: "All other objects have a specific content from which they derive their value. Money derives its content from its value; it is value turned into a substance, the value of things without the things themselves" (Simmel [1907] 1978: 121).

7. In this sense, money is "the counterpart to sacred objects in religious life" (Orléan 2014: 158); its value depends on collective beliefs, just as the power of a totem depends on the beliefs of clan members. The source of the "magic" of money is the collective order itself. Unsurprisingly, Marcel Mauss ([1914] 1974) asserts that religious talismans were actually the first circulating

currency. According to Mauss, the purchasing power of a talisman stems from the social status it confers on the person who carries it.

8. At the same time, the hoarding of wealth in the form of liquidity is never more than a short-run strategy for protecting wealth from the uncertainties of markets, and it cannot be used by all actors at the same time. The macro-effect of too many actors hoarding their money is an economic crisis (Ganßmann 2011: 3). But for a situation of deflation, monetary wealth can only be maintained and increased if it is invested. Inflation forces actors to invest, which implies exposing their wealth to the risks entailed in an unknown future.

9. This does not take into account the problem of counterfeit bank notes. If it circulates in large quantities, counterfeit money is a hazard to the stability of monetary value. A fascinating history of counterfeit money and its connection to the developing capitalist economy in the United States may be found in Mihm (2007). Surprisingly, Mihm shows that in a context of mostly local and regional money supply, such as that of the United States before the Civil War, counterfeit bills were a significant part of the money in circulation.

10. Parallels to this can be found in many other situations involving trust, in which a joint project whose (uncertain) success lies in the future may be undertaken because those actors imagine the project *as if* it had already been successfully completed (Wenzel 2002: 72). The project is imagined in the future perfect tense.

11. Georg Simmel, for instance, emphasized the decisive role of the state in establishing monetary stability when he wrote that money is "based on a guarantee represented by the central political power" (Simmel [1907] 1978: 184). Strong states have more stable currencies.

12. For detailed descriptions of regulatory rules in the international financial system, see, for instance, the contributions in Mayntz (2012).

13. Georg Simmel had a similar intuition when he wrote that "economic credit does contain an element of this supra-theoretical belief, and so does the confidence that the community will assure the validity of the tokens for which we have exchanged the products of our labor in an exchange against material goods" (Simmel [1907] 1978: 179).

14. Pragmatist thinking also offers helpful insight in this vein. To the pragmatists, beliefs and expectations are not merely subjective opinions but rather the outcome of an intersubjective process of deliberation among actors (Commons [1934] 1961: 153). From the pragmatist perspective, the expectation of the future value of money is communicatively established and maintained through speech acts and practices in the economic field.

15. The burning of a flag or of holy books are comparable examples of symbol destruction capable of sparking emotional reactions resembling those occurring when the actual social order is attacked.

16. See for instance Campbell et al. (2012) and Eusepi and Preston (2010). For a review of this literature see Blinder et al. (2008).

17. The two concepts differ in the following way. *Trust* denotes a situation in which the other party may make a deliberate decision to harm me for his own benefit. *Confidence* denotes a situation in which I engage in incalculable risks that emerge from an open future that is equally unforeseeable for both parties. A bank's deliberate misrepresentation of the risks in a loan would be a breach of trust; my expectation that Goldman Sachs will stay in business is an expression of confidence.

18. Although the willingness to grant credit also depends on interest rates, it would be short-sighted to see the expansion of credit as a function of this factor alone: in economic crises, even interest rates close to zero do not lead to an increase in lending. See, for comparison, Keynes ([1936] 1964). This can be observed empirically; for example, in the failure of low interest rates to stimulate investments in the wake of the financial crisis of 2008.

19. Since the functioning of institutions also depends on the "good will" of those regulated by the institutions, moral resources are an indispensable factor in capitalist dynamics (Streeck 2006: 17). This is also true for debt relationships because they too are maintained by a moral framework that assumes debtors are obligated to repay their debt. See Fourcade (2013) and Graeber (2011).

20. See Kalthoff (2005) and Prato and Stark (2012) on the role of interpretation in the valuation of financial assets.

21. Rona-Tas and Hiss (2011) make the interesting observation that the credibility of risk assessments of rating agencies depends itself on the morphological structure of the industry. They argue that it is no coincidence that the market is dominated by precisely three rating agencies. "The tripoly is the optimal solution for when coordination is necessary but a monopoly is not trusted" (243).

22. Wisniewski and Lambe (2013), in a study of equity prices in three countries, show that the intensification of pessimistic press coverage of financial institutions led to lower valuations of banks in the aftermath of the 2008 financial crisis. An "increase in negative coverage induces a statistically significant response in the future returns on banking stocks" (174).

23. See also Bryan and Rafferty (2013). Financial crises, and economic crises more generally, can also lead to the questioning of dominant economic paradigms or "economic imaginaries" (Jessop 2013). This could briefly be observed after 2008, when the magnitude of the crisis led some economists and politicians to question the free market assumptions that dominate the discipline and much of politics since the 1980s. The crisis disrupted actors' "sedimented views of the world" (Jessop 2013: 237). Other examples for this are the turn toward Keynesianism in the wake of the Great Depression and the

turn toward neoliberal imaginaries during the economic crisis of the 1970s (see Chapter 10). The destabilization of dominant economic imaginaries in times of crisis can also be interpreted as a change in expectations associated with specific institutions and policies.

24. One way of stabilizing expectations in times of crisis is to look backward, not forward. During the financial crisis of 2008, economists and politicians made frequent reference to the Great Depression, identifying parallels and differences between the two events and justifying contemporary responses by casting them as an attempt to avoid repeating the mistakes made in the 1930s. Monetary policy in Germany is regularly justified with reference to the hyperinflation of the 1920s and the necessity of avoiding the mistakes made then that led to the devaluation of money.

25. Gorton and Metrick (2012) argue that the crisis of 2007–2008 was a bank run on the repo market and that the U.S. banking system was effectively insolvent.

6. INVESTMENTS

1. For a discussion of the historical origins of discounted cash flow techniques in American industry see Dulman (1989).

2. John Sawyer (1952) argues that, paradoxically, ignorance or errors as to the real costs of an investment project can be a condition for its success. This is the case when capital budgeting underestimates the costs of a project that would never be undertaken if its real costs were known. Such projects may also be profitable when demand is underestimated, or when there is unexpected macroeconomic growth. Successful investments can be made for the wrong reasons, based on entrepreneurial "acts of faith."

3. George Shackle (1970), in his investigation on how businesses reach investment decisions, follows a similar line of thinking by considering several capital budgeting models that, given the uncertainty of the future, would make rational investment decisions possible: the idea of a discount for uncertainty (99) and the idea that investment decisions are made with the baseline criterion that even the worst possible outcome would not endanger the firm's existence (102). In the end, however, he concludes that in "a world where the consequences of deciding to do this or that are essentially and logically beyond the reach of observation and of calculation, where a guaranteed, exact and complete knowledge of them is unattainable, where history exercises in every age and generation her inexhaustible gift of irony and of surprise, no system of prophecy can give objectively sure guidance" (102).

4. For an investigation of the role of fictional expectations in entrepreneurial decisions see Bernasconi (2014). For research on the role of fictional expec-

tations in the negotiation of free trade agreements see de Ville and Siles-Brügge (2014).

5. Imaginaries about solar power date as far back as the late nineteenth century (Ergen 2015). In *The Romance of Modern Invention*, an especially vivid imagined scenario by the engineer Archibald Williams (1910: 209), the author queried: "Do many of us realize the enormous energy of a hot summer's day? The heat falling in the tropics on a single square foot of the earth's surface has been estimated as the equivalent of one-third of a horse power." The use of solar energy would be "so simple, so scientific, and so obvious, that it is easy to imagine it at no far distant date a dangerous rival to King Coal himself" (212).

6. I would like to thank Timur Ergen for making background information on the history of Desertec available to me. Ergen's (2015) excellent book on the development of solar energy since the nineteenth century shows that this industry has always been driven by visions, hopes, and dreams of a better future made possible through the use of the sun for energy production.

7. On this point see also Pongratz, Bernhard, and Abbenhardt (2014) and Geipel (2015).

8. See the documentary *Nicht ohne Risiko*, directed by Harun Farocki. http://www.youtube.com/watch?v=wskdx49AWgI. I would like to thank Fabian Muniesa for pointing me toward this film.

9. The distinction between investment in plant and equipment and in financial assets is not always clear-cut. Stocks and other forms of equity are a financial investment that at the same time constitute ownership rights in a company. Equity investments may be treated as financial investments if the investor does not exercise managerial control over the firm.

10. See also Esposito (2011). It is, however, necessary to distinguish among different classes of financial investments as well as the expectations associated with them. The yield can be calculated for a German government bond, and financial markets treat them as carrying de facto no risk. Future options, by contrast, are highly speculative investments.

11. This is, however, not unique to financial markets: it is true of investment decisions in general. Like a financial investor, an entrepreneur investing in plant and equipment is purchasing opportunities and risks whose magnitude can only be fully assessed once the investment has ended. Both types of investor are in the market, and are thus vulnerable to unexpected market turns.

12. Following John Searle's ([1969] 2011: 57ff) definition of promises, the promise-giver must be sincere in his intentions to act on his promise; fraud, in Searle's words, is an "insincere promise."

13. See the interview in the *Frankfurter Allgemeine Zeitung* from October 17, 2013.

14. This also bears a certain similarity to Harrison White's (1981) market theory, which sees producer decisions as anchored in producers' mutual observations of one another.

15. Charles Smith (2011) observes that the equity option traders he investigated are aware of their inability to anticipate market development. Instead of "making sense" of what is happening in the market by trying to find an ordering narrative to account for events, they "act sensibly in the market" (Smith 2011: 277), meaning that they deal with contingencies and uncertainties in spontaneous and intuitive ways. Smith argues that this form of acting does not replace the significance of narrative in financial markets; indeed, it should add to it.

16. Several conditions must be met for such a community of believers to form. First, there must be a vision of profitable new investment opportunities (a new economy, BRICS, nanotechnology, etc.). Second, the investment strategy must deviate from the norm. Third, the belief must be established that the investment opportunity will come to fruition only if the vision is followed (Kraemer 2010: 192). The investment idea is loaded with an imaginary of a better future: usually it is one of personal riches, but often includes a social vision of a better world.

17. Economists and economic sociologists have noted the importance of promissory stories in very distinct financial market settings. Brooke Harrington (2008), for instance, investigated the role of stories in the investment decisions of private investment clubs. She argues that, "like fiction, investment in stocks requires the construction of imaginative links between signifiers (like stocks) and the signified (value). This is why storytelling is so important in shaping understanding of the stock market: it is literally the lingua franca of investing" (48). Zsuzsanna Vargha (2013) shows how bank agents in Hungary use storytelling to sell home savings plans. In his work on microfinance, Philip Mader (2015) describes how the financial industry, in order to attract investors and borrowers, uses the personal stories of successful borrowers who found their way out of poverty thanks to microcredit. The boom in mortgages in the American housing market was fueled by narratives that promised widespread access to home ownership as a fulfillment of the American dream.

18. Warren Buffet famously called mark-to-model accounting practices for extreme cases as "mark-to-myth" (Berkshire Hathaway 2003: 13) in a clear parallel to the creation of fictional expectations through economic models described here (see Chapter 10). In the legal realm, Marion Fourcade (2011) demonstrates how different rules for the accounting of environmental damage lead to fundamentally different rulings on legal damages and compensation schemes. Like the value of a company, the value of nature depends on the accounting rules used.

19. The hype surrounding the BRICS concept and the disappointment that followed confirm that cognitive concepts are cyclical. As Deutschmann (1999) argues, an investment idea passes through what he calls a "spiral of myths," which may be broken down into five stages: creation, ascension, codification, institutionalization, and decline. At the outset, a myth may project spectacular market buoyancy, as did Glassman's and Hassett's *Dow 36,000,* or it may proclaim "megatrends" like the BRIC concept. At this stage, if the story is credible, it mobilizes financial investments by suspending disbelief. In the end, however, as retrospective analyses of stock market "megatrends" such as BRIC show, investors are often left with dashed hopes: the long-term performance of funds specialized in such investment strategies is lower than more general stock market indices such as the MSCI World (*Die Welt,* May 3, 2013, p. 15).

20. Prato and Stark (2012) argue that actors' valuations in financial markets are also shaped by their location within a network. Different actors evaluate the same situation in different ways because, based on their network positions, they pay attention to different issues. The concept of the *attention network,* while it does not consider assessments as matters of individual taste, pushes past the idea that categories or institutions shape actor cognition on their own. Prato and Stark show that "the same issue will be viewed differently when seen against a different background of other issues" (3).

21. I thank Bruce Carruthers for pointing me to this case.

22. Data for 2011–2012; source: US Department of Education; http://nces.ed.gov/fastfacts/display.asp?id=76].

23. The role of fictional expectations on the demand side of labor markets is not discussed here. In the production process, possessing qualifications is not sufficient: they must also be applied, a phenomenon that has been described as the *labor extraction problem.* Workers in all but the most controlled of work processes have discretion as to how they apply their skills. From the employer's perspective, it is difficult to assess a worker's productivity when making hiring decisions. The value of labor power cannot be determined ex ante. The technologies applied in the recruitment process aim at reducing this uncertainty by interpreting the signals sent by potential employees (Marchal 2013; Gerlach 2013). These technologies can be interpreted as instruments of imagination.

24. Such imaginaries of a future state of the world do not just influence career decisions: they are also strong predictors of school achievement. Social and demographic factors have significant impact on the actual realization of career aspirations (Schoon 2001; Yowell 2002).

25. In the postindustrial economy, work motivation seems to have become partly detached from income. Particularly in industries related to media or the

Internet, for example, participation in the work process seems to operate as a motivating force in itself. Employees (or interns and freelancers) see work as a means to "self-realization" (Deutschmann 2013: 12). Work is motivated by an imaginary of the undetermined results of harnessing one's creativity.

26. In a well-known passage, Max Weber describes the role of this nonrational, evocative excess with reference to academia: "whoever lacks the capacity to put on blinders, so to speak, and to come up to the idea that the fate of his soul depends upon whether or not he makes the correct conjecture at this passage of this manuscript may as well stay away from science. He will never have what one may call the 'personal experience' of science. Without this strange intoxication, ridiculed by every outsider; without this passion, this 'thousands of years must pass before you enter into life and thousands more wait in silence'—according to whether or not you succeed in making this conjecture; without this, you have no calling for science and you should do something else. For nothing is worthy of man as man unless he can pursue it with passionate devotion" (Weber [1922] 1946: 135).

27. Habitus refers to "a system of lasting, transposable dispositions which, integrating past experiences and actions, functions at every moment as a matrix of perceptions, appreciations, and actions" (Bourdieu [1972] 1977: 83).

28. This is also confirmed by Borghans and Golsteyn (2004), who show that schooling behavior depends on the quality of the image students have of the future. The authors do not relate this finding to social class background; rather, they argue that schooling itself has an effect on behaviorally consequential images, meaning that the better-educated make more beneficial investments in human capital.

29. Indeed, another area in which the role of fictional expectations in labor markets might be investigated is the imaginaries of the (socialist) future created in the labor movement (Hölscher 1989; Müller and Tanner 1988) and in social movements more generally (Appadurai 2013: 190ff). Only by convincing their members to measure the costs of collective action in nonutilitarian terms can labor organizations succeed in overcoming the free-rider problem and create the willingness to participate (Offe and Wiesenthal 1985: 183). Labor unions and labor parties often mobilized their members by evoking an "imagined community" (Anderson 1983) of workers in whose name the organization could legitimately demand solidarity. The depiction of imagined future states that collective action will help to bring about is a great motivator to engage with it. Song texts from the labor movement evoke imaginaries of victory in the struggle. A line in the 1863 anthem of the *Allgemeiner deutscher Arbeiterverein,* the ancestor of the current German social-democratic party, says, "all wheels are standing still, if your strong arms so will," describing a future situation in which the utopian state of a successful

strike has been achieved. The song personalizes this achievement by pointing to the necessary condition of the individual worker's participation. The refrain of *The International* declares: "This is the final struggle/ Let us group together, and tomorrow/ The International / Will be the human race." Here again, the lyrics hint at the utopian state to be reached and connect it to the need for collective action in the now, emphasizing that this is the "final struggle" and that the goal can be reached "tomorrow." The immediacy of the imagined success shortens the lapse of time between the present and the utopian future, thus making the end of the struggle seem imminent.

30. See for example Moen and Roehling (2005).

31. For an account of the consequences of hopelessness on individual aspirations, see the enduringly impressive study of the Austrian town of Marienthal conducted during the Depression (Jahoda, Lazarsfeld, and Zeisel [1933] 1971), in which the authors describe how the unemployed in Marienthal had lost all relationship to the future, had no long-term plans, and had lost all consciousness of time in their daily conduct. See also Katherine Newman's books (1993, 1999) on downward social mobility in America.

7. INNOVATION

1. Descriptions of technological development in forecasting models also often assume—contrary to all that is known about innovation processes—that technological development is linear, leading to stage models that provide generalized concepts of technological development.

2. This is also true of the approach by Lane and Maxfield (2005: 11), who claim that actors in innovation processes deal with ontological uncertainty using "narrative embedding." By this they mean that "actors hold ontological uncertainty temporarily at bay by interpreting the contexts in which they must act in terms of stories whose structure is familiar from their past experience, and then they follow *narrative logic*, enacting their role in the story."

3. This part of Schumpeter's book was not translated in the 1934 English edition. I am therefore quoting from the German edition, with my own translations.

4. Psychological theories (Beach and Mitchell 1987) distinguish between several mental "images" through which knowledge is represented: The *self-image*, consisting of personal beliefs and values; the *trajectory image*, depicting a desirable future; the *action image*, portraying the sequence of actions required to achieve the desirable future; and the *projected image*, which depicts an action's anticipated results.

5. See, for example, Adorno and Horkheimer ([1944] 2002).

6. See for instance Borup et al. (2006); Brown, Kraft, and Martin (2006); Jasanoff and Kim (2009); van Lente and Rip (1998). In England, an approach known as the "sociology of expectations" is investigating the innovation process using the notion of promissory expectations (Borup et al. 2006).

7. Analogically, one may investigate the role of organizational visions, often expressed in "mission statements" in creating imagined futures and orienting decisions.

8. Interesting empirical research on the promissory story of the driverless car is presented in Araujo, Mason, and Spring (2014).

9. See Chapter 8 for a description of a similar mechanism that drives the dynamics of consumer demand.

10. This should also qualify the claim of Sturken and Thomas (2004: 225) that "new social order is possible on the basis of the (heterogeneous) contents of collective-level projections of the future." While expectations are influential, their impact is disciplined by social institutions and existing cognitive and moral frames.

11. The translation in Koselleck (2004) is erroneous.

8. CONSUMPTION

1. The chapter is based on Beckert (2011).

2. For work on the valuation of consumer goods, see the contributions in Beckert and Aspers (2011) and Beckert and Musselin (2013) as well as Karpik (2010).

3. As Durkheim ([1912] 1965: 261) remarks with regard to totemistic emblems, the value "assumed by an object is not implied in the intrinsic properties of this latter: it is added to them." See also D. Marshall (2010: 64).

4. In his essay "Economic Possibilities for Our Grandchildren," Keynes turns briefly to the microfoundations of demand, distinguishing between two types of needs: "those needs which are absolute in the sense that we feel them whatever the situation of our fellow human beings may be, and those which are relative in the sense that we feel them only if their satisfaction lifts us above, makes us feel superior to, our fellows" (Keynes [1931] 1972: 326). While Keynes sees the first type of needs satisfied "much sooner perhaps than we are all of us aware" (326) the second type he sees as insatiable. This supports the argument that capitalist growth is ever more dependent on positional and imaginary value.

5. A few marginal remarks in the book relate vaguely to the economy, but the economy does not receive any systematic treatment.

6. The physical performance of goods is often referred to as "functional value" (Valtin 2005) or "utilitarian value" (Richins 1994). These terms appear misplaced to me because they seem to imply that other forms of value in products can emerge without having a function or utility.

7. Akerlof's analysis implies that a problem emerges from the asymmetric distribution of information, rather than a question of the social constitution of qualities. Following his reasoning, once everyone knows a good's qualities, an objective basis exists for judging the good and comparing it to all other goods. This fails to account for the fact that judgments of quality are socially constructed, and the criteria used to evaluate product qualities are based on social conventions. These judgments may be objective in cases where physical performance can be easily measured (such as the different chemical compositions of an oil), but in the case of objects so complex that qualities cannot be objectively established, or in cases where aesthetic qualities must be taken into account, quality is not merely measured through quality assessments—it is established by them. This phenomenon may, for instance, be observed in wine ratings (such as Parker's), which influence how consumers assess the quality of wine.

8. The distinction between positional and imaginative value is based partly on distinctions among forms of symbolic consumption introduced by Marsha Richins (1994).

9. For the sake of avoiding misunderstanding, it should be noted this does not imply that imaginative value is purely individual; to the contrary, preferences are culturally and socially rooted. The point of this distinction is that value does not necessarily emerge from the owner's calculations of how her purchase will position her in a given social space.

10. A good's positional performance is public in the sense that symbolic meaning must be attributed to it by a third party in order to classify the good's owner by bestowing a certain social identity upon him. This happens independent of the owner himself, although he may be aware of the positional effects of his purchasing choices and take them into consideration as he purchases. Imaginative value is private, in that the purchaser himself ascribes symbolic meaning, even if the meaning he ascribes reflects moral values and orientations that are socially constituted (Fischer and Benson 2006; Richins 1994). The social positioning of the owner by others' judgments of the objects he possesses is therefore significantly different from the "bridging of displaced meaning" (McCracken 1988: 104) through the imaginative performance of goods. Gambling is a useful example to clarify this difference: possessing a lottery ticket does not lead to social repositioning, but may link its owner to an imaginary in which his social position is transformed.

11. Because the purchase of lottery tickets has a defined negative monetary utility—the statistical value of a ticket is only about half of what it costs—lottery tickets should be considered to be a consumer product.

12. André Vereta Nahoum (2013) has written an excellent dissertation on this topic. He investigated how the Yawanawa culture, which is indigenous to the southwestern Amazon, is projected into the products of an American

cosmetics company that uses the seeds of the native Bixa Orellana plant in its products. The company markets its products using idealized images of the Yawanawa culture, which Vereta Nahoum analyzes as an instance of the commodification of culture.

13. See also Durkheim ([1912] 1965: 243ff.).

14. Schumpeter ([1912] 2006: 164) observes that from the moment an entrepreneur begins to seriously engage in a new project, its existence becomes perceptible to her.

15. This is not to say that identities are created and maintained through consumption patterns alone, but rather that all social groups make some demands on their members with regard to their consumption patterns, and sanction those who deviate from group norms. However, groups differ widely with regard to their tolerance for deviations and group membership involves more than consumption patterns.

16. Such secular-yet-sacred entities also informed later discussions of civil religion (Bellah 1967; Luckmann 1967).

17. The mystical and quasi-religious appearance of commodities is also an important part of Marx's analysis of commodity fetishism (Marx [1867] 1977). However, Marx attributes the exchange value of commodities to the employment of labor power in the production process, and he defines as fetishism actors' perceptions of the exchange of goods as a relationship among objects, rather than a relationship among the actors themselves. In the analysis developed here, the mystical character of goods is located in the attribution of symbolic value. Value is thus understood not from the perspective of the production process but from that of market exchange.

18. In this sense advertising is not merely manipulative, as a long tradition of cultural criticism maintains (Adorno and Horkheimer [1944] 2002; Galbraith [1958] 1998): it actually constitutes goods' symbolic content.

19. Here, one might speculate about whether societies such as the United States, in which class barriers are at least outwardly less forceful, are also societies in which imaginaries of a better future have a greater impact on consumer behavior as well as on investment decisions. If this is true, it may be an entry point in helping to explain growth differences among different countries.

20. See, for instance, Felipe Gonzales's excellent dissertation (2015) on the development of the market for consumer credit in Chile.

21. According to Belk, Wallendorf, and Sherry (1989: 30), there are four distinct ways the sacred status of goods is maintained: the separation of the sacred from the profane, ritual, bequests, and tangibilized contamination. It would be informative to investigate which types of products are more vulnerable to disillusionment than others. It could be hypothesized that products that can also be defined as investments (art, real estate, jewelry, etc.) are the least

vulnerable because they can evoke fantasies of increased wealth after their purchase.

22. The most comprehensive treatment of the role played by fantasies of a desired, better world is probably Ernst Bloch's *The Principle of Hope* (Bloch 1995). While Bloch focuses on the utopian political potential of the human ability to imagine a better future, he also discusses the experience of consumers daydreaming about new identities as they (window)shop. The transcending—that is, utopian—force of human imagination lies at the core of Bloch's analysis.

23. The two instruments of imagination discussed in Chapters 9 and 10 are not the only ones operating in the capitalist economy. More chapters could have been included in this book, for instance on the role of advertising and marketing as instruments for constructing the imaginaries of future satisfaction of consumers. Other instruments of imagination include accounting techniques, business plans (Giraudeau 2012; Doganova and Renault 2008), and business strategies. All these instruments are essential for the generation of fictional expectations regarding future outcomes in capitalist modernity.

9. FORECASTING

1. Although forecasting is used in other kinds of planning, such as economic development, environmental work, or international relations, these fields lie outside the scope of this book. For examples, see Andersson (2013) and Mallard and Lakoff (2011).

2. For a historiography of forecasting see Antholz (2006), Dominguez, Fair, and Shapiro (1988), Martino (1983), Makridakis, Wheelwright, and Hyndman (1998), Tooze (2001), W. Friedman (2014), and Reichmann (2011).

3. European countries began using macroeconomic forecasting at roughly the same time. In the United Kingdom, the Cambridge Economic Service was established in 1921. In France, the Statistical Institute of the University of Paris was founded in the same year. In Germany, the *Institut für Konjunkturforschung* (Institute for Business-Cycle Research) was inaugurated in 1925 (Tooze 2001: 103). Specialized institutes of this kind were also developed in Austria, Sweden, and the Soviet Union at this time (Favero 2007: 8).

4. I would like to thank Timur Ergen for making this information available to me.

5. See, for example, "Top 30 Failed Technology Predictions," http://listverse.com/2007/10/28/top-30-failed-technology-predictions/.

6. Dominguez, Fair, and Shapiro (1988) write that even with today's econometric techniques and access to data sets, it would have been impossible to predict the Great Depression.

7. Evaluation studies of predictions are somewhat problematic, particularly in that the criteria for success and failure have not been fully specified. Can a prediction be considered successful if it merely points in the right direction, or must it be precisely accurate? Which is more important, the methodology employed in the prediction or the accuracy of the outcome alone? "The interpretation of 'wrong' economic forecasts depends on the validating systems. The community of economists emphasizes the process; that is, they argue that a good forecast is one that was produced in the right way. For the public, only the results count" (Reichmann 2012: 11). Even if an observed result matches a prediction, it is not clear whether the outcome is the result of the causal mechanisms assumed in the model, or it comes about due to very different mechanisms. If the latter is the case, the model remains inadequate.

8. See also Popper ([1957] 1964, 1982).

9. Assessments of the failure of macroeconomic and technological forecasts try to distinguish situations in which accurate predictions are more likely to be made from those in which they are less likely. For instance, Davidson (2010) makes use of Samuelson's (1969) notion of ergodic processes. Good historical information about how the economic system works is available for ergodic processes, which makes it possible to use statistical results from those processes to extrapolate a pattern into the future in the form of a forecast. Such information is not available for nonergodic processes. Bronk (2013) argues that predictions become especially unreliable in times of rapid innovations in markets. De Laat (2000) states that "methods that focus on calculus, systems analysis, or any other parameterization, work only in settings in which they can work, i.e. in situations which for the greater part have been constructed and stabilized" (180). Furthermore, and not surprisingly, evaluation studies of forecasts show that the accuracy of predictions declines as the time span of the predictions increases (Kholodilin and Siliverstovs 2009; Taleb 2010).

10. This does not mean, however, that forecasts are the product of social judgments alone. As noted above, formal econometric models play a significant role; indeed, the judgments to which forecasters have recourse make sense only in the context of the formal modeling (R. Evans 2007: 693). There is "a broad consensus regarding the value of these instruments in framing interpretative discussions" (Holmes 2009: 400); furthermore, these models are the backbone of the narratives forecasts deliver.

11. In this sense, the value of forecasts is based on collective beliefs, which are the result of actors' involvement in discursive processes. In other words, their value is constructed in much the same way as that of money or consumer goods. This kind of value cannot exist independently of actors' assessments of it. Instead, it is the outcome of contingent evaluations of actors in a given field.

12. It is worth noting Ludwik Fleck ([1935] 1979) and his discussion of "thought collectives." Fleck argued that knowledge processes cannot be understood as a relationship between a subject and an object; rather, the creation of knowledge takes place through exchanges among multiple actors. His point was not that all participants converge on one perspective, but that the recognition of different perspectives within the field provides a basis from which an actor may form her own perspective. For Fleck, the interaction between scientific experts and an interested lay public also plays an important role in the production of scientific knowledge.

13. The fact that heightened economic uncertainty of today's liberalized economies is creating an ever-increasing demand for forecasts and projections highlights an interesting irony. The idea that markets are simply an alternative to planning as a coordination mechanism—as claimed by the Austrian economists cited earlier as well as by other proponents of market liberalization—does not hold. Planning is as central to market economies as it is to any other type of economy, the only difference being that planning in a market economy is decentralized and delegated from the state to the firm, which relies on fictitious projections of profit opportunities, rather than on policy goals, to make decisions.

14. Early on, Max Weber ([1906] 1988b) argued that counterfactuals make it possible to recognize causal influences. And Morgenstern (1928: 118) argued that deviations from prognoses can be virtuous because of the learning opportunities they provide.

15. Deception (Harrington 2009) occurs when the author of a forecast proclaims a future he does not believe in because doing so gives him an advantage. The behavior of some banks and rating agencies in the period before the financial crisis of 2008 may be interpreted as deceptive. Banks sold highly rated financial products they believed were worthless, and benefited both from the sale and from betting those products would fail.

16. In political contexts, forecasts may actually play a part in the governance of society. As Jenny Andersson writes with regard to projections at the RAND Corporation in the 1960s, scientists were "not primarily interested in the accuracy of prediction. Instead it was the communicative, indeed self-fulfilling, aspect of prediction that they found promising" (Andersson 2013: 7). "In futurology, therefore, concepts of scientific observation, and concepts of political action oftentimes seemed to merge" (5).

10. ECONOMIC THEORY

1. MacKenzie (2006) formulated the constitutive idea of performativity in the catchphrase "an engine, not a camera," meaning that economic theory is not

simply a photographic representation of economic reality. Instead, he argues, it should be compared to an engine, in that it is an instrument for *driving* the economy. Milton Friedman (1953: 35) also used this metaphor: Writing of the nineteenth-century economist Alfred Marshall, he says, "Marshall took the world as it is; he thought to construct an 'engine' to analyze it, not a photographic reproduction of it."

2. This also supports questions about the idea mentioned above that economic theories are performative. Theories may affect economic outcomes, but not necessarily in a way that increases their predictive capacity. The openness and uncertainty of the future make this impossible, at least as an overarching trend. Theories may be "engines" of the economy, as some have argued, but what the engines produce cannot be predicted.

3. See also Mäki (2002).

4. In his essay "How is society possible?" Georg Simmel ([1908] 2009) tackles the question of whether the Kantian postulate that nature is constituted through intellectual acts of categorization can also be applied to society. For Simmel, the chief difference between nature and society is that the elements constituting society (individuals) are conscious of their relatedness, independent from any observer, which is not the case in nature. The relatedness of individuals, in other words, is not imposed upon them from the outside. However, Simmel maintains that this does not rule out the possibility "of an observant third party crafting a well-founded subjective synthesis of the relations between persons, as between spatial elements" (41). This is exactly what theories of society and the economy do: they craft syntheses of the relations among persons.

5. Despite the gap he described between the apperception and the things-in-themselves, Vaihinger was not a scientific relativist. According to his thinking, scientific fictions should only be used as long they aid scientific progress. In the process of scientific inquiry, when fictions contradict one another, they must be altered: scientific fictions are "provisional representations which at some future time are to make room for better and more natural systems" (Vaihinger 1924: 19).

6. Vaihinger sees fictions as the necessary basis for the development of all higher forms of intellectual life—not just of the sciences, but of philosophy and religion, as well.

7. The concentration of masses in gravitational points is a fiction in physics that neglects many of the features of mass but is nevertheless useful for recognizing certain properties of physical systems. Other examples of such fictions are the notions of ideal gas, absolute zero, or the light ray (Ströker 1983: 113).

8. To see scientific models as abstracting from the manifold elements of the real world is assumed by the "isolation approach" (Mäki 1992b, 1994). Models

are seen as isolating the relevant explanatory features of reality from the complexity of the real world. Law-like propositions are made by removing many factors, which remain part of the theory only as *ceteris paribus* clauses. Though the isolation of factors makes the theory unrealistic, it may still be able to describe an aspect of reality.

9. For example, Chicago economist Gary Becker's well-known idea (1964) that families should be considered as a kind of human capital does not mean that the typical family—that complex mixture of love, convenience, and frustration—is a business enterprise (McCloskey 1985: 86). Rather, in the tradition of Friedman, economists using this postulate treat the family *as if* it were human capital, and consciously leave out many of the qualities families are known to possess. This doubling of reality is intended to provide insight into the functioning of the family that would otherwise remain obscured.

10. For a detailed discussion of the epistemology pursued by Friedman, particularly of the question of whether Friedman suggests an instrumentalist or a realist epistemology, see Uskali Mäki's excellent reconstructions (1992a, 2000, 2009b).

11. Durkheim claimed that the clan members were not capable of understanding the "fictional" character of their classification systems, which was revealed only through the scientific inquiry of the sociologist. It may be argued that the same is true of economists (or other social scientists) who claim that models are true representations of reality.

12. The speculator George Soros (1987) has developed an approach to understanding self-reinforcing processes in financial markets based on the reflexivity of social phenomena. Contrary to the assumption made by economic theory, he argues that expectations regarding the future value of an asset not only influence the price of the asset but also its underlying fundamental value. If this happens, expectations become self-reinforcing, leading to cycles of bubbles and busts. This contradicts the core idea of equilibrium theory that prices in markets are efficient and that markets tend toward equilibrium.

13. Note the implicit reference to the possible world approach of David Lewis (1986). Lewis sees fictional objects as *actually* existing in possible worlds.

14. Iser (1983) also sees the hiding of the fictional character of the text as a main difference between fictional and nonfictional texts (see Chapter 4).

15. McCloskey emphasizes that different scientific groups must overlap sufficiently, in order to avoid a balkanization of the scientific community and to maintain the standards of scientific inquiry (1985: 29).

16. In this sense, theory is akin to utopian thought, in that it emphasizes a gap between reality and the ideal. For the practical use of the efficient market hypothesis in financial markets see also Ortiz (2014).

17. Neither Vaihinger nor Durkheim paid attention to the role of power in the formation of expectations. To Vaihinger, the utility of scientific fictions was limited to their contribution to scientific progress. Vaihinger acknowledged social implications only with regard to fictions outside the realm of science: for example, he argued that belief in God was a useful fiction because it aided childrearing. Durkheim did not see symbolic representations as instruments that might be used in power struggles, either. He saw representations as collective, encompassing the whole clan, whose members had no consciousness of the contingent nature of their beliefs. When applied to modern societies, this homogenizing view of culture is a limit to Durkheim's theory.

18. See also Blyth (2002), Mirowski and Plehwe (2009), and Schmidt and Thatcher (2013).

19. Note the resemblance to Thomas Kuhn's assessment of scientific paradigm shifts.

20. Neil Fligstein (1990) offers a longer-term perspective on the influence of heuristic fictions on corporate governance in his study of changes in the corporate control of American firms over the twentieth century. Fligstein argues that at different points, managers have embraced distinct "conceptions of control," which they apply to organizing corporate activities. These conceptions of control can be interpreted as paradigms prompting imaginaries that motivate organizational changes in certain ways. At the beginning of the century, firms were organized around manufacturing; subsequently, they were structured around marketing, then around the model of multidivisional conglomerates, and, finally, around finance. Behind each of these strategy shifts—each of which fundamentally transformed the organizational structure of the firms—stood a new imaginary of how to succeed in the competitive struggle.

11. CONCLUSION

1. Of course, from the perspective of general sociology, the notion of fictional expectations lends itself also to a much broader research program investigating the role of expectations in the family, in politics, in religion, in law, and so forth.

REFERENCES

Abbott, Andrew. 2005. "Process and Temporality in Sociology: The Idea of Outcome in U.S. Sociology." In *The Politics of Method in the Human Sciences: Positivism and Its Epistemological Others,* edited by George Steinmetz, 393–426. Durham, NC: Duke University Press.

Abolafia, Mitchel Y. 2010. "Narrative Construction as Sensemaking: How a Central Bank Thinks." *Organization Studies* 31: 349–67.

Adam, Barbara, and Chris Groves. 2007. *Future Matters: Action, Knowledge, Ethics.* Leiden, Netherlands: Brill.

Admati, Anat R., and Martin F. Hellwig. 2013. *The Bankers' New Clothes: What's Wrong with Banking and What to Do about It.* Princeton, NJ: Princeton University Press.

Adolf, Marian, and Nico Stehr. 2010. "Zur Dynamik des Kapitalismus: Machtgewinner und Machtverlierer." In *Capitalism Revisited: Anmerkungen zur Zukunft des Kapitalismus. Festschrift für Birger Priddat,* edited by Alihan Kabalak, Karen van den Berg, and Ursula Pasero, 15–38. Marburg, Germany: Metropolis.

Adorno, Theodor W., and Max Horkheimer. (1944) 2002. *Dialectic of Enlightenment: Philosophical Fragments.* Translated by Edmund Jephcott. Stanford, CA: Stanford University Press.

Aglietta, Michel, and André Orléan. 1992. *La violence de la monnaie.* Paris: Presses Universitaires de France.

Akerlof, George A. 1970. "The Market for 'Lemons': Quality Uncertainty and the Market Mechanism." *Quarterly Journal of Economics* 84: 488–500.

Akerlof, George A., and Robert J. Shiller. 2009. *Animal Spirits: How Human Psychology Drives the Economy, and Why It Matters for Global Capitalism.* Princeton, NJ: Princeton University Press.

Almeling, Rene. 2014. "Medical Professionals, Relational Work, and Markets for Bodily Knowledge: The Case of Direct-to-Consumer Genetic Testing." American Sociological Association (ASA) Annual Meeting, August 10–13, 2013, New York.

Anderson, Benedict. 1983. *Imagined Communities: Reflections on the Origin and Spread of Nationalism.* London: Verso.

Andersson, Jenny. 2013. *Forging the American Future: RAND, the Commission for the Year 2000 and the Rise of Futurology.* Paris: Sciences Po.

Andreozzi, Luciano, and Marina Bianchi. 2007. "Fashion: Why People Like It and Theorists Do Not." In *The Evolution of Consumption: Theories and Practices,* edited by Marina Bianchi, 209–30. Amsterdam: Elsevier.

Ansari, Shahzad, and Raghu Garud. 2009. "Inter-generational Transitions in Socio-technical Systems: The Case of Mobile Communications." *Research Policy* 38: 382–92.

Ansell, Chris. 2005. "Pragmatism and Organization." Unpublished manuscript. Department of Political Science, University of California, Berkeley.

Antholz, Birger. 2006. "Geschichte der quantitativen Konjunkturprognose-Evaluation in Deutschland." *Vierteljahrshefte zur Wirtschaftsforschung* 75: 12–33.

Appadurai, Arjun. 1996. *Modernity at Large: Cultural Dimensions of Globalization.* Minneapolis: University of Minnesota Press.

———. 2013. *The Future as Cultural Fact: Essays on the Global Condition.* London: Verso.

Araujo, Luis, Katy Mason, and Martin Spring. 2014. "Performing the Future: Expectations of Driverless Cars." Presented at the 3rd Market Studies Workshop, Saint-Maximin-la-Sainte-Baume, France.

Arnould, Eric J., and Craig J. Thompson. 2005. "Consumer Culture Theory (CCT): Twenty Years of Research." *Journal of Consumer Research* 31: 868–82.

Arrow, Kenneth J. (1969) 1983. "The Organization of Economic Activity: Issues Pertinent to the Choice of Market versus Nonmarket Allocation." In *General Equilibrium.* Vol. 2 of *Collected Papers of Kenneth J. Arrow,* 133–55. Cambridge, MA: The Belknap Press of Harvard University Press.

———. 1985. "The Economic Implications of Learning by Doing." In *Production and Capital.* Vol. 5 of *Collected Papers of Kenneth J. Arrow,* 157–80. Cambridge, MA: The Belknap Press of Harvard University Press.

———. 2013. "Knowledge, Belief and the Economic System." *Monatsberichte des Österreichischen Instituts für Wirtschaftsforschung* 86: 943–51.

Arrow, Kenneth J., and Gerard Debreu. 1954. "Existence of an Equilibrium for a Competitive Economy." *Econometrica* 22: 265–90.

Augier, Mie, and Kristian Kreiner. 2000. "Rationality, Imagination and Intelligence: Some Boundaries in Human Decision-making." *Industrial and Corporate Change* 9: 659–81.

Aynsley, Sarah, and Barbara Crossouard. 2010. "Imagined Futures: Why Are Vocational Learners Choosing Not to Progress to HE?" *Journal of Education and Work* 23: 129–43.

Bacharach, Michael, and Diego Gambetta. 2001. "Trust in Signs." In *Trust in Society*, edited by Karen S. Cook, 148–84. New York: Russell Sage.

Backhouse, Roger E. 1985. *A History of Modern Economic Analysis.* Oxford: Blackwell.

———. 2010. *The Puzzle of Modern Economics: Science or Ideology?* New York: Cambridge University Press.

Ball, Stephen J., Sheila MacRae, and Meg Maguire. 1999. "Young Lives, Diverse Choices and Imagined Futures in an Education and Training Market." *International Journal of Inclusive Education* 3: 195–224.

Bandelj, Nina. 2009. "Emotions in Economic Action and Interaction." *Theory and Society* 38: 347–66.

Bandelj, Nina, and Frederick F. Wherry, eds. 2011. *The Cultural Wealth of Nations.* Stanford, CA: Stanford University Press.

Bar-Hillel, Yehoshua. 1966. "On a Misapprehension of the Status of Theories in Linguistics." *Foundations of Language* 2: 394–99.

Barbalet, Jack M. 1998. *Emotion, Social Theory, and Social Structure: A Macrosociological Approach.* Cambridge: Cambridge University Press.

———. 2009. "Action Theoretic Foundations of Economic Sociology." In *Wirtschaftssoziologie*, edited by Jens Beckert and Christoph Deutschmann, 143–57. Kölner Zeitschrift für Soziologie und Sozialpsychologie, Special Issue 49.

Bareis, Alexander J. 2008. *Fiktionales Erzählen: Zur Theorie der literarischen Fiktion als Make-Believe.* Gothenburg, Sweden: University of Gothenburg.

Barlow, John P. 2004. "The Future of Prediction." In *Technological Visions: The Hopes and Fears That Shape New Technologies*, edited by Marita Sturken, Douglas Thomas, and Sandra J. Ball-Rokeach, 177–85. Philadelphia: Temple University Press.

Baumol, William J. 2002. *The Free-Market Innovation Machine: Analyzing the Growth Miracle of Capitalism.* Princeton, NJ: Princeton University Press.

Bausor, Randall. 1983. "The Rational-Expectations Hypothesis and the Epistemics of Time." *Cambridge Journal of Economics* 7: 1–10.

Beach, Lee R., and Terence R. Mitchell. 1987. "Image Theory: Principles, Goals, and Plans in Decision Making." *Acta Psychologica* 66: 201–20.

Becker, Gary S. 1964. *Human Capital: A Theoretical and Empirical Analysis, with Special Reference to Education.* 2nd ed. New York: Columbia University Press.

Becker, Gary S., and Casey B. Mulligan. 1997. "The Endogenous Determination of Time Preference." *The Quarterly Journal of Economics* 112: 729–58.

Becker, Howard S. 1982. *Art Worlds.* Berkeley: University of California Press.

Beckert, Jens. 1996. "What Is Sociological about Economic Sociology? Uncertainty and the Embeddedness of Economic Action." *Theory and Society* 25: 803–40.

———. 1999. "Agency, Entrepreneurs and Institutional Change: The Role of Strategic Choice and Institutionalized Practices in Organizations." *Organization Studies* 20: 777–99.

———. 2002. *Beyond the Market: The Social Foundations of Economic Efficiency.* Princeton, NJ: Princeton University Press.

———. 2005. "Trust and the Performative Construction of Markets." *MPIfG Discussion Paper* 05/8. Cologne: Max Planck Institute for the Study of Societies.

———. 2006. "Was tun? Die emotionale Konstruktion von Zuversicht bei Entscheidungen unter Ungewissheit." In *Kluges Entscheiden: Disziplinäre Grundlagen und interdisziplinäre Verknüpfungen,* edited by Arno Scherzberg, 123–41. Tübingen, Germany: Mohr Siebeck.

———. 2009. "The Social Order of Markets." *Theory and Society* 38: 245–69.

———. 2010. "Institutional Isomorphism Revisited: Convergence and Divergence in Institutional Change." *Sociological Theory* 28: 150–66.

———. 2011. "The Transcending Power of Goods: Imaginative Value in the Economy." In *The Worth of Goods: Valuation and Pricing in the Economy,* edited by Jens Beckert and Patrik Aspers, 106–28. Oxford: Oxford University Press.

———. 2013a. "Capitalism as a System of Expectations: Toward a Sociological Microfoundation of Political Economy." *Politics and Society* 41: 323–50.

———. 2013b. "Imagined Futures: Fictional Expectations in the Economy." *Theory and Society* 42: 219–40.

Beckert, Jens, and Patrik Aspers, eds. 2011. *The Worth of Goods: Valuation and Pricing in the Economy.* Oxford: Oxford University Press.

Beckert, Jens, and David Dequech. 2006. "Risk and Uncertainty." In *International Encyclopedia of Economic Sociology,* edited by Jens Beckert and Milan Zafirovski, 582–87. London: Routledge.

Beckert, Jens, and Mark Lutter. 2009. "The Inequality of Fair Play: Lottery Gambling and Social Stratification in Germany." *European Sociological Review* 25:475–88.

———. 2013. "Why the Poor Play the Lottery: Sociological Approaches to Explaining Class-based Lottery Play." *Sociology* 47:1152–70.

Beckert, Jens, and Christine Musselin, eds. 2013. *Constructing Quality: The Classification of Goods in Markets.* Oxford: Oxford University Press.

Beckert, Jens, and Jörg Rössel. 2013. "The Price of Art: Uncertainty and Reputation in the Art Field." *European Societies* 15: 178–95.

Belk, Russell W., Melanie Wallendorf, and John F. Sherry. 1989. "The Sacred and the Profane in Consumer Behavior: Theodicy on the Odyssey." *The Journal of Consumer Research* 16: 1–38.

Bell, Daniel. (1976) 1978. *The Cultural Contradictions of Capitalism.* New York: Basic Books.

Bellah, Robert N. 1967. "Civil Religion in America." *Dædalus, Journal of the American Academy of Arts and Sciences* 96: 1–21.

Benford, Robert D., and David A. Snow. 2000. "Framing Processes and Social Movements: An Overview and Assessment." *Annual Review of Sociology* 26: 611–39.

Benjamin, Walter. 1991. "Kapitalismus als Religion." In *Gesammelte Schriften,* edited by Rolf Tiedemann and Hermann Schweppenhäuser, 100–102. Frankfurt am Main: Suhrkamp.

Berezin, Mabel. 2005. "Emotions and the Economy." In *The Handbook of Economic Sociology,* edited by Neil J. Smelser and Richard Swedberg, 109–27. Princeton, NJ: Princeton University Press.

Berkshire Hathaway. 2003: *2002 Annual Report.* http://www.berkshirehathaway.com/2002ar/2002ar.pdf#page=4&zoom=auto,-67,9.

Bernasconi, Oriana. 2014. "Testimonies, Manifestos and Motivational Anthems: How Fictional Narratives Disseminate the Entrepreneurial Regime in Current Neoliberal Chilean Society." Presented at the 7th Narrative Matters Conference, University of Paris Diderot.

Beunza, Daniel, and Raghu Garud. 2007. "Calculators, Lemmings or Framemakers? The Intermediary Role of Securities Analysts." In *Market Devices,* edited by Michel Callon, Yuval Millo, and Fabian Muniesa, 13–39. Malden, MA: Blackwell.

Biernacki, Richard. 1995. *The Fabrication of Labor: Germany and Britain, 1640–1914.* Berkeley: University of California Press.

Bilkic, Natasa, Thomas Gries, and Margarethe Pilichowski. 2012. "Stay in School or Start Working? The Human Capital Investment Decision under Uncertainty and Irreversibility." *Labour Economics* 19: 706–17.

Billeter-Frey, Ernst P. 1984. "Wirtschaftsprognosen im Lichte der Systemtheorie." *Jahrbücher für Nationalökonomie und Statistik* 199: 433–44.

Blinder, Alan S. 2004. *The Quiet Revolution: Central Banking Goes Modern.* New Haven, CT: Yale University Press.

Blinder, Alan S., Michael Ehrmann, Marcel Fratzscher, Jakob de Haan, and David-Jan Jansen. 2008. "Central Bank Communication and Monetary Policy: A Survey of Theory and Evidence." *Journal of Economic Literature* 46: 910–45.

Bloch, Ernst. 1995. *The Principle of Hope.* Translated by Neville Plaice, Stephen Plaice, and Paul Knight. Cambridge, MA: MIT Press.

Bloom, Paul. 2010. *How Pleasure Works: The New Science of Why We Like What We Like.* New York: Norton.

Blyth, Mark. 2002. *Great Transformations: Economic Ideas and Political Change in the Twentieth Century.* Cambridge: Cambridge University Press.

Bogdanova, Elena. 2013. "Account of the Past: Mechanisms of Quality Construction in the Market for Antiques." In *Constructing Quality: The Classification of Goods in Markets,* edited by Jens Beckert and Christine Musselin, 153–73. Oxford: Oxford University Press.

Boje, David M. 1995. "Stories of the Storytelling Organization: A Postmodern Analysis of Disney as 'Tamara-Land.'" *Academy of Management Journal* 38: 997–1035.

Bonus, Holger. 1990. *Wertpapiere, Geld und Gold: Über das Unwirkliche in der Ökonomie.* Graz, Austria: Styria.

Borghans, Lex, and Bart Golsteyn. 2004. "Imagination, Time Discounting and Human Capital Investment Decisions." Maastricht, Netherlands: Maastricht University.

Borup, Mads, Nick Brown, Kornelia Konrad, and Harro van Lente. 2006. "The Sociology of Expectations in Science and Technology." *Technology Analysis and Strategic Management* 18: 285–98.

Boudon, Raymond. 2012. *Croire et savoir: penser le politique, le moral et le religieux.* Paris: Presses Universitaires de France.

Boulding, Kenneth. (1956) 1961. *The Image: Knowledge in Life and Society.* Ann Arbor: University of Michigan Press.

Bourdieu, Pierre. (1972) 1977. *Outline of a Theory of Practice.* Translated by Richard Nice. Cambridge: Cambridge University Press.

———. 1973. "Cultural Reproduction and Social Reproduction." In *Knowledge, Education, and Cultural Change: Papers in the Sociology of Education,* edited by Richard K. Brown, 71–84. London: Tavistock.

———. 1979. *Algeria 1960.* Translated by Richard Nice. Cambridge: Cambridge University Press.

———. 1984. *Distinction: A Social Critique of the Judgement of Taste.* Translated by Richard Nice. Cambridge, MA: Harvard University Press.

———. 1993. *The Field of Cultural Production: Essays on Art and Literature.* Edited by Randal Johnson. New York: Columbia University Press.

———. 2000. *Pascalian Meditations.* Translated by Richard Nice. Stanford, CA: Stanford University Press.

———. 2005. *The Social Structures of the Economy.* Translated by Chris Turner. Cambridge: Polity Press.

Bowles, Samuel, and Herbert Gintis. 1975. "The Problem with Human Capital Theory: A Marxian Critique." *American Economic Review* 65: 74–82.

Boyer, Robert. 2012. "The Unfulfilled Promises, But Still the Power of Finance: An Invitation to a Post-Positivist Economics." Presented at the Annual CRESC Conference, Centre for Research of Socio-Cultural Change, Manchester.

———. 2013. "The Global Financial Crisis in Historical Perspective: An Economic Analysis Combining Minsky, Hayek, Fisher, Keynes and the Regulation Approach." *Accounting, Economics, and Law—A Convivium* 3: 93–193.

Braudel, Fernand. (1979) 1985. *Civilization and Capitalism, 15th-18th Century.* 3 vols. London: Fontana.

Braun, Benjamin. 2015. "Governing the Future: The ECB's Expectation Management during the Great Moderation." *Economy and Society* 44: 367–391.

Briggs, Asa. 2004. "Man-made Futures, Man-made Pasts." In *Technological Visions: The Hopes and Fears That Shape New Technologies,* edited by Marita Sturken, Douglas Thomas, and Sandra J. Ball-Rokeach, 92–109. Philadelphia: Temple University Press.

Bronk, Richard. 2009. *The Romantic Economist: Imagination in Economics.* Cambridge: Cambridge University Press.

———. 2013. "Reflexivity Unpacked: Performativity, Uncertainty and Analytical Monocultures." *Journal of Economic Methodology* 20: 343–49.

———. Forthcoming. "Epistemological Difficulties with Neo-Classical Economics." *Review of Austrian Economics.*

Bronner, Gérald. 2011. *The Future of Collective Beliefs.* Oxford: Bardwell Press.

Brown, John S., Stephen Denning, Katalina Groh, and Laurence Prusak. 2005. *Storytelling in Organizations: Why Storytelling Is Transforming 21st Century Organizations and Management.* Burlington, MA: Elsevier Butterworth-Heinemann.

Brown, Nik, Alison Kraft, and Paul Martin. 2006. "The Promissory Pasts of Blood Stem Cells." *Biosocieties* 1: 329–48.

Brown, Nik, Brian Rappert, and Andrew Webster, eds. 2000. *Contested Futures: A Sociology of Prospective Techno-Science.* Aldershot, UK: Ashgate.

Bryan, Dick, and Michael Rafferty. 2013. "Fundamental Value: A Category in Transformation." *Economy and Society* 42: 130–53.

Buchanan, James M., and Victor J. Vanberg. 1991. "The Market as a Creative Process." *Economics and Philosophy* 7: 167–86.

Buhite, Russell D., and David W. Levy, eds. 1992. *FDR's Fireside Chats.* Norman: University of Oklahoma Press.

BullionVault. 2011. "Gold News. Gold Price 'Will Reach $2400' Says Jim Rogers." Accessed May 3, 2012. http://goldnews.bullionvault.com/gold_price _111020117.

Bunia, Remigius. 2010. "Was ist Fiktion?" *Kunstforum International* 202: 46–52.

Burgdorf, Anna. 2011. "Virtualität und Fiktionalität: Überlegungen zur Finanzwelt als 'Vorstellungsraum.'" In *Finanzen und Fiktionen*, edited by Christine Künzel and Dirk Hempel, 107–18. Frankfurt am Main: Campus Verlag.

Calder, Lendol. 1999. *Financing the American Dream: A Cultural History of Consumer Credit*. Princeton, NJ: Princeton University Press.

Callon, Michel. 1998a. "Introduction: The Embeddedness of Economic Markets in Economics." In *The Laws of the Markets*, edited by Michel Callon, 1–57. Oxford: Blackwell.

———, ed. 1998b. *The Laws of the Markets*. Oxford: Blackwell.

Callon, Michel, Cécile Méadel, and Vololona Rabeharisoa. 2002. "The Economy of Qualities." *Economy and Society* 31: 194–217.

Cameron, Angus, and Ronen P. Palan. 2004. *The Imagined Economies of Globalization*. London: Sage.

Camic, Charles. 1986. "The Matter of Habit." *American Journal of Sociology* 91: 1039–87.

Campbell, Colin. 1987. *The Romantic Ethic and the Spirit of Modern Consumerism*. Oxford: Basil Blackwell.

Campbell, Jeffrey R., Charles Evans, Jonas D. M. Fisher, and Alejandro Justiniano. 2012. "Macroeconomic Effects of Federal Reserve Forward Guidance." Chicago: Federal Reserve Bank of Chicago. https://www.chicagofed.org/publications/working-papers/2012/wp-03.

Campbell, John L. 2004. *Institutional Change and Globalization*. Princeton, NJ: Princeton University Press.

Campbell, John L., and Ove K. Pedersen. 2014. *The National Origins of Policy Ideas: Knowledge Regimes in the United States, France, Germany, and Denmark*. Princeton, NJ: Princeton University Press.

Carr, Deborah. 1999. "Unfulfilled Career Aspirations and Psychological Well-Being." *PSC Research Reports* No. 99-432. Ann Arbor: University of Michigan, Population Studies Center.

Carruthers, Bruce G. 1996. *City of Capital: Politics and Markets in the English Financial Revolution*. Princeton, NJ: Princeton University Press.

———. 2013. "From Uncertainty toward Risk: The Case of Credit Ratings." *Socio-Economic Review* 11: 525–51.

Carruthers, Bruce G., and Laura Ariovich. 2010. *Money and Credit: A Sociological Approach*. Cambridge: Polity Press.

Carruthers, Bruce G., and Sarah Babb. 1996. "The Color of Money and the Nature of Value: Greenbacks and Gold in Postbellum America." *American Journal of Sociology* 101: 1556–91.

Carruthers, Bruce G., and Wendy N. Espeland. 1991. "Accounting for Rationality: Double-Entry Bookkeeping and the Rhetoric of Economic Rationality." *American Journal of Sociology* 97: 31–69.

Carruthers, Bruce G., and Arthur L. Stinchcombe. 1999. "The Social Structure of Liquidity: Flexibility, Markets, and States." *Theory and Society* 28: 353–82.

Cass, David, and Karl Shell. 1983. "Do Sunspots Matter?" *Journal of Political Economy* 91: 193–227.

Castoriadis, Cornelius. 1998. *The Imaginary Institution of Society.* Translated by Kathleen Blamey. Cambridge, MA: MIT Press.

Chinoy, Ely. 1955. *Automobile Workers and the American Dream.* Garden City, NY: Doubleday.

Chong, Kimberly, and David Tuckett. 2015. "Constructing Conviction through Action and Narrative: How Money Managers Manage Uncertainty and the Consequences for Financial Market Functioning." *Socio-Economic Review* 13: 309–30.

Chong, Kimberly, David Tuckett, and Claudia Ruatti. 2013. "Constructing Conviction through Action and Narrative: How Money Managers Manage Uncertainty and the Consequences for Financial Market Functioning." Unpublished manuscript.

Coleridge, Samuel T. 1817. "Biographia Literaria." Accessed May 3, 2012. http://www.gutenberg.org/cache/epub/6081/pg6081.html.

Commons, John R. (1934) 1961. *Institutional Economics: Its Place in Political Economy.* Madison: University of Wisconsin Press.

Cortes Douglas, Hernán. 2003. "Toward a New Understanding of Growth and Recession, Boom and Depression." In *Pioneering Studies in Socionomics*, edited by Robert R. Prechter, 256–65. Gainesville, GA: New Classics Library.

Costa, Vincent D., Peter J. Lang, Dean Sabatinelli, Francesco Versace, and Margaret M. Bradley. 2010. "Emotional Imagery: Assessing Pleasure and Arousal in the Brain's Reward Circuitry." *Human Brain Mapping* 31: 1446–57.

Czarniawska, Barbara. 1997. *Narrating the Organization: Dramas of Institutional Identity.* Chicago: University of Chicago Press.

d'Astous, Alain, and Jonathan Deschênes. 2005. "Consuming in One's Mind: An Exploration." *Psychology & Marketing* 22: 1–30.

Dahlén, Micael. 2013. *Nextopia: Freu dich auf die Zukunft—du wirst ihr nicht entkommen!* Translated by T. A. Wegberg. Frankfurt am Main: Campus Verlag.

Dahrendorf, Ralf. 1976. *Inequality, Hope, and Progress.* Liverpool: Liverpool University Press.

Dal Bó, Pedro. 2005. "Cooperation under the Shadow of the Future: Experimental Evidence from Infinitely Repeated Games." *American Economic Review* 95: 1591–604.

Daston, Lorraine. 1988. *Classical Probability in the Enlightenment.* Princeton, NJ: Princeton University Press.

David, Paul A. 1985. "Clio and the Economics of QWERTY." *American Economic Review* 75: 332–37.

Davidson, Paul. 1996. "Reality and Economic Theory." *Journal of Post Keynesian Economics* 18: 479–508.

———. 2010. "Risk and Uncertainty." In *The Economic Crisis and the State of Economics,* edited by Robert Skidelsky and Christian W. Wigström, 13–29. London: Palgrave.

———. 2011. *Post Keynesian Macroeconomic Theory.* 2nd ed. Cheltenham, UK: Edward Elgar.

de Laat, Bastiaan. 2000. "Scripts for the Future: Using Innovation Studies to Design Foresight Tools." In *Contested Futures: A Sociology of Prospective Techno-Science,* edited by Nik Brown, Brian Rappert, and Andrew Webster, 175–208. Aldershot, UK: Ashgate.

de Man, Reinier. 1987. *Energy Forecasting and the Organization of the Policy Process.* Delft: Ebouron.

de Ville, Ferdi, and Gabriel Siles-Brügge. 2014. "The EU–US Transatlantic Trade and Investment Partnership and the Role of Trade Impact Assessments: Managing Fictional Expectations." Presented at the 55th International Studies Association Annual Convention, Toronto.

Demange, Gabrielle, and Guy Laroque. 2006. *Finance and the Economics of Uncertainty.* Malden, MA: Blackwell.

Dequech, David. 1999. "Expectations and Confidence under Uncertainty." *Journal of Post Keynesian Economics* 21: 415–30.

———. 2000. "Fundamental Uncertainty and Ambiguity." *Eastern Economic Journal* 26: 41–60.

Derman, Emanuel. 2011. *Models. Behaving. Badly: Why Confusing Illusion with Reality Can Lead to Disaster, on Wall Street and in Life.* New York: Free Press.

Deuten, J. Jasper, and Arie Rip. 2000. "The Narrative Shaping of a Product Creation Process." In *Contested Futures: A Sociology of Prospective Techno-Science,* edited by Nik Brown, Brian Rappert, and Andrew Webster, 65–86. Aldershot, UK: Ashgate.

Deutschmann, Christoph. 1999. *Die Verheißung des absoluten Reichtums: Zur religiösen Natur des Kapitalismus.* Frankfurt am Main: Campus Verlag.

———. 2009. "Soziologie kapitalistischer Dynamik." *MPIfG Working Paper* 09/5. Cologne: Max Planck Institute for the Study of Societies.

———. 2011. "Social Rise as a Factor of Capitalist Growth." Presented at the 23rd SASE Conference, Madrid.

———. 2013. "Ideen und Interessen: Zum Verhältnis von Religion und wirtschaftlicher Entwicklung." In *Religion und Gesellschaft,* edited by Christof Wolf and Matthias Koenig, 359–82. Kölner Zeitschrift für Soziologie und Sozialpsychologie, Special Issue 53.

———. 2014. "Wirtschaft, Arbeit und Konsum." In *Handbuch der Soziologie,* edited by Jörn Lamla, Henning Laux, Hartmut Rosa, and David Strecker, 333–49. Constance, Germany: UVK Verlagsgesellschaft.

Devroop, Karendra. 2012. "The Occupational Aspirations and Expectations of College Students Majoring in Jazz Studies." *Journal of Research in Music Education* 59: 393–405.

Dewey, John. 1915. "The Logic of Judgments and Practise." *The Journal of Philosophy, Psychology and Scientific Methods* 12: 505–23.

———. (1922) 1957. *Human Nature and Conduct: An Introduction to Social Psychology.* New York: The Modern Library.

———. (1938) 1998. "The Pattern of Inquiry." In *The Essential Dewey,* edited by Larry A. Hickman and Thomas M. Alexander, 169–79. Bloomington: Indiana University Press.

Diaz-Bone, Rainer, and Gertraude Krell, eds. 2009. *Diskurs und Ökonomie: Diskursanalytische Perspektiven auf Märkte und Organisationen.* Wiesbaden, Germany: VS Verlag für Sozialwissenschaften.

DiMaggio, Paul J. 1988. "Interest and Agency in Institutional Theory." In *Institutional Patterns and Organizations: Culture and Environment,* edited by Lynne G. Zucker, 3–22. Cambridge, MA: Ballinger.

———. 2002. "Endogenizing 'Animal Spirits': Toward a Sociology of Collective Response to Uncertainty and Risk." In *The New Economic Sociology: Developments in an Emerging Field,* edited by Mauro F. Guillén, Randall Collins, Paula England, and Marshall Meyer, 79–100. New York: Russell Sage.

DiMaggio, Paul J., and Walter W. Powell. 1983. "The Iron Cage Revisited: Institutional Isomorphism and Collective Rationality in Organizational Fields." *American Sociological Review* 48: 147–60.

———, eds. 1991. *The New Institutionalism in Organizational Analysis.* Chicago: University of Chicago Press.

Djelic, Marie-Laure, and Antti Ainamo. 1999. "The Coevolution of New Organizational Forms in the Fashion Industry: A Historical and Comparative Study of France, Italy, and the United States." *Organization Science* 10: 622–37.

———. 2005. "The Telecom Industry as Cultural Industry? The Transposition of Fashion Logics into the Field of Mobile Telephony." In *Transformation in Cultural Industries,* edited by Candace Jones and Patricia H. Thornton, 45–80. Amsterdam: Elsevier JAI.

Dobbin, Frank. 2001. "How Institutional Economics Is Killing Micro-economics." *Economic Sociology Listserve* April 2001.

Dobbin, Frank, and Jiwook Jung. 2010. "The Misapplication of Mr. Michael Jensen: How Agency Theory Brought Down the Economy and Why It Might Again." In *Markets on Trial: The Economic Sociology of the U.S. Financial*

Crisis, edited by Michael Lounsbury and Paul M. Hirsch, 29–64. Bingley, UK: Emerald Group.

Dodd, Nigel. 2011. "'Strange Money': Risk, Finance and Socialized Debt." *The British Journal of Sociology* 62: 175–94.

———. 2014. *The Social Life of Money.* Princeton, NJ: Princeton University Press.

Doganova, Liliana. 2011. "Necessarily Untrue: On the Use of Discounted Cash Flow Formula in Valuation of Exploratory Projects." Presented at the 7th Critical Management Studies Conference, Naples.

Doganova, Liliana, and Peter Karnoe. 2012. "Controversial Valuations: Assembling Environmental Concerns and Economic Worth in Clean-tech Markets." Presented at the 2nd Interdisciplinary Market Studies Workshop, Dublin.

Doganova, Liliana, and Marie Renault. 2008. "What Do Business Models Do? Narratives, Calculation and Market Exploration." *CSI Working Paper* 012. Paris: Centre de Sociologie de L'Innovation, Ecole des Mines de Paris.

Dominguez, Kathryn M., Ray C. Fair, and Matthew D. Shapiro. 1988. "Forecasting the Depression: Harvard versus Yale." *American Economic Review* 78: 595–612.

Dosi, Giovanni, and Massimo Egidi. 1991. "Substantive and Procedural Uncertainty: An Exploration of Economic Behaviours in Changing Environments." *Journal of Evolutionary Economics* 1: 145–68.

Dosi, Giovanni, and Luigi Orsenigo. 1988. "Coordination and Transformation: An Overview of Structures, Behaviors and Change in Evolutionary Environments." In *Technical Change and Economic Theory,* edited by Giovanni Dosi, Christopher Freeman, Richard Nelson, Gerald Silverberg, and Luc L. Soete, 13–37. London: Pinter.

Douglas, Mary. 1986. *How Institutions Think.* Syracuse, NY: Syracuse University Press.

Dreher, Axel, Silvia Marchesi, and James R. Vreeland. 2007. "The Politics of IMF Forecasts." *CESifo Working Paper* 012. Munich: Ludwig Maximilian University, Center for Economic Studies and Ifo Institute.

Dubuisson-Quellier, Sophie. 2013. "From Qualities to Value: Demand Shaping and Market Control in Mass Consumption Markets." In *Constructing Quality: The Classification of Goods in Markets,* edited by Jens Beckert and Christine Musselin, 247–67. Oxford: Oxford University Press.

Dulman, Scott P. 1989. "The Development of Discounted Cash Flow Techniques in U.S. Industry." *The Business History Review* 63: 555–87.

Dupuy, Jean-Pierre, François Eymard-Duvernay, Olivier Favereau, Robert Salais, and Laurent Thévenot. 1989. "Introduction." *Revue économique* 40: 141–46.

Durkheim, Emile. (1893) 1984. *The Division of Labour in Society.* Translated by W. D. Halls. London: Macmillan.

———. (1911) 1974. "Value Judgments and Judgments of Reality." In *Sociology and Philosophy*, 80–97. Translated by D. F. Peacock. New York: Free Press.

———. (1912) 1965. *The Elementary Forms of the Religious Life*. Translated by Joseph Ward Swain. New York: Free Press.

———.(1957) 1992. *Professional Ethics and Civic Morals*. Translated by Cornelia Brookfield. New York: Routledge.

Eckersley, Michael. 1988. "The Form of Design Processes: A Protocol Analysis Study." *Design Studies* 9: 86–94.

Elias, David. 1999. *Dow 40,000: Strategies for Profiting from the Greatest Bull Market in History*. New York: McGraw-Hill.

Elliott, Graham, and Allan Timmermann. 2008. "Economic Forecasting." *Journal of Economic Literature* 46: 3–56.

Elster, Jon. 1989. *Nuts and Bolts for the Social Sciences*. Cambridge: Cambridge University Press.

———. 2009. "Excessive Ambitions." *Capitalism and Society* 4: 1–30.

Emirbayer, Mustafa, and Ann Mische. 1998. "What Is Agency?" *American Journal of Sociology* 103: 962–1023.

Ergen, Timur. 2015. *Große Hoffnungen und brüchige Koalitionen: Industrie, Politik und die schwierige Durchsetzung der Photovoltaik*. Frankfurt am Main: Campus Verlag.

Esposito, Elena. 2007. *Die Fiktion der wahrscheinlichen Realität*. Frankfurt am Main: Suhrkamp.

———. 2011. *The Future of Futures: The Time of Money in Financing and Society*. Cheltenham, UK: Edward Elgar.

Etzioni, Amitai. 1988. *The Moral Dimension: Toward a New Economics*. New York: Free Press.

Eusepi, Stefano, and Bruce Preston. 2010. "Central Bank Communication and Expectations Stabilization." *Macroeconomics* 2: 235–71.

Evans, Jeanne. 1995. *Paul Ricoeur's Hermeneutics of the Imagination*. New York: Peter Lang.

Evans, Robert. 1997. "Soothsaying or Science? Falsification, Uncertainty and Social Change in Macroeconomic Modelling." *Social Studies of Science* 27: 395–438.

———. 1999. *Macroeconomic Forecasting: A Sociological Appraisal*. London: Routledge.

———. 2007. "Social Networks and Private Spaces in Economic Forecasting." *Studies in History and Philosophy of Science* 38: 686–97.

———. 2014. "Expert Advisers: Why Economic Forecasters Can Be Useful When They Are Wrong." In *Experts and Consensus in Social Science*, edited by Carlo Martini and Marcel Boumans, 233–52. Cham, Switzerland: Springer International Publishing.

Ezrahi, Yaron. 2012. *Imagined Democracies: Necessary Political Fictions.* Cambridge: Cambridge University Press.

Fama, Eugene F. 1965a. "The Behavior of Stock-Market Prices." *The Journal of Business* 38: 34–105.

———. 1965b. "Random Walks in Stock Market Prices." *Financial Analysts Journal* 21: 55–59.

Faulkner, Robert R., and Andy B. Anderson. 1987. "Short-Term Projects and Emergent Careers: Evidence from Hollywood." *American Journal of Sociology* 92: 879–909.

Favero, Giovanni. 2007. "Weather Forecast or Rain-dance? On Inter-war Business Barometers." *Research Paper* 14/WP/07. Ca' Foscari University of Venice.

Fenn, Jackie, and Mark Raskino. 2008. *Mastering the Hype Cycle: How to Choose the Right Innovation at the Right Time.* Cambridge, MA: Harvard Business Press.

Ferguson, Niall. 2008. *The Ascent of Money: A Financial History of the World.* New York: Penguin.

Fischer, Edward F. 2014. *The Good Life: Aspiration, Dignity, and the Anthropology of Wellbeing.* Stanford, CA: Stanford University Press.

Fischer, Edward F., and Peter Benson. 2006. *Broccoli and Desire: Global Connections and Maya Struggles in Postwar Guatemala.* Stanford, CA: Stanford University Press.

Fisher, Irving. 1930. *The Theory of Interest: As Determined by Impatience to Spend Income and Opportunity to Invest It.* New York: Macmillan.

Fleck, Ludwik. (1935) 1979. *The Genesis and Development of a Scientific Fact.* Chicago: University of Chicago Press.

Fligstein, Neil. 1990. *The Transformation of Corporate Control.* Cambridge, MA: Harvard University Press.

———. 2001. *The Architecture of Markets: An Economic Sociology of Twenty-First-Century Capitalist Societies.* Princeton, NJ: Princeton University Press.

Fligstein, Neil, Jonah S. Brundage, and Michael Schultz. 2014. "Why the Federal Reserve Failed to See the Financial Crisis of 2008: The Role of 'Macroeconomics' as a Sense-making and Cultural Frame." *IRLE Working Paper* 111–14. University of California, Berkeley, Department of Sociology.

Fligstein, Neil, and Doug McAdam. 2012. *A Theory of Fields.* Oxford: Oxford University Press.

Foskett, Nicholas, and Jane Hemsley-Brown. 2001. *Choosing Futures: Young People's Decision-making in Education, Training and Careers Markets.* London: Routledge.

Foucault, Michel. 1975. *Discipline and Punish: The Birth of the Prison.* New York: Random House.

Fourcade-Gourinchas, Marion, and Sarah L. Babb. 2002. "The Rebirth of the Liberal Creed: Paths to Neoliberalism in Four Countries." *American Journal of Sociology* 108: 533–79.

Fourcade, Marion. 2009. *Economists and Societies: Discipline and Profession in the United States, Britain and France, 1890s to 1990s.* Princeton, NJ: Princeton University Press.

———. 2011. "Cents and Sensibility: Economic Valuation and the Nature of 'Nature.'" *American Journal of Sociology* 116: 1721–77.

———. 2013. "The Economy as Morality Play, and Implications for the Euro-zone Crisis." *Socio-Economic Review* 11: 620–27.

Fournier, Susan, and Michael Guiry. 1993. "'An Emerald Green Jaguar, a House on Nantucket, and an African Safari': Wish Lists and Consumption Dreams in Materialist Society." *Advances in Consumer Research* 20: 352–58.

Frank, Robert H. 1999. *Luxury Fever: Weighing the Cost of Excess.* New York: Free Press.

Frank, Robert H., and Philip J. Cook. 1995. *The Winner-Take-All Society: Why the Few at the Top Get So Much More than the Rest of Us.* New York: Penguin.

Freeman, Christopher. 1974. *The Economics of Industrial Innovation.* Harmonds-worth, UK: Penguin.

———. 1987. "Innovation." In *The New Palgrave: A Dictionary of Economics,* edited by John Eatwell, Murray Milgate, and Peter Newman, 858–60. London: Macmillan.

Friedman, Milton. 1953. *Essays in Positive Economics.* Chicago: University of Chicago Press.

Friedman, Walter A. 2009. "The Harvard Economic Service and the Problems of Forecasting." *History of Political Economy* 41: 57–88.

———. 2014. *Fortune Tellers: The Story of America's First Economic Fore-casters.* Princeton, NJ: Princeton University Press.

Fritz, Claudia, Joseph Curtin, Jacques Poitevineau, Palmer Morrel-Samuels, and Fan-Chia Tao. 2012. "Player Preferences among New and Old Violins." *Proceedings of the National Academy of Science* 109: 760–63.

Froud, Julie, Sukhdev Johal, Adam Leaver, and Karel Williams. 2006. *Financial-ization and Strategy: Narrative and Numbers.* London: Routledge.

Frydman, Roman, and Michael D. Goldberg. 2007. *Imperfect Knowledge Eco-nomics: Exchange Rates and Risk.* Princeton, NJ: Princeton University Press.

Gabriel, Yiannis. 2000. *Storytelling in Organizations: Facts, Fictions, and Fan-tasies.* Oxford: Oxford University Press.

Galbraith, John Kenneth. (1958) 1998. *The Affluent Society.* New York: Houghton Mifflin.

Gall, Alexander. 2012. "Mediterrane Stromvisionen: Von Atlantropa zu DE-SERTEC?" In *Technology Fiction: Technische Visionen und Utopien in der*

Hochmoderne, edited by Uwe Fraunholz and Anke Woschech, 165–91. Bielefeld, Germany: Transkript Verlag.

Ganßmann, Heiner. 2011. *Doing Money: Elementary Monetary Theory from a Sociological Standpoint.* London: Routledge.

———. 2012. "Geld und die Rationalität wirtschaftlichen Handelns." In *Wirtschaftliche Rationalität: Soziologische Perspektiven,* edited by Anita Engels and Lisa Knoll, 221–39. Wiesbaden, Germany: VS Verlag für Sozialwissenschaften.

Garcia-Parpet, Marie-France. 2011. "Symbolic Value and the Establishment of Prices: Globalization of the Wine Market." In *The Worth of Goods: Valuation and Pricing in the Economy,* edited by Jens Beckert and Patrik Aspers, 131–54. Oxford: Oxford University Press.

Garfinkel, Harold. 1967. *Studies in Ethnomethodology.* Cambridge: Polity Press.

Garud, Raghu, and Peter Karnoe. 2001. "Path Creation as a Process of Mindful Deviation." In *Path Dependence and Creation,* edited by Raghu Garud and Peter Karnoe, 1–40. Mahwah, NJ: Erlbaum.

Garvía, Roberto 2007. "Syndication, Institutionalization, and Lottery Play." *American Journal of Sociology* 113: 603–53.

Geipel, Julian. 2015. "Fiktionen und Märkte: Entscheidungen unter Unsicherheit am Beispiel von strategischen M&A-Prozessen." In *Bewegungen in Unsicherheit / Unsicherheit in Bewegung: Ökonomische Untersuchungen,* edited by Birger P. Priddat, 9–116. Marburg, Germany: Metropolis.

Gerlach, Philipp. 2013. "Evaluation Practices in Internal Labor Markets: Constructing Engineering Managers' Qualification in French and German Automotive Firms." In *Constructing Quality: The Classification of Goods in Markets,* edited by Jens Beckert and Christine Musselin, 126–50. Oxford: Oxford University Press.

Gibson, David R. 2012. *Talk at the Brink: Deliberation and Decision During the Cuban Missile Crisis.* Princeton, NJ: Princeton University Press.

Giddens, Anthony. 1984. *The Constitution of Society: Outline of the Theory of Structuration.* Berkeley: University of California Press.

———. 1994. "Living in a Post-traditional Society." In *Reflexive Modernization: Politics, Tradition and Aesthetics in the Modern Social Order,* edited by Ulrich Beck, Anthony Giddens, and Scott Lash, 56–109. Stanford, CA: Stanford University Press.

———. 1999. "Risk." *BBC Reith Lecture* No. 2. BBC Online Network. http://news.bbc.co.uk/olmedia/video/events99/reith_lectures/riskvi.ram.

Gigerenzer, Gerd. 2013. *Risiko: Wie man die richtigen Entscheidungen trifft.* Munich: Bertelsmann.

Gigerenzer, Gerd, and Henry Brighton. 2009. "Homo Heuristicus: Why Biased Minds Make Better Inferences." *Topics in Cognitive Science* 1: 107–43.

Giorgi, Simona, and Klaus Weber. 2015. "Marks of Distinction: Framing and Audience Appreciation in the Context of Investment Advice." *Administrative Science Quarterly* 20: 1–35.

Giraudeau, Martin. 2012. "Imagining (the Future) Business: How to Make Firms with Plans?" In *Imagining Organizations: Performative Imagery in Business and Beyond*, edited by François-Régis Puyou, Paolo Quattrone, Chris McLean, and Nigel Thrift, 213–29. New York: Routledge.

Glassman, James K., and Kevin A. Hassett. 1999. *Dow 36,000: The New Strategy for Profiting from the Coming Rise in the Stock Market*. New York: Times Business.

Goffman, Erving. 1959. *The Presentation of Self in Everyday Life*. New York: Doubleday.

Gonzales, Felipe. 2015. "Micro-foundations of Financialization: Status Anxiety and the Expansion of Consumer Credit in Chile." PhD diss., University of Cologne.

González-Páramo, José Manuel. 2007. "Expectations and Credibility in Modern Central Banking: A Practitioner's View." Frankfurt am Main: European Central Bank.

Gorton, Gary. 2009. "Slapped in the Face by the Invisible Hand: Banking and the Panic of 2007." Presented at Federal Reserve Bank of Atlanta's Financial Markets Conference.

Gorton, Gary, and Andrew Metrick. 2012. "Securitized Banking and the Run on Repo." *Journal of Financial Economics* 104: 425–51.

Graeber, David. 2011. *Debt: The First 5,000 Years*. Brooklyn, NY: Melville House.

Gravelle, Hugh S. E., and Ray Rees. 1992. *Microeconomics*. 2nd ed. London: Longman.

Guerrien, Bernard, and Ozgur Gun. 2011. "Efficient Market Hypothesis: What Are We Talking About?" *Real-World Economics Review* 56: 19–30.

Güth, Werner, and Hartmut Kliemt. 2010. "(Un)Eingeschränkt rational entscheiden in Geschäft und Moral." In *Preis der Berlin-Brandenburgischen Akademie der Wissenschaften gestiftet von der Commerzbank Stiftung. Preisverleihung am 19. Oktober 2009: Weyma Lübbe*, edited by Berlin-Brandenburgische Akademie der Wissenschaften, 17–28. Berlin: Berlin-Brandenburg Academy of Sciences.

Hahn, Frank. 1980. "General Equilibrium Theory." *Public Interest*, Special Issue: 123–38.

Haldane, Andrew G. 2015. "Growing, Fast and Slow." Lecture at University of East Anglia, Norwich. London: Bank of England.

Hall, Peter A. 1993. "Policy Paradigms, Social Learning, and the State: The Case of Economic Policymaking in Britain." *Comparative Politics* 25: 275–96.

Hall, Peter A., and David Soskice. 2001a. "Introduction." In *Varieties of Capitalism: The Institutional Foundations of Comparative Advantage,* edited by Peter Hall and David Soskice, 1–45. Oxford: Oxford University Press.

———. 2001b. *Varieties of Capitalism: The Institutional Foundations of Comparative Advantage.* Oxford: Oxford University Press.

Hall, Peter A., and Rosemary C. R. Taylor. 1996. "Political Science and the Three New Institutionalisms." *Political Studies* 44: 936–57.

Hall, Rodney B. 2008. *Central Banking as Global Governance: Constructing Financial Credibility.* Cambridge: Cambridge University Press.

Halliday, Terence C., and Bruce G. Carruthers. 2009. *Bankrupt: Global Lawmaking and Systemic Financial Crisis.* Stanford, CA: Stanford University Press.

Harrington, Brooke. 2008. *Pop Finance: Investment Clubs and the New Investor Populism.* Princeton, NJ: Princeton University Press.

———. 2009. *Deception: From Ancient Empires to Internet Dating.* Stanford, CA: Stanford University Press.

Harvey, David. 1982. *The Limits to Capital.* Oxford: Basil Blackwell.

Hayek, Friedrich A. von. (1968) 1969. "Wettbewerb als Entdeckungsverfahren." In *Wirtschaftswissenschaftliche und wirtschaftsrechtliche Untersuchungen.* Vol. 5 of *Freiburger Studien: Gesammelte Aufsätze,* 249–65. Tübingen, Germany: Mohr Siebeck.

———. 1973. *Rules and Order.* Vol. 1 of *Law, Legislation and Liberty: A New Statement of the Liberal Principles of Justice and Political Economy.* Chicago: University of Chicago Press.

———. 1974. "The Pretence of Knowledge." Prize Lecture. Nobelprize.org. Accessed March 18, 2013.

Hellwig, Martin. 1998. "Discussion on International Contagion: What Is It and What Can Be Done Against It?" *Swiss Journal of Economics and Statistics* 134: 715–39.

Hinze, Jörg. 2005. "Konjunkturprognosen: Falsche Erwartungen an Treffgenauigkeit." *Wirtschaftsdienst* 85: 117–23.

Hirschle, Jochen. 2012. *Die Entstehung des transzendenten Kapitalismus.* Constance, Germany: UVK Verlagsgesellschaft.

Hirschman, Albert O. 1982. *Shifting Involvements: Private Interest and Public Action.* Princeton, NJ: Princeton University Press.

———. 1986. *Rival Views of Market Society and Other Recent Essays.* New York: Viking Press.

———. 1991. *Rhetoric of Reaction: Perversity, Futility, Jeopardy.* Cambridge, MA: Harvard University Press.

Hirshleifer, Jack, and John G. Riley. 1992. *The Analytics of Uncertainty and Information.* Cambridge: Cambridge University Press.

Hodgson, Geoffrey M. 2011. "The Eclipse of the Uncertainty Concept in Mainstream Economics." *Journal of Economic Issues* 45: 159–75.

Holbrook, Morris, B., and Elizabeth C. Hirschman. 1982. "The Experimential Aspects of Consumption: Consumer Fantasies, Feelings, and Fun." *Journal of Consumer Research* 9: 132–40.

Holmes, Douglas R. 2009. "Economy of Words." *Cultural Anthropology* 24: 381–419.

———. 2014. *Economy of Words: Communicative Imperatives in Central Banks.* Chicago: University of Chicago Press.

Hölscher, Lucian. 1989. *Weltgericht oder Revolution: protestantische und sozialistische Zukunftsvorstellungen im deutschen Kaiserreich.* Edited by Reinhart Koselleck and Rainer Lepsius. Stuttgart, Germany: Klett-Cotta.

———. 1999. *Die Entdeckung der Zukunft.* Edited by Wolfgang Benz. Frankfurt am Main: Fischer.

———. 2002. "The History of the Future: The Emergence and Decline of a Temporal Concept in European History." *History of Concepts Newsletter* 5: 10–15.

Horton, Donald, and R. Richard Wohl. 1956. "Mass Communication and Para-Social Interaction: Observations on Intimacy at a Distance." *Psychiatry* 19: 215–29.

Hutter, Michael. 2011. "Infinite Surprises: On the Stabilization of Value in the Creative Industries." In *The Worth of Goods: Valuation and Pricing in the Economy,* edited by Jens Beckert and Patrik Aspers, 201–20. Oxford: Oxford University Press.

Ingham, Geoffrey. 2003. "Schumpeter and Weber on the Institutions of Capitalism: Solving Swedberg's 'Puzzle.'" *Journal of Classical Sociology* 3: 297–309.

———. 2004. *The Nature of Money.* Malden, MA: Polity Press.

———. 2008. *Capitalism.* Cambridge: Polity Press.

Innes, Mitchell A. (1914) 2004. "The Credit Theory of Money." In *Credit and State Theories of Money: The Contributions of A. Mitchell Innes,* edited by Randall L. Wray, 50–78. Cheltenham, UK: Edward Elgar.

International Monetary Fund. 2013. *World Economic Outlook Update.* Washington, DC: IMF.

Iser, Wolfgang. 1983. "Akte des Fingierens: Oder: Was ist das Fiktive im fiktionalen Text?" In *Funktionen des Fiktiven,* edited by Dieter Henrich and Wolfgang Iser, 121–51. Munich: Fink.

———. 1991. *Das Fiktive und das Imaginäre: Perspektiven literarischer Anthropologie.* Frankfurt am Main: Suhrkamp.

———. 1993. *The Fictive and the Imaginary: Charting Literary Anthropology.* Baltimore: Johns Hopkins University Press.

Issing, Otmar. 1997. "Monetary Targeting in Germany: The Stability of Monetary Policy and of the Monetary System." *Journal of Monetary Economics* 39: 67–79.

Jahoda, Marie, Paul. F. Lazarsfeld, and Hans Zeisel. (1933) 1971. *Marienthal: A Sociography of an Unemployed Community.* London: Tavistock.

Jasanoff, Sheila, and Sang-Hyun Kim. 2009. "Containing the Atom: Sociotechnical Imaginaries and Nuclear Power in the United States and South Korea." *Minerva* 47: 119–46.

Jensen, Michael C., and William H. Meckling. 1976. "Theory of the Firm: Managerial Behavior, Agency Costs and Ownership Structure." *Journal of Financial Economics* 3: 305–60.

Jessop, Bob. 2013. "Recovered Imaginaries, Imagined Recoveries: A Cultural Political Economy of Crisis Construals and Crisis Management in the North Atlantic Financial Crisis." In *Beyond the Global Economic Crisis: Economics, Politics and Settlement,* edited by Mats Benner, 234–54. Cheltenham, UK: Edward Elgar.

Joas, Hans. 1996. *The Creativity of Action.* Translated by Jeremy Gaines and Paul Keast. Cambridge: Polity Press.

———. 2000. *The Genesis of Values.* Translated by Gregory Moore. Cambridge: Polity Press.

Joas, Hans, and Wolfgang Knöbl. 2009. *Social Theory: Twenty Introductory Lectures.* Translated by Alex Skinner. Cambridge: Cambridge University Press.

Johnes, Geraint. 1993. *The Economics of Education.* London: Macmillan.

Kadlec, Charles W. 1999. *Dow 100,000: Fact or Fiction.* Paramus, NJ: Prentice Hall.

Kahl, Joseph A. 1953. "Educational and Occupational Aspirations of 'Common Man' Boys." *Harvard Educational Review* 23: 186–203.

Kaldor, Nicholas. 1957. "A Model of Economic Growth." *The Economic Journal* 67: 591–624.

Kalecki, Michal. 1943. "Political Aspects of Full Employment." *The Political Quarterly* 14: 322–30.

Kalthoff, Herbert. 2005. "Practices of Calculation: Economic Representations and Risk Management." *Theory, Culture & Society* 22 (2): 69–97.

Kant, Immanuel. (1787) 1911. *Kritik der reinen Vernunft.* 2nd ed. Vol. 3 of *Kant's Gesammelte Schriften.* Berlin: Georg Reimer.

Karpik, Lucien. 2010. *Valuing the Unique: The Economics of Singularities.* Princeton, NJ: Princeton University Press.

Keynes, John Maynard. (1931) 1972. *Essays in Persuasion.* Vol. 9 of *The Collected Writings of John Maynard Keynes.* London: Macmillan.

———. (1936) 1964. *The General Theory of Employment, Interest, and Money.* London: Macmillan.

————. 1937. "The General Theory of Employment." *Quarterly Journal of Economics* 51: 209–23.

Kholodilin, Konstantin A., and Boriss Siliverstovs. 2009. "Geben Konjunkturprognosen eine gute Orientierung?" *Wochenbericht des DIW* 13: 207–13.

Kim, Jongchul. 2012. "How Politics Shaped Modern Banking in Early Modern England: Rethinking the Nature of Representative Democracy, Public Debt, and Modern Banking." *MPIfG Discussion Paper* 12/11. Cologne: Max Planck Institute for the Study of Societies.

Kindleberger, Charles P., and Robert Z. Aliber. (1978) 2005. *Manias, Panics, and Crashes: A History of Financial Crises.* Hoboken, NJ: Wiley.

Kinnier, Richard T., Teresa A. Fisher, Maria U. Darcy, and Tad Skinner. 2001. "The Fate of Career Dreams: A Test of Levinson's Theory." *Australian Journal of Career Development* 10 (3): 25–27.

Kirzner, Israel M. 1985. *Discovery and the Capitalist Process.* Chicago: University of Chicago Press.

Knapp, Georg F. 1924. *The State Theory of Money.* London: Macmillan.

Knight, Frank H. (1921) 2006. *Risk, Uncertainty, and Profit.* Mineola, NY: Dover Publications.

Knorr Cetina, Karin. 1994. "Primitive Classification and Postmodernity: Towards a Sociological Notion of Fiction." *Theory, Culture and Society* 11 (3): 1–22.

————. 1999. *Epistemic Cultures: How the Sciences Make Knowledge.* Cambridge, MA: Harvard University Press.

————. 2003. "From Pipes to Scopes: The Flow Architecture of Financial Markets." *Distinktion* 7 (2): 7–23.

————. 2015. "What Is a Financial Market? Global Markets as Weird Institutional Forms." In *Re-Imagining Economic Sociology,* edited by Patrik Aspers and Nigel Dodd, 103–24. Oxford: Oxford University Press.

Knorr Cetina, Karin, and Urs Bruegger. 2002. "Global Microstructures: The Virtual Societies of Financial Markets." *American Journal of Sociology* 107: 905–50.

Knorr Cetina, Karin, and Alex Preda, eds. 2004. *The Sociology of Financial Markets.* Oxford: Oxford University Press.

————, eds. 2012. *The Oxford Handbook of the Sociology of Finance.* Oxford: Oxford University Press.

Kocka, Jürgen. 2013. *Geschichte des Kapitalismus.* Munich: C.H. Beck.

Kormann, Eva. 2011. "Dr. Real and Mr. Hype: Die Konstrukte der Kaufleute." In *Finanzen und Fiktionen: Grenzgänge zwischen Literatur und Wissenschaft,* edited by Christine Künzel and Dirk Hempel, 91–105. Frankfurt am Main: Campus Verlag.

Korpi, Walter. 1985. "Power Resources Approach vs. Action and Conflict: On Causal and Intentional Explanations in the Study of Power." *Sociological Theory* 3 (2): 31–45.

Koselleck, Reinhart. 1979. *Vergangene Zukunft: Zur Semantik geschichtlicher Zeiten.* Frankfurt am Main: Suhrkamp.

————. 2004. *Futures Past: On the Semantics of Historical Time.* Translated by Keith Tribe. New York: Columbia University Press.

Kraemer, Klaus. 2010. "Propheten der Finanzmärkte: Zur Rolle charismatischer Ideen im Börsengeschehen." *Berliner Journal für Soziologie* 20: 179–201.

Künzel, Christine. 2014. "Imaginierte Zukunft: Zur Bedeutung von Fiktion(en) in ökonomischen Diskursen." In *Literarische Ökonomik*, edited by Iuditha Balint and Sebastian Zilles, 143–57. Paderborn: Fink.

Lamont, Michèle, and Laurent Thévenot. 2000. "Introduction: Toward a Renewed Comparative Cultural Sociology." In *Rethinking Comparative Cultural Sociology: Repertoires of Evaluation in France and the United States,* edited by Michèle Lamont and Laurent Thévenot, 1–22. Cambridge: Cambridge University Press.

Landes, David S. 1969. *The Unbound Prometheus: Technological Change and Industrial Development in Western Europe from 1750 to the Present.* Cambridge: Cambridge University Press.

Lane, David A., and Robert R. Maxfield. 2005. "Ontological Uncertainty and Innovation." *Journal of Evolutionary Economics* 15: 3–50.

Latour, Bruno. 1993. *We Have Never Been Modern.* Cambridge, MA: Harvard University Press.

Lawrence, Thomas B., and Nelson Phillips. 2004. "From Moby Dick to Free Willy: Macro-Cultural Discourse and Institutional Entrepreneurship in Emerging Institutional Fields." *Organization* 11: 689–711.

Lawrence, Thomas B., and Roy Suddaby. 2006. "Institutions and Institutional Work." In *Handbook of Organization Studies,* edited by Stewart Clegg, C. Hardy, W. R. Nord, and T. Lawrence, 215–54. London: Sage.

Lazarus, Jeanne. 2012. "Prévoir la défaillance de credit: l'ambition du scoring." *Raisons politiques* 48: 103–18.

Le Goff, Jacques. 1960. "Au moyen âge: temps de l'église et temps du marchand." *Annales* 15: 417–33.

Lepsius, Rainer M. 1995. "Institutionenanalyse und Institutionenpolitik." In *Politische Institutionen im Wandel,* edited by Birgitta Nedelmann, 392–403. Kölner Zeitschrift für Soziologie und Sozialpsychologie, Special Issue 35.

Levy, Sidney J. 1959. "Symbols for Sale." *Harvard Business Review* 37: 117–24.

Lewis, David. 1986. *On the Plurality of Worlds.* Malden, MA: Blackwell.

Lindblom, Charles E. 1982. "The Market as Prison." *The Journal of Politics* 44: 324–36.

Lucas, Robert E. 1972. "Expectations and the Neutrality of Money." *Journal of Economic Theory* 4: 103–24.

———. 1975. "An Equilibrium Model of the Business Cycle." *Journal of Political Economy* 83: 1113–44.

———. 1981. *Studies in Business Cycle Theory.* Cambridge, MA: MIT Press.

Luckmann, Thomas. 1967. *The Invisible Religion: The Problem of Religion in Modern Society.* New York: Macmillan.

Luhmann, Niklas. 1976. "The Future Cannot Begin: Temporal Structures in Modern Society." *Social Research* 43: 130–52.

———. 1988. *Die Wirtschaft der Gesellschaft.* Frankfurt am Main: Suhrkamp.

———. 1995. *Social Systems.* Stanford, CA: Stanford University Press.

———. 1996. *Die Realität der Massenmedien.* 2nd ed. Opladen, Germany: Westdeutscher Verlag.

Lukes, Steven. 1973. *Emile Durkheim: His Life and Work. A Historical and Critical Study.* London: Penguin.

Lutter, Mark. 2012a. "Anstieg oder Ausgleich? Die multiplikative Wirkung sozialer Ungleichheiten auf dem Arbeitsmarkt für Filmschauspieler." *Zeitschrift für Soziologie* 41: 435–57.

———. 2012b. "Tagträume und Konsum: Die imaginative Qualität von Gütern am Beispiel der Nachfrage für Lotterien." *Soziale Welt* 63: 233–51.

Lyman, Peter. 2004. "Information Superhighways, Virtual Communities, and Digital Libraries: Information Society Metaphors as Political Rhetoric." In *Technological Visions: The Hopes and Fears That Shape New Technologies,* edited by Marita Sturken, Douglas Thomas, and Sandra J. Ball-Rokeach, 201–18. Philadelphia: Temple University Press.

MacKenzie, Donald. 2006. *An Engine, Not a Camera: How Financial Models Shape Markets.* Cambridge, MA: MIT Press.

———. 2011. "The Credit Crisis as a Problem in the Sociology of Knowledge." *American Journal of Sociology* 116: 1778–841.

———. 2012. "Visible, Tradeable Carbon: How Emissions Markets are Constructed." In *Imagining Organizations: Performative Imagery in Business and Beyond,* edited by François-Régis Puyou, Paolo Quattrone, Chris McLean, and Nigel Thrift, 53–81. New York: Routledge.

MacKenzie, Donald, and Yuval Millo. 2003. "Constructing a Market, Performing Theory: The Historical Sociology of a Financial Derivatives Exchange." *American Journal of Sociology* 109: 107–45.

Maddison, Angus. 2001. *The World Economy: A Millennial Perspective.* Paris: Organisation for Economic Co-operation and Development.

Mader, Philip. 2015. *The Political Economy of Microfinance: Financializing Poverty.* Basingstoke, UK: Palgrave Macmillan.

Mahoney, James. 2000. "Path Dependence in Historical Sociology." *Theory and Society* 29: 507–48.

Mäki, Uskali. 1989. "On the Problem of Realism in Economics." *Ricerche Economiche* 43: 176–98.

———. 1992a. "Friedman and Realism." *Research in the History of Economic Thought and Methodology* 10: 171–95.

———. 1992b. "On the Method of Isolation in Economics." In *Idealization IV: Intelligibility in Science,* edited by Craig Dilworth, 317–51. Amsterdam: Rodopi.

———. 1994. "Isolation, Idealization, and Truth in Economics." In *Idealization VI: Idealization in Economics,* edited by Bert Hamminga and Neil B. De Marchi, 147–68. Amsterdam: Rodopi.

———. 2000. "Kinds of Assumptions and Their Truth: Shaking an Untwisted F-Twist." *Kyklos* 53: 317–36.

———, ed. 2002. *Fact and Fiction in Economics: Models, Realism and Social Construction.* Cambridge: Cambridge University Press.

———. 2009a. "MISSing the World: Models as Isolations and Credible Surrogate Systems." *Erkenntnis* 70: 29–43.

———. 2009b. "Unrealistic Assumptions and Unnecessary Confusions: Rereading and Rewriting F53 as a Realistic Statement." In *The Methodology of Positive Economics: Reflections on the Milton Friedman Legacy,* edited by Uskali Mäki, 90–116. Cambridge: Cambridge University Press.

Makridakis, Spyros, and Michèle Hibon. 2000. "The M3-Competition: Results, Conclusions and Implications." *International Journal of Forecasting* 16: 451–76.

Makridakis, Spyros, Robin M. Hogarth, and Anil Gaba. 2009. "Forecasting and Uncertainty in the Economic and Business World." *International Journal of Forecasting* 25: 794–812.

Makridakis, Spyros, Steven C. Wheelwright, and Rob J. Hyndman. 1998. *Forecasting: Methods and Applications.* 3rd ed. New York: Wiley.

Mallard, Grégoire. 2013. "From Europe's Past to the Middle East's Future: The Constitutive Purpose of Forward Analogies in International Security." Unpublished manuscript.

Mallard, Grégoire, and Andrew Lakoff. 2011. "How Claims to Know the Future Are Used to Understand the Present: Techniques of Prospection in the Field of National Security." In *Social Knowledge in the Making,* edited by Charles Camic, Neil Gross, and Michèle Lamont, 339–77. Chicago: University of Chicago Press.

March, James G. 1995. "The Future, Disposable Organizations and the Rigidities of Imagination." *Organization* 2: 427–40.

Marchal, Emmanuelle. 2013. "Uncertainties Regarding Applicant Quality: The Anonymous Resume Put to the Test." In *Constructing Quality: The Classifi-*

cation of Goods in Markets, edited by Jens Beckert and Christine Musselin, 103–25. Oxford: Oxford University Press.

Markus, Hazel, and Paula Nurius. 1986. "Possible Selves." *American Psychologist* 41: 954–69.

Marshall, Alfred. (1920) 1961. *Principles of Economics.* 2 vols. London: Macmillan.

Marshall, Douglas A. 2010. "Temptation, Tradition, and Taboo: A Theory of Sacralization." *Sociological Theory* 28: 64–90.

Martin, Paul, Nik Brown, and Andrew Turner. 2008. "Capitalizing Hope: The Commercial Development of Umbilical Cord Blood Stem Cell Banking." *New Genetics and Society* 27: 127–43.

Martinez, Matias, and Michael Scheffel. 2003. *Einführung in die Erzähltheorie.* 4th ed. Munich: C.H. Beck.

Martino, Joseph P. 1983. *Technological Forecasting for Decision Making.* 2nd ed. New York: North-Holland.

Marx, Karl. (1867) 1977. *Capital: A Critique of Political Economy.* Vol. 1. New York: Vintage.

———. (1885) 1993. *Capital: A Critique of Political Economy.* Vol. 2. London: Penguin.

Marx, Karl, and Friedrich Engels. (1846) 1976. "The German Ideology." In *Marx and Engels: 1845–47.* Vol. 5 of *Collected Works.* London: Lawrence & Wishart.

Maurer, Bill. 2002. "Repressed Futures: Financial Derivatives' Theological Unconscious." *Economy and Society* 31: 15–36.

Mauss, Marcel. (1914) 1974. "Les origines de la notion de monnaie." In *Représentations collectives et diversité des civilisations.* Vol. 2 of *Oeuvres,* 106–12. Paris: Les Editions de Minuit.

Mayntz, Renate. 2012. "Erkennen, was die Welt zusammenhält: Die Finanzmarktkrise als Herausforderung für die soziologische Systemtheorie." *MPIfG Discussion Paper* 13/2. Cologne: Max Planck Institute for the Study of Societies.

McCloskey, Deirdre. 2011. *Bourgeois Dignity: Why Economics Can't Explain the Modern World.* Chicago: University of Chicago Press.

McCloskey, Donald N. 1985. *The Rhetoric of Economics.* Madison: The University of Wisconsin Press.

———. 1990. *If You're So Smart: The Narrative of Economic Expertise.* Chicago: The University of Chicago Press.

McCracken, Grant. 1988. *Culture and Consumption: New Approaches to the Symbolic Character of Consumer Goods and Activities.* Bloomington: Indiana University Press.

McDermott, Rose. 2004. "Prospect Theory in Political Science: Gains and Losses from the First Decade." *Political Psychology* 25: 289–312.

McKinsey Global Institute. 2015. "Debt and (Not Much) Deleveraging." London. http://www.mckinsey.com/insights/economic_studies/debt_and_not_much_deleveraging.

Mead, George H. (1932) 2002. *The Philosophy of the Present.* Amherst, NY: Prometheus.

Mears, Ashley. 2011. *Pricing Beauty: The Making of a Fashion Model.* Berkeley: University of California Press.

Menger, Carl. (1883) 1963. *Problems of Economics and Sociology.* Urbana: University of Illinois Press.

———. 1892. "On the Origin of Money." *The Economic Journal* 2: 239–55.

Menger, Pierre-Michel. 1999. "Artistic Labor Markets and Careers." *Annual Review of Sociology* 25: 541–74.

———. 2009. *Le travail créateur: s'accomplir dans l'incertain.* Paris: Gallimard.

———. 2014. *The Economics of Creativity: Art and Achievement under Uncertainty.* Cambridge, MA: Harvard University Press.

Merton, Robert K. 1957. *Social Theory and Social Structure.* Glencoe, IL: Free Press.

Mihm, Stephen. 2007. *A Nation of Counterfeiters: Capitalists, Con Men, and the Making of the United States.* Cambridge, MA: Harvard University Press.

Miller, Daniel. 1998. *A Theory of Shopping.* Ithaca, NY: Cornell University Press.

Minsky, Hyman P. 1982. "The Financial-Instability Hypothesis: Capitalist Processes and the Behavior of the Economy." In *Financial Crises: Theory, History, and Policy,* edited by Charles P. Kindleberger and Jean-Pierre Laffargue, 13–39. Cambridge: Cambridge University Press.

Mirowski, Philip. 1989. *More Heat than Light: Economics as Social Physics, Physics as Nature's Economics.* Cambridge: Cambridge University Press.

———. 1991. "Postmodernism and the Social Theory of Value." *Journal of Post Keynesian Economics* 13: 565–82.

Mirowski, Philip, and Dieter Plehwe, eds. 2009. *The Road from Mont Pèlerin: The Making of the Neoliberal Thought Collective.* Cambridge, MA: Harvard University Press.

Mische, Ann. 2009. "Projects and Possibilities: Researching Futures in Action." *Sociological Forum* 24: 694–704.

———. 2014. "Measuring Futures in Action: Projective Grammars in the Rio+20 Debates." *Theory and Society* 43: 437–64.

Miyazaki, Hirokazu. 2003. "The Temporalities of the Market." *American Anthropologist* 105: 255–65.

———. 2004. *The Method of Hope: Anthropology, Philosophy, and Fijian Knowledge.* Stanford, CA: Stanford University Press.

Moen, Phyllis, and Patricia Roehling. 2005. *The Career Mystique: Cracks in the American Dream.* Lanham, MD: Rowman & Littlefield.

Möllering, Guido. 2010. "Collective Market-making Efforts at an Engineering Conference." *MPIfG Discussion Paper* 10/2. Cologne: Max Planck Institute for the Study of Societies.

Moreira, Tiago, and Paolo Palladino. 2005. "Between Truth and Hope: On Parkinson's Disease, Neurotransplantation and the Production of the 'Self.'" *History of the Human Sciences* 18 (3): 55–82.

Morgan, Mary S. 2002. "Models, Stories and the Economic World." In *Fact and Fiction in Economics: Models, Realism and Social Construction,* edited by Uskali Mäki, 178–201. Cambridge: Cambridge University Press.

———. 2012. *The World in the Model: How Economists Work and Think.* Cambridge, MA: Cambridge University Press.

Morgan, Stephen L. 2007. "Expectations and Aspirations." In *The Blackwell Encyclopedia of Sociology,* edited by George Ritzer, 1528–31. Oxford: Blackwell.

Morgenstern, Oskar. 1928. *Wirtschaftsprognose: Eine Untersuchung ihrer Voraussetzungen und Möglichkeiten.* Vienna: Julius Springer.

———. (1935) 1976. "Perfect Foresight and Economic Equilibrium." In *Selected Economic Writings of Oskar Morgenstern,* edited by Andrew Schotter, 169–83. New York: New York University Press.

Müller, Felix, and Jakob Tanner. 1988. "'. . . im hoffnungsvollen Licht einer besseren Zukunft': Zur Geschichte der Fortschrittsidee in der schweizerischen Arbeiterbewegung." In *Solidarität, Widerspruch, Bewegung: 100 Jahre Sozialdemokratische Partei der Schweiz,* edited by Karl Lang, Peter Hablützel, Markus Mattmüller, and Heidi Witzig, 325–67. Zürich: Limmat Verlag.

Muniesa, Fabian. 2011. "A Flank Movement in the Understanding of Valuation." In *Measure and Value,* edited by Lisa Adkins and Celia Lury, 24–38. Sociological Review Monograph Series. *The Sociological Review* 59 (S2).

———. 2014. *The Provoked Economy: Economic Reality and the Performative Turn.* Abingdon: Routledge.

Muniesa, Fabian, and Liliana Doganova. 2015. "Setting the Habit of Capitalization: The Pedagogy of Earning Power at the Harvard Business School, 1920–1940." Unpublished manuscript. Ecole des mines, Paris.

Münnich, Sascha. 2011. "Interest-Seeking as Sense-Making: Ideas and Business Interests in the New Deal." *European Journal of Sociology* 52: 277–311.

Munro, John H. 2003. "The Medieval Origins of the Financial Revolution: Usury, Rentes, and Negotiability." *The International History Review* 25: 505–62.

Muth, John F. 1961. "Rational Expectations and the Theory of Price Movements." *Econometrica* 29: 315–35.

Mützel, Sophie. 2010. "Koordinierung von Märkten durch narrativen Wettbewerb." In *Wirtschaftssoziologie,* edited by Jens Beckert and Christoph Deutschmann, 87–106. Kölner Zeitschrift für Soziologie und Sozialpsychologie, Special Issue 49.

Nahoum, André Vereta. 2013. "Selling 'Cultures': The Traffic of Cultural Representations from the Yawanawa". PhD diss., University of São Paulo.

Nama, Yesh, and Alan Lowe. 2013. "Due-Diligence of Private Equity Funds: A Practice Based View." Presented at Management Accounting Research Group (MARG) Conference in association with the Management Control Association at Aston Business School, November 15–16, 2012, Birmingham, UK.

Nelson, Richard R., and Sidney G. Winter. 1982. *An Evolutionary Theory of Economic Change.* Cambridge, MA: The Belknap Press of Harvard University Press.

Nelson, Stephen C., and Peter J. Katzenstein. 2010. Uncertainty, Risk and the Crisis of 2008. Unpublished manuscript. Cornell University, Ithaca, NY.

———. 2014. "Uncertainty, Risk, and the Financial Crisis of 2008." *International Organization* 68: 361–92.

Newman, Katherine S. 1993. *Declining Fortunes: The Withering of the American Dream.* New York: Basic Books.

———. 1999. *Falling from Grace: Downward Mobility in the Age of Affluence.* Berkeley: University of California Press.

Nierhaus, Wolfgang. 2011. "Wirtschaftskonjunktur 2010: Prognose und Wirklichkeit." *Ifo Schnelldienst* 64 (2): 22–25.

North, Douglass C. 1990. *Institutions, Institutional Change and Economic Performance.* Cambridge: Cambridge University Press.

———. 1999. "Dealing with a Non-Ergodic World: Institutional Economics, Property Rights, and the Global Environment." *Duke Environmental Law & Policy Forum* 10 (1): 1–12.

Nye, David E. 2004. "Technological Prediction: A Promethean Problem." In *Technological Visions: The Hopes and Fears That Shape New Technologies,* edited by Marita Sturken, Douglas Thomas, and Sandra Ball-Rokeach, 159–76. Philadelphia: Temple University Press.

O'Neill, Jim. 2013. "Enttäuschende Bilanz." *Handelsblatt,* July 30, 2013, 48.

Offe, Claus. 1975. "The Capitalist State and the Problem of Policy Formation." In *Stress and Contradiction in Modern Capitalism,* edited by Leon N. Lindberg, Robert Alford, Colin Crouch, and Clause Offe, 125–44. Lexington: D.C. Heath.

Offe, Claus, and Helmut Wiesenthal. 1985. "Two Logics of Collective Action." In *Disorganized Capitalism: Contemporary Transformations of Work and Politics,* edited by John Keane and Claus Offe, 170–220. Cambridge, MA: MIT Press.

Orléan, André. 2012. "Knowledge in Finance: Objective Value versus Convention." In *Handbook of Knowledge and Economics,* edited by Richard Arena, Agnès Festré, and Nathalie Lazaric, 313–37. Cheltenham, UK: Edward Elgar.

———. 2013. "Money: Instrument of Exchange or Social Institution of Value?" In *Financial Crises and the Nature of Capitalist Money: Mutual Developments from the Work of Geoffrey Ingham,* edited by Jocelyn Pixley and Geoffrey C. Harcourt, 46–69. Basingstoke, UK: Palgrave Macmillan.

———. 2014. *The Empire of Value: A New Foundation for Economics.* Cambridge, MA: MIT Press.

Ortiz, Horacio. 2009. "Investors and Efficient Markets: The Everyday Imaginaries of Investment Management." *Economic Sociology: The European Electronic Newsletter* 11 (1): 34–40.

———. 2014. "The Limits of Financial Imagination: Free Investors, Efficient Markets, and Crisis." *American Anthropologist* 116: 38–50.

Ortmann, Günther. 2004. *Als Ob: Fiktionen und Organisationen.* Wiesbaden, Germany: VS Verlag für Sozialwissenschaften.

Otte, Max. 2011. "Fiktion und Realität im Finanzwesen." In *Finanzen und Fiktionen: Grenzgänge zwischen Literatur und Wissenschaft,* edited by Christine Künzel and Dirk Hempel, 27–43. Frankfurt am Main: Campus Verlag.

Oudin-Bastide, Caroline, and Philippe Steiner. 2015. *Calcul et Moral: Coûts de l'esclavage et valeur de l'émancipation (XVIIIe–XIXe siècle).* Paris: Editions Albin Michel.

Palan, Ronan. 2012. "The Financial Crisis and Intangible Value." *Capital & Class* 37: 65–77.

Parsons, Talcott. (1937) 1949. *The Structure of Social Action: A Study in Social Theory with Special Reference to a Group of Recent European Writers.* Glencoe, IL: Free Press.

———. 1951. *The Social System.* Glencoe, IL: Free Press.

———. (1959) 1964. "The School Class as a Social System: Some of Its Functions in American Society." In *Social Structure and Personality,* 129–54. New York: Free Press.

———. 1963. "On the Concept of Political Power." *Proceedings of the American Philosophical Society* 107: 232–62.

Parsons, Talcott, and Neil J. Smelser. (1956) 1984. *Economy and Society: A Study in the Integration of Economic and Social Theory.* London: Routledge.

Partnoy, Frank. 2014. "Is Herbalife a Pyramid Scheme?" *The Atlantic Monthly* June.

Patalano, Roberta. 2003. "Beyond Rationality: Images as Guide-Lines to Choice." *Working Paper* 05/2003. Torino: Università di Torino.

Pelzer, Peter. 2013. *Risk, Risk Management and Regulation in the Banking Industry: The Risk to Come.* London: Routledge.

Pénet, Pierre, and Grégoire Mallard. 2014. "From Risk Models to Loan Contracts: Austerity as the Continuation of Calculation by Other Means." *Journal of Critical Globalisation Studies* 7: 4–47.

Pieri, Elisa. 2009. "Sociology of Expectation and the E-Social Science Agenda." *Information, Communication & Society* 12: 1103–18.

Piotti, Geny. 2009. "German Companies Engaging in China: Decision-Making Processes at Home and Management Practices in Chinese Subsidiaries." *MPIfG Working Paper* 09/14. Cologne: Max Planck Institute for the Study of Societies.

Pixley, Jocelyn. 2004. *Emotions in Finance: Distrust and Uncertainty in Global Markets.* Cambridge: Cambridge University Press.

Podolny, Joel M. 2005. *Status Signals: A Sociological Study of Market Competition.* Princeton, NJ: Princeton University Press.

Polanyi, Karl. (1944) 1957. *The Great Transformation.* Boston: Beacon Press.

Polillo, Simone. 2011. "Money, Moral Authority, and the Politics of Creditworthiness." *American Sociological Review* 76: 437–64.

———. 2013. *Conservatives versus Wildcats: A Sociology of Financial Conflict.* Stanford, CA: Stanford University Press.

Pongratz, Hans J., Stefan Bernhard, and Lisa Abbenhardt. 2014. "Fiktion und Substanz: Praktiken der Bewältigung zukunftsbezogener Ungewissheit wirtschaftlichen Handelns am Beispiel der Gründungsförderung." *Berliner Journal für Soziologie* 24: 397–423.

Poovey, Mary. 2008. *Genres of the Credit Economy: Mediating Value in Eighteenth- and Nineteenth-Century Britain.* Chicago: University of Chicago Press.

Popper, Karl. (1949) 1963. "Prediction and Prophecy in the Social Sciences." In *Conjectures and Refutations: The Growth of Scientific Knowledge,* 336–46. London: Routledge & Kegan Paul.

———. (1957) 1964. *The Poverty of Historicism.* New York: Harper Torchbooks.

———. 1982. *The Open Universe: An Argument for Indeterminism.* London: Routledge.

Portes, Alejandro, and Julia Sensenbrenner. 1993. "Embeddedness and Immigration: Notes on the Determinants of Economic Action." *American Journal of Sociology* 98: 1320–50.

Postlewaite, Andrew. 1987. "Asymmetric Information." In *The New Palgrave: A Dictionary of Economics,* edited by John Eatwell, Murray Milgate, and Peter Newman, 133–35. London: Macmillan.

Prato, Matteo, and David Stark. 2012. "Attention Structures and Valuation Models: Cognitive Networks among Securities Analysts." *COI Working Paper* December 2011. New York: Columbia University, Center on Organizational Innovation.

Preda, Alex. 2006. "Socio-Technical Agency in Financial Markets: The Case of the Stock Ticker." *Social Studies of Science* 36: 753–82.

Priddat, Birger P. 2012. *Diversität, Steuerung, Netzwerke: Institutionenökonomische Anmerkungen.* Marburg, Germany: Metropolis.

———. 2013. *Unentschieden: Wirtschaftsphilosophische Anmerkungen zur Ökonomie.* Marburg, Germany: Metropolis.

———. 2014. "Prognose als plausible Narratio." In *Die Ordnung des Kontingenten: Beiträge zur zahlenmäßigen Selbstbeschreibung der modernen Gesellschaft,* edited by Alberto Cevolini, 251–79. Wiesbaden, Germany: Springer VS.

Putnam, Ruth A. 2006. "Democracy and Value Inquiry." In *A Companion to Pragmatism,* edited by John R. Shook and Joseph Margolis, 278–89. Malden, MA: Blackwell.

Radner, Roy. 1968. "Competitive Equilibrium under Uncertainty." *Econometrica* 36: 31–58.

Ravasi, Davide, Violina Rindova, and Ileana Stigliani. 2011. "Valuing Products as Cultural Symbols: A Conceptual Framework and Empirical Illustration." In *The Worth of Goods: Valuation and Pricing in the Economy,* edited by Jens Beckert and Patrik Aspers, 297–316. Oxford: Oxford University Press.

Reichmann, Werner. 2011. "The Future-informed Market: The Contribution of Economic Forecast to the Stability of Markets." Unpublished manuscript. Cologne: Max Planck Institute for the Study of Societies.

———. 2012. "Scientific Failure: The Meanings of Economic Forecasts." Presented at 107th Meeting of the American Sociological Association, Denver.

———. 2013. "Epistemic Participation: How to Produce Knowledge about the Economic Future." *Social Studies of Science* 43: 852–77.

———. 2015. "Wissenschaftliches Zukunftswissen: Zur Soziologie der Wirtschaftsprognostik." Unpublished manuscript. University of Konstanz.

Reinhart, Carmen M., and Kenneth S. Rogoff. 2009. *This Time Is Different: Eight Centuries of Financial Folly.* Princeton, NJ: Princeton University Press.

———. 2010. "Growth in a Time of Debt." *American Economic Review* 100: 573–78.

Reisch, Lucia A. 2002. "Symbols for Sale: Funktionen des symbolischen Konsums." In *Die gesellschaftliche Macht des Geldes,* edited by Christoph Deutschmann, 226–50. Leviathan, Special Issue 21.

Rescher, Nicholas. 1998. *Predicting the Future: An Introduction to the Theory of Forecasting.* Albany: State University of New York Press.

Richins, Marsha L. 1994. "Valuing Things: The Public and Private Meanings of Possessions." *Journal of Consumer Research* 21: 504–21.

Ricoeur, Paul. 1979. "The Function of Fiction in Shaping Reality." *Man and World* 12: 123–41.

———. 1991. "Imagination in Discourse and in Action." Translated by Kathleen Blamey. In *From Text to Action,* 168–87. London: Athlone.

———. 2002. "Cinque lezioni: Dal linguaggio all'immagine." *Aesthetica Preprint* 66. Palermo: University of Palermo, International Centre for the Study of Aesthetics.

Ridgeway, Cecilia L. 2001. "Gender, Status, and Leadership." *Journal of Social Issues* 57: 637–55.

Riles, Annelise. 2010. "Collateral Expertise: Legal Knowledge in the Global Financial Markets." *Current Anthropology* 51: 795–818.

Robin, Corey. 2013. "Nietzsche's Marginal Children: On Friedrich Hayek." *The Nation* May 27, 2013: 27–36.

Roehrkasse, Alexander. 2013. "Discipline and Coerce? Imprisonment for Debt in the Market Revolution." Presented at Economic Moralities Conference, Max Planck Sciences Po Center, Paris.

Roemer, Paul. M. 1990. "Endogenous Technological Change." *Journal of Political Economy* 98: 71–102.

Rona-Tas, Akos, and Alya Guseva. 2014. *Plastic Money: Constructing Markets for Credit Cards in Eight Postcommunist Countries.* Stanford, CA: Stanford University Press.

Rona-Tas, Akos, and Stefanie Hiss. 2011. "Forecasting as Valuation: The Role of Ratings and Predictions in the Subprime Mortgage Crisis in the United States." In *The Worth of Goods: Valuation and Pricing in the Economy,* edited by Jens Beckert and Patrik Aspers, 223–46. Oxford: Oxford University Press.

Rorty, Richard. 1980. *Philosophy and the Mirror of Nature.* Princeton, NJ: Princeton University Press.

Rosa, Hartmut. 2005. *Beschleunigung: Die Veränderung der Zeitstrukturen in der Moderne.* Frankfurt am Main: Suhrkamp.

Rosenberg, Nathan. 1976. "On Technological Expectations." *The Economic Journal* 86: 523–35.

Rössel, Jörg. 2007. "Ästhetisierung, Unsicherheit und die Entwicklung von Märkten." In *Märkte als soziale Strukturen,* edited by Jens Beckert, Rainer Diaz-Bone, and Heiner Ganßmann, 167–82. Frankfurt am Main: Campus.

Rothschild, Kurt W. 2005. "Prognosen, Prognosen: Eine kleine Prognosendiagnose." *Wirtschaft und Gesellschaft* 31: 125–33.

Sabel, Charles F., and Jonathan Zeitlin. 1997. "Stories, Strategies, Structures: Rethinking Historical Alternatives to Mass Production." In *World of Possibilities: Flexibility and Mass Production in Western Industrialization,* edited by Charles F. Sabel and Jonathan Zeitlin, 1–33. Cambridge: Cambridge University Press.

Sahlins, Marshall. 1972. *Stone Age Economics.* New York: Aldine.

Salmon, Christian. 2007. *Storytelling: la machine à fabriquer des histoires et à formater les esprits.* Paris: La Découverte.

Samuelson, Paul. 1969. "Classical and Neoclassical Monetary Theory." In *Monetary Theory: Selected Readings,* edited by Robert Clower, 171–90. Harmondsworth, UK: Penguin Books.

Sargent, Thomas J. 2008. "Rational Expectations." In *Concise Encyclopedia of Economics,* edited by David R. Henderson, 432–34. Indianapolis: Liberty Fund.

Savage, Leonard J. 1954. *The Foundations of Statistics.* New York: Wiley.

Sawyer, John E. 1952. "Entrepreneurial Error and Economic Growth." *Explorations in Entrepreneurial History* 4 (4): 199–204.

Schmidt, Vivien A., and Mark Thatcher, eds. 2013. *Resilient Liberalism in Europe's Political Economy.* Cambridge: Cambridge University Press.

Schneider, Steven. 2009. The Paradox of Fiction. In *Internet Encyclopedia of Philosophy.* http://www.iep.utm.edu/fict-par/.

Schön, Donald A. 1983. *The Reflective Practitioner: How Professionals Think in Action.* New York: Basic Books.

Schoon, Ingrid. 2001. "Teenage Job Aspirations and Career Attainment in Adulthood: A 17-year-Follow-up Study of Teenagers Who Aspired to Become Scientists, Health Professionals, or Engineers." *International Journal of Behavioral Development* 25: 124–32.

Schularick, Moritz, and Alan M. Taylor. 2012. "Credit Booms Gone Bust: Monetary Policy, Leverage Cycles, and Financial Crises 1870–2008." *American Economic Review* 102: 1029–61.

Schumpeter, Joseph A. (1912) 2006. *Theorie der wirtschaftlichen Entwicklung.* Berlin: Duncker & Humblot.

———. (1927) 1952. "Die goldene Bremse an der Kreditmaschine: Die Goldwährung und der Bankkredit." In *Aufsätze zur ökonomischen Theorie,* 158–84. Tübingen, Germany: Mohr.

———. 1934. *Theory of Economic Development: An Inquiry into Profits, Capital, Credit, Interest and the Business Cycle.* Cambridge, MA: Harvard University Press.

———. 1939. *Business Cycles: A Theoretical, Historical, and Statistical Analysis of the Capitalist Process.* 2 vols. New York: McGraw-Hill.

———. (1942) 2014. *Capitalism, Socialism and Democracy.* 2nd ed. Floyd, VA: Impact Books.

Schütz, Alfred. 1962. *Collected Papers I: The Problem of Social Reality.* The Hague: Martinus Nijhoff.

———. 2003. "Das Problem der Personalität in der Sozialwelt: Bruchstücke." In *Theorie der Lebenswelt 1: Die pragmatische Schichtung der Lebenswelt.* Vol. 1 of *Alfred Schütz Werkausgabe,* edited by Martin Endreß and Ilja Srubar, 95–162. Constance, Germany: UVK Verlagsgesellschaft.

Searle, John R. (1969) 2011. *Speech Acts: An Essay in the Philosophy of Language.* Cambridge: Cambridge University Press.

———. 1975. "The Logical Status of Fictional Discourse." *New Literary History* 6: 319–32.

———. 1995. *The Construction of Social Reality.* New York: Free Press.

Seligman, Adam B. 1997. *The Problem of Trust.* Princeton, NJ: Princeton University Press.

Sewell, William H. 1996. "Three Temporalities: Toward an Eventful Sociology." In *The Historic Turn in the Human Sciences,* edited by Terrence J. McDonald, 245–80. Ann Arbor: University of Michigan Press.

———. 2008. "The Temporalities of Capitalism." *Socio-Economic Review* 6: 517–37.

———. 2010. "The Empire of Fashion and the Rise of Capitalism in Eighteenth-Century France." *Past and Present* 206: 81–120.

Sewell, William H., Archie O. Haller, and Murray A. Straus. 1957. "Social Status and Educational and Occupational Aspiration." *American Sociological Review* 22: 67–73.

Sewell, William H., and Robert M. Hauser. 1975. *Education, Occupation, and Earnings: Achievement in the Early Career.* New York: Academic Press.

Shackle, George L. S. 1958. "The Economist's Model of Man." *Occupational Psychology* 32: 191–96.

———. 1964. "General Thought-Schemes and the Economist." *Woolwich Economic Paper* 2. Woolwich, UK: Woolwich Polytechnic Department of Economics and Management.

———. 1970. *Expectation, Enterprise and Profit: The Theory of the Firm.* Edited by Charles Carter. London: George Allen & Unwin.

———. 1972. *Epistemics & Economics: A Critique of Economic Doctrines.* Cambridge: Cambridge University Press.

———. 1979. *Imagination and the Nature of Choice.* Edinburgh: Edinburgh University Press.

———. 1983. "The Bounds of Unknowledge." In *Beyond Positive Economics: Proceedings of Section F (Economics) of the British Association for the Advancement of Science, York, 1981,* edited by Jack Wiseman, 28–37. London: Macmillan.

Shapin, Steven. 2008. *The Scientific Life: A Moral History of a Late Modern Vocation.* Chicago: University of Chicago Press.

Shepsle, Kenneth. 2006. "Rational Choice Institutionalism." In *The Oxford Handbook of Political Institutions,* edited by R. A. W. Rhodes, Sarah A. Binder, and Bert A. Rockman, 23–38. Oxford: Oxford University Press.

Shiller, Robert J. 2000. *Irrational Exuberance.* Princeton, NJ: Princeton University Press.

———. 2003. "From Efficient Markets Theory to Behavioral Finance." *Journal of Economic Perspectives* 17 (1): 83–104.

Simiand, François. 1934. "La monnaie, réalité sociale." *Annales sociologiques,* série D. Fascicule 1: 1–58.

Simmel, Georg. (1904) 1971. "Fashion." In *On Individuality and Social Forms: Selected Writings,* edited by Donald N. Levine, 294–323. Chicago: Chicago University Press.

———. (1907) 1978. *The Philosophy of Money.* Translated by Tom Bottomore and David Frisby. London: Routledge & Kegan Paul.

———. (1908) 2009. *Sociology: Inquiries into the Construction of Social Forms,* Vol. 1. Translated and edited by Anthony J. Blasi, Anton K. Jacobs, and Mathew Kanjirathinkal. Leiden, Netherlands: Brill.

Simon, Herbert A. 1957. *Models of Man.* New York: Wiley.

Smart, Graham. 1999. "Storytelling in a Central Bank: The Role of Narrative in the Creation and Use of Specialized Economic Knowledge." *Journal of Business and Technical Communication* 13: 249–73.

Smith, Adam. (1776) 1976. *An Inquiry into the Nature and Causes of the Wealth of Nations.* Chicago: University of Chicago Press.

Smith, Charles W. 2011. "Coping with Contingencies in Equity Option Markets: The 'Rationality' of Pricing." In *The Worth of Goods: Valuation and Pricing in the Economy,* edited by Jens Beckert and Patrik Aspers, 272–94. Oxford: Oxford University Press.

Snow, David A., and Robert D. Benford. 1992. "Master Frames and Cycles of Protest." In *Frontiers in Social Movement Theory,* edited by Aldon D. Morris and Carol McClurg Mueller, 133–55. New Haven: Yale University Press.

Solow, Robert M. 1957. "Technical Change and the Aggregate Production Function." *Review of Economics and Statistics* 39: 312–20.

Sombart, Werner. (1902) 1969. *Die vorkapitalistische Wirtschaft,* Part 2. Vol. 1.2 of *Der moderne Kapitalismus: Historisch-systematische Darstellung des gesamteuropäischen Wirtschaftslebens von seinen Anfängen bis zur Gegenwart.* Berlin: Duncker & Humblot.

Sotheby's. 2011. Auction Results. Russian Art. 12 April 2011. http://www.sothebys .com/en/auctions/ecatalogue/2011/russian-works-of-art-n08733/lot.254 .html.

Soros, George. 1987. *The Alchemy of Finance.* Hoboken, NJ: Wiley.

———. 1998. *The Crisis of Global Capitalism: Open Society Endangered.* New York: PublicAffairs.

Speer, Nicole K., Jeremy R. Reynolds, Khena M. Swallow, and Jeffrey M. Zacks. 2009. "Reading Stories Activates Neural Representations of Visual and Motor Experiences." *Psychological Science* 20: 989–99.

Staff, Jeremy, Angel Harris, Ricardo Sabates, and Laine Briddell. 2010. "Uncertainty in Early Occupational Aspirations: Role Exploration or Aimlessness?" *Social Forces* 89: 659–83.

Stark, David. 2009. *The Sense of Dissonance: Accounts of Worth in Economic Life.* Princeton, NJ: Princeton University Press.

Starr, Ross M. 1997. *General Equilibrium Theory: An Introduction.* Cambridge: Cambridge University Press.

Stehr, Nico. 2007. *Moral Markets: How Knowledge and Affluence Change Consumers and Products.* Boulder, CO: Paradigm.

Stehr, Nico, Christoph Henning, and Bernd Weiler, eds. 2006. *The Moralization of the Markets.* New Brunswick, NJ: Transaction.

Steiner, Philippe. 2006. "Sociology of Economic Knowledge." In *International Encyclopedia of Economic Sociology,* edited by Jens Beckert and Milan Zafirovski, 185–88. London: Routledge.

Strange, Susan. 1998. *Mad Money.* Manchester, UK: Manchester University Press.

Streeck, Wolfgang. 2006. "Wirtschaft und Moral: Facetten eines unvermeidlichen Themas." In *Moralische Voraussetzungen und Grenzen wirtschaftlichen Handelns,* edited by Wolfgang Streeck and Jens Beckert, 11–21. *MPIfG Working Paper* 07/6. Cologne: Max Planck Institute for the Study of Societies.

———. 2011. "E Pluribus Unum? Varieties and Commonalities of Capitalism." In *The Sociology of Economic Life,* edited by Mark Granovetter and Richard Swedberg, 419–55. Boulder, CO: Westview.

———. 2012. "How to Study Contemporary Capitalism." *European Journal of Sociology* 53: 1–28.

———. 2014. *Buying Time: The Delayed Crisis of Democratic Capitalism.* Translated by Patrick Camiller. London: Verso.

Ströker, Elisabeth. 1983. "Zur Frage der Fiktionalität theoretischer Begriffe." In *Funktionen des Fiktiven,* edited by Dieter Henrich and Wolfgang Iser, 95–118. Munich: Fink.

Sturken, Marita, and Douglas Thomas. 2004. "Introduction: Technological Visions and the Rhetoric of the New." In *Technological Visions: The Hopes and Fears That Shape New Technologies,* edited by Marita Sturken, Douglas Thomas, and Sandra J. Ball-Rokeach, 3–18. Philadelphia: Temple University Press.

Sugden, Robert. 2000. "Credible Worlds: The Status of Theoretical Models in Economics." *Journal of Economic Methodology* 7: 1–31.

———. 2009. "Credible Worlds, Capacities and Mechanisms." *Erkenntnis* 70: 3–27.

———. 2013. "How Fictional Accounts Can Explain." *Journal of Economic Methodology* 20: 237–43.

Swedberg, Richard. 2007. "The Sociological Study of Hope and the Economy: Introductory Remarks." Presented at Hope Studies Conference, Institute of Social Science, University of Tokyo.

Taleb, Nassim N. 2010. *The Black Swan: The Impact of the Highly Improbable.* 2nd ed. New York: Random House.

Tappenbeck, Inka. 1999. *Phantasie und Gesellschaft: Zur soziologischen Relevanz der Einbildungskraft.* Würzburg, Germany: Königshausen & Neumann.

Tavory, Iddo, and Nina Eliasoph. 2013. "Coordinating Futures: Toward a Theory of Anticipation." *American Journal of Sociology* 118: 908–42.

Taylor, Charles. 2004. *Modern Social Imaginaries.* Durham, NC: Duke University Press.

Taylor, George H. 2006. "Ricoeur's Philosophy of Imagination." *Journal of French Philosophy* 16: 93–104.

ter Horst, Klaus W. 2009. *Investition.* 2nd rev. ed. Stuttgart, Germany: Kohlhammer.

Thelen, Kathleen, and Sven Steinmo. 1992. "Historical Institutionalism in Comparative Politics." In *Structuring Politics. Historical Institutionalism in Comparative Analysis,* edited by Kathleen Thelen, Sven Steinmo, and Frank Longstreth, 1–32. Cambridge: Cambridge University Press.

Théret, Bruno. 2008. "Les trois états de la monnaie: approche interdisciplinaire du fait monétaire." *Revue économique* 59: 813–42.

Thompson, Edward P. 1967. "Time, Work-Discipline, and Industrial Capitalism." *Past and Present* 38: 56–97.

Thrift, Nigel. 2001. "'It's the Romance, Not the Finance, That Makes the Business Worth Pursuing': Disclosing a New Market Culture." *Economy and Society* 30: 412–32.

Tillich, Paul. 1986. *Symbol und Wirklichkeit.* Göttingen, Germany: Vandenhoeck & Ruprecht.

Tilly, Charles. 2006. *Why? What Happens When People Give Reasons . . . And Why.* Princeton, NJ: Princeton University Press.

Tognato, Carlo. 2012. *Central Bank Independence: Cultural Codes and Symbolic Performance.* New York: Palgrave.

Tooze, Adam J. 2001. *Statistics and the German State 1900–1945: The Making of Modern Economic Knowledge.* Cambridge: Cambridge University Press.

Traube, Klaus. 1999. "Kernspaltung, Kernfusion, Sonnenenergie: Stadien eines Lernprozesses." Lecture, November 29, 1999, Philipp University of Marburg.

TREC Development Group. 2003. "Paper for Arab Thought Forum and Club of Rome." Amman, Jordan.

Trigilia, Carlo. 2006. "Why Do We Need a Closer Dialogue between Economic Sociology and Political Economy?" Presented at the First Max Planck Summer Conference on Economy and Society, Villa Vigoni, Italy.

Troy, Irene. 2012. "Patent Transactions and Markets for Patents: Dealing with Uncertainty." PhD diss., Utrecht University.

Trumbull, Gunnar. 2012. "Credit Access and Social Welfare: The Rise of Consumer Lending in the United States and France." *Politics and Society* 40: 9–34.

Tuckett, David. 2012. "Financial Markets Are Markets in Stories: Some Possible Advantages of Using Interviews to Supplement Existing Economic Data Sources." *Journal of Economic Dynamics & Control* 36: 1077–87.

Turkle, Sherry. 2004. "'Spinning' Technology: What We Are Not Thinking about When We Are Thinking about Computers." In *Technological Visions: The Hopes and Fears That Shape New Technologies*, edited by Marita Sturken, Douglas Thomas, and Sandra Ball-Rokeach, 19–33. Philadelphia: Temple University Press.

Ullrich, Wolfgang. 2006. *Habenwollen: Wie funktioniert die Konsumkultur?* Frankfurt am Main: Fischer.

Uzzi, Brian. 1997. "Social Structure and Competition in Interfirm Networks: The Paradox of Embeddedness." *Administrative Science Quarterly* 42: 35–67.

Vaihinger, Hans. 1924. *The Philosophy of "As-If": A System of the Theoretical, Practical and Religious Fictions of Mankind.* London: Routledge & Kegan Paul.

Valtin, Alexandra. 2005. *Der Wert von Luxusmarken: Determinanten des konsumentenorientierten Markenwerts und Implikationen für das Luxusmarkenmanagement.* Wiesbaden, Germany: Deutscher Universitätsverlag.

van Lente, Harro. 1993. *Promising Technology: The Dynamics of Expectations in Technological Development.* Delft: Eburon.

———. 2000. "Forceful Futures: From Promise to Requirement." In *Contested Futures: A Sociology of Prospective Techno-Science*, edited by Nik Brown, Brian Rappert, and Andrew Webster, 43–63. Aldershot, UK: Ashgate.

van Lente, Harro, and Arie Rip. 1998. "Expectations in Technological Developments: An Example of Prospective Structures to Be Filled in by Agency." In *Getting New Technologies Together: Studies in Making Sociotechnical Order*, edited by Cornelis Disco and Barend van der Meulen, 203–29. Berlin: de Gruyter.

Vargha, Zsuzsanna. 2013. "Realizing Dreams, Proving Thrift: How Product Demonstrations Qualify Financial Objects and Subjects." In *Constructing Quality: The Classification of Goods in the Economy*, edited by Jens Beckert and Christine Musselin, 31–57. Oxford: Oxford University Press.

Veblen, Thorstein. (1899) 1973. *The Theory of the Leisure Class.* Boston: Houghton Mifflin.

Velthuis, Olav. 2005. *Talking Prices: Symbolic Meanings of Prices on the Market for Contemporary Art.* Princeton, NJ: Princeton University Press.

Verganti, Roberto. 2009. *Design-Driven Innovation: Changing the Rules of Competition by Radically Innovating What Things Mean.* Boston: Harvard Business Press.

Vickers, Douglas. 1994. *Economics and the Antagonism of Time: Time Uncertainty and Choice in Economic Theory.* Ann Arbor: University of Michigan Press.

Wagner-Pacifici, Robin. 2010. "Theorizing the Restlessness of Events." *American Journal of Sociology* 115: 1351–86.

Wagner, Peter. 2003. "Social Science and Social Planning during the Twentieth Century." In *The Modern Social Sciences.* Vol. 7 of *The Cambridge History of Science,* edited by Theodore M. Porter and Dorothy Ross, 591–607. Cambridge: Cambridge University Press.

Waldby, Catherine. 2002. "Stem Cells, Tissue Cultures and the Production of Biovalue." *Health* 6: 305–23.

Walton, Kendall L. (1978) 2007. "Furcht vor Fiktionen." In *Fiktion, Wahrheit, Wirklichkeit: Philosophische Grundlagen der Literaturtheorie,* edited by Maria E. Reicher, 94–119. Paderborn, Germany: Mentis.

———. 1990. *Mimesis as Make Believe: On the Foundations of the Representational Arts.* Cambridge, MA: Harvard University Press.

Wansleben, Leon. 2011. "Wie wird bewertbar, ob ein Staat zu viele Schulden hat? Finanzexperten und ihr Bewertungswissen in der griechischen Schuldenkrise." *Berliner Journal für Soziologie* 21: 495–519.

———. 2013. "'Dreaming with BRICs': Innovating the Classificatory Regimes of International Finance." *Journal of Cultural Economy* 6: 453–71.

Ward, Thomas B. 1994. "Structured Imagination: The Role of Category Structure in Exemplar Generation." *Cognitive Psychology* 27: 1–40.

Warde, Alan. 2005. "Consumption and Theories of Practice." *Journal of Consumer Culture* 5: 131–53.

Weber, Max. (1894) 1988a. "Die Börse." In *Gesammelte Aufsätze zur Soziologie und Sozialpolitik,* edited by Marianne Weber, 256–322. Tübingen, Germany: J. C. B. Mohr.

———. (1906) 1988b. "Kritische Studien auf dem Gebiet der kulturwissenschaftlichen Logik." In *Gesammelte Aufsätze zur Wissenschaftslehre,* edited by Johannes Winckelmann, 215–90. Tübingen, Germany: Mohr.

———. (1913) 1981. "Some Categories of Interpretive Sociology." *The Sociological Quarterly* 22: 151–80.

———. (1922) 1978. *Economy and Society. An Outline of Interpretive Sociology.* 2 vols. Edited by Guenther Roth and Claus Wittich. Translated by Ephraim Fischoff. Berkeley: University of California Press.

———. (1922) 1946. *From Max Weber: Essays in Sociology.* Translated and edited by H. H. Gerth and C. Wright Mills. New York: Oxford University Press.

———. (1927) 2003. *General Economic History.* 8th ed. Translated by Frank H. Knight. Mineola, NY: Dover.

———. (1930) 1992. *The Protestant Ethic and the Spirit of Capitalism.* Translated by Talcott Parsons. London: Routledge.

Weintraub, E. Roy. 1974. *General Equilibrium Theory.* London: Macmillan.

Wenzel, Harald. 2002. "Vertrauen und die Integration moderner Gesellschaften." In *Politisches Vertrauen: Soziale Grundlagen reflexiver Kooperation,* edited by Rainer Schmalz-Bruns and Reinhard Zintl, 61–76. Baden-Baden, Germany: Nomos.

White, Harrison C. 1981. "Where Do Markets Come From?" *American Journal of Sociology* 87: 517–47.

———. 1992. *Identity and Control: A Structural Theory of Social Action.* Princeton, NJ: Princeton University Press.

White, Hayden V. 1973. *Metahistory: The Historical Imagination in Nineteenth-Century Europe.* Baltimore: Johns Hopkins University Press.

———. 1978. *Tropics of Discourse: Essays in Cultural Criticism.* Baltimore: Johns Hopkins University Press.

———. 1980. "The Value of Narrativity in the Representation of Reality." *Critical Inquiry* 7: 5–27.

Whitford, Josh. 2002. "Pragmatism and the Untenable Dualism of Means and Ends: Why Rational Choice Theory Does Not Deserve Paradigmatic Privilege." *Theory and Society* 31: 325–63.

Wieland, Volker. 2012. "Model Comparison and Robustness: A Proposal for Policy Analysis after the Financial Crisis." In *What's Right with Macroeconomics?,* edited by Robert M. Solow and Jean-Philippe Touffut, 33–67. Cheltenham, UK: Edward Elgar.

Wiesenthal, Helmut. 1990. "Unsicherheit und Multiple-Self-Identität: Eine Spekulation über die Voraussetzungen strategischen Handelns." *MPIfG Discussion Paper* 90/2. Cologne: Max Planck Institute for the Study of Societies.

Williams, Archibald. 1910. *The Romance of Modern Invention.* London: Seeley.

Wilson, Dominic, and Roopa Purushothaman. 2003. "Dreaming with BRICs. The Path to 2050." *Goldman Sachs Global Economics Paper* 99. London: Goldman Sachs.

Wisniewski, Tomasz Piotr, and Brendan Lambe. 2013. "The Role of Media in the Credit Crunch: The Case of the Banking Sector." *Journal of Economic Behavior and Organization* 85: 163–75.

Witt, Ulrich. 2001. "Learning to Consume: A Theory of Wants and the Growth of Demand." *Journal of Evolutionary Economics* 11: 23–36.

Woll, Cornelia. 2014. *The Power of Inaction: Bank Bailouts in Comparison.* Ithaca, NY: Cornell University Press.

Woodruff, David M. 1999. *Money Unmade: Barter and the Fate of Russian Capitalism.* Ithaca, NY: Cornell University Press.

Wray, L. Randall. 1990. *Money and Credit in Capitalist Economies: The Endogenous Money Approach.* Aldershot, UK: Edward Elgar.

Yip, Francis Ching-Wah. 2010. *Capitalism as Religion? A Study of Paul Tillich's Interpretation of Modernity.* Cambridge, MA: Harvard Theological Studies.

Yowell, Constance M. 2002. "Dreams of the Future: The Pursuit of Education and Career Possible Selves among Ninth Grade Latino Youth." *Applied Developmental Science* 6 (2): 62–72.

Yuran, Noam. 2014. *What Money Wants: An Economy of Desire.* Stanford, CA: Stanford University Press.

Zachmann, Karin. 2014. "Risk in Historical Perspective: Concepts, Contexts, and Conjunctions." In *Risk: A Multidisciplinary Introduction,* edited by Claudia Klüppelberg, Daniel Straub, and Isabell M. Welpe, 3–35. Cham, Switzerland: Springer.

Zelizer, Viviana. 2004. "Circuits of Commerce." In *Self, Social Structure, and Beliefs: Explorations in Sociology,* edited by Jeffrey C. Alexander, Gary T. Marx, and Christine L. Williams, 122–44. Berkeley: University of California Press.

Zipfel, Frank. 2001. *Fiktion, Fiktivität, Fiktionalität: Analysen zur Fiktion in der Literatur und zum Fiktionsbegriff in der Literaturwissenschaft.* Edited by Ulrich Ernst, Dietrich Weber, and Rüdiger Zymner. Berlin: Erich Schmidt Verlag.

Zittoun, Tania, Jaan Valsiner, Dankert Vedeler, João Salgado, Miguel M. Gonçalves, and Dieter Ferring. 2013. *Human Development in the Life Course: Melodies of Living.* Cambridge: Cambridge University Press.

Zuckerman, Ezra W. 1999. "The Categorical Imperative: Securities Analysts and the Illegitimacy Discount." *American Journal of Sociology* 104: 1398–438.

INDEX